HUMAN RIGHTS AND HEALTHCAⵕ

Human Rights and Healthcare looks at medical law perspective. Almost all issues traditionally taught und significant human rights issues inherent within then in bringing those human rights implications to the fore. Th _nclude established fundamental rights such as the right to life, th _spect for a private life, and the right to physical integrity, as well as c controversial 'rights' such as a 'right to reproduce' and a 'right to die'. The human rights perspective of this book enables new light to be cast upon familiar medico-legal cases and issues. As such the book provides a genuine merging of human rights law and medical law and will be of value to all students and academics studying medical law, as well as to those interested in the broader issues raised by the growing human rights culture within the UK and worldwide.

Human Rights and Healthcare

Elizabeth Wicks

·HART·
PUBLISHING

OXFORD AND PORTLAND, OREGON
2007

Published in North America (US and Canada) by
Hart Publishing
c/o International Specialized Book Services
920 NE 58th Avenue, Suite 300
Portland, OR 97213-3786
USA
Tel: +1 503 287 3093 or toll-free: (1) 800 944 6190
Fax: +1 503 280 8832
E-mail: orders@isbs.com
Website: www.isbs.com

Hart Publishing, 16C Worcester Place, OX1 2JW
Telephone: +44 (0)1865 517530 Fax: +44 (0)1865 510710
E-mail: mail@hartpub.co.uk
Website: http://www.hartpub.co.uk

British Library Cataloguing in Publication Data

Data Available

ISBN-13: 978-1-84113-580-9

Typeset by Columns Ltd, Reading
Printed and bound in Great Britain by
TJ International Ltd, Padstow, Cornwall

Acknowledgements

I am grateful to my colleague in the School of Law, Dr Stephen Smith, who read and commented upon Chapters 11 and 12. Chapter 8 is partly based upon my talk at the University of Birmingham's Institute of Medical Law Inaugural Conference in September 2005 and I am grateful to the delegates at that conference for constructive feedback. I should also acknowledge the contribution to this book made by the students on the Law and Medicine module over a number of years who have been enthusiastic and engaged with the topics discussed in this book and have thereby helped me to develop my understanding and evaluation of many issues. As always, I am grateful to my Mum and Dad for continued support and encouragement and to my partner Frank for tolerating many long discussions about medical law and human rights and for the valuable advice he invariably provides.

Medical law is a notoriously fast moving subject but I have sought to state the law as of January 2007.

Liz Wicks
Birmingham, March 2007

Contents

Table of Cases

Australia

Canada

Council of Europe

European Union

Ireland

Netherlands

United States of America

Table of Legislation

European Union

Germany

Netherlands

New Zealand

1

Introduction: Human Rights in Healthcare

Medical law is unusual amongst legal subjects as there is considerable academic debate over whether it is a distinct subject at all. The growth in healthcare during the 20th century, both in terms of technological advances and social expectations, means that we are all likely to encounter doctors, nurses and other healthcare workers on a professional basis at some point in our lives. As with any human relationship, the law seeks to regulate it but the discipline of medicine brings with it specific emotive and moral complications. Our encounter with healthcare may involve one of our most intimate interests: mortality; reproduction; a life free of pain and suffering. In a democratic society governed by the rule of law, the law must step in to regulate these issues but it does not, and should not, do so in a moral vacuum. Abortion, euthanasia, transplants, assisted conception, and so on, are ethical, as well as legal, issues and an entire philosophical subject of medical ethics has developed to study them. The question remains, however, whether there is a distinct legal subject which focuses on the law regulating healthcare.

Doubt has arisen because medical law is an academic version of the cuckoo. When a medico-legal problem arises, medical law utilises the principles and remedies of other branches of law. So, traditionally, if you wanted to know about the legal duties imposed upon your doctor – his legal standard of care in providing treatment – you would need to refer to the law of torts; if you wanted to know whether you would face legal liability for helping a terminally ill loved one to die, you would need to consult the criminal law; if you wanted to know whether an underage child could obtain contraceptives or an abortion without parental consent or knowledge, you would need to refer to the principles of family law. A medical lawyer needed to be a jack of all trades but, as the issues specific to healthcare increased (for example because the terminally ill could be kept alive for longer or because new technology enabled new uses of the human body), the traditional rules of these other branches of law had to be adapted. A tentative new and distinct branch of law emerged. With it came the question of whether there was any underlying theme or themes which ensured internal coherence of the subject. There are certain ethical principles which could play this role: autonomy, beneficence, sanctity of life, dignity of the human person, but consideration of these concepts has only opened the door to questions of the relationship between rights of the patient and duties of the doctor. And from this debate has emerged a strong argument that the conceptual unity of medical law is human rights.

Kennedy and Grubb, leading authorities in medical law, famously describe medical law as 'a subset of human rights law'[1] and this is the view adopted in this book. Thus while medical law continues to borrow from various legal subjects, it can now be seen against a backdrop of human rights law which prioritises the self-determination and dignity of the patient. The value of human rights in this context can be seen when we acknowledge, as we must, the unique relationship between doctor and patient which has an imbalance of power at its core. This point is well described by Sir Ian Kennedy, one of the early advocates for the role of human rights law in this field:

> As between the doctor and the patient there is an inevitable imbalance or disequilibrium of power. The doctor has information and skill which the patient, who lacks these, wishes to employ for his benefit. When it is remembered that among the powers possessed by the doctor is the privilege to touch and even invade the body of another and as a consequence exercise control to a greater or lesser extent over that person, it will be clear that, with the best will in the world, and conceding the good faith of the doctors, such powers must be subject to control and scrutiny, from an abundance of caution. This is the role of patients' rights, whereby the permissible limits are set by ethics and law to the exercise of the doctor's power.[2]

As convincing as this argument may seem, and it is certainly adopted and advocated throughout this book, it must be noted that the role of human rights in medicine has encountered some strong opposition. What is widely regarded as the leading textbook on medical law, Mason and McCall Smith's *Law and Medical Ethics*, remains somewhat sceptical about the influence of human rights on this field of medical law. In the sixth edition of the textbook in 2002, the influence of human rights on medical law was described as little more than 'tinkering at the edges'[3] and, although this comment seems to have been removed in the 2006 edition, the authors (now Mason and Laurie) continue to expressly cast doubt upon both the influence which human rights has had upon the subject,[4] and upon the desirability of such influence.[5] This book will seek to counter both of

---

[1]   I Kennedy and A Grubb, *Medical Law*, 3rd edn (London, Butterworths, 2000), p 3.

[2]   I Kennedy, *Treat Me Right: Essays in Medical Law and Ethics* (Oxford, Clarendon Press, 1991), p 387.

[3]   JK Mason, A McCall Smith and G Laurie, *Law and Medical Ethics*, 6th edn (London, Butterworths, 2002), p 31.

[4]   'Initial predictions of wide-sweeping changes have not been borne out in practice' (JK Mason and GT Laurie, *Mason and McCall Smith's Law and Medical Ethics*, 7th edn (Oxford, Oxford University Press, 2006), p 44).

[5]   'Our concern . . . is that disproportionate weight will be accorded to overly-individualistic notions of autonomy'. (Mason and McCall Smith, *ibid* pp 46-47.)

these assertions by cataloguing the myriad of influences introduced into medical law from the sphere of human rights law in recent years and by arguing in favour of the prioritisation of individual autonomy and rights as an underlying value in English medical law.

The scepticism of some legal academics is magnified in respect of medical professionals who fear the practical implications of the introduction of human rights into the legal regulation of medical practice. As Kennedy explains, 'talk of rights is often represented to the doctor as if it inevitably involves confrontation, legalism, and strict or rigid restrictions on what the doctor may do'.[6] As such, it is not surprising that doctors may regret the law's, and especially human rights law's, intrusion into what was traditionally broad medical discretion. However, as Kennedy also notes, the involvement of human rights enables medical discretion to be set within a legal framework to ensure that it is properly exercised.[7] Montgomery makes a more subtle criticism of the influence of human rights in medical law by arguing that patients' rights have been given fuller attention by the institutions of healthcare than by the courts[8] and that 'the traditional paradigm that sees the health professions and the institutions of the NHS as the principal problem, forces to be countered, needs to be replaced by a broader paradigm that sees them as part of the solution'.[9] Montgomery argues that the underlying theme of healthcare law is not rights and duties but the creation of moral values within the professional communities and their reinforcement by law.[10] He is correct to identify a traditional judicial tendency to 'regulate medical ethics through the filter of peer review'.[11] However, even though there are examples of the law enforcing professional ethics in this way, it is now outdated and widely regarded as inconsistent within a modern democratic state committed to human rights in international and domestic law. Peer review is too close to self-regulation which is simply not appropriate for a discipline such as medicine which, by its nature, interferes with individual rights to privacy, dignity and autonomy. We can acknowledge that most of these interferences are for the good of the patient without needing to admit unfettered professional discretion.

A final criticism of the utility of human rights law in this field is one which could be similarly directed towards all human rights law: that individual rights claims 'have an insidious history of gravitating towards those who are articulate and affluent'.[12] Morgan paints a vivid picture of 'patients staggering home with

---

[6]   Kennedy, n 2 above, p 386.

[7]   *Ibid*, pp 386-87. Kennedy argues that 'the history of mankind and even of doctors, is that some sort of social system for overseeing the activities of those who enjoy privileges as regards others is appropriate, indeed is essential' (p 386).

[8]   J Montgomery, 'Time for a Paradigm Shift? Medical Law in Transition' (2000) 53 *CLP* 363, at p 365.

[9]   *Ibid*, p 407.

[10]   *Ibid*, p 385.

[11]   *Ibid*, p 405.

[12]   D Morgan, *Issues in Medical Law and Ethics* (London, Cavendish, 2001), p 23.

copies of the Human Rights Act, the Patients' Charter and the Bar List bulging in their Louis Vuitton, Gucci and Dolce and Gabbana shopping bags'[13] but, even if there is an element of truth in the assertion that human rights are more likely to be relied upon by articulate and educated patients, this is hardly an argument in favour of ignoring the human rights of all patients. The very people Morgan fears will be excluded from the benefit of human rights – 'the poor, the illiterate and the sick'[14] – are exactly the people that the healthcare system may fail. Without individual rights – fundamental concepts such as a right to life, a right to be free from degrading and inhuman treatment, a right to autonomy – these vulnerable individuals may have no legal recourse. Pieces of legislation or lists of rights in themselves are of limited use but in conjunction with the development of a human rights culture, they can benefit every member of society when the other branches of law let them down. Such a human rights culture is increasing in the UK due to a diverse range of sources of human rights. It will now be helpful to identify these main sources, before moving on to consider which particular rights are relevant in the healthcare context.

I.   Sources of Human Rights Law

(a)   International Human Rights Treaties

The international protection of human rights is a relatively recent development. Prior to the Second World War, international law had only dabbled in a piecemeal manner into human rights issues.[15] During the course of the Second World War, the concept of universal individual rights began to evolve. The Four Freedoms set out by US President Roosevelt in January 1941,[16] the Atlantic Charter in August 1941 and the United Nations Declaration in January 1942 all began to hint at the protection of human rights as an Allied war aim. When the structure and purposes of a post-war international organisation were debated from August 1944 onwards, the role of human rights in this new organisation became the source of heated debate. Finally, on 26 June 1945, the Charter of the United Nations was signed with human rights prominent in two major ways. First, respect for human rights was elevated to a basic purpose of the new organisa-tion.[17] Second, the establishment of a Human Rights Commission was mandated

---

[13]   *Ibid.*

[14]   *Ibid,* p 23.

[15]   For example, in the form of humanitarian laws of war, laws on piracy and slavery, and treaties for the protection of minorities.

[16]   The Four Freedoms encompassed a wide range of modern day rights: freedom of expression and religion and freedom from want and fear.

[17]   Human rights are referred to in the Preamble ('to reaffirm faith in fundamental human rights, in the dignity and worth of the human person, in the equal rights of men and women and of nations

under the Economic and Social Council. Once established, this Commission, chaired by Eleanor Roosevelt, was keen to move on to the next phase of international protection of human rights: the drafting of an international Bill of Rights. The first stage of this was quickly achieved with the drafting of a non-binding declaration, the Universal Declaration of Human Rights, adopted by the General Assembly of the new United Nations on 10 December 1948. Forty-eight states, including the United Kingdom, agreed to this wide-ranging list of rights. The Declaration has had great rhetorical significance but, as a non-binding declaration, it could not be legally enforced and so had little practical impact. It was only intended as a first stage, however, and the Human Rights Commission proceeded to draft a legally enforceable covenant. This was considerably delayed by disagreement about the means of implementation and ultimately the only way to secure agreement was to create two distinct covenants: one on civil and political rights (ICCPR) and one on economic, social and cultural rights (ICESCR). The former, including rights such as freedom of expression and freedom of conscience, is implemented by means of a compulsory reporting system[18] and optional inter-state and individual complaints.[19] The ICESCR contains rights which impose greater positive obligations upon the states, such as a right to housing and a right to food, and their implementation is therefore more controversial, especially in many western states.[20] Before these international agreements were concluded, a group of European states had already decided to draft a regional human rights treaty which would seek, in the words of its preamble, to 'take the first steps for the collective enforcement of certain of the Rights stated in the Universal Declaration'.

In the post-war years, there was a concerted effort to unite the states of Western Europe in order to preserve the peace and counter the growing influence of the communist Soviet Union. One of the earliest successes in this effort was the establishment of the Council of Europe. The Statute of the Council of Europe which was signed in London in May 1949 included a strong emphasis on human rights. The process of drafting a human rights convention by this body, and the UK's role in it, has been documented extensively elsewhere.[21] The document which eventually emerged after months of negotiations was a compromise. It contained the narrowly defined form of rights favoured by common law states

---

large and small . . '.) and twice in Art 1: 'To develop friendly relations among nations based on respect for the principle of equal rights and self-determination of peoples' (Art 1(2)); 'To achieve international co-operation in . . . promoting and encouraging respect for human rights and for fundamental freedoms for all without distinction as to race, sex, language or religion . . '. (Art 1(3)).

[18] Article 40(1) ICCPR.

[19] Article 41 and Optional Protocol respectively.

[20] The UK has not ratified this covenant.

[21] A Lester, 'Fundamental Rights: The United Kingdom Isolated?' [1984] *PL* 46; G Marston, 'The United Kingdom's Part in the Preparation of the European Convention on Human Rights, 1950' (1993) 42 *ICLQ* 796; E Wicks, 'The UK Government's Perceptions of the European Convention on Human Rights at the Time of Entry' [2000] *PL* 438; AWB Simpson, *Human Rights and the End of Empire: Britain and the Genesis of the European Convention* (Oxford, Oxford University Press, 2001).

such as the UK, but also included radical implementation methods including the establishment of a European Court of Human Rights and individual petition. These implementation methods were optional and not originally accepted by the UK but in 1966 both the possibility of individual petition and the compulsory jurisdiction of the Court were accepted by the then UK government. Since that time, the European Convention on Human Rights (ECHR) has been the most important source of human rights law for the UK. The UK has been bound at international law to respect the Convention rights (including rights to life, liberty and privacy and freedoms of expression, conscience and association) of everyone within its jurisdiction. While at times the UK government has regretted the influence imposed from this external source of rights, it has never failed to comply with a finding that its law or practice is in violation of the Convention. In addition to the finding of many violations by the European Court of Human Rights in Strasbourg,[22] the ECHR has also had some direct influence upon domestic law by means of the courts' use of it as a guide to interpretation.[23]

More recently, the Council of Europe has drafted a more specific human rights convention which has particular relevance to the issues arising in this book. The European Convention on Human Rights and Biomedicine (ECHRB)[24] was opened for signature at Oviedo in Spain in April 1997. Although an initiative of the Council of Europe, other non-European states also participated in its formation (and are permitted to sign it) including Australia, Canada, Japan, United States and the Vatican. The European Court of Human Rights may give advisory opinions concerning the interpretation of the ECHRB at the request of a state government or the steering committee on bioethics,[25] and the Court may also, at the request of the Secretary-General of the Council of Europe, require any party to explain the manner in which its law ensures effective implementation of the ECHRB. Examples of matters covered by the ECHRB include consent, the human genome, scientific research and transplantation of tissue and organs from living donors. In addition more detailed issues in the biomedical field are dealt with in five additional protocols on cloning, transplantation, biomedical research, the human embryo and foetus and human genetics. The UK is not yet a signatory to the ECHRB and so the Convention's principles and provisions are of persuasive authority only.

---

[22] A few examples include *McCann v United Kingdom* Series A, No 324, (1996) 21 EHRR 97 (violation of Art 2 in relation to shooting of suspected terrorists in Gibraltar); *Ireland v United Kingdom* Series A, No 25, (1978) 2 EHRR 25 (violation of Art 3 due to interrogation methods in Northern Ireland amounting to inhuman treatment or punishment); *Smith v United Kingdom* (2000) 29 EHRR 493 (violation of Art 8 in relation to prohibition on homosexuals serving in the armed forces).

[23] See MJ Beloff and H Mountfield, 'Unconventional Behaviour: Judicial Uses of the European Convention in England and Wales' [1996] *EHRLR* 467 for domestic uses of the Convention pre-HRA.

[24] The full title is Convention for the Protection of Human Rights and Dignity of the Human Being with Regard to the Application of Biology and Medicine.

[25] Article 29 ECHRB.

As will be apparent, the Council of Europe has been a vital source of human rights documentation over the last fifty years. There is also another important European organisation, the European Union, which may also have some relevance as a source of human rights. Traditionally the EU and its predecessor organisations focused more upon economic and trade matters than on individual rights. However, increasingly the organisation's competence has been extended to encompass aspects of human rights. Respect for human rights is now regarded as one of the values on which the Union is founded and the Treaty of Amsterdam extended the exercise of the European Court of Justice's powers to include the issue of fundamental rights. Perhaps most significantly, an EU Charter of Fundamental Rights has been created which comprises an extensive and wide-ranging list of the rights already available to EU citizens, deriving from member states' constitutions as well as the laws of the EU. The Charter's legal status has been somewhat ambiguous but it represents an important step in the direction of EU involvement in human rights. There is little doubt that the EU, having dipped its toes into the sea of human rights protection, will in the future move further into that already somewhat overcrowded environment. As EU law has supremacy over domestic law in the British Constitution, any involvement of the EU in human rights issues will have profound implications for British law and practice.

(b)   The British Constitution and Common Law Rights

The British Constitution has traditionally favoured, in Feldman's words, 'an undifferentiated mass of liberty'[26] rather than codified lists of individual rights. This meant that each individual retained the freedom to act in any way not prohibited by the law. The major shortcoming of this approach was that the rights and liberties enjoyed were residual, gradually eroded by the sovereign Parliament's legislative competence.[27] Increasingly during the 20th century this was regarded as too precarious a means of protecting individual freedom and thus a number of senior judges sought alternative means of securing more meaningful protection for individuals. One means relied upon was reference to the growing number of international human rights documents, including most powerfully the European Convention on Human Rights. Another means of increasing protection for rights was more domestically-based however: a concept of fundamental common law rights. Legal academics and senior judges writing

---

[26]   DJ Feldman, *Civil Liberties and Human Rights in England and Wales*, 2nd edn (Oxford, Oxford University Press, 2002), p 70.

[27]   Parliamentary sovereignty is a core part of the British Constitution. The traditional conception of it is that of Dicey writing in the nineteenth century: 'the right to make or unmake any law whatever; and further, that no person or body is recognised by the law of England as having a right to override or set aside the legislation of Parliament' (AV Dicey, *Introduction to the Study of the Law of the Constitution*, 10th edn (London, Macmillan, 1959), at pp 39–40).

extra-judicially developed the notion of common law rights protected as fundamental law by the UK's uncodified constitution.[28] Sir John Laws was particularly
influential in this regard, arguing for constitutional limits to Parliament's competence to infringe individual rights.[29] His basis for this argument is a logical belief
that the constitution, rather than Parliament, is truly sovereign:

> Ultimate sovereignty rests, in every civilised constitution, not with those who wield
> governmental power, but in the conditions under which they are permitted to do so . . .
> In Britain those conditions should now be recognised as consisting in a framework of
> fundamental principles which include the imperative of democracy itself and those
> other rights, prime among them freedom of thought and expression, which cannot be
> denied save by a plea of guilty to totalitarianism.[30]

This argument is not universally accepted. The United Kingdom has a long
history of belief in a common law constitution and a sovereign Parliament with
unlimited legislative competence. The idea of common law, or constitutional,
rights being entrenched against removal by the sovereign Parliament has been
rejected by most judges and legal writers. However, the UK's constitution is an
evolving one and the modern constitutional framework leaves little room for a
legally unlimited legislature. The supremacy of European Community law and
devolution of legislative power to a Scottish Parliament in particular suggest that
a Parliament sovereign *under* the constitution rather than *over* the constitution is
a more realistic proposition.[31] Members of the House of Lords have even
recognised this in their judicial capacity in *Jackson v Attorney-General*.[32] Lord
Steyn regarded the traditional Diceyan view of parliamentary sovereignty as 'out
of place in the modern United Kingdom' and suggested that parliamentary
sovereignty is a 'construct of common law' which could be changed if necessary,[33]
while Lord Hope held that although the British constitution is dominated by the
sovereignty of Parliament, 'parliamentary sovereignty is no longer, if it ever was,
absolute'.[34] Such views, from such an authoritative position, suggest that the

---

[28] See, for example, J Laws, 'Is the High Court the Guardian of Fundamental Constitutional
Rights?' [1993] *PL* 59.

[29] In *Thoburn v Sunderland City Council* [2002] 4 All ER 156 Laws LJ attempted to reconcile his
judicial and extra-judicial thinking by expressly recognising the existence of constitutional rights and
suggesting that 'constitutional statutes' cannot be impliedly repealed. It is not a complete reconciliation, however, as his extra-judicial writing appears to go further and suggest that certain constitutional rights cannot even be expressly infringed. The concept of constitutional rights can also be seen
in a number of other cases: *R v Secretary of State for the Home Department, ex p Simms* [2000] 2 AC
115 at 131 per Lord Hoffmann; *Pierson v Secretary of State for the Home Department* [1998] AC 539; *R
v Lord Chancellor, ex p Witham* [1998] QB 575.

[30] J Laws, 'Law and Democracy' [1995] *PL* 72, at p 92.

[31] I have argued this elsewhere: E Wicks, *The Evolution of a Constitution: Eight Key Moments in
British Constitutional History* (Oxford, Hart Publishing, 2006).

[32] [2005] 3 WLR 733.

[33] *Ibid*, para 102.

[34] *Ibid*, para. 104.

concept of a sovereign Parliament limited in some respects is a viable possibility under the British constitution and, if Parliament is to be limited, it seems fitting that fundamental rights may join other concepts such as democracy, European legal supremacy and the rule of law in limiting it.

Regardless of the position taken in this ongoing constitutional debate, it cannot be denied that the common law has for many years served as a protector of human rights, albeit one often working under the shadows of a sovereign legislature. Important rights such as free speech and a right to life have been recognised by the courts as existing within the common law. Furthermore, the enactment of the Human Rights Act (discussed below) has served to encourage the recognition of pre-existing and independent common law rights often mirroring those found in the HRA. A common law right to privacy, long denied by the courts, has now developed externally to the HRA[35] and similarly a right to life was recognised in *Re A (children)(conjoined twins: surgical separation)* as existing before the HRA came into force and, in *Venables and Thomson v News Group Newspapers*, as applying beyond the restraints of HRA liability.[36]

In short, and to put some of the constitutional issues discussed in this section in context, there is no doubt that the common law protects a number of individual rights. However, there exists at least two limitations upon this form of human rights protection. First, the protection is offered under a constitution which is commonly thought to prioritise a sovereign Parliament and therefore any rights at common law can, arguably, be overridden by primary legislation. Second, the unwritten and uncodified nature of the common law means that the exact content of the rights protected at common law, and the extent of their enforcement, remains uncertain. Fortunately, the common law source of human rights is now of only secondary importance in contemporary Britain due to the enactment of the Human Rights Act in 1998.

(c) The Human Rights Act 1998

It was explained above that the United Kingdom has been bound by the ECHR at international law since 1953 (and subject to the jurisdiction of the European Court of Human Rights since 1966). The dualist nature of the UK constitution, under which international law is not automatically a part of domestic law, meant that the Convention rights could not be directly relied upon in domestic courts. (Although the ECHR did at times serve as a judicial guide to interpretation if there was an ambiguity in legislation.) For decades a debate ensued in political and legal circles as to whether the Convention should be incorporated into domestic law (or indeed whether an original domestic Bill of Rights should be drafted). When Blair's New Labour government took office in 1997, it came

---

[35] *Douglas v Hello! Ltd* [2001] QB 967.
[36] [2000] 4 All ER 961; [2001] 2 WLR 1038.

armed with extensive manifesto commitments to enact wide-ranging constitutional reform. In addition to devolution, electoral reform and House of Lords reform, the new government was committed to incorporating the ECHR into domestic law. The means by which it did so, in 1998, was the enactment of the Human Rights Act (HRA). This Act is in essence a compromise. It seeks to 'bring rights home' (in the political rhetoric of the government) by enabling their enforcement by domestic courts while also ensuring that the fundamental principles of the existing constitution remain unchanged. Most importantly, the government was not prepared to undermine the constitutional principle of parliamentary sovereignty (and leading members of the government demonstrated a very traditional understanding of the concept).[37]

This might have been thought to present a significant difficulty for the government because the legal protection of human rights may not seem compatible with a sovereign parliament unencumbered in its legislative freedom. However, the HRA adopts a number of ingenious solutions to this difficulty, in what the Home Secretary admitted was 'a British answer to a British problem'.[38] The emphasis in the Act is on statutory interpretation, declaratory remedies, parliamentary scrutiny and judicial review of public authorities. Section 3 imposes an obligation on domestic courts to interpret legislation in a manner compatible with the Convention rights 'so far as it is possible to do so'.[39] Section 4 introduces an innovative declaratory power under which a higher court, if it is unable to interpret primary legislation in a manner compatible with the Convention rights, may issue a declaration of incompatibility. Crucially this declaration 'does not affect the validity, continuing operation or enforcement of the provision in respect of which it is given'.[40] Through these means, Parliament's sovereignty can be retained while political pressure is brought to bear on Parliament to remedy the incompatibility identified by the court. Section 19 requires that a minister must either make a statement of compatibility (not to be confused with the judicial declaration of incompatibility under section 4) when introducing a new Bill or, if unable to do so, must explain that he wishes the Bill to proceed notwithstanding its incompatibility. Again this provision serves to discourage Parliament from violating the Convention rights while also ensuring that Parliament retains the constitutional ability to do so. Finally, section 6 compels all public authorities to act compatibly with Convention rights. While there remains room for argument as to which bodies qualify as 'public authorities', section 6

---

[37]   The Home Secretary at the time, Jack Straw, described his Diceyian understanding of the doctrine: 'Parliament must be competent to make any law on any matter of its choosing' (HC Deb, Vol 306, col 770, 16 February 1998).

[38]   HC Debs, Vol 313, col 420, 3 June 1998.

[39]   In the view of the then Lord Chancellor, Lord Irvine, this rule 'goes far beyond' the previous interpretative rule under which a statutory ambiguity was required (Lord Irvine of Lairg, 'The Development of Human Rights in Britain under an Incorporated Convention on Human Rights' [1998] *PL* 221 at 228).

[40]   Section 4(6)(a).

makes clear that Parliament is not caught within this category but that the courts are public authorities and will act unlawfully if they violate a Convention right.

The HRA introduces the Convention rights into domestic law and enables individuals to rely upon them before domestic courts rather than undergoing the long and costly journey to Strasbourg.[41] It has gone some way towards introducing a rights culture into the UK[42] although the Act continues to have its critics.[43] Some important and valuable judgments have been made under the Act[44] but it is limited both in terms of enforcement and coverage. While public authorities, including significantly for our purposes NHS Trusts and bodies such as the Human Fertilisation and Embryology Authority, are bound to comply with the Convention rights, Parliament can still choose to legislate in contravention of the rights if it wishes to do so and the courts continue to be denied the power to subject Acts of Parliament to substantive review. Furthermore, the HRA incorporates only the rights contained in the ECHR (with the notable exception of Article 13, the right to an effective remedy) and its First Protocol. Given that the Convention was drafted in 1949-1950, the HRA can be accused of being rather outdated in terms of the specific rights protected and more generally in terms of the concept of human rights apparent within its provisions. It is for these reasons that other international human rights treaties, including those more specific to the medical law field (ECHRB) and those of an economic and social nature (ICESCR), as well as rights inherent under the common law constitution, continue to be relevant sources of human rights law and/or principle for the United Kingdom. Having identified the main sources of human rights in English law, it will now be useful to consider which particular rights may be of most relevance in the medical law context.

---

[41]   The European Court of Human Rights retains its jurisdiction and this serves as a last resort after domestic remedies, including under the HRA, have been exhausted.

[42]   The government has acknowledged that this is one of the Act's primary aims: 'The Act is intended, over time, to help bring about the development of a culture of rights and responsibilities across the UK. This involves looking beyond questions of technical compliance. The Convention rights need to be seen as a set of broad basic values which are accessible to and integrated into the democratic policy making process'. (Home Office Memorandum to the Joint Parliamentary Committee on Human Rights, *Implementation and Early Effects of the Human Rights Act 1998*, para 6.)

[43]   The Conservative party has threatened to repeal the HRA if it wins the next general election.

[44]   For example, a declaration of incompatibility was issued in respect of the detention without trial of suspected international terrorists (*A v Secretary of State for the Home Department* [2006] 2 AC 221); another declaration led to a change in the mental health laws to ensure that a mental health review tribunal has to discharge a patient from detention in hospital where it can not be proven that he suffers from a mental disorder warranting detention (*R v Mental Health Tribunal, ex p H* [2002] QB 1); and statutory protection for tenants after a spouse has died has been interpreted to include homosexual couples (*Mendoza v Ghaidan* [2004] 2 AC 557).

II. The Human Rights Relevant to Medical Law

The potential relevance of human rights to the field of medical law was not overlooked when the HRA was enacted. Lord Irvine, the Lord Chancellor at the time, admitted that the number of Convention rights which are relevant in the medical field is 'more than you might guess'.[45] Largely this is because the medical field is itself so diverse – from issues of duties of care to doctor-patient confidentiality; from assisted conception to end of life decisions – that the nature of rights which apply varies accordingly. We may, however, identify four broad categories of rights which have the most relevance here:

(1) Privacy-related rights, including to self-determination, bodily integrity and confidentiality.
(2) The Right to Life (but does this include positive rights to treatment and to assistance in dying?)
(3) The Right to Dignity, incorporating most significantly a right to be free from degrading treatment.
(4) Reproductive autonomy, including both positive and negative aspects: a right to reproduce and a right not to do so.

In addition, some rights which do not fall into these categories may also have direct application, such as a freedom of conscience in respect of medical treatment. We will now look briefly at each of these four main categories.

(a) Privacy-related Rights

The concept of privacy is protected in Article 8 ECHR in an extremely broad fashion. It is drafted in terms of 'a right to respect for private life' and this has been interpreted as including a general right to self-determination or autonomy. In other words, this includes a right to determine for ourselves how we live our lives, free from state interference, including in respect of what medical treatment we receive. Such broadly based autonomy rights derive from other sources beyond Article 8. Indeed, it could be argued that the entirety of the ECHR serves as the legal embodiment of the principle of autonomy. However, in practice Article 8 will offer the most effective protection for individual autonomy, even though, as with many of the Convention rights, it is a right which has to be balanced against conflicting societal interests.[46] An example of the application of a right to self-determination or autonomy in the medical context is the apparently irrational choice of a competent patient to refuse life-sustaining medical treatment. If the treatment is continued against the patient's wishes, a violation of

---

[45]   Lord Irvine, 'The Patient, the Doctor, the Lawyers and the Judge: Rights and Duties' (1999) 7 *Med L Rev* 255 at p 261.
[46]   See Art 8(2).

the patient's autonomy and thus his or her Article 8 rights will have occurred.[47] The right to respect for private life within Article 8 ECHR has also been interpreted by the European Court of Human Rights as including a right to physical integrity.[48] A non-consensual invasion of a patient's bodily integrity, even if in the form of beneficial medical treatment, may violate this aspect of Article 8. This mirrors English law in which, as we shall see in Chapter 4, medical treatment can only be imposed with consent or, for a patient unable to consent, under the doctrine of necessity. Any other imposition of invasive treatment will amount to a battery for which damages may be available against the hospital.[49] Another aspect of Article 8's privacy-related rights of relevance in the medical field is the protection of doctor-patient confidentiality. There is no doubt that a right to respect for private life includes a right of non-disclosure of confidential information and both the European Court of Human Rights and the House of Lords has confirmed the particular importance of confidentiality in respect of medical matters.[50] Once more, however, a balance will need to be struck against competing interests necessary in a democratic society, such as the rights and freedoms of others and the prevention of crime.

(b)   The Right to Life

The right to life is nowadays regarded as one of the most fundamental human rights although its recognition and enforcement is of relatively recent development. It is protected in Article 2 ECHR as well as Article 6 ICCPR and through the common law. It is of obvious relevance in the medical law context because of the nature of decisions taken at both the beginning and the end of life. Debate is ongoing about when the right to life begins: at conception; implantation; viability; birth; or at some other stage in the process of life's commencement? The answer to this question, one that the law avoids and ethics remains ambiguous upon, will have profound implications for the treatment available to a pregnant woman, both in terms of the legality of a termination of pregnancy and in terms of the woman's right to refuse necessary medical treatment during pregnancy and labour. The right to life is no less controversial at the end of life because debate rages as to whether the right implies that life is always sacred or whether the quality of a person's life detracts from a state's obligations to preserve and prolong that life. For example, if a patient is rendered severely brain damaged and irreversibly comatose, does his life still have value? Does he continue to have an enforceable (by others) right to life? Does that include a right to receive

---

[47]   See *Re T (adult: refusal of medical treatment)* [1992] 4 All ER 649; and *Re C (adult: refusal of medical treatment)* [1994] 1 All ER 819.

[48]   *X and Y v Netherlands* (1986) 8 EHRR 235 at para 22.

[49]   See *Re B (adult: refusal of medical treatment)* [2002] 2 All ER 449.

[50]   See *Z v Finland* (1997) 25 EHRR 371 and *Campbell v Mirror Group Newspapers* [2004] 2 All ER 995 respectively.

life-sustaining treatment? In addition, it has been queried whether a right to life not only protects the value of life but also incorporates an element of self-determination about issues of life and death. If this view is correct, it suggests that a person's choice to end his life should receive legal protection and perhaps even assistance. In other words, is it possible that there is a 'right to die' lying hidden beneath the veneer of a right to life?[51] One other aspect of the right to life which has huge significance in the healthcare context is the issue of a positive obligation upon the state to preserve life and the possibility that this may be the basis for a 'right to treatment'. In a state with a publicly funded, but chronically under funded, national health service, it is the possibility of a right to receive necessary or beneficial medical treatment which may be of greatest value to many ill or injured citizens. This issue will be considered in the next chapter and we will see there that the potential application of individual rights can never be completely removed from considerations of the society in which the individual lives.

(c)   The Right to Dignity

Dignity, along with autonomy, is regarded as one of the concepts underlying modern human rights law. As with autonomy, the value of dignity can be seen influencing many of the Convention rights, but it is Article 3 ECHR which is of most relevance here as this Article prohibits 'inhuman or degrading treatment'. The concept of dignity may lend some support to the withdrawal of treatment from terminally ill patients and thus provides support to quality of life considerations as opposed to the sanctity of life considerations prioritised in the right to life. Dignity is notoriously subjective, however, and could sometimes be used to strengthen both sides of a single argument. For example, if the brain damaged and irreversibly comatose patient mentioned above is being kept alive by medical treatment, a principle of dignity could be utilised to support a decision to withdraw the treatment and allow nature to take its course. If withdrawal of the treatment in effect means removing artificial hydration and nutrition, however, dignity could also be used to argue against an undignified death from dehydration.[52] Furthermore, while some may see no dignity in prolonging a life of pain and suffering, others may find dignity in fighting for life as long as possible. The law, therefore, faces a difficult task in regulating these issues. A final utilisation of the concept of dignity in the medical context, and one increasingly regarded as vital, is the need to preserve the dignity of the human body, both living and deceased. This particularly cautions against the commercialisation of the human body or its parts, but may also preclude other uses of the body perceived by some

---

[51]   This is one of the arguments raised in the *Pretty* case: *R (on application of Pretty) v Director of Public Prosecutions* [2002] 1 All ER 1; *Pretty v United Kingdom* (2002) 35 EHRR 1.

[52]   These were some of the issues facing the House of Lords in *Airedale NHS Trust v Bland* [1993] 1 All ER 821.

as being undignified, such as surrogate pregnancy or retention of human tissue after a post-mortem for research purposes.

(d) Reproductive Autonomy

The principle of autonomy has already been mentioned in the context of privacy-related rights, but also has specific resonance in the context of reproduction. Reproductive autonomy is a concept developed through human rights law and academic theory and it prioritises the right to choose if, when, and how to reproduce. The concept, therefore, has application both in a negative sense (a right to choose not to reproduce by the use of contraceptives or by a termination of pregnancy) and in a positive sense (a right to found a family, if necessary by means of assisted conception methods such as IVF). Both of these aspects of reproductive autonomy generate heated political and legal debate. States, including the United Kingdom, impose legal regulation onto reproductive treatment far more than any other medical treatment and perhaps this is understandable. However, as the legal regulation is increased in these matters, so the potential for human rights abuses grows. In addition to being an aspect of the general right to autonomy, reproductive autonomy, at least in its positive sense, also finds legal force through the right to found a family in Article 12 ECHR (and perhaps a right to reproduce at common law) although, as we will see, this is one of the most limited of all the Convention rights.

This brief overview of the human rights of most relevance in the medical field should merely serve to whet the appetite for what follows. As will become apparent, legal issues arising in the context of the provision of healthcare almost invariably involve potential rights violations. The remainder of the book seeks both to describe and analyse the involvement of human rights law in medicine and simultaneously to justify its application to this field of human interaction. While it is in the nature of medico-legal issues that there are no easy answers when the disciplines of law and medicine collide, human rights law at least provides a useful framework in which to consider the dilemmas and the one most fitting in a democratic society.

Recommended Further Reading

DJ Feldman, *Civil Liberties and Human Rights in England and Wales*, 2nd edn (Oxford, Oxford University Press, 2002), Chapters 1 and 2.
I Kennedy, 'Patients, Doctors and Human Rights' in *Treat Me Right: Essays in Medical Law and Ethics* (Oxford, Clarendon Press, 1991).

Lord Irvine, 'The Patient, the Doctor, their Lawyers and the Judge: Rights and Duties' (1999) 7 *MedLRev* 255.

J Montgomery, 'Time for a Paradigm Shift? Medical Law in Transition' (2000) 53 *CLP* 363

2

A Right to Treatment? The Allocation of Resources in the National Health Service

This chapter discusses the preliminary issue of whether there is a right to receive medical treatment within the UK. This topic resides within the broader issue of the allocation of resources within the National Health Service. Limited public funding puts extreme pressures upon health authorities and medical professionals and inevitably results in some patients being denied the medical treatment which they need. Does such a situation engage the human rights of the patient? This chapter will answer this question by looking, first, at the applicable rights to healthcare, and then at the government's legal duties to promote a free and comprehensive health service and the allocation of resources within it. Finally, attention will turn to the courts' approach to the question of a right to treatment and it will be seen that, despite a judicial reluctance to become involved in such notoriously problematic issues, the courts have recently acknowledged the need to protect in law certain interests of the patient in need of, and denied, treatment.

I. Rights, Health and Resources

(a) Rights to Healthcare

It will be evident throughout the pages of this book that the administration of healthcare engages a number of human rights. For example, a patient in receipt of medical treatment is entitled to respect for his or her autonomy (through the law on consent), physical integrity (through consent and negligence) and privacy (through the law on confidentiality), but the entirety of such rights' protection presupposes that the patient has access to the necessary medical treatment. In today's world of limited public funding and a growing, and aging, population, it is far more likely that a person's interests will be detrimentally affected by a place at the bottom of a long waiting list than they would be by an abuse of rights during the administration of the treatment. Therefore, an appropriate starting point for the entire issue of human rights and healthcare is whether there is any legally recognised and enforceable *right to* healthcare.

The European Convention on Human Rights offers protection for an individual's right to life. This is derived from Article 2 which declares that 'Everyone's right to life shall be protected by law. No one shall be deprived of his life intentionally . . .' A number of exceptions to this prohibition on intentional deprivation of life are then listed relating to the death penalty[1] and the use of lethal force during law enforcement. Outside of these exceptions, a state is prohibited from intentionally killing its citizens. The key question for our purposes, however, is whether a state is also obliged to take positive steps to preserve life. An affirmative answer was provided by the European Court of Human Rights in the case of *Osman v United Kingdom*.[2] The Court took the view that Article 2 'enjoins the state not only to refrain from the intentional and unlawful taking of life, but also to take appropriate steps to safeguard the lives of those within its jurisdiction'.[3] The case concerned a failure on the part of the police to prevent a death, but the principle extends to the provision of life-saving medical treatment. In *Osman*, it was held that there must be a 'real and immediate' risk to life before the duty to take positive steps to preserve life is engaged.[4] Furthermore, the Court explicitly recognised the need to balance resources within the context of policing and concluded that the obligation to safeguard lives 'must be interpreted in a way which does not impose an impossible or disproportionate burden on the authorities'.[5] This requirement of proportionality would also need to serve as a constraint upon any right to life-saving medical treatment under Article 2, and may have particular significance given the limits of public funding of healthcare.[6] As McBride explains, 'Although it is clear that there is a very substantial duty to protect life, it is also evident that this is not one that is to be fulfilled regardless of all other considerations'.[7] Article 2 undoubtedly offers the potential for a right to treatment (at least a right to life-saving treatment and perhaps more if we accept the old maxim that 'life depends upon health'[8]) but it also reflects the crucial reality that, when imposing positive obligations upon state authorities, there must be recognition of the need to balance conflicting demands upon the public purse. This is a consideration which permeates this entire chapter, as will soon become obvious.

---

[1]   The death penalty is now prohibited by Protocol 6.

[2]   (2000) 29 EHRR 245.

[3]   *Ibid*, at para 115.

[4]   Because the police did not have knowledge of such a risk, there was no violation found in this case.

[5]   See n 2 above, para 116.

[6]   See J McBride, 'Protecting Life: A Positive Obligation to Help' (1999) 24 *Eur Law Rev HR Survey* 43, at p 54.

[7]   *Ibid*, at p 52.

[8]   See *R v Bourne* [1939] 1 KB 687.

There is also an argument that we should not seek to infer too much from the ECHR in this context given that the provision of healthcare is a matter specifically reserved for the European Social Charter (ESC) rather than the Convention.[9] Both are documents stemming from the auspices of the Council of Europe but the Charter, which protects economic and social rights, does not have the effective implementation methods of the Convention. Nevertheless, the United Kingdom has signed the ESC and is thus committed at international law to its terms including, under Article 13, 'to ensure that any person who is without adequate resources . . . be granted adequate assistance, and, in case of sickness, the care necessitated by his condition'.[10] By contrast, the European Convention on Human Rights and Biomedicine (ECHRB) protects only equitable access to healthcare by requiring that state parties 'taking into account health needs and available resources, shall take appropriate measures with a view to providing, within their jurisdiction, equitable access to healthcare of appropriate quality'.[11] It is perhaps noteworthy that the relevant provisions in both the ESC and the ECHRB are framed in terms of duties upon the state rather than rights of the citizen. The need to take into account issues of resources places discretion firmly in the hands of the state and its healthcare authorities.

Perhaps a stronger protection for an individual's right of access to healthcare may be detected within the laws of the European Union. Although the EC Treaty does not specifically mention healthcare, the free movement provisions coupled with the principle of equal treatment have enabled the issue to be raised under the laws of the EC. Furthermore, the Treaty of Maastricht recognises access to healthcare as an EU competence,[12] and the EU Charter of Fundamental Rights and Freedoms protects a limited right of access to healthcare.[13] The potential application of EC law to this issue was recently considered in the case of *R (Watts) v Bedford Primary Care Trust*.[14] This case concerned a pensioner who obtained a hip replacement in France within three months of referral in order to avoid a waiting time of twelve months in Bedford. The primary care trust refused to pay for the treatment in France on the grounds that the waiting time of twelve months was normal for NHS patients and thus did not amount to the 'undue delay' which would have required the authorisation of the treatment in another member state. The Court of Appeal referred the case to the European Court of Justice (ECJ) on the issue of whether patients can legitimately 'queue jump' NHS waiting lists by going abroad for treatment even if this means straining NHS

---

[9] A Maclean, 'The Individual's Right to Treatment under the Human Rights Act 1998' in A Garwood-Gowers, J Tingle and T Lewis (eds), *Healthcare Law: The Impact of the Human Rights Act 1998* (London, Cavendish Publishing, 2001), p 87.

[10] Article 13(1) ESC.

[11] Article 3 ECHRB.

[12] Article 152.

[13] Article 35: 'everyone has the right of access to preventative healthcare and the right to benefit from medical treatment under the conditions established by national laws and practices'.

[14] (2004) 77 BMLR 26.

budgets to the disadvantage of others on the list. The ECJ held[15] that, in order for the member state to refuse to pay for the treatment abroad, it would have to be clearly established that the waiting time in the original country did not exceed a period which is acceptable on the basis of an objective medical assessment of the patient's clinical needs.[16] If the waiting time does appear to be excessive, then it was held that the member state cannot refuse to pay for the treatment merely on the grounds that jumping the waiting list queue would distort the normal order of priorities. Therefore, the response of the ECJ seems to favour the individual in this classic dilemma of individual versus society. It also makes clear that closer political and economic integration across Europe means that a right of access to healthcare need no longer be confined to NHS care within the UK. The implications for healthcare throughout Europe are profound.[17]

Within the United Kingdom, and with the exception of the Human Rights Act's incorporation of Article 2, there is little protection for a right to healthcare. The Patients' Charter introduced by John Major in 1992 did include a number of 'rights' relevant to this topic, including a right to healthcare on the basis of clinical need; a right to receive emergency medical care at any time; and a right to be guaranteed admission for treatment by a specific date no later than two years from being placed on waiting list. There was no legal remedy for a failure to respect these 'rights', however, and the patient's only recourse would be a complaint to the Chief Executive of the NHS.[18] Even this limited protection has now been largely superseded by the 'NHS Plan' of 2000[19] and the establishment of a National Institute for Clinical Excellence (NICE) in 1999 which sets uniform standards across the country. As this discussion of legal rights has now strayed into the territory of professional duties, it is time to investigate the core legal duty upon the government to provide a free and comprehensive health service.

(b)   The Ministerial Duty to Promote a Comprehensive and Free Health Service

The National Health Service Act 1977 obliges the Secretary of State for Health to promote 'a comprehensive health service designed to secure improvements (a) in the physical and mental health of the people ... and (b) in the prevention, diagnosis and treatment of illness'.[20] The Act further requires that these services

---

[15]   *R v Bedford Primary Care Trust* (C-372/04) (2006).

[16]   This was held to require consideration of the patient's medical condition, the history and probable course of the illness and the degree of pain and/or nature of disability suffered by the patient.

[17]   See TK Hervey and JV McHale, 'Law, Health and the European Union' (2005) 25 *LS* 228 for further discussion.

[18]   See M Brazier, 'Rights of Healthcare' in R Blackburn (ed), *Rights of Citizenship* (London, Mansell Publishing, 1994), p 57.

[19]   Cm 4818 – I, 2000.

[20]   Section 1(1) NHS Act 1977.

must be provided free of charge unless the law expressly permits charges to be made.[21] Examples of such exceptions include the recouping of costs after road traffic accidents, and charges for wigs, drugs, and optical and dental appliances. Section 3 of the 1977 Act further specifies the types of services which it is the Secretary of State's duty to provide 'to such extent as he considers necessary to meet all reasonable requirements'; these include hospital accommodation and medical, dental, nursing and ambulance services. However, case law has established that the Secretary of State's duty under this section is subject to the need to take into account limited financial resources.[22] Furthermore, the Court of Appeal has confirmed that it is permissible for the Secretary of State to exclude some services from the NHS if they are to be provided by the social services instead. Thus, in *R v North and East Devon Health Authority, ex p Couglan*[23] it was held that nursing care provided in connection with residential accommodation under the National Assistance Act 1948 could be excluded from the NHS and means tested by the social services. The only requirements are that the nursing services are incidental or ancillary to the provision of accommodation, and of a nature which it can be expected that a local authority, whose primary responsibility is to provide social services, can be expected to provide.[24] When making such decisions, however, the Secretary of State must bear in mind his overall duty in the 1977 Act to promote a comprehensive, free health service and he must not exclude a service merely because the social services will fill the gap.[25]

Mason, McCall Smith and Laurie note that there are three potential measures of a free health service: comprehensiveness, quality and availability, and recognise that 'the goal of fully comprehensive, high quality medical care that is freely available to all on the basis of medical need is unattainable in the face of steadily increasing costs; the temptation is to lower one standard in favour of the other two'.[26] The problem of seeking a compromise between demand and supply is only becoming more acute.[27] When the NHS was founded in 1948,[28] society's expectations of medicine were far more limited: life expectancy was lower (66 rather than today's 78); infant death six times more likely; and there was less focus on the long-term treating of chronic, as opposed to acute, illness.[29] The demands upon a 'comprehensive' health service have increased drastically. In addition, the evolving definitions of health and illness continue to raise questions as to the

---

[21] Section 1(2) NHS Act 1977.

[22] *R v Secretary of State for Health, West Midlands Regional Health Authority and Birmingham Area Health Authority, ex p Hincks* [1980] 1 BMLR 93.

[23] [2000] 3 All ER 850.

[24] *Ibid*, at para 30.

[25] *Ibid*.

[26] Mason, McCall Smith and Laurie, *Law and Medical Ethics*, 7th edn (Oxford, Oxford University Press, 2006) pp 416-417.

[27] *Ibid*, at p 412.

[28] By means of the National Health Service Act 1946.

[29] See C Newdick, *Who Should We Treat? Rights, Rationing and Resources in the NHS*, 2nd edn (Oxford, Oxford University Press, 2005), pp 5-6.

appropriate boundaries of healthcare. If treatments are available for conditions such as obesity, alcoholism, hyper-activity and drug addiction, does this mean they are illnesses?[30] The World Health Organisation defines health as a 'state of complete physical, mental and social well-being and not merely the absence of disease and infirmity'.[31] If such a definition is accepted, the demands upon a 'comprehensive' health service will continue to escalate.

Some commentators query the inevitability of increasing demand for health-care, however. Frankel, Ebrahim and Smith make the sound point that neither increased life expectancy nor new technologies necessarily require increased provision of healthcare.[32] As an example, they point out that most people want to die at home (despite the fact that more and more are dying in institutions). Meeting public expectations does not always involve the provision of greater treatment; it may involve withdrawing treatment to give effect to the patient's wishes. Furthermore, these commentators point out that 'there is also a strand of professional self interest in the common focus on failure. The NHS is one of the largest employers in the United Kingdom. Evidence of unsatisfied demand is not necessarily disinterested. Bidding for extra resources is a competitive process for which ordered coping is rarely rewarded'.[33] This argument, despite its cynicism, introduces an important new perspective to the issue of a free and comprehensive health service: while resources to provide this may be finite, so too is demand, not least because the population is finite and only a proportion of the population will want and benefit from medical treatment at any one time.[34] This is undoubtedly true, but the recognition that demand is finite does not resolve the issue of resource allocation because, while both resources and demand are finite, demand may still outstrip resources and present the Secretary of State with an impossible task under his statutory duty to provide comprehensive and free healthcare.

Interestingly, while the commentators above define demand, as well as resources, as finite, John Harris takes the unusual view that resources are not finite at all and that the difficult issues of resource allocation are surmountable with sufficient political will. Harris argues, with undeniable logic, that 'Any given budget may be increased if other budgets are traded off against it. This means that priorities can always be reassessed.'[35] The argument here is that the resources available to the Secretary of State for providing a free and comprehensive health service are only limited because the healthcare budget is subject to other

---

[30]   Newdick, *ibid* p 6.

[31]   The definition of health can be found in the Constitution of the World Health Organisation.

[32]   S Frankel, S Ebrahim and GD Smith, 'The Limits to Demand for Healthcare' (2000) 321 *BMJ* 40.

[33]   *Ibid.*

[34]   *Ibid.*

[35]   J Harris, 'Micro-Allocation: Deciding Between Patients' in H Kuhse and P Singer (eds), *A Companion to Bioethics* (Oxford, Blackwell, 1998), p 293.

competing claims to the public purse. But, as Harris notes elsewhere, financial resources for life-saving treatment seem a strong candidate for prioritisation over other government spending:

> any rubric for resource allocation should examine the national budget afresh to see whether there are any headings of expenditure that are more important to the community than rescuing citizens in mortal danger. For only if all other claims on funding are plausibly more important than that, is it true that resources for life-saving are limited.[36]

It might be assumed, therefore, that a state with Harris as Prime Minister would prioritise public funding of life-saving treatment (and perhaps life-improving treatment?) and thus face greatly reduced issues of resource allocation within the NHS. However desirable such a policy may be, real life PMs take a different view and the present day reality of an under-funded health service is unavoidable: long waiting lists, a shortage of beds, and hard choices are the everyday working conditions of the NHS. Access to healthcare within the UK is, in effect, rationed. If hard choices have to be made, who is to make them and on what principles should such choices rest?

(c) Ethical Issues in Resource Allocation

Resource allocation decisions are taken at three levels: by government when deciding the healthcare budget and when issuing guidance as to particular priorities; by health authorities when allocating their budget to individual hospitals; and by medical staff within hospitals when choosing how best to use the limited resources available to them. It is at the final level that choices between specific patients needing treatment may have to be faced and, therefore, it is this level which most directly impacts upon individuals. One obvious means of choosing between two patients in equal clinical need of the treatment is to treat the one most deserving. For example, if a patient has contributed to his condition through obesity, smoking, alcohol or drugs, it could be argued that he has relinquished his right to receive healthcare at the expense of a more 'innocent' patient. It is clear, however, that this would be a moral decision and one which doctors or health authorities are not necessarily well suited to make. The fundamental principle underlying access to healthcare must be equality and any factors which encourage a moral assessment of the patient's previous actions or status should be disregarded. As Harris points out, we are seeking to make moral assessments whenever we ask the following questions:

> whether priority for treatment should be given to the productive executive or to the chronically unemployed, or when we compare the claims of the young mother of four

---

[36] J Harris, 'QALYfying the Value of Life' (1987) 13 *J Med Eth* 117, at p 122.

to that of the friendless loner, or when we consider whether the drunken driver or his victim should be treated first, or when we allocate a low priority to smokers . . .[37]

While choices such as these make good medical drama for television, they so undermine the idea of equality of access to treatment that they must play no role in real-life decisions of who to treat. To value the life of the 'friendless loner' as worth less than that of the 'single mother of four' is to seek to value a life solely in terms of its value to others in society. The individual, and his or her desire to live the only life (s)he knows, is lost in this social focus. And yet it is a vital consideration if such ideas as an individual's right to life (equal to all others) and individual autonomy (to live life as one chooses) are to have meaning.[38]

It might be argued, of course, that factors such as smoking raise specific issues of clinical benefit. If treatment is less likely to be successful because, for example, the patient is a smoker, this might be a justifiable distinction based on clinical issues between two patients needing the same treatment.[39] The General Medical Council (GMC) guidance on this matter recognises the distinction between taking account of 'the likely effectiveness of treatment'[40] and views about the patient's 'lifestyle, culture, beliefs, race, colour, gender, sexuality, disability, age, or social or economic status', which must not prejudice the decision. In addition, the GMC confirms that treatment must not be refused or delayed because of the doctor's belief that the 'patient's actions have contributed to their condition'.[41]

One of the factors mentioned above which the GMC guidance excludes from consideration is age (unless, of course, the age impacts upon the likely effectiveness of the treatment). The public seem less concerned about such discrimination, however. Research by Lewis and Charney reveals that when asked to choose between two patients with identical clinical needs, a huge majority of the public will choose the younger patient.[42] This preference for the younger patient was given official recognition in New Zealand where guidelines issued under the Health and Disability Services Act 1993 included an assumption that patients over 75 should not be accepted for end stage renal failure programmes, as well as categorising the existence of other serious diseases or disabilities likely to affect

---

[37]   Harris (1998), n 35 above, p 298.

[38]   As Harris argues, 'each person's wish to have the treatment that will offer him the chance of continued flourishing to the extent that his personal health status permits is as urgent and important as that of any other person' (*ibid*, p 304).

[39]   It should always be borne in mind, however, that many of us participate in behaviour potentially harmful to our health. Newdick gives examples such as stress, sport and driving (n 29 above, p 24).

[40]   *Good Medical Practice* (GMC, 2001) para 5: treatment must be provided 'based on your clinical judgment of the patient's needs'.

[41]   *Ibid.*

[42]   P Lewis and M Charney, 'Which of Two Individuals Do You Treat When Only their Ages are Different and You Can't Treat them Both?' (1989) 15 *J Med Eth* 28. Interestingly, this general preference does not hold true beneath a certain age. Thus, when asked to choose between a two year old and an eight year old, the majority chose the older child for treatment, suggesting that the choice is rather more complex than it might at first appear.

the patient's survival or quality of life as reasons for exclusion from the programmes.[43] Publicised cases under these guidelines include the exclusion of a 63
year old man with renal failure, diabetes and dementia who subsequently died
once dialysis ceased, and the exclusion of a 76 year old man also suffering from
coronary artery disease and prostate cancer. The latter patient complained to the
New Zealand Human Rights Commission of age discrimination, inspiring the
Chief Executive of the hospital to order the doctors to review the case. Treatment
commenced and the patient died eighteen months later of his other conditions.[44]
It is obvious from these cases that the distinction between age discrimination and
clinical decisions based on the patient's overall health is notoriously difficult to
draw.

An attempt to achieve fairness in rationing is evident in the discipline of
healthcare economics where 'QALYs' are proposed as a helpful framework for
difficult allocation of resource issues. A QALY is a 'quality adjusted life year'. A
numerical value is placed on the quality of an individual's life and this is then
multiplied by his expected lifespan. The cost of the treatment is then taken into
account so that different treatments for different patients can be compared on a
purely numerical basis. A year of full health is valued as 1; death is valued at 0. A
year of reduced health will be valued at somewhere between 0 and 1. This
attempt to value life and ensure that the allocation of resources achieves the
greatest number of 'life years' is controversial, to say the least. Perhaps the most
obvious criticism is that it discriminates against the elderly patient who, by
definition, has a lower QALY due to his shorter life expectancy, and yet this
patient's loss if life-saving treatment is withheld is just as complete as a young
patient's loss, namely the loss of the rest of his or her life.[45] QALYs also
discriminate against the sick and disabled. There is a sense of 'double jeopardy'
here[46] in that a patient who has already suffered a condition leaving him with a
poor quality of life will be regarded by the QALY approach as having a lower
value in continued life and thus a healthier person may be preferred for
treatment. Harris notes the inherent unfairness in this approach:

> QALYs dictate that because an individual is unfortunate, because she has once become
> a victim of disaster, we are required to visit upon her a second and perhaps graver
> misfortune. The first disaster leaves her with a poor quality of life and QALYs then
> require that in virtue of this she should be ruled out as a candidate for life-saving
> treatment, or at best, that she be given little or no chance of benefiting from what little

---

[43]   See CM Feek, W McKean, L Heneveld, G Barrow, W Edgar and RJ Paterson, 'Experience with
Rationing Healthcare in New Zealand' (1999) 318 *BMJ* 1346.

[44]   See *ibid* for a fuller discussion. The conclusion of the authors is that New Zealand benefits from
the existence of clear guidelines and that while rationing may not always be palatable 'it can be made
understandable and fair'.

[45]   Harris (1998), n 35 above, p 304.

[46]   See Harris (1987), n 36 above, p 120.

amelioration her condition admits of. Her first disaster leaves her with a poor quality of life and when she presents herself for help, along come QALYs and finish her off![47]

Perhaps the greatest problem with the QALY, however, is that it does not value life itself but rather 'quality adjusted life years'. Thus, it does not prioritise the saving of as many lives as possible, even though this is usually the aim of a society which values life. Harris explains the need to save lives rather than life-years:

> To think that life is valuable, that in most circumstances the worst thing that can happen to an individual is that she loses her life when this need not happen, and the worst thing we can do is make decisions, a consequence of which, is that others die prematurely, we must think that each life is valuable. Each life counts for one and that is why more count for more. For this reason we should give priority to saving as many lives as we can, not as many life-years.[48]

A similar approach is also inherent in a rights-based conception of the issue. The right to life – a core fundamental human right – is enjoyed by all individuals and the quality of a person's life does not lead to a reduction in the value of that person's life.[49] Everyone's right to life must be protected by law, regardless of life expectancy, regardless of quality of life, and regardless of the conflicting needs of healthier, younger and more viable individuals. Equality of rights protection is vital, and while all effective schemes of human rights protection ensure a balance between individual rights and societal interests (such as national security, prevention of crime, and the rights of others), the greater good of society (ie the maximisation of 'life years' throughout a community) must never be regarded as detracting from the need to protect each individual's fundamental right to life. A QALY approach would legitimise the giving of many life years to a few at the expense of a few life years to many. A rights-based approach will view each life as equally deserving of protection.

So, while the QALY may have some uses at a macro level – ie to provide guidance to planners at central, regional or district levels[50] – it should not be used to distinguish between individual patients awaiting treatment. If we accept that resources are limited, however, how should we choose between patients if all cannot be treated? The underlying principle must be therapeutic merit: the patient in greatest clinical need must receive the treatment. If this factor does not resolve the issue (because two patients are in equal clinical need), no others are relevant and therefore a randomised approach is the only justifiable way forward.

---

[47]   *Ibid.*

[48]   *Ibid.*

[49]   See *Re A (children)(conjoined twins: surgical separation)* [2000] 4 All ER 961. This issue will be discussed in greater detail in Chapter 11.

[50]   See Newdick, n 29 above, p 31.

This will not, however, prevent complaints of the violation of the unlucky patient's right to treatment. We must now turn to this issue and the courts' approach to such complaints.

II. The General Rule: No Right to Treatment

The reality of inadequate resources within the NHS has led to a number of complaints about a refusal or delay of necessary medical treatment. The courts have shown great sympathy but little inclination to be dragged into such a morally difficult and emotive issue. As was mentioned above, the first judicial recognition of the issue of limited resources came in the 1980 case of *R v Secretary of State for Health, West Midlands Regional Health Authority and Birmingham Area Health Authority, ex p Hincks*[51] when the Court of Appeal approved Wien J's view at first instance that the statutory duty of the Secretary of State to promote and provide a free and comprehensive health service is subject to the need to take into account the financial resources available. Thus, the statutory duty, which could have provided a means to enforcing individual rights to healthcare, is subject to the implied limitation of finite resources.

It might, of course, remain open to a patient denied medical care to make an application for judicial review of that refusal. Unless there is some illegality or procedural impropriety in the decision, however, the patient will face an uphill struggle because irrationality will be very hard to prove. For example, in *R v Secretary of State for Social Services, ex p Walker*,[52] the Court of Appeal refused leave to apply for judicial review of decisions to postpone a non-urgent operation on a premature baby. Sir John Donaldson MR explained the predominant judicial approach to this issue:

> It is not for this court, or indeed any court, to substitute its own judgment for the judgment of those who are responsible for the allocation of resources. This court could only intervene where it was satisfied that there was a prima facie case ... of a failure to allocate resources to an extent which was Wednesbury unreasonable ...

The term 'Wednesbury unreasonable' refers to a decision so unreasonable that no responsible body could make it.[53] This is an extremely strict burden to discharge. Provided that a decision about allocating limited funding has been taken with clinical advice, it will be difficult to challenge, not least because the courts will be aware that, by forcing a doctor to treat one patient, it may be requiring the denial of treatment to other patients considered in more urgent need by the medical

---

[51] [1980] 1 BMLR 93.
[52] [1987] 3 BMLR 32.
[53] *Associated Provincial Picture Houses Ltd v Wednesbury Corpn* (1948) 1 KB 223.

experts. Brazier has also noted that the issue may not be, and indeed was not in *Walker*, as simple as a lack of funds. The problem in *Walker* was a lack of specially trained nurses in intensive care paediatric units and, as Brazier argues, 'The Court of Appeal could not wave a magic wand and procure more nurses. The core problem was the inadequate pay and career structure in nursing, something beyond the control of the authority . . .'[54] As Brazier also notes, the Court of Appeal was being asked to decide that Baby Walker should be treated as a priority over other babies who were regarded by the paediatricians as being in greater need of immediate surgery: 'In the absence of evidence that that judgment was manifestly wrong, the judges were largely helpless. They were impaled on the horns of the healthcare dilemma; defending A's right to treatment may itself be a violation of B's concurrent right.'[55]

Laws J's first instance decision in *R v Cambridge District Health Authority, ex p B*[56] did offer some comfort but only for a matter of hours until it was overruled by the Court of Appeal on the same day.[57] B was a 10 year old girl suffering from leukaemia who was refused further treatment that might have prolonged her life. The health authority's refusal was based on its categorisation of the treatment as experimental and as having only a small chance of success[58] and the likelihood of debilitating side effects. These factors led the health authority to regard the treatment as not in B's best interests. The total cost of the two stages of the procedure was £75,000 but the health authority emphasised that the decision to refuse treatment was based on clinical, rather than financial, grounds. Laws J, in a judgment characteristic of his commitment to common law rights, emphasised B's right to life and held that this required, at the very least, an explanation from the health authority as to the conflicting priorities which had led it to refuse potentially life-saving treatment: 'Where the question is whether the life of a 10 year-old child might be saved, by however slim a chance, the responsible Authority must . . . do more than toll the bell of tight resources. They must explain the priorities that have led them to decline to fund the treatment.'[59] The Court of Appeal regarded it as unrealistic, however, to require a health authority to present its accounts to the court and seek to demonstrate that, if treatment were provided to B, another specified patient would be denied treatment.[60] It was sufficient for the Court of Appeal to recognise that '[d]ifficult and agonising judgments have to be made as to how a limited budget is best allocated to the maximum advantage of the maximum number of patients' and, in the opinion of

---

[54] Brazier, n 16 above, p 62.
[55] *Ibid.*
[56] [1995] 25 BMLR 5.
[57] [1995] 2 All ER 129.
[58] The chances of success were between 1% and 4%.
[59] Note 56 above, pp 16-17 of judgment.
[60] Note 57 above, p 137 (Sir Thomas Bingham MR).

the Court of Appeal, '[t]hat is not a judgment which the court can make'.[61] Fundamentally, the Court of Appeal was determined to live in the real world:

> I have no doubt that in a perfect world any treatment which a patient, or a patient's family, sought would be provided if doctors were willing to give it, no matter how much it cost, particularly when a life was potentially at stake. It would however, in my view, be shutting one's eyes to the real world if the court were to proceed on the basis that we do live in such a world.[62]

So, do the realities of a publicly-funded health service prevent any positive duty on the state to preserve individual lives where life-saving treatment is available but expensive? Is there any potential for the application of a right to treatment within the UK? As the next section will demonstrate, recent case law suggests that such a right may exist, albeit in an extremely limited form.

III. Procedural Aspects of a Right to Treatment

Despite the judicial reluctance to become involved in questions of allocating scarce resources, described in the previous section, there have recently been indications that individuals are entitled to expect certain minimal procedural requirements when their access to healthcare is determined by the medical profession. It will immediately be obvious, however, that these still fall far short of a legally enforceable right to treatment. As Newdick explains, the focus has shifted from what treatment a patient should receive to how the decision is reached: 'The essential question is not what we can have, but who decides the matter and how? This focuses attention not on over-arching rights of access, but on processes which illuminate how decisions are made and highlight the need for consistency between patients.'[63]

(a) The Equality Principle

The first aspect of entitlement in respect of access to healthcare is that of equality. Any blatant discrimination in decisions of who to treat will be illegal. If the discrimination relates to sex or race, the discrimination laws will come into play. Since the enactment of the Human Rights Act 1998, however, there is a much broader requirement that a patient's rights are respected in a non-discriminatory fashion.[64] Article 14 prohibits discrimination in the enjoyment of the Convention

---

[61] *Ibid.*
[62] *Ibid.*
[63] Newdick, n 29 above, pp 43-44.
[64] See J Montgomery, *Healthcare Law*, 2nd edn (Oxford, Oxford University Press, 2003), pp 72-73.

rights and freedoms on the basis of 'any ground such as sex, race, colour, language, religion, political or other opinion, national or social origin, association with a national minority, property, birth or other status'.[65] This means that even less obvious discrimination may be unlawful if it relates to the exercise of an individual's right to life or, perhaps, right to respect for private life. In a case pre-HRA, it was held that, while the exclusion of, for example, all Jews from IVF treatment may well be illegal, the refusal of treatment for a woman based on her previous convictions for prostitution was not unreasonable.[66] Even though the provision of IVF treatment raises specific issues (including, under the Human Fertilisation and Embryology Act 1990, passed subsequent to the case cited, the need to take account of the welfare of any child born as a result of the treatment), an exclusion of a woman because of her status as a convicted prostitute may well now violate Article 14 (provided always that another Convention right is in issue). Brazier has described a right to healthcare as 'a right to a fair share of what is available'.[67] This is a very useful definition because, while acknowledging that limited resources will mean rationing of treatment, it emphasises that we are all entitled to an equal chance of receiving treatment. This will require both that a patient's need or condition receives a fair deal and also that a patient is personally given equality of opportunity with other patients with similar needs.[68] This idea of equality of opportunity thus raises the second aspect of entitlement to healthcare: procedural propriety.

(b) Procedural Propriety

Although the courts have remained unwilling to substitute their judgment for that of the health authorities, who are guided by clinical advice, on questions of who to treat, there has recently been a willingness to review treatment decisions for their procedural propriety. This can be seen most clearly in the case of *R v North West Lancashire Health Authority, ex p A*.[69] The case concerned three transsexuals, A, D and G, who were refused gender reassignment surgery by the health authority. The Authority had a policy in place which allocated a low priority for public funding to procedures considered to be clinically ineffective. The policy was entitled 'Medical Procedures of No Beneficial Health Gain or No Proven Benefit' and included cosmetic plastic surgery, reversal of sterilisation, correction of short-sightedness, alternative medicine and homeopathy, as well as gender reassignment, as treatments which would not be funded except in cases of overriding clinical need. The Court of Appeal accepted the legitimacy of such a policy given the need to allocate limited funding:

---

[65]   Article 14 ECHR.
[66]   *R v Ethical Committee of St Mary's Hospital (Manchester), ex p H* [1988] 1 FLR 512.
[67]   Brazier, n 16 above, p 67.
[68]   *Ibid.*
[69]   [2000] 1 WLR 977.

it is an unhappy but unavoidable feature of state funded healthcare that regional health authorities have to establish certain priorities in funding different treatments from their finite resources. It is natural that each Authority, in establishing its own priorities, will give greater priority to life threatening and other grave illnesses than to others obviously less demanding of medical intervention. The precise allocation of weighting of priorities is clearly a matter of judgment for each Authority . . . It makes sense to have a policy for the purpose . . . and it makes sense too that, in settling on such a policy, an Authority would normally place treatment of transsexualism lower in its scale of priorities than, say, cancer or heart disease or kidney failure.[70]

Despite this, the Court of Appeal emphasised that such a policy must 'genuinely recognise the possibility of there being an overriding clinical need and require each request for treatment to be considered on its individual merits'.[71] This is where the North West Lancashire Health Authority's application of its policy failed to meet the necessary standard. Rather than being a 'genuine application of a policy subject to individually determined exceptions', it amounted to an 'over rigid application' of a near 'blanket policy'.[72] The Court of Appeal doubted whether the Authority really regarded transsexualism as an illness, despite its claims that it did so,[73] and required the Authority to reformulate its policy, giving proper weight to the acknowledgement that transsexualism is an illness and making effective provision for exceptions in individual cases to the general policy limiting funding of treatment for it.[74]

Despite the Court of Appeal's criticism of the way in which the Health Authority made its decision to refuse to fund treatment in this case, Buxton LJ made clear that the decision itself was acceptable. He explained that, although the Authority must make its decision again, it could legitimately come to the same conclusion for a second time because it was proper for the Authority to take account of (a) the cost of the procedure; (b) the comparatively small number of patients needing this treatment; and (c) the costs and demands of other procedures.[75] All of these factors suggest that refusing to provide public funding for gender reassignment surgery is an appropriate and lawful decision. The wider significance of this Court of Appeal judgment is, therefore, limited: it does not entitle any patient to any particular treatment. It does, however, require health authorities to avoid blanket policies refusing to fund treatment and to consider each case on its individual merits. This is an important public law principle and

---

[70]   *Ibid*, p 991 (per Auld LJ).
[71]   *Ibid*.
[72]   *Ibid*, p 993.
[73]   *Ibid*, p 992.
[74]   *Ibid*, pp 994-95.
[75]   *Ibid*, pp 999-1000.

its application to decisions of allocation of healthcare resources is a vital development in the protection of patients' healthcare rights.[76]

The debate surrounding the funding of Herceptin for early stage breast cancer raised similar issues of resource allocation and received a great deal of media and public attention. The Secretary of State for Health intervened by issuing a weekly bulletin to NHS Chief Executives stating that Primary Care Trusts should not refuse to fund Herceptin solely on the grounds of its cost and they must consider the individual circumstances of each patient. This political intervention is controversial, particularly as Herceptin had not at the time been licensed for early stage breast cancer. It led regrettably to a so-called postcode lottery as some PCTs interpreted it as an instruction to fund Herceptin and others, including Swindon PCT, did not. In *Rogers v Swindon NHS Primary Care Trust*, a woman refused this treatment challenged the refusal.[77] At first instance, Bean J upheld Swindon PCT's policy of only funding this treatment if an individual patient presents an exceptional need for treatment. However, on appeal, the Court of Appeal took a very different view and held that the PCT's policy was irrational. The key to this finding was that the case was held not to be about the allocation of scarce resources.[78] If it had been, the PCT's policy of refusing funding except in exceptional circumstances may have been lawful provided that it was possible to envisage such exceptional circumstances.[79] The difficulty faced by the PCT was that financial considerations had been ruled out: 'the PCT developed a policy which treated financial considerations as irrelevant. It thus had funds available for all women within the eligible group whose clinician prescribed Herceptin.'[80] In this situation, the Court of Appeal held that the only relevant factors for consideration by the PCT are the clinical needs of the patients: 'Where the clinical needs are equal, and resources are not an issue, discrimination between parties in the same eligible group cannot be justified on the basis of personal characteristics not based on healthcare.'[81] Therefore, the policy of requiring exceptional personal circumstances in order to choose between patients all in need of Herceptin was held to be irrational and thus unlawful.

On the surface, this judgment seems to be almost the antithesis of *A, D and G*, where a policy permitting exceptional circumstances exceptions was actually required by the court. However, it was clear in that case that it was exceptional clinical needs which were sought, rather than clinically irrelevant exceptional personal circumstances, and thus the two cases together illustrate that only

---

[76] Newdick summarises the requirements in respect of process as follows: 'the process should be robust, fair, and consistent and always admit the possibility of individual patients presenting exceptional circumstances which merit access to care notwithstanding a policy guideline to the contrary' (n 29 above, p 94).

[77] [2006] 1 WLR 2649.

[78] *Ibid*, para 57.

[79] *Ibid*, para 62.

[80] *Ibid*, para 78.

[81] *Ibid*, para 79.

considerations of clinical need can help to justify a general policy to decline funding for treatment. The requirement for rational and lawful policies is an important step towards establishing procedural rights in respect of access to healthcare as a patient can legally challenge a policy denying treatment if it does not meet the strict standards of public law. However, even if successful, the PCT or health authority will only be required to reformulate a policy: no court has yet compelled the provision of treatment. Are there any substantive guarantees of treatment under English law?

IV. A Right to Basic Life-Sustaining Treatment?

In a case which gained much publicity at the time, Oliver Burke, a 45 year old man suffering from a congenital degenerative brain condition, sought a court declaration that artificial nutrition and hydration (ANH) would not be withdrawn as his condition inevitably deteriorated. At first instance, Munby J granted the declarations sought,[82] including declaring a number of paragraphs of the GMC's guidance on withholding and withdrawing life-prolonging treatment to be unlawful.[83] His judgment, 225 paragraphs in length, appeared to create and uphold a right to treatment. The Court of Appeal, however, was extremely critical of this judgment, particularly as many of the issues decided by Munby J did not relate directly to Mr Burke,[84] and set aside Munby J's declarations.

On the question of a right to treatment, the Court of Appeal was adamant that there was no such right:

> Autonomy and the right of self-determination do not entitle the patient to insist on receiving a particular medical treatment regardless of the nature of the treatment. Insofar as a doctor has a legal obligation to provide treatment this cannot be founded simply upon the fact that the patient demands it. The source of the duty lies elsewhere.[85]

The source of the doctor's duty to treat a patient lies in the legal requirement that a doctor treat in the best interests of the patient. To omit to do so leaves a doctor open to a charge of murder or manslaughter should the patient die from the lack

---

[82] *R (on the application of Burke) v General Medical Council* [2005] QB 424.

[83] *Withholding and Withdrawing Life-Prolonging Treatment: Good Practice in Decision Making* (GMC, 2002).

[84] As Lord Phillips MR said in his Court of Appeal judgment, 'The Judge himself observed that it is not the task of a judge when sitting judicially – even in the Administrative Court – to set out to write a text book or practice manual. Yet the judge appears to have done just that' (2005) 3 WLR 1132, at para 19.

[85] *Ibid*, para 31.

of treatment.[86] Patient autonomy overrules this duty, however, in the sense that if a competent adult patient refuses consent to treatment, there is no power, and therefore no duty, to treat the patient. Therefore, a patient who refuses consent to ANH, whether contemporaneously or in advance, will have the treatment withheld.[87] If, however, as in the case of Mr Burke, a patient requests ANH, the request will not be the source of the doctor's duty to provide it, but will merely 'underscore' that duty.[88] The Court of Appeal also held that if a patient requests specific treatment which is not regarded as clinically indicated by his doctors, the doctors will not face any legal obligation to provide that treatment, although the Court did suggest that a second opinion should be offered to the patient.[89] So far, this is very clear and logical. However, the Court of Appeal did not address the question of whether there is any legal obligation to provide treatment which is (a) requested by the patient; and (b) regarded as clinically indicated by the doctors; but (c) regarded as too expensive by the health authority.

The Court restricted itself to considering ANH and held in this context that:

> where life depends upon the continued provision of ANH there can be no question of the supply of ANH not being clinically indicated unless a clinical decision has been taken that the life in question should come to an end. That is not a decision that can lawfully be taken in the case of a competent patient who expresses the wish to remain alive.[90]

This suggests that a competent patient wishing to remain alive is legally entitled to receive the basic life-sustaining treatment of ANH. Such a conclusion is given added weight by the Court of Appeal's conclusion that Article 2 ECHR's protection of the right to life would be infringed if life-sustaining treatment is withdrawn contrary to a competent patient's wishes.[91] This looks very much like a substantive right to treatment, albeit only in respect of life-sustaining treatment.[92] Therefore, the Court of Appeal's judgment in *Burke* is no less significant and controversial than that of Munby J. It appears that a patient who is competent, wishes to remain alive, and needs artificial nutrition and hydration to do so, has a legal right to receive that treatment.

---

[86]   The corollary of this is also true: a doctor will be liable for assault if he treats a patient in a way which is not in the patient's best interests.

[87]   Not to do so would be an assault. See Chapter 4.

[88]   CA judgment, n 84 above, para 32.

[89]   *Ibid*, para 50.

[90]   *Ibid*, para 53.

[91]   *Ibid*, para 39.

[92]   The Court of Appeal confirmed, as previous case law had suggested, that Art 2 is not violated by the withdrawal of life-sustaining treatment either in accordance with a competent patient's wishes or if the treatment is no longer in the best interests of an incompetent patient. This issue is discussed further in Chapter 11.

There remains some doubt about whether ANH is a form of medical treatment. It was held to be so by the House of Lords in *Airedale NHS Trust v Bland*[93] but this was largely in order that it could be withdrawn and Keown has queried poignantly what exactly ANH is supposed to be treating.[94] In *Burke*, the Court of Appeal does not confront this issue at all but merely assumes that ANH is treatment (which, given the House of Lords precedent, is a safe course of action). The Court of Appeal also does not grapple with the issue of whether a withdrawal of life-sustaining treatment is legally distinct from the withholding of it. It is possible that, while a patient in the situation described above has a right not to have life-sustaining treatment withdrawn once it has commenced, there may be no comparable right to require the treatment to commence in the first place. This is not a sustainable distinction, however, because if the right derives, as it appears to, from Article 2's right to life, the state's obligation to preserve life will be indistinguishable in these two situations.

The procedural aspects of a right to treatment seem, post-*Burke*, to have been joined by a substantive aspect even if the Court of Appeal was reluctant to admit that it was authorising such a development. There are some reservations about a substantive right to treatment. Newdick, for example, who has written extensively on the right to treatment under the NHS, is wary of the development of substantive rights: 'The tendency to promote individual rights to healthcare resources will benefit those who shout loudest. But it will not protect less articulate groups and, without additional investment in the NHS, will distort healthcare policy.'[95] These two concerns have some merit but both can be countered. First, it is inevitable that a right to treatment will benefit most those patients 'who shout loudest' but this is true of all human rights: unless an individual who is wronged is willing and able to complain, the violation will go unremedied and, quite possibly, undetected. This is not usually regarded as a reason for not offering legal protection for individual rights. It is, however, a reason for developing a broader human rights culture, providing education on rights and citizenship, and ensuring that equality of opportunity and procedural fairness remain central to the implementation of healthcare decisions. Second, the concern about distorting healthcare policy is lessened by the apparent inherent restriction, or at least prioritisation, of the right to life-sustaining treatment. We can recall here Harris's argument against the QALY approach to allocating resources, namely that a state serious about its obligations to preserve the life of its citizens will seek to preserve as many lives as possible rather than the optimum number of quality-adjusted life years. Providing basic life-sustaining treatment for a patient who needs and desires it is a basic obligation upon a state and an important aspect of that patient's right to life and autonomy.

---

[93] [1993] 1 All ER 831.

[94] J Keown, 'Restoring Moral and Intellectual Shape to the Law after *Bland*' (1997) 113 *LQR* 481, at p 491.

[95] Newdick, n 29 above, p 261.

IV. Conclusion

A right to treatment is the most controversial of all the healthcare rights. It imposes positive, and potentially very expensive, obligations upon the state and in practice it may well require infringing the rights of other patients to receive the treatment they also require. In a world where healthcare resources are limited – whether inevitably or, as some commentators argue, through a policy choice – an absolute right to receive whatever treatment is wanted or needed is simply unrealistic. However, a patient is not entirely without rights-based protection when decisions about allocating limited resources result in a refusal of treatment. The patient is entitled to equal consideration with other patients in the same position; he is entitled not to have a refusal of treatment decided upon a discriminatory basis; and to have his request for treatment assessed on the basis of individual need. Blanket policies refusing funding for treatments are no longer acceptable and the courts, while retaining a reluctance to become too immersed in such difficult resource decisions, will require health authorities to make decisions in a procedurally fair manner. Furthermore, within the context of life-sustaining treatment, specifically ANH, there are recent hints of a more substantive right for competent patients to receive this treatment. Within a healthcare system, and a democratic society, based upon patient autonomy, there is a natural desire to enable a patient to receive the treatment he or she requests and needs. However, while that healthcare system continues to work within a very limited budget, the courts have probably gone as far as they can in providing patients with procedural (and some limited substantive) interests in a broader right to treatment which remains, by necessity, denied to users of the NHS.

Recommended Further Reading

C Newdick, *Who Should We Treat? Rights, Rationing and Resources in the NHS*, 2nd edn (Oxford, Oxford University Press, 2005) especially chapters 2 and 5.

J Harris, 'QALYfying the Value of Life' (1987) 13 *J Med Eth* 117.

M Brazier, 'Rights of Healthcare' in R Blackburn (ed), *Rights of Citizenship* (London, Mansell Publishing, 1994).

S Frankel, S Ebrahim and GD Smith, 'The Limits to Demand for Healthcare' (2000) 321 *BMJ* 40.

3

Ensuring Quality Healthcare: An Issue of Rights or Duties?

If a patient overcomes the hurdles presented by the shortage of NHS resources, discussed in the previous chapter, and obtains medical treatment, the law's focus will turn to the quality of that treatment. A certain minimum standard of care is imposed upon medical professionals and legal liability might ensue if treatment falling below that standard causes some harm to the patient. The regulation of healthcare quality has traditionally been a matter for the law of torts, specifically negligence, and therefore the bulk of this chapter will discuss the legal requirements of negligence. However, the main significance of negligence from the perspective of this book is its shortcoming as sole cause of action for vindicating patient rights. Therefore this chapter will also focus upon the problems inherent in proving negligence against a doctor and recent judicial attempts to rectify these, before culminating in a discussion of potential non-fault alternatives to negligence for use in the healthcare context.

I. The Doctor-Patient Relationship

The development of a human rights culture in the United Kingdom is a relatively recent occurrence. Therefore, the central role of human rights in healthcare has only recently been recognised by the UK courts. Traditionally, the regulation of the provision of healthcare and its requisite quality has been regarded as primarily an aspect of tort law. The emphasis on doctors' duties rather than patients' rights is infamous and carries with it intrinsic dangers. If a doctor performs his professional duties competently but the patient suffers some injury as a result of the medical treatment, there is no scope for a vindication of the patient's rights. Similarly, even if a doctor fails in his professional duty and provides treatment in a negligent fashion, unless the patient can prove that this negligence caused physical harm to the patient, the law of torts will fail to compensate the patient for the negligent treatment of the doctor. Of course, these consequences are justified, indeed essential, if the doctor-patient relationship is to continue to be regulated on the basis of a doctor's duty of care, because in neither situation has the doctor's breach of his duty of care caused an injury to the patient and to hold the doctor liable to compensate the patient in such circumstances would be unjust. And yet, increasingly, the courts, as well as academic commentators and politicians, are recognising that the primary goal of healthcare law must be to vindicate the healthcare rights of the patient.[1] This will inevitably necessitate an evolution of the traditional judicial emphasis on a professional standard of care. As Lord Irvine noted when the Human Rights Act was enacted: 'if incorporation of the European Convention of Human Rights encourages the courts to focus more on the patient's rights, this may prove not entirely compatible with what the doctors have traditionally seen as their duties'.[2]

The doctor-patient relationship is unique because of the inherent imbalance of power. A patient is by definition in a vulnerable position. This does not imply that a doctor is in any way assuming a threatening or malevolent role but rather that he or she is exercising professional skills upon an ill or injured individual whose very life may lie in the doctor's hands. Any legal regulation of the doctor-patient relationship which fails to take account of this inherent imbalance will be flawed. It has been suggested that a doctor-patient relationship is of a fiduciary nature,[3] ie a relationship of trust and confidence. MacLachlin J of the Canadian Supreme Court categorised a doctor as a fiduciary in *Norberg v Wynrib*,[4] which would impose duties of loyalty and good faith upon the doctor in order to protect, preserve and further the interests of the patient.[5] As Kennedy notes, such a fiduciary relationship would be appropriate because 'it embodies a recognition of the imbalance of power between doctor and patient'.[6] However, the English courts have not accepted such a classification of the doctor-patient relationship and instead have focused upon implying a duty of care into such a relationship by virtue of its character. The standard of care expected of the doctor will traditionally be that of his professional colleagues and therefore when the European Convention on Human Rights and Biomedicine (ECHRB) states that any intervention in the health field 'must be carried out in accordance with relevant professional obligations and standards'[7], it is requiring little more than the traditional British negligence approach to healthcare quality. If a patient

---

[1]   See, for example, Lord Hope in *Chester v Afshar*: 'the function of the law is to enable rights to be vindicated and to provide remedies when duties have been breached' [2004] 4 All ER 587, at para 87.

[2]   Lord Irvine of Lairg, 'The Patient, the Doctor, their Lawyers and the Judge: Rights and Duties' (1999) 7 *Med L Rev* 255, at p 267.

[3]   See IM Kennedy, 'The Fiduciary Relationship – Doctors and Patients' in P Birks (ed), *Wrongs and Remedies in the Twenty First Century* (Oxford, Clarendon Press, 1996). See also P Bartlett, 'Doctors as Fiduciaries: Equitable Regulation of the Doctor-Patient Relationship' (1997) 5 *Med L Rev* 193.

[4]   (1992) 92 DLR (4th) 449.

[5]   See Kennedy, n 3 above, p 121.

[6]   *Ibid*, p 122. Kennedy ultimately rejects the argument as a 'false dawn' however: 'It is confused jurisprudentially, it infantilises patients, it leaves doctors unsure. Most important, it extends the carte blanche of 'best interests' . . .' (p 140).

[7]   Article 4 ECHRB.

suffers harm as a result of the failure of a healthcare professional to meet his or her professional standards, the patient will be entitled to some compensation for that harm. Increasingly, however, a patient can also expect some vindication of his or her rights to quality healthcare regardless of whether the doctor met his professional standards. While negligence continues to be the focus of legal regulation of healthcare quality in the UK, it is no longer the bar to patient's rights that it once was. Given that studies show that there is a surprisingly high risk of being the victim of a preventable error when in hospital,[8] there is no doubt that the question of healthcare quality is central to the law's involvement with medicine.

II.   The Legal Requirements of Negligence

In order for a patient to succeed in a claim for negligence against a doctor he must satisfy three requirements: he must establish that a duty of care was owed by the doctor or hospital to himself; he must prove that the doctor breached that duty of care by failing to reach the standard of care required by the law; and finally the patient must prove that his injury or harm was caused by the doctor's negligent act. Each of these requirements for negligence will now be considered in detail, with particular emphasis upon the way in which the strict requirements have evolved to incorporate some consideration for the rights of the patient suffering an adverse event in a medical context.

(a)   Establishing a Duty of Care

Generally, in negligence cases, the establishment of a duty of care is a complex issue. In the healthcare context, however, the burden on the claimant to prove that a duty of care was owed to him is considerably lessened due to a general assumption that a doctor will inevitably owe a duty of care to his patient.[9] This assumption is based on the fundamental nature of the doctor-patient relationship which incorporates an obligation of caring as an inherent feature of it. The duty of care is easy to establish in the healthcare context and indeed will usually be conceded. Therefore, a patient seeking to prove medical negligence on the part

---

[8]   A US study suggests that there are adverse events in 3.7% of admissions (TA Brennan, LL Leape et al, 'Incidence of Adverse Events and Negligence in Hospitalised Patients: Results of the Harvard Medical Practice Study I and II' (1991) 324 *New Eng. J of Med* 370 and 377) and an Australian study suggests an even higher level of adverse events in 16.6% of hospital admissions (with 51% of these judged to be highly preventable) (R McL Wilson and WB Runciman et al, 'The Quality in Australian Health Care Study' (1995) 163 *Med J of Aus* 458).

[9]   A health authority will also be vicariously liable for the actions of its employees.

of his doctors will usually jump the first hurdle with ease. Establishing that the doctor's duty of care has been breached and has caused harm will be more challenging.

The fact that a duty of care is usually easily established does not mean that there are not some more problematic issues at the margins of the topic. In particular, there are two controversial issues stemming from the fact that, although it is established that a doctor owes a duty of care to his patient, it is less clear when a person becomes the doctor's patient. Is presenting oneself at a hospital accident and emergency department sufficient to impose a duty of care upon the hospital doctors? And if a person becomes ill in a public place where a doctor is present, does a doctor-patient relationship ensue?

The answers to both of these questions stem from the important 1969 case of *Barnett v Chelsea and Kensington Hospital Management Committee*.[10] This case arose from the fact that three night watchmen, feeling unwell after drinking some tea, arrived at their local casualty department seeking medical assistance. They told a nurse about their situation and she consulted a doctor by telephone. The doctor was himself feeling unwell, however, and merely advised over the telephone that the men should go home and visit their GP if their symptoms persisted. The doctor did not personally examine the men. They left as instructed and one of them subsequently died from arsenic poisoning. An action in negligence was brought and the first question facing the court (another vital question of causation will be discussed later in this chapter) was whether the doctor had owed the deceased man a duty of care. The court held that the key to answering this question was whether there had been an undertaking of responsibility by the hospital. It was held that on the facts such an undertaking had been given, presumably by the telephone consultation although the court's reasoning is not entirely clear. The requirement of an undertaking of responsibility means that a doctor who does not respond to a call for a doctor in a theatre or an aeroplane when somebody is taken ill, could not be held to be negligent as he has not assumed any duty of care. If, however, a doctor does identify himself in such circumstances and attempts to assist the ill person, he will assume a duty of care and could potentially be found negligent if the medical assistance which he offers falls below the requisite standard. In other words, the law positively discourages the Good Samaritan. If a doctor follows his conscience and ethical obligations and offers assistance to a person in need, he opens the door to a claim for negligence. If he stays silent, he owes no legal duties at all. The one exception to this general rule is a GP who probably does owe a duty of care to any emergency case within, but not outside, his practice area.[11]

---

[10]   [1969] 1 QB 428, [1968] 1 All ER 1068.

[11]   It appears that the ambulance service owes a duty of care to any identifiable person who is in need of an ambulance and has summoned one. Curiously, this places the ambulance service in a very different legal position to the other emergency services that have consistently been held not to be negligent by failing to respond to a 999 call. In *Kent v Griffiths, Roberts and London Ambulance Service*

In general, the task of establishing a duty of care will be of minimal difficulty within the context of a doctor-patient relationship. The assumption that a legal duty is owed to a patient when receiving medical care is a sensible means of protecting the patient's rights to healthcare of a reasonable quality. The fact that such a duty only arises once a doctor has undertaken professional responsibility for the patient is a logical concession to the need to protect the medical professional from legal repercussions for events over which they had no influence. As easy as it usually is to establish a duty of care owed by a doctor, it must be remembered that this is of no legal significance unless the patient is also able to prove that the doctor breached this duty. It is to this more problematic issue to which we will now turn.

(b)   Proving that the Doctor has Breached his Duty of Care

(i)   The traditional *Bolam* test

In order for a doctor to breach his duty of care he must fall below the standard of care imposed by the law. The question of what this standard is, and who determines it, has been a major preoccupation of medical law for over half a century. The starting point for discussion of this issue is the case of *Bolam v Friern Hospital Management Committee*.[12] The patient in this case was suffering from mental illness and was subjected to electro-convulsive therapy (ECT). During this treatment, the patient was not given any relaxant drugs and was largely unrestrained. The patient's convulsive movements during the treatment resulted in dislocation of both hip joints and fractures of the pelvis. The patient alleged negligence but there were two bodies of opinion on the correct procedure for ECT: one body of opinion required restraint of the patient in order to avoid such injuries and the other did not. The judge, McNair J, set out what has become known as the *Bolam* test: a doctor is not guilty of negligence if he has acted in accordance with a practice accepted as proper by a responsible body of medical men skilled in that particular art. On the facts of the case, because a body of medical opinion supported the application of ECT without restraint, there was held to be no breach of the doctor's duty of care and thus no negligence.

At the core of the infamous *Bolam* test is the controversial proposition that the standard of care required of a doctor in order to avoid negligence is that of his professional colleagues. While it may be entirely reasonable to judge professional behaviour on the basis of the standards of that profession, the consequence of

[2000] 2 All ER 474, a pregnant woman suffering from asthma called her GP because she was feeling out of breath. Her GP called an ambulance but it took 40 minutes to arrive despite further calls from the woman's husband. While in the ambulance, she suffered a respiratory arrest which resulted in serious brain damage and a miscarriage. The Court of Appeal held that a duty of care was owed. This duty requires that the ambulance service respond to calls reasonably promptly. It was recognised, however, that limited resources may mean that some cases are prioritised over others.

[12]   [1957] 2 All ER 118.

such an approach is that it is doctors rather than judges who are perceived to be setting the standard. This is undesirable for a number of reasons, including the danger of the medical profession closing ranks to avoid findings of negligence and the possibility that dangerous practices may be tolerated by the law because they have widespread support among professional bodies.

One issue meriting some discussion here is the question of whether all doctors are held to an identical standard of care or whether, for example, a junior doctor will only be expected to meet a lower standard. In *Wilsher v Essex Health Authority*,[13] a baby was born prematurely and suffering from oxygen deficiency. A junior doctor mistakenly placed a catheter in a vein rather than an artery and then asked the senior registrar to check it. The more senior doctor failed to spot the mistake, which led to incorrect oxygen readings causing the baby to be given excess oxygen which may have caused later blindness. The court held that the standard of care expected was that of a junior doctor working in a special baby care unit. It is therefore an objective standard which is not based on the individual doctor's experience or ability, but is related to the position in which the doctor is employed. The junior doctor in this case was held not to be negligent because he had satisfied his standard of care by consulting his senior colleague. If anyone was negligent here it was the senior doctor who should have spotted the mistake (although the negligence action failed on the causation requirement).

One significant feature derived from the *Bolam* test was that the courts would not choose between two conflicting bodies of medical opinion: the existence of one body supporting the doctor's actions is sufficient to negate any claims of negligence. This point was seen most clearly in *Maynard v West Midlands Regional Health Authority* when the House of Lords approved and applied the *Bolam* test.[14] This case concerned two consultants who examined a patient with symptoms which could indicate either TB (the most likely) or Hodgkin's disease (which would have more serious implications). They recommended that the patient undergo an exploratory operation in order to rule out Hodgkin's disease but this operation itself ran a risk of causing damage to the patient's vocal cords. The patient underwent the operation and Hodgkin's disease was ruled out but her vocal cords were damaged. The medical profession was divided on whether the doctors had acted negligently. One body of opinion held that a diagnosis of TB should have been made without the operation, while another body of opinion held that it was correct to recommend the operation even with its inherent risks given the seriousness of Hodgkin's disease. The judge at first instance compared these two bodies of medical opinion and decided that he preferred the body of opinion which held that the operation was negligent but on appeal the House of Lords refused to choose between these two views. Applying the *Bolam* test, the

---

[13]   [1999] 3 AC 1074.
[14]   [1985] 1 All ER 635.

House of Lords held that there can be no negligence if there is a responsible body of medical opinion which supports the doctors' actions. The fact that there is also an opposing body of opinion is legally irrelevant. The body of opinion supporting the doctors' actions need not be a majority view and indeed it need not even comprise a substantial number of doctors. This point was seen clearly in *Defreitas v O'Brien*[15] in which only 4 or 5 out of 250 specialists in neurosurgery supported the doctor's actions and yet the court held that this was sufficient to qualify as a responsible body of medical opinion and thus preclude a finding of negligence. In this context it is easy to see why the Bolam test has proved controversial. It was 'out of control', frequently applied 'out of context',[16] and 'came close to acquiring demonic status in some quarters'.[17]

(ii) *Bolitho*: reasserting the role of the courts

In the 1998 case of *Bolitho v City & Hackney Health Authority*,[18] an attempt was made to re-assert the judiciary's role in determining the standard of care in medical negligence in contrast to the perception that doctors were judged only by their peers. *Bolitho* concerned a young boy suffering from respiratory distress while in hospital. Despite being called, the senior registrar failed to attend and the boy suffered a cardiac arrest and brain damage and subsequently died. The key question for the court was one of causation because the health authority admitted that the doctor had been in breach of her duty of care by not attending. The complicating factor in this case was that, even if she had attended the patient (as she should have done), she would not have intubated him. As intubation was the only procedure which would have prevented the injury, there was considerable doubt over whether the doctor's failure to attend 'caused' the injury. (Causation is discussed in more detail below.) The court thus enquired into whether a failure to intubate would have been a breach of the doctor's duty of care. Medical opinion was divided on this issue but, as there was one body of medical opinion supporting the doctor's actions, a strict application of *Bolam* would have found her not negligent. However, the House of Lords was not willing to blindly accept this professional opinion without first being convinced that the opinion rested on a 'logical' basis. On the facts it was held that the expert evidence in favour of not intubating was indeed logical and therefore the doctor was found not to be negligent. The judicial inquiry into the logic of the medical

---

[15] [1993] 4 Med LR 281.

[16] Originally the *Bolam* test applied only to the standard of care in medical negligence cases but subsequently a judicial philosophy of 'when in doubt Bolamise' has arisen. (M Davies, 'The 'New *Bolam*': Another False Dawn for Medical Negligence' (1996) 12 *PN* 10) and the *Bolam* test has been applied to questions of the treatment of incompetent patients (*Re F (mental patient: sterilisation)* [1990] 2 AC 1) and the withdrawal of life-sustaining treatment (*Airedale NHS Trust v Bland* [1993] 1 All ER 821).

[17] M Brazier and J Miola, 'Bye-Bye Bolam: A Medical Litigation Revolution?' (2000) 8 *Med L Rev* 85, at p 85.

[18] [1998] AC 232.

opinion has wide-ranging significance, however. It was widely seen as a reasser-
tion of the judiciary's role in determining the standard of care in medical
negligence cases and a denial of the criticism that doctors were free to set their
own standard which the courts would accept without scrutiny.

The point cannot be ignored, however, that 'logic' is a very curious test to
introduce into medical negligence. A number of criticisms can be made in respect
of it. First, the House of Lords admitted in *Bolitho* that it would be extremely rare
for a body of medical opinion to be regarded as not resting on a logical basis, and
therefore the logic test can be criticised as an insufficient restraint upon medical
discretion in respect of the standard of care. Second, in the absence of a medical
qualification it may remain extremely difficult for a judge to sincerely assess the
logic of a medical practice. Finally, and most obviously, logic just seems the
wrong test for the courts to apply. Perhaps all three of these criticisms can best be
illustrated by querying whether a medical practice which has the support of a
body of professionals is ever likely to be illogical: if a number of specialists abide
by it then the practice will almost inevitably have the internal consistency
necessary to satisfy a logic test to the extent that judges can assess the matter and
thus may still be an unreasonable practice to have adopted, particularly when
regard is given to patients' rights. As Teff has argued, '[t]o speak of logic in this
context suggests an appeal to the internal consistency of the expert's testimony
rather than a more extensive, pragmatic assessment of what the court deems
reasonable'.[19] Teff is correct to regard such a test as still very much in the domain
of credibility rather than reasonableness.[20] Thus the logic gloss placed upon the
Bolam test by *Bolitho* could be regarded as an insufficient means of restraining
medical discretion.

It could be, however, that the label of 'logic' hides a more substantial change in
the law. Teff notes that the nomenclature could be seen as 'a residue of deference'
but that courts may in future 'deploy their own sense of reasonableness as the
operative criterion'.[21] There is some evidence for this view of the message of
Bolitho as Lord Browne-Wilkinson placed great prominence upon the *Edward
Wong* case,[22] a case concerning conveyancing practice in Hong Kong, which held
that even if a practice has widespread adherence of virtually all the members of a
profession, it may still be found to be negligent. The contrast with the *Defreitas*
case discussed above, where the support of a mere handful of doctors was
sufficient to prevent a finding of negligence, is obvious. Brazier and Miola share
Teff's view that the *Bolitho* judgment has the potential to be hugely significant. It
is perhaps illuminating that the significance foreseen is merely to place the
medical profession on the same footing as other professions: '*Bolitho* has set in

---

[19]   H Teff, 'The Standard of Care in Medical Negligence: Moving on from *Bolam?*' (1998) 18 *OJLS*
473, at p 481.
[20]   *Ibid.*
[21]   *Ibid.*
[22]   *Edward Wong Finance v Johnson Stokes* [1984] 1 AC 296.

train a process whereby judges scrutinise medical evidence, using the same mixture of common sense and logical analysis that they use to scrutinise other expert evidence in negligence claims against professionals such as architects and accountants'.[23] That this is the most optimistic interpretation of *Bolitho* demonstrates just how weak judicial scrutiny of the medical profession was pre-*Bolitho*. In a healthcare system, and a legal system, in which the rights of patients are increasingly being recognised as a vital component of healthcare quality, the pre-*Bolitho* deference can no longer withstand scrutiny.[24]

A good example of the post-Bolitho environment for medical negligence cases is provided by the 1999 case of *Marriott v West Midlands Health Authority*.[25] A patient attended hospital after suffering a head injury. After being discharged the patient continued to suffer headaches and visited his GP eight days later. The GP conducted some simple neurological tests but found no abnormalities and merely recommended painkillers. Four days later the patient was readmitted to hospital and underwent a major operation for a large extradural haematoma and internal bleeding. The patient was left paralysed and with a speech disorder and claimed negligence against both the hospital and the GP. The medical evidence was divided on whether the GP should have sent the patient back to the hospital. Pre-*Bolitho*, the mere existence of a body of medical opinion supporting the GP would have been sufficient to prevent a finding of negligence, even if the wisest course would have been readmittance. Post-*Bolitho*, the judge felt justified in undertaking a risk assessment exercise, concluding that, with the small risk of a very serious consequence, the only reasonably prudent course would have been to readmit the patient. This reasoning was upheld in the Court of Appeal. Reasonableness, rather than logic, was at the core of this decision, suggesting that there is some merit to the argument, outlined above, that *Bolitho's* reliance upon the label of logic may merely disguise a greater shift in the law's approach to the medical profession.

(iii)   Errors: negligence or just human?

One issue that has caused problems for both the courts and commentators in recent decades is whether a mere error amounts to negligence. In the 1981 case of *Whitehouse v Jordan*,[26] the doctor had tried to deliver a baby by using forceps before deciding that this would not be possible and proceeding to a Caesarean section delivery. The baby was born with severe and irreparable brain damage and it was alleged that this was caused by the doctor's failed attempts to use

---

[23]   Brazier and Miola, n 17 above, p 103.

[24]   It should be noted that many commentators view *Bolitho* as merely seeking to restore the *Bolam* test to its original limits. The emphasis, after all, in McNair J's test is on a 'responsible' body of medical opinion, and it is doubtful that he ever intended 'to give doctors carte blanche to clothe inadequate practice with some sort of official blessing, thereby effectively sanctioning negligent practice' (Brazier and Miola, n 17 above, p 98).

[25]   [1999] Lloyd's Rep Med 23.

[26]   [1981] 1 All ER 267.

forceps. The judge made a finding of negligence but this was overturned on appeal. Lord Denning argued forcefully in the Court of Appeal that a mere error of judgement, as was evident in this case, could never amount to negligence. The House of Lords, however, took a different view and held that errors of judgement can be negligent but only if it is an error which would not be made by a reasonably competent doctor acting with ordinary care. On the facts of the case, the doctor did not fall below this standard and thus was not negligent.

More generally, Merry and McCall Smith have argued that errors are inevitable in the human condition and should not be regarded as negligence. It was noted above that recent studies have indicated that medical errors are more widespread than was previously known. Merry and McCall Smith explain that, while the chances of an individual patient during one hospital admission suffering an adverse event are quite low, the chances of an individual doctor over the course of his career accidentally causing an adverse event are extremely high.[27] If this is true – if it is highly likely that every doctor will occasionally make a mistake – we must ask whether it is appropriate to regard that as something which a reasonably competent doctor would not do. For example, it is never reasonable to give a patient the wrong drug but a reasonable doctor over the course of his career may well do so at least once. If we look at the adverse event in isolation, we see merely a wronged patient but if we look at the career of the doctor, the error becomes less of a reason for blame and more of an unfortunate inevitability. Often an error may not be the subject of complaint, as negligence depends greatly upon moral luck – ie whether the breach of the duty of care actually causes any significant harm to the patient. Merry and McCall Smith argue that the inevitability of errors at some point in a career – any career – mean that it is extremely harsh to find a doctor negligent when one of those errors causes harm. The writers are careful to distinguish 'errors' from 'violations' which they do regard as culpable. A violation is a deliberate deviance from safe practice while errors are entirely unintentional: misreading the label on a drug would be classified as an error, for example, but not bothering to read the label in order to save time would be a violation. This argument is sound in the sense that it acknowledges that there are different levels of blame attached to adverse events but the distinction fails to adequately focus upon the harm done to the patient. As Merry and McCall Smith do recognise, 'however blameless the doctor, the patient is even less to blame for the injury'.[28] This point perhaps suggests that a fault based system such as negligence does not strike the necessary balance between protecting the patient's rights while not attaching blame to a professional who has done nothing other than act as a reasonably competent doctor, but inevitably flawed human being. Alternative means to regulate the quality of healthcare are discussed below.

---

[27]   A Merry and A McCall Smith, *Errors, Medicine and the Law* (Cambridge, Cambridge University Press, 2001) p 45.

[28]   *Ibid*, p 204.

(iv)   Conclusion on breach of a duty of care

In conclusion on the breach of a duty of care requirement for negligence, it can be seen that the courts have recently been less willing to defer to medical opinion and will attempt at least some scrutiny of medical evidence before accepting it. This is a move consistent with developments in other areas of medical law as the focus is shifting onto patients' rights in a number of contexts. However, it will still be rare for a court to dismiss expert evidence that a doctor has acted in a manner consistent with professional standards and practice. As Teff has argued, 'shopping around' for a sympathetic expert is common and 'differential resources, of funding and access to expertise, will typically favour institutional defendants such as health authorities or hospital trusts'.[29] The patient still faces an uphill struggle to prove a breach of a doctor's duty of care.

(c)   The Final Hurdle: Did the Breach Cause the Harm?

(i)   From *Barnett* to *Chester*: relaxation of the causation requirement

It was mentioned above that moral luck plays a part in a negligence finding. This is because, even if a doctor breaches his duty of care by falling below the requisite standard of care, a patient will only be able to recover damages if that breach can be regarded as causing some harm. If the doctor breaches his duty of care but the patient is unharmed or would have suffered identical harm regardless of the doctor's failings, then the doctor is not negligent. This can be seen most clearly in the outcome of the *Barnett v Chelsea and Kensington Hospital Management Committee* case, discussed above in the duty section.[30] In this case, it was established that the doctor had breached his duty of care to the deceased man by not examining him personally but the action for negligence failed because, even if the patient had been seen by the doctor, the arsenic poisoning was regarded as too far advanced for an antidote to be effective. In other words, by the time the patient arrived at the hospital he was destined to die regardless of the actions, or negligent omissions, of the doctors. The fact that his doctor failed to meet the requisite standard of care in treating him did not in itself cause any harm.

There are two ways of viewing this causation requirement. On the one hand, it embodies the sound principle that a person should not be held liable for damage which he did not cause. On the other hand, there is no legal remedy for incompetent medical care unless the patient can prove on the balance of probabilities that the doctor's actions caused some identifiable harm. The patient in *Barnett* should have been seen by a doctor but the fact that he was not was not susceptible to legal recompense. In recent years, the English courts have recognised that a very strict application of the causation requirement can result in

---

[29]   Teff, n 19 above, p 48.
[30]   [1969] 1 QB 428, [1968] 1 All ER 1068

injustice for the patient and thus there have been stuttering moves towards a relaxation of this requirement. In *Bolitho*,[31] for example, a strict application of the traditional causation test of 'but for' – i.e. the harm would not have been caused but for the doctor's negligence – was self-evidently not satisfied. It will be recalled that in this case the doctor failed to attend the patient but argued that, if she had attended, she would not have provided the one treatment (intubation) which could have saved the child. Therefore, it is clear that the harm of the child's death would have occurred even if the doctor had met her duty of care by attending the patient. Nevertheless, the court was not willing to settle for this conclusion and instead enquired into whether the doctor's intended failure to intubate if she had attended would have been negligent in itself. The court's conclusion on this issue was discussed above in the breach section. The fact that it was considered by the court at all is an indication that, if some serious harm has occurred, the courts will look at the entire circumstances of the case before coming to a conclusion as to whether the causation requirement has been satisfied.

The approach can be seen even more starkly, and controversially, in the 2004 case of *Chester v Afshar*.[32] This case involved a doctor's negligent failure to warn a patient about the risks inherent in a procedure. The need for a patient's consent to medical treatment to be fully informed is discussed in detail in the next chapter. At this stage, however, it is merely necessary to discuss the causation aspects of this case. The complication in respect of causation arose because the patient admitted that she would have still undergone the operation (albeit after some further time for reflection) even if she had been warned about the risks of paralysis which unfortunately materialised during the procedure. Therefore, the doctor's failure to disclose this risk, although a breach of his duty of care, did not on the strict application of the causation requirement, cause the harm suffered by the patient. When *Chester* reached the House of Lords, the House was divided on the issue of causation. The two dissenting Lords emphasised that Miss Chester had failed to prove that the doctor caused her injury. Lord Bingham said that 'she cannot show that the negligence proved against Mr Afshar was, in any ordinary sense, a cause of her loss'[33] and Lord Hoffman noted that 'on ordinary principles of tort law, the defendant is not liable'.[34] Both of these judges therefore held that Miss Chester could not recover damages in respect of Mr Afshar's negligent non-disclosure. Even the judges in the majority acknowledged that the traditional causation requirement had not been satisfied in this case. Lord Hope, for example, who gave the leading judgment, accepted that 'a solution to this problem which is in Miss Chester's favour cannot be based on conventional

---

[31]   See n 18 above.
[32]   [2004] 4 All ER 587.
[33]   *Ibid*, para 9.
[34]   *Ibid*, para 32.

causation principles'.[35] Nevertheless, the majority allowed Miss Chester to recover damages on the basis of somewhat vague policy reasons. Lord Hope explained that the key question for the House was 'whether, in the unusual circumstances of this case, justice requires the normal approach to causation to be modified'.[36] Lord Hope further explained that 'the function of the law is to enable rights to be vindicated and to provide remedies when duties have been breached. Unless this is done the duty is a hollow one, stripped of all practical force and devoid of all content'.[37] Lord Steyn shared this view that the vindication of the patient's rights was the overriding consideration: 'Her right of autonomy and dignity can and ought to be vindicated by a narrow and modest departure from traditional causation principles ... This result is in accord with one of the most basic aspirations of the law, namely to right wrongs.'[38] On policy grounds, therefore, Lords Hope, Steyn and Walker held that the test of causation had been satisfied, even though they agreed with Lords Bingham and Hoffman that this required a departure from traditional principles. The mere fact that the patient's injury was 'intimately involved with the duty to warn' was sufficient for Lord Hope,[39] while Lord Walker emphasised that the doctor had failed in his professional duty and the patient 'has suffered injury directly within the scope and focus of that duty'.[40]

The adaptation of the causation requirement in *Chester v Afshar* has been the subject of considerable debate and some criticism.[41] Green, for example, argues that the law of torts 'is concerned not with compensating all those who have suffered loss, but only with compensating those who have suffered loss as a result of the defendant's breach of duty'.[42] This very point is emphasised by Lord Bingham in his dissent when he argues that 'a claimant is not entitled to be compensated, and a defendant is not bound to compensate the claimant, for damage not caused by the negligence complained of'.[43] To some extent this is a convincing argument. Miss Chester was awarded full damages for the injury she suffered even though this injury was not really caused by the doctor's actions, and this seems unjust. However, the point that is being missed here is that the doctor's negligent non-disclosure did cause a different loss to Miss Chester. Green argues that Miss Chester 'lost nothing of value'[44] but this is not true: she lost her right to make an autonomous choice about medical treatment.

---

[35]   *Ibid*, para 81.
[36]   *Ibid*, para 85.
[37]   *Ibid*, para 87.
[38]   *Ibid*, para 24-25.
[39]   *Ibid*, para 87.
[40]   *Ibid*, para 101.
[41]   Indeed, in the following chapter, the vagueness surrounding the rights being vindicated in this case is criticised.
[42]   S Green, 'Coherence of Medical Negligence Cases: A Game of Doctors and Purses' (2006) 14 *Med L Rev* 1, at p 4.
[43]   *Chester v Afshar*, n 32 above, para 9.
[44]   Green, n 42 above, p 14.

As is explained in much more detail in the next chapter, autonomy in respect of healthcare requires that a patient is fully informed about the treatment before he or she can consent to it. The right to refuse consent to medical treatment, protected in both English common law and international human rights law, requires that an informed choice be made by the patient. Miss Chester was denied this right. She agreed to undergo treatment in ignorance of its risks and true nature. Her right to autonomy was denied. Green's opposing view is best explained as follows:

> A patient's dignity and right to decide is protected by the law of tort's recognition that a doctor has a duty to warn, not by the readiness to override causal considerations in the claimant's favour. If a breach of that duty to warn causes the patient no loss, then a finding of no liability does not violate that right. It merely serves as an acknowledgment that the patient's inability to exercise that right did not, on this occasion, cause any harm.[45]

A fundamentally different view of the situation is taken in this book. The inability to exercise a right to autonomy is regarded as a harm in itself, regardless of the ultimate physical consequences. This rights-based approach does mean, however, that Mason and Brodie are correct to regard the award of full damages to Miss Chester as inconsistent with the House of Lords' modified approach to causation:

> One can understand the concern to allow the plaintiff to vindicate her rights. However, the measure of damages allowed does not, in truth, reflect the loss suffered because, at the end of the day, the loss lay in an invasion of autonomy per se, and an award of full damages can be said to over-compensate.[46]

The House of Lords judgment in *Chester v Afshar* represents a significant departure from the traditional requirements of a negligence action. It is a flawed judgment because the policy grounds relied upon remain largely unarticulated and the emphasis upon vindication of the patient's rights is insufficiently explained and justified. But, it is also encouraging from a human rights perspective to see this judicial recognition at the highest level that causation requirements should no longer act as a bar to recovery where a patient's rights have been infringed during the provision of healthcare. Mason and Laurie refer to a trend to 'assist the plaintiff over the causation hurdle in medico-legal cases'[47] and, given the tall hurdle still in place in respect of proving a breach of the duty of care, this is overall to be welcomed. It is a trend which is not confined to the United

---

[45]   *Ibid*, pp 9-10.

[46]   K Mason and D Brodie, 'Bolam, Bolam – Wherefore Art Thou Bolam?' (2005) 9 *Edin LR* 298, at p 305.

[47]   JK Mason, A McCall Smith and G Laurie, *Law and Medical Ethics*, 7th edn (Oxford, Oxford University Press, 2006), p 339.

Kingdom.[48] However, the House of Lords has not been entirely consistent in applying this more relaxed approach and therefore in the recent case of *Gregg v Scott*[49] a patient fell at the causation hurdle in tragic circumstances.

(ii) *Gregg v Scott*: reassertion of the need to prove causation

The case of *Gregg v Scott* involved a loss of chance of a recovery situation. A similar issue had arisen in the earlier case of *Hotson v East Berkshire Area Health Authority*[50] when a hospital initially incorrectly diagnosed a child's injured hip and permanent disability ensued. The health authority admitted negligence in the delay in providing a correct diagnosis but denied that the delay had in law caused the disability. The judge found that there was a 75% chance that the disability would have developed anyway and so he awarded damages based on the loss of a 25% chance of recovery. The House of Lords, however, overturned this decision on the logical grounds that a 25% chance that the injury was caused by the negligent act does not satisfy the general causation test of 'but for' (which would require a greater than 50% chance). In *Gregg v Scott*, this approach was confirmed even though *Chester v Afshar* had previously suggested that the House of Lords would be more flexible on the causation test. In *Gregg*, there was a negligent delay of nine months in diagnosing and treating the patient's cancer. During this period, the patient's chance of recovery was regarded as having dropped from 42% to 25%.[51] The House of Lords, by a 3-2 majority, refused to allow the patient to recover for this loss of chance because, on the balance of probabilities, the patient would have died regardless of the negligence.[52] The majority were not prepared to amend the traditional causation test. Lord Phillips explained his view that 'there is a danger, if special tests of causation are developed piecemeal to deal with perceived injustices in particular factual situations, that the coherence of our common law will be destroyed'.[53] In particular, the introduction of possible rather than probable causation was denied.[54]

However, this decision can be subjected to criticism because there seems little doubt that the significant reduction in the chance of recovering from cancer in this case represented a very real loss to the patient. The harshness of the 'but for', or balance of probabilities, causation requirement is evident here. As Lord Nicholls explained in his dissenting judgment:

---

[48] *Rufo v Hoskins* [2004] NSWCA 391; *Philip v Ryan* [2004] 1 IESC 105.

[49] [2005] 2 AC 176.

[50] [1987] AC 750.

[51] Lord Phillips rejected these simplistic figures, regarding them as 'fallacious' (para 147) and emphasises that 'deductions cannot safely be drawn from statistics without expert evidence' (para 170). However, the other four Law Lords accepted, and based their judgments upon, these figures.

[52] The matter was somewhat complicated (although happily so) by the fact that the patient was still alive at the time of the trial, nine years later.

[53] *Gregg v Scott*, n 49 above, para 172.

[54] See Lord Hoffman's comments at *ibid*, para 90, that this would be 'so radical a change in our law as to amount to a legislative act'.

> The present state of the law is crude to an extent bordering on arbitrariness. It means that a patient with a 60% chance of recovery reduced to a 40% prospect by medical negligence can obtain compensation. But he can obtain nothing if his prospects were reduced from 40% to nil. This is rough justice indeed.[55]

The fact that a patient already has only a slim chance of recovery will inevitably mean that it is all the more valuable to him. If a patient is told, as was Mr Gregg, that he has only a 42% chance of recovery – ie more than a 1 in 3 chance – and then, due to a doctor's negligence, that chance is taken away from him so that he is left with only a 1 in 4 chance (25%), the patient will be perfectly entitled to feel that the doctor's negligence has caused him some loss. As Lord Nicholls says:

> a doctor's duty to act in the best interests of his patient involves maximising the patient's recovery prospects, and doing so whether the patient's prospects are good or not so good . . . To this end the law should recognise the existence and loss of poor and indifferent prospects as well as those more favourable.[56]

He continues by making the sensible suggestion that 'the difference between good and poor prospects is a matter going to the amount of compensation fairly payable, not to liability to make payment at all'.[57]

Lord Hope also dissented but, although he said that he was in agreement with Lord Nicholls, his dissent is actually based on rather different reasoning. Lord Hope did not see the case as concerning a mere loss of chance. Instead, he regarded the inevitable enlargement of the cancerous tumour which occurred after the doctor's negligence as the actionable injury.[58] The existence of this injury could be established on the balance of probabilities and thus avoids the need to make radical changes to the causation test. However, this ingenious solution was not adopted by the other Law Lords. It should be noted that despite the majority refusing to compensate the patient for the loss of a chance of recovery, Lord Phillips and Baroness Hale both made the point that they would have awarded damages for the additional pain, suffering and distress caused by the doctor's negligence.[59] Unfortunately, these additional grounds of damage were not claimed and therefore the House of Lords decision had the harsh result of denying any compensation for the doctor's negligence. *Gregg v Scott* is a good example of the injustice which can arise as a result of the traditional negligence requirements. It suggests that *Chester v Afshar* was a false dawn and that the traditional strict causation test will still need to be satisfied before a patient can be compensated for suffering from medical treatment which falls below the requisite standard of care.

---

[55]   *Gregg v Scott*, n 49 above, para 46.
[56]   *Ibid*, para 42.
[57]   *Ibid*, para 43.
[58]   *Ibid*, para 113.
[59]   *Ibid*, Lord Phillips, at para 191; Baroness Hale at para 227.

(d)   Negligence: Conclusion

Overall, there is little doubt that the rights of a patient suffering a preventable adverse event while in hospital have been increasingly recognised by the courts. When the traditional rules of negligence have failed to provide a remedy as in *Marriott* or *Chester*, the higher courts have been willing to develop these rules to enable a vindication of the patient's rights. The clear message in *Bolitho* that medical discretion has its limits was a significant turning point in the relationship between medicine and law. The utilisation of negligence to regulate the doctor-patient relationship still has its inherent flaws, however. Its intricate duty, breach and causation requirements continue to present a difficult challenge for patients and its allocation of blame to an individual doctor for a non-intentional mistake can operate unduly harshly upon the medical profession. Increasingly, therefore, the rights of both the patients and the doctors suggest that an alternative non-fault system of compensation for medical errors may be desirable. The arguments for this will now be considered.

III.   Non-fault Compensation: Escaping the Blame Culture

The concept of non-fault compensation is not new, nor is it restricted to medical injuries. The question is whether compensation should be awarded irrespective of blame and, as Merry and McCall Smith note, the real barrier to doing so is cultural: 'an excessive readiness to respond to misfortune by blaming others'.[60] Nevertheless, some countries have been able to overcome the blame culture, or at least set it to one side in this context. In New Zealand, a non-fault system for all accident injuries compensation has existed since the 1972 Accident Compensation Act. This Act established an Accident Compensation Corporation to award compensation and removed the right to sue. Originally, the system put in place did not distinguish healthcare injuries from accidental injuries caused in any other context. However, in 1992, the Accident and Rehabilitation and Compensation Insurance Act distinguished 'medical misadventures' from other injuries. These were defined as either (a) 'medical error': the failure to observe a standard of care and skill reasonably to be expected in the circumstances;[61] or (b) 'medical mishap': an adverse consequence of treatment which is severe and where the likelihood of it occurring was rare.[62] These two types of medical misadventure had caused considerable debate in New Zealand before the 1992 Act and

---

[60]   Merry and McCall Smith, n 27 above, p 206.
[61]   Section 5(1) Accident and Rehabilitation and Compensation Insurance Act 1992.
[62]   *Ibid*, as amended by the Accident Rehabilitation and Compensation Amendment Act (No 2) 1993.

continued to do so subsequently. The concept of medical error refers back to negligence as it requires that the doctor has failed to meet an adequate standard of care but a medical mishap is, by definition, a non-negligent injury, although both a rare and severe one. Therefore, even non-negligent injuries can be the subject of compensation in New Zealand, although only if they satisfy the requirements of the 1992 Act. Oliphant notes a worrying lack of clarity in respect of this provision and concludes that 'at present, doctrinal confusion as to the nature of 'medical mishap' threatens to obscure the ethical concerns which underlie the non-fault endeavour and to imperil the achievement of its goals'.[63]

Such ethical concerns are not unfamiliar to UK lawyers. Lord Woolf, in his 1996 Access to Justice Report, singled out medical negligence as an area in which civil justice was 'failing most conspicuously'.[64] Lord Woolf identified the excessive cost, inherent delay, low success rate and lack of co-operation between parties in medical negligence cases as particular causes for concern. Lord Woolf personally favours the introduction of a non-fault system[65] and further heavyweight support for this change came with the Report of the Bristol Inquiry in 2001.[66] This Report, commonly known as the Kennedy Report after the chairman of the Inquiry, resulted from a high profile public inquiry into the care of children undergoing cardiac surgery at Bristol Royal Infirmary between 1984 and 1995. The situation being investigated was the performance of two cardiac surgeons who performed 53 operations during this period on children with congenital heart abnormalities. Twenty nine of these children died and four more suffered brain damage. These tragic results were considerably worse than in other hospitals but the surgeons continued with the operations, even after concerns had been raised by others in the hospital, and quoted the normal risks to parents rather than the actual results of their unit. Disciplinary proceedings before the GMC led to the de-registration of the surgeons but the problems went far deeper than two negligent doctors. The Kennedy Report emphasised that:

> This is not an account of bad people, nor of people who did not care. It is certainly not an account of people who wilfully harmed patients. Rather, it is an account of how people who were well motivated, failed to work together effectively for the interests of their patients, through lack of insight, poor leadership, and lack of teamwork . . . And it is an account of a system of hospital care which was poorly organised and beset with uncertainty from top to bottom as to how to get things done, such that when concerns were raised, it took years for them to be taken seriously.[67]

---

[63]   K Oliphant, 'Defining 'Medical Misadventure': Lessons from New Zealand' (1996) 4 *Med L Rev* 1, at p 28.

[64]   'Access to Justice: Final Report to the Lord Chancellor on the Civil Justice System in England and Wales' (1996) para 15.2.

[65]   Lord Woolf, 'Clinical Negligence: What is the Solution? How can we Provide Justice for Doctors and Patients?' (2004) 4 *Med Law Int* 133, at p 134.

[66]   'The Report of the Public Inquiry into Children's Heart Surgery at the Bristol Royal Infirmary 1984-1995: Learning from Bristol' (Cmnd 5207 (I) 2001.)

[67]   *Ibid*, para 13.8.

The Report found that the traditional tort approach was unhelpful in such complex circumstances and favoured a systems analysis approach in which failures are understood in the context of the system as a whole rather than by the allocation of individual blame and sanctions.[68] Bridgeman explains that:

> the Kennedy Report argues that the current tort-based adversarial system of negligence liability supports a culture of blame and fear, encourages a code of silence amongst professionals, and results in errors being covered up. The panel were clearly of the view that abolition of clinical negligence litigation is necessary if openness and candour to patients and between professionals are to prevail.[69]

Such openness and candour is a vital element of vindicating the rights of patients who suffer injury as a result of a failure on the part of medical professionals or the NHS system as a whole. But it is not, of course, the only element and this is why steps towards the introduction of a non-fault based system in the UK have been so very slow. While the removal of the blame culture inherent in a tort-based approach brings many advantages for both patient and doctor, it could also deny an injured patient a full vindication of his or her rights.

A Report by the Chief Medical Officer in 2003[70] investigated these issues in some detail and helpfully identified both advantages and disadvantages in the current system. The main problems identified echoed Lord Woolf's criticisms seven years earlier: the fault-based system is complex, slow, costly and can be unfair. It also diverts clinical staff from clinical care, damages both staff morale and public confidence, and encourages defensiveness and secrecy. Patients can be left dissatisfied with the lack of explanation or apology or reassurance that steps have been taken to prevent a repetition, with this dissatisfaction being intensified by potentially huge legal fees. However, despite this ringing condemnation of medical negligence as a means of ensuring quality healthcare and rectifying any adverse incidents, the 'Making Amends Report' concluded against the introduction of a non-fault system because of inherent dangers in such a change. A potentially huge increase in claims and therefore higher overall costs, leading to lower levels of compensation, was the main concern, but the difficulty in distinguishing harm to a patient from the natural progression of a disease (a lingering causation requirement which even the removal of 'fault' can not entirely extinguish) was also identified as a concern. Furthermore, the removal of fault will not in itself improve processes for learning from errors or reduce the risk of further harm to future patients. Indeed, it is arguable that the removal of blame may actually reduce the chances of this.

---

[68] J Bridgeman, '"Learning from Bristol": Healthcare in the Twenty First Century' (2002) 65 *Med L Rev* 241, at p 245.

[69] *Ibid*, p 252.

[70] Department of Health, 'Making Amends: A Consultation Paper Setting Out Proposals for Reforming the Approach to Clinical Negligence in the NHS' (2003).

Despite these concerns, the Report was adamant that the current system could not be left unchanged and therefore a compromise solution was proposed. This would entail the creation of a new NHS-based system of redress. This recommendation is being implemented through the NHS Redress Act 2006. There are four main elements to this proposed redress: an offer of compensation; an explanation; an apology; and a report on action taken, or to be taken, to prevent similar cases arising in the future.[71] Such redress will be available only if there is qualifying liability in tort, meaning that a breach of the duty of care is required.[72] Significantly the new NHS Redress scheme will not remove a patient's right to sue for negligence unless a package of care and compensation under the scheme has already been accepted. Therefore, unlike in New Zealand, a patient will have a choice of suing for negligence or pursuing redress without a finding of fault. The choice is likely to depend upon the patient's priorities. While some injured patients may need to prioritise monetary compensation, others may favour an apology or explanation or reassurance that it will not happen again. Others may seek a finding of blame by means of a judicial hearing. Their goals will help determine the redress sought, as unfortunately will their monetary situation, as legal fees may be a relevant factor. There is no doubt that greater choice will be available to patients harmed by medical treatment and this can only be an improvement on the current situation. The ultimate goal, however, must be the improvement of healthcare quality, and neither a fault-based nor a non-fault based system has yet found the key to unlock this door. As the Bristol Report identified, healthcare quality is today dependent upon a number of interlocking factors of which the individual doctor is often the least significant component: 'The Bristol scandal was a symptom of a National Health Service which had lost direction: dominated by a culture which is no longer socially acceptable, thrown into disarray by the attempt to apply market economics and consumer values to a chronically under-funded service'.[73] Until these problems are tackled at their roots, patients will still face the need to attempt to vindicate their rights in an imperfect system.

IV.   Conclusion

In the context of healthcare quality, there are few legally enforceable patient rights. The ECHRB gives patients a right to have any medical intervention carried out in accordance with relevant professional obligations and standards[74] and English law similarly holds doctors legally accountable for failing to meet a

---

[71]   Section 3(2) NHS Redress Act 2006.
[72]   Section 1(4) NHS Redress Act 2006.
[73]   Bridgeman, n 68 above, p 255.
[74]   Article 4 ECHRB.

professional standard of care. However, this provides little protection for a patient and recent court judgments have focused upon asserting the role of the courts in reviewing the professional standard of care to ensure that the standard has the basic features of logic and reason. In a similar vein, the courts have shown some signs of relaxing the traditional negligence requirements in the healthcare context expressly in order to vindicate the rights of patients. Therefore, falling at the traditional causation hurdle is no longer inevitably destructive of a patient's claim for compensation. The judicial recognition of the need for protection of patients' rights is to be welcomed but, in the quality of healthcare context, it is ultimately unproductive because the rights in question have thus far remained unarticulated and vague. Debate surrounding the possibility of removing fault from the legal equation and instead prioritising compensation for avoidable adverse outcomes of medical care has culminated in legislative moves towards an alternative to suing for negligence through the courts, but even this does not address the issue of patients' rights in a convincing manner. By sidestepping the issue of breach of duty without replacing it with enforceable patient rights, the NHS Redress scheme fails to provide a definitive answer to the problem of ensuring quality of healthcare in a human rights age and, therefore, is unlikely to be the final word on the subject of rights and duties in healthcare.

Recommended further reading

A Merry and A McCall Smith, *Errors, Medicine and the Law* (Cambridge, Cambridge University Press, 2001).

M Brazier and J Miola, 'Bye-Bye Bolam: A Medical Litigation Revolution?' (2000) 8 *Med L Rev* 85.

H Teff, 'The Standard of Care in Medical Negligence: Moving on from *Bolam*?' (1998) 18 *OJLS* 473.

J Bridgeman, "Learning from Bristol': Healthcare in the Twenty First Century' (2002) 65 *Med L Rev* 241, at p 245.

Department of Health, 'Making Amends: A Consultation Paper Setting Out Proposals for Reforming the Approach to Clinical Negligence in the NHS' (2003).

4

Autonomy and Consent to Medical Treatment

The need for consent to medical treatment is the underlying principle of English medical law. It is also the epitome of the human rights aspect of the subject for it is the principle of individual autonomy which provides the theoretical foundation for both the need for consent and human rights. This chapter will begin by introducing the principle of autonomy, in both its ethical and legal forms, and will then proceed to consider the nature of the principle of consent. Particular focus will be placed upon the need for actual, voluntary, competent and informed consent under the English common law and the hurdles that these requirements sometimes present for patient autonomy.

I. Autonomy, Consent and Choices

(a) Autonomy: The Ethical Principle

'I wish my life and decision to depend on myself, not on external forces of whatever kind. I wish to be the instrument of my own, not of other men's acts of will. I wish to be a subject, not an object; to be moved by reasons, by conscious purposes, which are my own, not by causes which affect me, as it were, from outside. I wish to be somebody, not anybody; a doer – deciding not being decided for, self-directed and not acted upon by external nature or by other men . . . I wish, above all, to be conscious of myself as a thinking, willing, active being, bearing responsibility for his choices and able to explain them by reference to his own ideas and purposes'.[1]

Such sentiments are at the core of our humanity and philosophers throughout history have sought to emphasise and justify this sense of free choice, self-determination or 'autonomy'.[2] For example, JS Mill, in his famous treatise *On*

[1] I Berlin, *Two Concepts of Liberty* (Oxford, Clarendon Press, 1969) p 123.
[2] The word 'autonomy' is derived from autos (self) and nomes (rule or law).

Liberty, argued that it is the hallmark of individuality that each person be allowed to make free choices (provided only that they do not cause harm to others).[3] Kant also asserted the importance of free choice in his famous theory that an agent is an end in himself and should never be used as a means to an end.[4] More recently, Gerald Dworkin has developed a detailed thesis on autonomy.[5] In Dworkin's view of autonomy, an ability to be reflective on one's own desires is at the core of the principle. Thus, autonomy is a second-order capacity to reflect critically upon first-order preferences, wishes and desires.[6] For example, an individual may have not only a desire to smoke but also simultaneously a desire that he not have that desire. This capacity to reflect upon our instant desires distinguishes autonomy from mere voluntariness.[7]

Dworkin also explains why this concept of autonomy is valuable: 'What makes an individual the particular person he is his life-plan, his projects. In pursuing autonomy, one shapes one's life, one constructs its meaning. The autonomous person gives meaning to his life.'[8] In no context is this more true than within the healthcare context. Our identity as a person is closely linked to the integrity of our bodies. As Dworkin notes, 'one's body is irreplaceable and inescapable . . . In addition because my body *is* me, failure to respect my wishes concerning my body is a particularly insulting denial of autonomy'.[9] Furthermore, the choices one has to make within the healthcare context often touch upon the fundamentals of life: reproduction, a life free of pain, the dying process. One may have to choose, for example, whether as a Jehovah's Witness one will accept a life-saving blood transfusion; whether as a pregnant woman one will accept treatment to terminate the pregnancy; whether as a tetraplaegic, with no hope of recovery, one wishes to continue to receive life-sustaining ventilation. These are examples of the hardest choices a person will ever have to make and when he or she has agonised over the choice and finally reached a conclusion, it should be respected by others.

Autonomy is not the only ethical principle at issue here, however. Just as autonomy seems to have special significance in the healthcare context, so too does paternalism: the idea of making a decision for another in order to promote the other's benefit. There are situations where paternalism is vital, for example in relation to minors and also (perhaps) those who are not mentally competent to make an autonomous choice, but paternalism has a larger and disputed role in healthcare stemming from a doctor's ethical obligation to 'prescribe regimens for

[3]   JS Mill, *On Liberty* (Cambridge, Cambridge University Press, 1989, S Collini (ed)) p 13.
[4]   I Kant, *Foundations of the Metaphysics of Morals* (RP Wolff (ed), 1969) p 52.
[5]   G Dworkin, *The Theory and Practice of Autonomy* (Cambridge, Cambridge University Press, 1988)
[6]   *Ibid*, p 20.
[7]   *ibid*, p 15.
[8]   *Ibid*, p 31.
[9]   *Ibid*, p 113.

the good of my patients according to my ability and my judgment'.[10] This may bring the medical profession into conflict with patient autonomy. A reconciliation is needed which prioritises the patient's needs, needs both of a medical nature and also, no less crucially, needs in relation to autonomous choice. Few would deny that a patient has a right to autonomy, but its application in practice within the context of saving lives is a far more challenging concept. For example, we may readily accept a general right of self-determination but not wish it to incorporate a patient's right to refuse life-saving treatment for purely irrational reasons. If the right is to have any meaning, however, it must apply even in the most difficult of circumstances. In seeking a reconciliation between the ethical principles of autonomy and paternalism, the law must play a crucial role. As we will now investigate, the principle of autonomy is inherent in the civil and political rights and freedoms protected at international law by human rights treaties such as the ECHR and the ICCPR, and protected in domestic law by both the Human Rights Act 1998 and pre-existing common law.

(b)   Autonomy: The Legal Principle

(i)   International Human Rights Law

As a traditional first generation human rights treaty, the ECHR has the principle of autonomy implicit and central in its terms. The rights protected in the convention – freedom of expression and religion, freedom from torture, right to life and liberty of the person and respect for private life etc – are no more and no less than aspects of a broader freedom to determine how to live one's own life. The general ethos of the Convention thus prioritises autonomy but individual articles also implicitly protect autonomous choices within the healthcare context.[11] Article 3 ECHR prohibits torture and inhuman or degrading treatment or punishment. The imposition of medical treatment without the patient's consent may amount to degrading treatment under the terms of this Article. The European Commission of Human Rights held in *X v Denmark* that 'medical treatment of an experimental character and without the consent of the person involved may under certain circumstances be regarded as prohibited by Article 3'.[12] The requirement of an experimental treatment will not be easily satisfied, however. This protection against medical experimentation is echoed in the ICCPR where Article 7 (the equivalent provision to Article 3 ECHR) expressly states that 'no one shall be subjected without his free consent to medical or scientific experimentation'. This protection clearly has its roots in a post-war response to Nazi atrocities and prevents the imposition of non-consensual

---

[10]   Hippocratic Oath.

[11]   See generally, E Wicks, 'The Right to Refuse Medical Treatment under the European Convention on Human Rights' (2001) 9 *Med L Rev* 17.

[12]   *X v Denmark* (1988) 32 DR 282 at 283.

treatment which is of a non-therapeutic or dangerous nature and which is done for the purpose of furthering medical knowledge rather than for the purpose of benefiting the patient in question. At the other extreme of the spectrum of medical treatment, the imposition of non-consensual medical treatment which is a therapeutic necessity will not be prohibited by Article 3. The European Court of Human Rights made this clear in the 1992 case of *Herczegfalvy v Austria*.[13] In this case the forcible treatment of a mental patient, including force-feeding and restraint, was held not to be in breach of Article 3 because of its therapeutic necessity. The Court did emphasise, however, that such a medical necessity must be 'convincingly shown to exist'.[14] Thus we can see that, under Article 3, imposing medical treatment without consent may, under certain circumstances, be regarded as degrading, but therapeutic necessity, if proven, will provide a sufficient justification.

This limited protection for autonomy within the healthcare context is overshadowed by the protection offered under Article 8 ECHR. This Article protects a right to respect for private life. As such, it is the ultimate embodiment of a right to be free from external intervention, including in the form of therapeutic medical treatment. The European Court of Human Rights has held in *X & Y v Netherlands* that Article 8 incorporates a right to physical integrity of the person[15] and the European Commission of Human Rights has stated explicitly that a compulsory medical intervention must be considered an interference with this right.[16] More recently, the European Court of Human Rights has affirmed the applicability of Article 8 to the issue of consent to medical treatment. In *Pretty v United Kingdom*, the Court made clear that it considers the notion of personal autonomy to be an important principle underlying the interpretation of Article 8's guarantees[17] and declared that 'the imposition of medical treatment, without the consent of a mentally competent adult patient, would interfere with a person's physical integrity in a manner capable of engaging the rights protected under Article 8(1) of the Convention'.[18] Despite this clear guarantee of the need for consent to medical treatment under Article 8(1), it should be noted that Article 8 is not an absolute right and limitations to the right are permissible under Article 8(2) provided that they can be justified as prescribed by law and necessary in a democratic society for one of a number of specified legitimate aims including protection of the rights and freedoms of others, protection of health and morals and prevention of disorder and crime. It is unlikely, however, that a non-consensual medical intervention solely for paternalistic reasons would be justified under any of these grounds.

---

[13]   (1992) Series A, No 244, para 82.
[14]   *Ibid.*
[15]   (1986) 8 EHRR 235 at para 22.
[16]   *X v Austria* (1980) 18 DR 154 at 156.
[17]   *Pretty v United Kingdom* (2002) 35 EHRR 1, at para 61.
[18]   *Ibid*, para 63.

One further Article of the ECHR may offer some legal protection for the right to choose whether to consent to medical treatment. Article 9 protects freedom of thought, conscience and religion, including a right to manifest a religion or belief in worship, teaching, practice and observance. If a decision to refuse consent to treatment is a consequence of the patient's religious beliefs – as, for example, with a Jehovah's Witness's refusal of a blood transfusion – Article 9 issues may arise. There has been no case directly on this point before the Strasbourg institutions and it is clear that not every act which is motivated by a religion will be regarded as a manifestation of religion and thus protected under Article 9.[19] Nevertheless, a refusal of treatment which is as central to a religious belief as the Jehovah's Witnesses' rejection of blood transfusions seems likely to fall within the ambit of the Article. As with Article 8, however, Article 9 is far from absolute and permits such limitations as are necessary in a democratic society, reflecting the balance between the rights of individuals and the interests of society inherent in the terms of the Convention.

While both the overall ethos and the specific terms of the ECHR offer protection for individual autonomy in the healthcare context as well as in other contexts, more subject-specific protection is apparent within the European Convention on Human Rights and Biomedicine (ECHRB).[20] As discussed in Chapter 1, this Convention is an initiative of the Council of Europe which seeks to reflect the application of the core human rights of the ECHR to the rapidly evolving field of biomedicine. Article 5 ECHRB declares that 'An intervention in the health field may only be carried out after the person concerned has given free and informed consent to it. The person shall beforehand be given appropriate information as to the purpose and nature of the intervention as well as on its consequences and risks. The person concerned may freely withdraw consent at any time.'[21] The Explanatory Report explains that this Article 'affirms at the international level an already well-established rule, that is that no one may in principle be forced to undergo an intervention without his or her consent'.[22] The Report continues by explaining that 'This rule makes clear patients' autonomy in their relationship with healthcare professionals and restrains the paternalist approaches which might ignore the wish of the patient.'[23] This strong emphasis upon autonomy is to be welcomed although, as in the ECHR, there is a balancing with other competing societal interests. In addition to the specific exceptions to Article 5 relating to incapacity and emergency, all the rights in the ECHRB are

---

[19]   See *Arrowsmith v United Kingdom* (1978) 19 DR 5 at 19.

[20]   Convention for the Protection of Human Rights and Dignity of the Human Being with regard to the Application of Biology and Medicine.

[21]   The Explanatory Report defines 'free and informed' consent as consent 'given on the basis of objective information from the responsible healthcare professional as to the nature and the potential consequences of the planned intervention or of its alternatives, in the absence of any pressure from anyone' (para 35).

[22]   *Ibid*, para 34.

[23]   *Ibid.*

subject to limitations prescribed by law and necessary in a democratic society in the interests of public safety, prevention of crime, protection of public health or protection of rights and freedoms of others.[24]

(ii)   Domestic Common Law

In addition to the persuasive authority of these international agreements and the incorporation of the convention rights into the Human Rights Act 1998 (including the requirement that domestic courts 'take account' of the judgments and decisions of the Strasbourg institutions[25]), English common law explicitly recognises the need for consent to any medical intervention on a competent adult patient. As Kennedy has explained, the legal principle of consent is the conceptual mechanism through which the patient's right to self-determination is guaranteed and safeguarded.[26] Perhaps the most famous assertion of the need for consent to medical treatment was provided by Lord Donaldson MR in the 1992 case of *Re T*:

> An adult patient who, like Miss T, suffers from no mental incapacity has an absolute right to choose whether to consent to medical treatment, to refuse it or to choose one rather than another of the treatments being offered . . . This right of choice is not limited to decisions which others might regard as sensible. It exists notwithstanding that the reasons for making the choice are rational, irrational, unknown or even non-existent.[27]

This principle was subsequently affirmed by the House of Lords in *Airedale NHS Trust v Bland*:

> it is established that the principle of self-determination requires that respect must be given to the wishes of the patient, so that if an adult patient of sound mind refuses, however unreasonably, to consent to treatment or care by which his life would or might be prolonged, the doctors responsible for his care might give effect to his wishes, even though they do not consider it to be in his best interests to do so . . .[28]

The English courts have perhaps been understandably reluctant to grapple with the ethical foundations which underlie the need for consent but it seems clear that autonomy, or 'self-determination' as the English courts prefer to describe it, provides the foundational principle for the law on consent to medical treatment. In *Re T*, Lord Donaldson argued that the patient's interest, consisting of 'his right to self-determination – his right to live his own life how he wishes, even if it will

---

[24]   Article 26 ECHRB.

[25]   Section 2(1). So, for example, the European Court's declaration in *Pretty* that non-consensual treatment upon a competent patient amounts to an interference with the patient's right to respect for private life should be taken into account by any domestic courts considering the issue.

[26]   I Kennedy, 'The Legal Effect of Requests by the Terminally Ill and Aged not to Receive Further Treatment from Doctors' in I Kennedy, *Treat Me Right* (Oxford, Clarendon Press, 1988) p 347.

[27]   *Re T (adult: refusal of treatment)* [1992] 4 All ER 649, at pp 652-653.

[28]   [1993] AC 789 at p 864 (per Lord Goff).

damage his health or lead to his premature death', conflicts with society's interest in upholding the sanctity of life.[29] Although noting that the right of the individual is 'paramount', Lord Donaldson argues that if there is any doubt about the exercise of that right, it should be resolved in favour of the preservation of life 'for if the individual is to override the public interest he must do so in clear terms'.[30] This approach is unsatisfactory because it fails to give adequate protection to the right to self-determination which is at the core of the whole breadth of civil and political rights. Furthermore, by pitting the individual against society, Lord Donaldson fails to recognise that society also has an interest in individual self-determination.

Within a democratic society, individual freedom is vital and will be ensured by the protection of human rights and the rule of law. The imperative of individual autonomy is well described by Judge LJ in the case of *St George's Healthcare NHS Trust v S; R v Collins, ex S*:

> how can a forced invasion of a competent adult's body against his will even for the most laudable of motives (the preservation of life) be ordered without immediately damaging the principle of self-determination? When human life is at stake the pressure to provide an affirmative answer authorising unwanted medical intervention is very powerful. Nevertheless, the autonomy of each individual requires continuing protection even, perhaps particularly, when the motive for interfering with it is readily understandable, and indeed to many would appear commendable . . .[31]

The importance of autonomy within the healthcare context cannot be more clearly asserted than this. Having established the underlying ethical and legal principle of autonomy and its application through the conceptual mechanism of consent, we must now turn to consider the nature of consent in greater detail.

II.   The Nature of Consent

(a)   To what can we consent?

We have seen that the requirement of consent for medical treatment ensures that a patient's autonomy is protected within the healthcare context. But what legal purposes does this need for consent achieve? As many forms of medical treatment involve an assault upon the physical integrity of the patient, consent relieves healthcare professionals of legal liability for battery under the law of crime and tort. The issue is rather more complex than it may at first appear, however. This is

---

[29]   *Re T*, n 27 above, p 661.
[30]   *Ibid.*
[31]   [1998] 3 All ER 673 at p 688.

because under the general criminal law a victim of physical harm amounting to actual or grievous bodily harm (or death) cannot consent to such harm. This point was made clear in the infamous case of *R v Brown* in which the purported consent of victims of sado-masochist sexual activities was held not to be capable of relieving the criminal liability of the perpetrators.[32] Therefore, if consent of the patient is to protect a doctor against allegations of assault occasioning actual bodily harm or worse, medical treatment must be regarded as an exception to the general criminal law. This was the view taken by Lord Lane CJ in *A-G's Reference (No 6 of 1980)*[33] where he specified a number of exceptions to the general criminal law rule that a victim cannot consent to actual bodily harm, including 'properly conducted games and sports, lawful chastisement or correction, reasonable surgical interference, dangerous exhibitions etc'.[34] Lord Lane explained that these exceptions are justified as such because they all involve 'the exercise of a legal right, in the case of chastisement or correction, or as needed in the public interest, in the other cases'.[35] From this important statement we can see that reasonable surgical interference is justified as an exception to the general criminal rule that a victim cannot consent because such interference is necessary in the public interest. More recently in the case of *Airedale NHS Trust v Bland*, Lord Mustill considered the difficulty caused by the general criminal rule on this issue and held that 'bodily invasions in the course of proper medical treatment stand completely outside the criminal law'.[36] We may note, of course, that both 'reasonable' and 'proper' are terms open to interpretation and apparently impose some limitations on the type of procedures to which a patient can consent, but such issues have not been crucial in the case law. Lord Mustill noted that the consent of the patient 'is usually essential to the propriety of medical treatment'[37] but this is a somewhat circular argument given that it is the propriety of the treatment which enables the consent of the patient to be taken into account in the first place. Nevertheless, it is clear that standard medical procedures will not amount to a criminal offence if the consent of the patient is forthcoming. Thus, unusually, a patient can consent to activity which amounts to actual bodily harm provided it is done within the healthcare context.

There are, however, some types of medical intervention to which a patient cannot either consent or, crucially, refuse consent – ie treatments for which

---

[32]   [1994] 1 AC 212. This ruling had serious human rights implications in that the activities in question all took place in private as well as with the consent of all involved. The European Court of Human Rights did not, however, regard the convictions as a violation of Article 8's right to respect for private life, holding that it was a justified interference as necessary in a democratic society for the protection of health. Indeed, some members of the Court even doubted whether there had been an interference with private life, arguing that 'not everything that takes place behind closed doors is private' (*Laskey, Jaggard and Brown v United Kingdom* (1997) 24 EHRR 39, at para 36).

[33]   [1981] QB 715.

[34]   *Ibid*, at p 719.

[35]   *Ibid.*

[36]   *Bland*, n 28 above, p 891.

[37]   *Ibid.*

consent, and patient autonomy, are regarded as irrelevant issues. The most common of these is treatment for a mental disorder under the Mental Health Act 1983. Under section 63 of the 1983 Act[38] consent is not needed for any medical treatment which is for the patient's mental disorder even if the patient is mentally competent to provide consent, unless the treatment is one of those specified in sections 57 or 58.[39] Given the serious infringement of autonomy inherent in such compulsory treatment, it is worrying that the courts have interpreted this category of 'medical treatment for a mental disorder' so broadly. It has been held to include, for example, force-feeding of an anorexic patient[40] and a Caesarean section delivery.[41] While there are sound reasons for some legal provision for the compulsory treatment of the mentally disordered, it should be very narrowly defined to ensure that it is only treatment of a mental disorder, and not all treatment of the mentally disordered, which is authorised without the need for consent. If a mentally disordered patient requires other treatment, such as a Caesarean section operation, the usual rules on competence should be adequate. Other situations in which consent for treatment is irrelevant exist under the Public Health (Control of Diseases) Act 1984 in which the removal to hospital of a person with a notifiable disease (including cholera, plague, smallpox and AIDS) is permitted without the need for consent.[42] This provision does not, however, expressly authorise treatment without consent and, as Kennedy and Grubb have argued, such a violation of fundamental rights ought not to be implied into the legislation.[43] The National Assistance Act 1948 also permits the removal to suitable premises of persons in need of care and attention but again there is no express authorisation of treatment without consent.[44]

Finally it should be noted that, other than those three statutory exceptions to the need for consent (and ignoring for now the common law and statutory law on incompetent patients who can be treated without consent), all medical treatment requires the consent of the adult patient. This raises the question of what constitutes medical treatment. For example, the fluoride added to the drinking water in some regions could be regarded as an attempt to treat the population en masse and yet it is done without consent. Is this an infringement of our autonomy? While it is true that we can choose not to drink the fluoridated

---

[38]   The mental health laws have been the subject of proposals for reform for a number of years but the challenges in striking an appropriate balance between protection of the patients' rights and public safety have proved difficult. See now the Mental Health Bill 2006.

[39]   Section 57 requires the patient's consent AND a second medical opinion and applies to psychosurgery and treatments specified in Department of Health regulations; s 58 requires the patient's consent OR a second medical opinion and applies to electro-convulsive therapy and treatment given for longer than three months.

[40]   *B v Croydon Health Authority* (1994) 22 BMLR 13.

[41]   *Tameside & Glossop Acute Services Trust v CH* (1996) 31 BMLR 93.

[42]   Section 37.

[43]   I Kennedy and A Grubb, *Medical Law*, 3rd edn (London, Butterworths, 2000) p 909.

[44]   Section 47. This provision is intended to provide protection to those suffering from grave chronic disease and aged, infirm or physically incapacitated persons living in insanitary conditions.

water, so too could we choose not to take self-administered medicines. Does this mean that it is only those treatments which are administered by a healthcare professional which require consent? Or is it the fact that there is no infringement of physical integrity which is the crucial issue? While there is no strictly legal need for consent in the absence of physical contact, the need for consent to medical treatment operates, as we have seen, on a number of levels, including safeguarding the ethical principle of autonomy and ensuring protection of our right to self-determination. As such, it cannot simply be defined in terms of the legal principles relating to bodily contact. It is a manifestation of a far more important value – that of autonomy – and should be treated with due respect because of this.

(b)   How do we consent?

(i)   The Form of Consent

Having established that a (competent adult) patient must consent to all medical treatment, the question of how a patient does this now arises. Obviously, one possibility is for the patient to expressly and verbally give consent. This is unlikely in the vast majority of situations where medical treatment is given as, for example, when a blood test is taken. In this situation, the patient is unlikely to say (or be asked to say) 'I consent to you taking a sample of blood from my arm'. Instead, a doctrine of implied consent comes into play: by being present in the room and presenting an arm to the nurse, the patient's consent to the procedure can be implied.[45] Kennedy and Grubb prefer to see this in terms of a mere estoppel from subsequent complaint rather than a positive implication of consent,[46] but the latter view is to be preferred given that it is the patient's right to make a choice regarding medical treatment. The law should seek to deduce evidence of that choice (the presenting of the arm for a blood test, for example) rather than merely prevent the patient's subsequent complaint due to the lack of resistance to the procedure at the time.

In respect of more serious medical procedures, the evidence of consent will need to be much clearer and the doctrine of implied consent has little role to play. This does not mean that the signing of a written hospital consent form is essential. Contrary to medical practice, it is the fact of consent which is vital rather than its form.[47] Thus a patient who has not signed a consent form may still have given consent in verbal terms and that will be sufficient. By contrast, the fact

---

[45]   Lord Donaldson in *Re T* confirmed that consent 'may sometimes be inferred from the patient's conduct in the context of the surrounding circumstances' (n 27 above, p 653).

[46]   Kennedy and Grubb, n 43 above, p 589.

[47]   See Lord Donaldson in *Re T*, n 27 above, at p 653.

that a patient has signed a consent form is not decisive on the question of whether he has in fact consented (although in the huge majority of cases it will be convincing evidence of actual consent).

(ii)   The Timing of Consent

The patient's consent can be given in advance of the treatment, and so can a valid refusal of consent. In *Re AK* a patient suffering from motor neurone disease and gradually losing the ability to communicate was able to indicate (by moving an eyelid) that he wanted his respiration to be switched off (ie he wished to refuse consent to continued ventilation) two weeks after his ability to communicate ceased. When his doctors applied to the courts for a declaration that it would be lawful to abide by his wishes, the declaration was granted but the court made it clear that such a declaration was unnecessary: the refusal of consent was valid and must be respected even though it was given in advance.[48] There is a significant hurdle to the enforceability of advance refusals of consent, however, and this is that the refusal must be meant to apply in the exact situation which subsequently arises. This was the basis for the first instance decision in *Re T* to authorise a blood transfusion which had been refused in advance by the patient. Ward J held that the patient had refused consent in a competent and voluntary manner but, because she had not been informed of the risks of a refusal of a blood transfusion, her refusal did not apply in the emergency which had subsequently arisen. The Court of Appeal reached the same result but on very different grounds although Lord Donaldson MR confirmed that, 'If the factual situation falls outside the scope of the refusal or if the assumption upon which it is based is falsified, the refusal ceases to be effective.'[49] Thus, although a refusal of consent to a medical procedure can be made at a point of time in advance of when it would take effect, this will only be effective if the patient was able to foresee any changing circumstances, especially a deterioration in the patient's condition. Of course, for a patient to foresee this, he must be provided with advice and information by the doctors who are more likely to be able to predict any change in circumstances. However, if a doctor disagrees with the patient's chosen course of action, the patient may in practice be deprived of the information necessary to preserve the validity of the advance directive.

(iii)   The Voluntariness of Consent

The case of *Re T* also raises another vital issue, namely that, regardless of whether the consent or refusal of consent is verbal or written; in advance or contemporary, it must be voluntary. It will be useful to look now in more detail at this important Court of Appeal decision. T was injured in a road traffic accident when 34 weeks pregnant. She had been brought up by her mother who was a

---

[48]   *Re AK (medical treatment: consent)* [2001] 1 FLR 129.
[49]   *Re T*, n 27 above, p 663.

Jehovah's Witness but T was not herself a member of this faith. After being alone with her mother, T told the medical staff that she did not want a blood transfusion and she signed a form to that effect. T was not told at that time that a blood transfusion might be necessary in order to save her life and indeed she was reassured by medical staff that other solutions could be used. A Caesarean section operation was performed but resulted in a stillbirth. T's condition deteriorated. At this point, a blood transfusion was in her best interests but the doctors felt restrained by her refusal of consent. T's father and boyfriend applied to the courts for assistance. At an emergency hearing Ward J, following the medical advice available to him at the time, found T to be mentally incompetent and thus authorised treatment in her best interests.[50] By the time of a full hearing two days later, the medical evidence was (strangely) different and Ward J held that T was competent to refuse consent and, despite some possible pressure from her mother, had done so voluntarily. However, as mentioned above, Ward J held that the refusal was not effective in the current emergency because T had not been informed of the risks of her refusal. On appeal to the Court of Appeal alternative reasoning was adopted. Lord Donaldson MR held that there was evidence which would have justified the court finding that T was not mentally competent at the time in question and even if, contrary to that view, she was competent, 'the influence of her mother was such as to vitiate the decision which she expressed'.[51]

The Court of Appeal was not clear in substituting its reasoning for that of Ward J, Butler-Sloss LJ expressly preferring not to do so and Staughton LJ merely concluding that there was no valid refusal of consent without specifying why this was so. Even Lord Donaldson does not labour the point and this is perhaps wise as Ward J's initial reasoning seems far preferable to that of the Court of Appeal. This is because Ward J regards T's refusal of consent as valid at the time that she expressed it but, due to the failure of medical staff to give T full and accurate information regarding the potential consequences of her refusal, a blood transfusion was now justified. Lord Donaldson's first possible justification – lack of competence – is potentially far more damaging to individual autonomy as he seems willing to take into account the road traffic accident four days previously, the pregnancy, pain and narcotic drugs as contributing to a lack of competence.[52] The second possible justification – undue influence – could be regarded as an aspect of the general rule, noted above, that what matters is that consent exists in fact rather than merely in form. As Lord Donaldson points out, the only relevant question when considering undue influence is whether the decision is in form rather than reality.[53] If it appears that a patient has consented (or refused consent) but they have done so only because their will has been overborne by

---

[50]   The issue of treating the mentally incompetent will be dealt with below and in the subsequent chapter.

[51]   *Re T*, n 27 above, p 660.

[52]   *Ibid.*

[53]   *Ibid*, p 662.

another, or because of deception or misinformation,[54] the patient has not in reality exercised a free choice. This seems a sensible theory but the Court of Appeal in *Re T* was unable to define undue influence in any detailed manner. Staughton LJ said that 'there must be such a degree of external influence as to persuade the patient to depart from her own wishes, to an extent that the law regards as undue', adding that 'I can suggest no more precise test than that'.[55] The difficulty with this ambiguous definition, and indeed the concept as a whole, is that it fails to appreciate the extent of influence which will be exercised by the doctor. Is influence only 'undue' if it stems from a relative rather than a professional? While it is essential that an individual's choice as to whether to consent to treatment or not is a genuinely free choice in order to ensure that autonomy is upheld and the right to respect for private life under the ECHR is not infringed, this must equally apply to undue influence from doctors in favour of treatment, particularly taking into account the unbalanced power relationship between doctor and patient. Whether the courts are ready to intervene to undermine the influence of a trained professional remains doubtful at this time.

A further aspect of the requirement of voluntariness in the context of consent to medical treatment is the question of whether consent can ever be voluntary within an institutional setting. This issue was raised in *Freeman v Home Office (No 2)*[56] concerning a prisoner's consent to medical treatment within prison. The Court of Appeal rejected arguments that a prisoner cannot make a free choice and thus give valid consent but did accept that an institutional setting may raise some doubts about the issue. It would, therefore, be wise to apply particularly stringent requirements of voluntariness within a prison or mental hospital in order to ensure that a purported choice is freely arrived at. It is important, however, that the autonomy of detained patients, even though restricted in many ways, is maximised so far as possible and that the clearly expressed wishes of a competent patient are given adequate respect even if true freedom of choice is curtailed within the institutional setting. We have seen in this section that a patient's consent to medical treatment must be voluntary and not subject to the undue influence of another. In addition, there are two further more problematic requirements in order for a consent or refusal of consent to be valid: (1) the patient must be competent to give consent; and (2) the consent given must be adequately informed. We will now consider each of these issues in turn.

---

[54]   See Butler-Sloss LJ, *ibid*, at p 665.
[55]   Staughton LJ, *ibid*, at p 669.
[56]   [1984] QB 524.

III. Competent Consent

(a) Assessing Capacity

In order to give a valid consent (or refusal) to medical treatment, the patient must be regarded as mentally competent to make an autonomous decision. The concept of capacity (used interchangeably here with competence) is therefore the 'gate-keeper of "who decides"'.[57] If a patient has capacity, his right to autonomy ensures (or should ensure) that his choices are respected but if the patient lacks (or loses) capacity, decisions as to his treatment will be taken by his doctors acting in what they perceive as his best interests. Given the significance of a finding of incapacity for a person's autonomy, it is unfortunate that the concept is shrouded in uncertainty. While it is clear that a patient can be deprived of capacity either by long-term mental incapacity or by temporary factors such as unconsciousness, confusion, fatigue, shock, pain or drugs, it is difficult to know how to define the concept:[58]

> Capacity/incapacity are not concepts with clear a priori boundaries. They appear on a continuum which ranges from full capacity at one end to full incapacity at the other end. There are, therefore, degrees of capacity. The challenge is to choose the right level to set as the gateway to decision-making and respect for persons and autonomy.[59]

In order to enable as many patients as possible to make their own treatment decisions (and thereby maximise their autonomy), the test for capacity should not be too stringent. However, it is also important to ensure that patients whose decisions might be affected by their mental incompetence are able to receive the treatment which is in their best interests.

In seeking to strike an appropriate balance between these two concerns, courts have had to choose between two potential approaches to determining capacity: an understanding of the issues involved, or rationality or reasonableness of the decision reached.[60] Or, in other words, the law must choose between a process approach or an outcome approach to capacity. A process approach would look at whether the patient was competent to participate in a decision-making process, particularly looking at whether the patient was able to understand the issues involved in reaching a decision. If such an approach were adopted, a further question would be whether a mere ability to understand was required or whether actual understanding must be proved. Alternatively, an outcome approach to capacity would focus upon the decision which was reached and whether it is one

---

[57]   Kennedy and Grubb, n 43 above, p 596.
[58]   See Lord Donaldson MR in *Re T*, n 27 above, p 664.
[59]   M Gunn, 'The Meaning of Incapacity' (1994) 2 *Med L Rev* 8, at p 14.
[60]   See M Jones and K Keywood, 'Assessing the Patient's Competence to Consent to Medical Treatment' (1996) 2 *Med Law Int* 107.

which is objectively appropriate in the circumstances, either looking at its rationality or, even stricter, its reasonableness. The danger with an outcome approach is that it fails to protect the right to make an irrational decision. The exercise of autonomy does not, could not, need to be rational for we all make objectively irrational decisions on a daily basis. For example, any decision based upon religious belief is likely to be regarded as irrational by others (for it is not based upon rationality but faith) and yet a manifestation of religious belief is regarded as so important that it is protected expressly by Article 9 ECHR as a human right. Likewise, the protection of private life in Article 8 does not imply that only objectively reasonable behaviour and choices will be protected but rather the fact of self-determination. The need to protect irrational decisions has also been recognised by the Court of Appeal in *Re T*.[61] Indeed, freedom to choose has at its core the freedom to choose wrongly. If it did not, it would be meaningless. An outcome approach to capacity would undermine the principle of individual autonomy in treatment decisions. So rationality of outcome is not an appropriate test in a purportedly autonomy-based healthcare system (and democratic state). Rationality may still play a role, however, in ensuring that the decision-making process is a rational process. A third alternative approach to capacity would be a status approach. This would look solely at the category of patient involved before determining the patient's capacity to consent – ie a patient suffering from a mental disorder would automatically and without exception be rendered incompetent to make treatment decisions. Again this is not an appropriate test because it potentially violates the rights of the mentally disordered patient. If that patient remains capable of understanding the issues involved in making a decision about treatment and can initiate a rational decision-making process, he should not be prohibited from exercising his autonomy in this way. Furthermore, patient involvement in the decision-making process has been proven to have therapeutic benefits for the treatment and therefore should be encouraged wherever possible.

Thus we return to the process approach which is the only one compatible with patient autonomy. If a patient is unable to make a decision then he is unable to exercise his autonomy and it is appropriate at that time for beneficial treatment to be provided on another legal basis.[62] English law has adopted a process approach to the issue of competence. This was first defined by Thorpe J in the case of *Re C*.[63] This case concerned a paranoid schizophrenic who was suffering from gangrene in his foot. He refused consent to an amputation of the foot even though the doctors told him that this was the only way to save his life. He sought a declaration from the court that his foot would not be amputated without his consent, arguing forcefully that he would rather die with two feet than live with one. The key issue for the court was whether C was mentally competent to refuse

---

[61] *Re T*, n 27 above, p 653.
[62] The nature of this legal basis will be discussed in the following chapter.
[63] *Re C (adult: refusal of medical treatment)* [1994] 1 All ER 819.

consent to the treatment despite his mental disorder. Thorpe J adopted the analysis of one of the doctors giving evidence who had divided the decision-making process into three stages: (1) comprehending and retaining treatment information; (2) believing it; and (3) weighing it in the balance to arrive at a choice. This is the *Re C* test and it remains the authoritative common law test for capacity. Thorpe J applied the test to C and concluded that he was:

> completely satisfied that the presumption that C has the right of self-determination has not been displaced. Although his general capacity is impaired by schizophrenia, it has not been established that he does not sufficiently understand the nature, purpose and effects of the treatment he refuses. Indeed, I am satisfied that he has understood and retained the relevant treatment information, that in his own way he believes it, and that in the same fashion he has arrived at a clear choice.[64]

There is some doubt whether C really satisfied the second requirement of belief given that he believed himself to be a world class doctor and seemingly did not believe the doctors' warning that he would die without amputation. However, the fault may be less with Thorpe J's application of the competency test and more with the test itself, in that a requirement that the patient believe the doctors' advice could be regarded as inappropriate. Many patients may retain false hope that their doctor is mistaken. This does not seem a satisfactory reason for denying the patient the competence to make an autonomous choice, particularly if the patient satisfies the other requirements of comprehending, retaining and balancing the treatment information. Indeed, when the *Re C* test was approved by the Court of Appeal in *Re MB*, Butler-Sloss LJ omitted the second requirement of belief when describing the test.[65] Although she did not expressly exclude it, the *Re C* test is a stronger, more justifiable test without the unnecessary and potentially overly prescriptive requirement of belief, particularly as belief will be almost impossible to prove.

The Mental Capacity Act 2005 also omits the belief requirement while adopting the remainder of the *Re C* test as the statutory test for mental capacity. Section 2(1) declares that a person lacks capacity if 'at the material time he is unable to make a decision' due to 'an impairment of or disturbance in the functioning of, the mind or brain'. Section 3(1) then proceeds to define 'unable to make a decision' as unable to understand the information relevant to the decision; unable to retain that information; unable to use or weigh that information as part of the process of making the decision; or unable to communicate the decision. It will be noted that this is a process-based test, remarkably similar to the *Re C* test with the important exception that the inability to make a decision must be caused by an impairment or disturbance in the mind or brain. Explanatory notes to the Act make clear that this requirement will encompass psychiatric

[64]   *Ibid*, at p 824.
[65]   *Re MB (adult: medical treatment)* (1997) 38 BMLR 175.

illness, learning disability, dementia, brain damage and even toxic confusional state,[66] but it is clear that it will not necessarily cover all of the causes of incapacity and thus this is to some extent a status based approach to capacity despite denials.

(b) The Capacity Test in Practice

In *Re MB*, Butler-Sloss LJ also raised a further interesting point by claiming that 'the graver the consequences of the decision, the commensurately greater the level of competence is required to take the decision'.[67] This was confirmation of a similar point made by Lord Donaldson MR in *Re T* that capacity must be 'commensurate with the gravity of the decision which he [the patient] purported to make'.[68] This suggests that it will be far harder for a patient validly to refuse (or even to consent to) life-saving treatment than other less serious treatments. This does seem to have been the view of Thorpe J at the time that he developed the *Re C* test. Thorpe rejected the medical evidence of one doctor who held the view that C lacked capacity on the basis that this doctor was not aware that the danger to C's life had faded by the time of the court hearing. (Interestingly, this very fact adds further credence to the criticisms of the requirement that the patient believe the doctor's treatment advice as C was entirely correct to disbelieve the warnings that he would die without the operation because they proved erroneous.) Thorpe J argued that the doctor in question:

> was unaware of the dramatic aversion of the risk of death over the preceding four weeks ... She still regarded the limb as dead below the knee and death within a maximum of two years as certain without amputation. She did not know that amputation carried a significant mortality risk. I have no doubt that this lack of information influenced her appraisal of the critical equation and of C's approach to it.[69]

Thus Thorpe J seems to be indicating that he would have accepted the medical evidence that C was not competent if the treatment he was purporting to reject was necessary to save his life. This suggests that if the amputation had remained a life-saving measure C would somehow be regarded as less competent, even though his mental state and ability to comprehend, retain, believe and weigh the information remained unchanged. This is a clear indication that the consequences of the choice made are regarded as relevant to the capacity to choose. There is no theoretical justification for such an approach. It is apparent that the fact that C was right to disbelieve his doctors' opinion that the treatment was necessary to save his life was the conclusive factor in the court's willingness to

---

[66] Explanatory Notes, para 22.
[67] *Re MB*, n 65 above, p 15 of judgment.
[68] *Re T*, n 27 above, p 661.
[69] *Re C*, n 63 above, p 823.

regard him as competent. However, especially given that the court used a requirement of belief in its competency test, this is completely illogical. Whether C made the right choice in hindsight should not impact upon his capacity to choose. As noted above, the capacity to choose must include the capacity to choose wrongly. The decision in *Re C* undermines this vital aspect of autonomy and sets a dangerous precedent. Gunn makes the sound point that some medical procedures may be easier to understand than others and therefore easier to give consent to,[70] but to this extent only should the requirement for capacity vary.

An understanding of the issues involved in taking the treatment decision is a justified requirement for capacity and thus autonomous choice. Beyond this, the level of capacity should not be variable, regardless of the consequences of a refusal. Unfortunately, the English courts have shown a willingness to take into account the consequences of the patient's decision in determining capacity. Therefore, there is a danger that a patient saying no to objectively necessary treatment may be regarded as incompetent to do so merely because of the irrational choice made. The English courts deny that this occurs and yet even in *Re T* Lord Donaldson accepted that the fact that a choice is 'contrary to what is to be expected of the vast majority of adults' may be relevant, provided that there are also some other reasons for doubting the patient's capacity to decide. In this situation, 'the nature of his choice or the terms in which it is expressed may then tip the balance'.[71] Again, this is a very dangerous precedent. It suggests that a refusal of consent to treatment which is objectively in the patient's best interests will be less likely to be effective than a consent to treatment proposed by the doctors. As Jones and Keywood explain, the question of competence tends to arise only where the patient is refusing treatment in an apparently unreasonable or irrational decision because, '[i]f an apparently competent patient agrees with medical recommendations this will tend to confirm the doctors' view that the patient has the appropriate capacity to make the decision'.[72] Thus, by agreeing to the proposed treatment the patient '"demonstrates" rational behaviour'.[73] It is, therefore, easier to say yes to treatment than to choose to say no, and this illustrates that patient autonomy, which is founded upon choice, is precariously situated in the English law on consent to medical treatment. As Kennedy has described, 'It is as if there existed a right to free speech, but that, before exercising it, one must submit to someone with a practically unchallengeable power of censorship a copy of one's proposed speech for approval.'[74]

Thankfully, despite indications in *Re C* and *Re T* that a patient would face an uphill struggle in attempting to say no to treatment against the advice of his or her doctors, the more recent case of *Re B* asserts, and significantly is willing to

---

[70]   Gunn, n 59 above, p 14.
[71]   *Re T*, n 27 above, p 662.
[72]   Jones and Keywood, n 60 above, p 108.
[73]   *Ibid*, p 111.
[74]   Kennedy, n 26 above, p 336.

apply, a more autonomy-based reasoning on consent.[75] Ms B was suffering from tetraplegia – complete paralysis from the neck down – and was sustained on an artificial ventilator. She was fully conscious and requested that the ventilator be switched off. While this may appear at first glance to be a euthanasia-type case, comparable perhaps to the situation of Dianne Pretty who requested assistance to commit suicide, it should not be so regarded. Ms B was merely refusing consent to continued artificial ventilation.[76] If she was mentally competent, this refusal would, as has been discussed, have to be respected and treatment withdrawn leading to Ms B's death. The crucial issue was whether Ms B had capacity. Initially, in April 2001, the medical view was that Ms B did not possess capacity due to depression but subsequently a re-assessment in August 2001 decided that she was competent and from then on the hospital treated her as having capacity to make decisions. Nevertheless, from August 2001 until March 2002 the hospital refused to respect Ms B's wish that ventilation cease. In evidence to the court, Ms B explained her frustration at this lack of respect for her wishes:

> I felt that I was being treated as if I was being unreasonable by putting people in this awkward position. I fully accept the doctor's right to say, 'I personally will not do it,' and I respect that position, but I was angered at the arrogance and complete refusal to allow me access to someone that would. I felt my path was being blocked . . . I felt that my rights were being eroded . . .[77]

The President of the Family Division, Dame Butler-Sloss, investigated the medical evidence and agreed with the hospital's own assessment that Ms B had been competent since August 2001. Commenting on the hospital's refusal to respect the autonomous choice of this competent patient, Butler-Sloss recognised 'a serious danger, exemplified in this case, of a benevolent paternalism which does not embrace recognition of the personal autonomy of the severely disabled patient'.[78] She re-iterated that 'the right of the competent patient to request cessation of treatment must prevail over the natural desire of the medical and nursing professions to try to keep her alive'.[79] The danger of this 'natural desire' to save lives renders the law on competence vulnerable to manipulation. As Butler-Sloss acknowledged, the general law on mental capacity is 'clear and easily to be understood by lawyers'. However, its 'application to individual cases in the context of a general practitioner's surgery, a hospital ward and especially in an intensive care unit is infinitely more difficult to achieve'.[80] This is undoubtedly true but, if the law on capacity is not applied unambiguously in these ethically complex situations, there will be a serious cause for concern as to whether patient

---

[75] *Re B (adult: refusal of medical treatment)* [2002] 2 All ER 449.
[76] End of life issues will be considered in more detail in Chapter 11.
[77] *Re B*, n 75 above, quoted at para 50.
[78] *Ibid*, para 94.
[79] *Ibid*, para 27.
[80] *Ibid*, para 14.

autonomy is being sacrificed to paternalism. While both ethical principles have their merits, as we have seen, English law, as influenced by international law, has adopted an autonomy-based law on consent to medical treatment, as is entirely appropriate within a democratic state. Butler-Sloss sent a clear message in her judgment in *Re B* that the good intentions of the medical profession must not be allowed to undermine the effectiveness of this approach. Nominal damages were awarded against the hospital for the ventilation against Ms B's wishes which was, in effect, a battery upon her person and, we might note, also a possible violation of her right to physical integrity under Article 8 ECHR. Butler-Sloss also re-iterated that the issue of mental capacity should not be confused with the nature of the decisions made by the patient.[81] As she explained, the view of the patient 'may reflect a difference in values rather than an absence of competence'.[82] However mistaken, irrational or ridiculous are the values underlying the patient's choice, they are worthy of legal respect because they are the patient's values and it is her choice to make. Reassuringly, the guiding principles of the Mental Capacity Act 2005, listed in section 1, include that a person is not to be treated as unable to make a decision merely because he makes an unwise one.[83]

Two final points of concern arise in respect of the *Re C* competency test. First, it has been argued by Robertshaw and Thacker that a doctor can 'infantilise' a patient so that he is no longer competent and can be treated in his best interests.[84] They give the example of *Re T* in which, following the Caesarean section operation, T was sedated and given paralysing drugs without specific consent, thus rendering her incompetent. It is undoubtedly true that 'both consciousness and articulation may be medically orchestrated'[85] but to accept that this is done in practice requires a certain cynicism about doctors' motives. While it is entirely possible that healthcare professionals may show a reluctance to respect the wishes of a patient such as Ms B due to prioritising paternalism over autonomy, it is less likely that a doctor would take a deliberate decision to render a patient incompetent through medical measures. The second, more realistic, concern is that a failure to provide sufficiently detailed information to a patient regarding the risks and consequences of a treatment, again motivated by well-meaning paternalism, may result in the patient lacking competence to make a decision regarding the treatment. This danger was apparent in a case concerning a minor, *Re L*, in which a failure to adequately inform the patient of the consequences of a refusal of treatment enabled Sir Stephen Brown P to declare her incompetent because she did not actually understand what was involved in

---

[81]   *Ibid*, para 100.
[82]   *Ibid*.
[83]   Section 1(4) Mental Capacity Act 2005.
[84]   P Robertshaw and R Thacker, 'Consent, Autonomy and the Infantilised Patient' (1993) 1 *Med Law Int* 33, at p 51.
[85]   *Ibid*.

her refusal.[86] In this way, a doctor may prevent a patient having the information required to act autonomously. The question of adequate provision of information is a significant, and expanding, area of English medical law.

IV. Informed Consent

(a) The Meaning of Informed Consent

A vital aspect of the right to make autonomous decisions in respect of medical treatment is a right to all relevant information necessary in order to make an informed choice. As Lesser has argued:

> If patients have a right to make all the appropriate decisions, they must also have a right to all the information necessary for decision-making: the limits are set, not by what it is medically advisable or beneficial for them to know, but by what they need to know in order to make an informed assessment before deciding what to do.[87]

The provision of relevant information is vital, not just because without it a patient's autonomy may be compromised due to the uninformed nature of the decision reached, but also because, as noted above, a patient who makes a choice based upon insufficient information may be regarded as incompetent to choose. The importance of the right to information in a healthcare context is recognised in the ECHRB. Article 5 states that a patient shall be given 'appropriate information as to the purpose and nature of the intervention as well as on its consequences and risks'. The Explanatory Report on the Convention also makes clear that this list is not exhaustive and emphasises that the information provided:

> must be sufficiently clear and suitably worded for the person who is to undergo the intervention. The patient must be put in a position, through the use of terms he or she can understand, to weigh up the necessity or usefulness of the aim and methods of the intervention against its risks and the discomfort or pain it will cause.[88]

This correctly indicates that the key is that the patient understands the information provided rather than merely that it is disclosed. Thus the provision of information should be in a form and manner comprehensible to the patient. This also means that too much information may be just as bad as not enough if it is in a technical and detailed form incomprehensible to the patient.

---

[86] *Re L (medical treatment: Gillick competency)* [1998] 2 FLR 810. Although this case involved a minor, there is no reason why the principle would not also be applied to an adult patient.

[87] H Lesser, 'The Patient's Right to Information' in M Brazier and M Lobjoit (eds), *Protecting the Vulnerable: Autonomy and Consent in Healthcare* (London, Routledge, 1991), p 152.

[88] ECHRB Explanatory Report, para 36.

The GMC guidance on seeking patients' consent recognises that patients 'must be given sufficient information, in a way that they can understand, in order to enable them to exercise their right to make informed decisions about their care'.[89] In addition to ensuring respect for patient autonomy and enabling a genuine free choice regarding treatment, the provision of adequate information to the patient may also have therapeutic benefits.[90] Teff has emphasised this point: 'Within medicine it is increasingly acknowledged that mutual participation in treatment can offer therapeutic benefits, while affording due respect for the patient's moral agency.'[91] To view the provision of information as solely a rights and autonomy issue, therefore, is misleading as paternalism and beneficence also require an informed patient participating voluntarily and freely in the recommended treatment.

(b)   The Legal Consequences of a Failure to Inform of Risks

Having established the importance of consent being appropriately informed, it is now necessary to investigate what will be the legal consequences of a failure to inform the patient. In *Chatterton v Gerson*, Bristow J set out an important general principle: 'In my judgment once the patient is informed in broad terms of the nature of the procedure which is intended, and gives her consent, that consent is real, and the cause of action on which to base a claim for failure to go into risks and implications is negligence not trespass.'[92] This principle was approved by Hirst J in the 1983 case of *Hills v Potter*[93] and by Sir John Donaldson MR in the Court of Appeal judgment in *Sidaway v Bethlem Royal Hospital Governors*.[94] Interestingly, it creates a dual level of information disclosure. On the first level, a patient must be informed 'in broad terms of the nature of the procedure'. If he is not so informed, any purported consent will not be valid and thus the procedure will amount to a battery upon the patient. In this way, the patient's physical integrity and right to autonomy are well protected. On the second level, a failure to inform the patient of the risks and implications of treatment will not vitiate the consent but may justify a claim against the doctor for negligence. This dichotomy between nature and risk can be subjected to a number of criticisms. First, it excludes other relevant information such as alternative treatments, benefits of the proposed treatment and advice on the underlying ailment.[95]

---

[89]   *Seeking Patients' Consent: The Ethical Considerations* (GMC, 1998), para 1.

[90]   H Teff, 'Consent in Medical Procedures: Paternalism, Self-determination or Therapeutic Alliance?' (1985) 101 *LQR* 432, at p 437.

[91]   *Ibid.* See also M Brazier, 'Patient Autonomy and Consent to Treatment: The Role of the Law?' (1987) 7 *Legal Studies* 169, at p 176.

[92]   [1981] QB 432 at p 443.

[93]   [1983] 3 All ER 716.

[94]   [1985] AC 871, [1985] 1 All ER 643.

[95]   See TK Feng, 'Failure of Medical Advice: Trespass or Negligence?' (1987) 7 *Legal Studies* 149, at p 156.

Second, it drastically reduces the role of battery in English law. As Kennedy and Grubb have noted, the residual role left for battery 'is virtually vestigial'[96] and yet in their view it remains a 'powerful symbolic and actual deterrent against doctors ignoring the right of autonomy of their patients'.[97] While this may be true, the fact remains that the most fitting legal mechanism for protecting a patient's physical integrity and autonomous choice regarding their body is excluded from the question of a failure to disclose the risks of a proposed treatment. This is an unfortunate limitation upon the patient's rights, and raises the third criticism of the *Chatterton v Gerson* principle, namely that negligence as a means for protecting a patient's right to know is seriously flawed. A negligence claim can only be brought if some harm results from the failure to disclose. So, for example, if a patient is not told of a 1% risk inherent in a procedure and that risk materialises, a claim in negligence against the doctor is a possibility (the details will be considered below) but in an apparently illogical contrast, in the 99% of cases where the 1% risk does not materialise, there is no possibility of a legal remedy for the non-disclosure. The patient's autonomy – the right to decide freely and in possession of all relevant information necessary to make a choice – will have been infringed regardless of whether any injury results from the treatment, and yet the availability of a legal remedy rests entirely upon the unrelated issue of whether the risk which was not disclosed materialises or not. This seems to represent a misconception of the significance of a failure to disclose necessary information – ie the damage which is done thereby to the patient's autonomy. Finally, the fourth criticism of the *Chatterton v Gerson* principle is that there is no inherent difference between information as to the nature of a procedure and information as to its risks and consequences. The nature/ risk dichotomy is therefore misplaced.[98] Feng has argued that a failure to disclose risks should also sometimes vitiate consent and this indeed would be more consistent with protection of patient autonomy.[99] As English law currently stands, however, once information as to the broad nature of the procedure has been disclosed to the patient (in a form which enables the patient to understand it), a claim in negligence remains the only legal claim possible. Therefore, we must now look in some detail at the law on negligence, and specifically at the level of disclosure necessary in order to satisfy the doctor's standard of care.

---

[96]   Kennedy and Grubb, n 43 above, p 672.
[97]   *Ibid.*
[98]   Feng, n 95 above, p 156.
[99]   *Ibid,* p 160. Feng's argument that focus should be shifted to the degree of non-disclosure rather than the type of medical information not disclosed is not entirely convincing.

(c)   The Doctor's Standard of Care

(i)   A Patient-Oriented Test

Three possible options exist. First, the law could require that all information which the patient in question desires must be disclosed. This has the advantage of extending the patient's autonomy to the issue of what level of information disclosure is needed in order to enable a free choice as to whether to consent or not. It faces the difficulty, however, that the patient will not know what information he will consider relevant until it has been disclosed. It will, therefore, be impossible to ask the appropriate questions or indicate in other ways the information desired before the disclosure has occurred. The second option is that the law could require disclosure of all the information which the reasonable patient would consider relevant. This is the approach adopted in some jurisdictions in the United States, first developed in the case of *Canterbury v Spence*,[100] and favoured by Lord Scarman in his powerful dissent in the landmark English case of *Sidaway*. Lord Scarman recognised that in cases concerning a failure to disclose risks, 'the court is concerned primarily with a patient's right'.[101] He continued:

> The doctor's duty arises from the patient's rights. If one considers the scope of the doctor's duty by beginning with the right of the patient to make his own decision whether he will or will not undergo the treatment proposed, the right to be informed of significant risk and the doctor's corresponding duty are easy to understand, for the proper implementation of the right requires that the doctor be under a duty to inform his patient of the material risks inherent in the treatment.[102]

This is clearly a rights-based approach to the issue of informed consent and, given that the judgment was delivered in 1985 and pre-dates the recent surge in human rights awareness, it is a prescient approach. Unfortunately the other Law Lords in *Sidaway* did not share Lord Scarman's view. Subsequently, however, the High Court of Australia had to choose between following Lord Scarman's approach or that of the majority in *Sidaway* and unequivocally preferred the reasonable patient test. The Australian case of *Rogers v Whittaker*[103] involved a patient who was almost totally blind in her right eye and was not warned of a risk of becoming blind in the left eye as a result of an operation to correct the right eye. Clearly this risk would be of huge significance for a reasonable patient in this patient's position when deciding whether to consent to this elective surgery. The case presented a stark choice for the High Court: if they adopted the US prudent patient approach, the doctor would be liable for negligent non-disclosure; if,

---

[100]   464 F 2d 772 (DC, 1972)
[101]   Sidaway, n 94 above, p 654.
[102]   *Ibid.*
[103]   (1992) 109 ALR 625.

however, the court choose to adopt the *Sidaway* test, which, as we will see, depends upon the application of the *Bolam* test, the doctor would not be liable because other doctors would also not have disclosed the risk. The High Court of Australia chose the reasonable patient test:

> The law should recognise that a doctor has a duty to warn a patient of a material risk inherent in the proposed treatment; a risk is material if, in the circumstances of the particular case, a reasonable person in the patient's position, if warned of the risk, would be likely to attach significance to it or if the medical practitioner is or should reasonably be aware that the particular patient, if warned of the risk, would be likely to attach significance to it.[104]

It will be noted that the final part of this quote indicates that the Australian approach actually goes beyond Lord Scarman's reasonable patient test and requires disclosure of information to which the particular patient in question would be likely to attach significance. It seems clear that the Australian judges favoured a rights-based approach to the question of a doctor's standard of care on issues of non-disclosure and yet, strangely, they chose to deny this. As Chalmers and Schwartz have noted, the High Court was 'perhaps overzealous to distinguish itself' from the US approach[105] and rejects the US term 'informed consent' and further claimed that the right of self-determination was of little assistance to the question. But, as these writers point out, the entire High Court judgment is based upon self-determination because, while rejecting the American justification for a patient-oriented test, the court adopts 'the principle and, almost verbatim, the substantive language of *Canterbury v Spence*'.[106] It is, as Chalmers and Schwartz argue, a pity that the High Court did not feel able to assert patient rights as its justification for the reasonable patient test, as this would stand Australian law on a firmer theoretical foundation.[107] Nevertheless, there is no doubt that the case of *Rogers v Whittaker* establishes Australian law as the most patient- and risk-oriented of the common law jurisdictions.[108] This is particularly so because of the inclusion of an actual patient test beyond that of the reasonable patient. Despite the practical difficulties in this noted above, it ensures greater protection for patient autonomy because, as Brazier has noted, 'the right to be wrong, to act on individual preferences, to act against one's best interests as perceived by others, is unprotected even by a 'reasonable patient' test'.[109] Unfortunately the majority of the Law Lords in *Sidaway* were not willing to go even as far as a reasonable patient test.

---

[104]   *Ibid*, at p 52.
[105]   D Chalmers and R Schwartz, '*Rogers v Whittaker* and Informed Consent in Australia: A Fair Dinkum Duty of Disclosure' (1993) 1 *Med L Rev* 139, at p 148.
[106]   *Ibid*, p 158.
[107]   *Ibid*, p 149.
[108]   *Ibid*, p 139.
[109]   Brazier, n 91 above, p 187.

(ii) A Doctor-Oriented Test

The third and final option for the standard of care is to require disclosure only of what the medical profession considers appropriate. The case of *Sidaway* concerned an operation on the cervical vertebrae in order to remove the patient's recurrent pain. The operation carried a 2% risk of damage to the nerve root and a 1% risk of damage to the spinal cord. This latter risk would have more serious consequences if it materialised but, unlike the 2% risk, was not disclosed to the patient. Nor was the fact that the operation was one of choice rather than necessity disclosed to the patient. When the 1% risk of damage to the spinal cord materialised, the patient brought a claim in negligence. The majority of the House of Lords concluded that the level of disclosure required should be decided on the basis of the *Bolam* test. This test, which we encountered in the previous chapter, holds that a doctor will not be negligent if he follows a practice accepted as proper by a responsible body of medical opinion. Its application to a risk disclosure case means that a doctor need only disclose those risks which other doctors would also disclose. No room is left in this test for consideration of what the patient needs to know in order to make an autonomous choice. It is not, therefore, an approach consistent with patient autonomy or the right to self-determination.

It should be noted, however, that only Lord Diplock in *Sidaway* applied *Bolam* in its pure form. Lord Diplock held that:

> no convincing reason has in my view been advanced before your Lordships that would justify treating the *Bolam* test as doing anything less than laying down a principle of English law that is comprehensive and applicable to every aspect of the duty of care owed by a doctor to his patient in the exercise of his healing functions as respects that patient.[110]

Lord Diplock, therefore, sees no reason to treat a risk disclosure case as in any way distinct from other negligence cases. He fails to appreciate the significance of the patient's rights in respect of receiving information which enables an informed and autonomous choice to be made. In contrast to Lord Scarman's rights-based judgment, Lord Diplock's judgment is entirely in terms of doctors' duties.[111] The other three Law Lords take less extreme views. Lord Bridge, with whom Lord Keith agrees, holds only that the level of disclosure should be decided 'primarily' on the basis of medical evidence: 'a decision what degree of disclosure of risks is best calculated to assist a particular patient to make a rational choice whether or

---

[110] *Sidaway*, n 94 above, p 658.

[111] Lord Diplock even goes so far as to say that 'The only effect that mention of risks can have on the patient's mind, if it has any at all, can be in the direction of deterring the patient from undergoing the treatment which in the expert opinion of the doctor it is in the patient's interest to undergo' (*ibid*, p 659). It is clear from this that Lord Diplock entirely fails to recognise the right to make an informed choice.

not to undergo a particular treatment must primarily be a matter of clinical judgment'.[112] Quite what 'primarily' means in this context is not entirely clear. Lord Bridge does proceed, however, to hold open the possibility that, even where no medical expert condemns the non-disclosure as being in conflict with accepted and responsible medical practice, the court may conclude that disclosure of a particular risk 'was so obviously necessary that no reasonably prudent medical man would fail to make it'.[113] This is clearly beyond the strict limits of the *Bolam* test and indicates an appreciation of the shortcomings of this test. It is clear that, at the very least, Lord Bridge and Lord Keith would ensure that the courts retain the final say on what risks should be disclosed to patients. The fifth Law Lord, Lord Templeman, delivered a judgment described by Kennedy and Grubb as 'to say the least, idiosyncratic'.[114] He refers to neither the *Bolam* test nor the US prudent patient test.

It is clear that the ratio of *Sidaway* was not a simplistic application of *Bolam* to cases of risk-disclosure (as only Lord Diplock favoured this approach). Nevertheless, this seemed initially to be *Sidaway's* legacy as the Court of Appeal in *Gold v Haringey Health Authority*[115] and *Blyth v Bloomsbury Health Authority*[116] relied entirely upon Lord Diplock's judgment and *Bolam* seemed to be emerging as the final word on information disclosure. Subsequent to the *Bolitho* case, however, in which, as was discussed in the previous chapter, it was held that a responsible medical opinion must rest upon a logical basis in order to be relied upon,[117] the Court of Appeal has rethought the application of *Bolam* to this issue. In *Pearce v United Bristol Healthcare NHS Trust*,[118] Lord Woolf MR, giving the opinion of the court, considered the impact of *Bolitho* upon *Sidaway* and concluded that:

> if there is a significant risk which would affect the judgment of a reasonable patient, then in the normal course it is the responsibility of a doctor to inform the patient of that significant risk, if the information is needed so that the patient can determine for him or herself as to what course he or she should adopt.[119]

It will be immediately apparent that this approach is comparable to the reasonable patient test adopted by the Australian High Court in *Rogers v Whittaker*. As Kennedy and Grubb note, it is interesting that 'the Australian High Court thought it was rejecting *Bolam* . . . while the Court of Appeal applied it, at least in its new-variant form post-*Bolitho*'[120] to reach the same result. The approach in *Pearce* is certainly an improvement upon Lord Diplock's strict application of

---

[112] *Ibid*, pp 662-663.
[113] *Ibid*, p 663.
[114] Kennedy and Grubb, n 43 above, p 693.
[115] [1987] 2 All ER 888, [1988] QB 481.
[116] [1993] 4 Med LR 151.
[117] *Bolitho v City & Hackney Health Authority* [1998] AC 232.
[118] (1998) 48 BMLR 118.
[119] *Ibid*.
[120] Kennedy and Grubb, n 43 above, p 709.

Bolam in that it pays some regard to the information needed by the patient in order to exercise a free choice. This approach has subsequently been approved by the House of Lords in *Chester v Afshar* in which Lord Steyn concluded that:

> A surgeon owes a legal duty to a patient to warn him or her in general terms of possible serious risks involved in the procedure . . . In modern law medical paternalism no longer rules and a patient has a prima facie right to be informed by a surgeon of a small, but well established, risk of serious injury as a result of surgery.[121]

There is no mention here of disclosing only those risks which no responsible body of medical opinion would withhold. Instead, Lord Steyn adopts a very rights-based approach, comparable to Lord Scarman's judgment in *Sidaway*. He argues, for example, that 'a patient's right to an appropriate warning from a surgeon when faced with surgery ought normatively to be regarded as an important right which must be given effective protection whenever possible'.[122] Such a principled approach bodes well for the future protection of patients' rights in this context.

(iii)   Asking Questions

We will return to the important and somewhat unsatisfactory case of *Chester v Afshar* shortly but first one final issue in respect of the appropriate standard of care regarding information disclosure must be considered. Should the standard of care and level of disclosure vary depending upon whether the patient asks specific questions about potential risks? In *Sidaway* Lord Bridge said, obiter, that a doctor's duty when asked a question is 'to answer both truthfully and as fully as the questioner requires'.[123] Subsequently in *Blyth v Bloomsbury Health Authority*, however, the Court of Appeal applied the *Bolam* test even to the issue of asking questions. Thus, Kerr LJ held that:

> The question of what a plaintiff should be told in answer to a general enquiry cannot be divorced from the Bolam test, any more than when no such enquiry is made . . . Indeed I am not convinced that the Bolam test is irrelevant even in relation to the question of what answers are properly to be given to specific enquiries.[124]

It should be noted, however, that in the case in question the doctor did not himself know of the risk which was not disclosed and was held not to be negligent. It could be argued, therefore, that this case is distinguishable on its facts from the cases where doctors have known of risks but withheld them from the patient. Subsequently, in *Pearce*, Woolf LJ confirmed that 'if a patient asks a

---

[121]   [2005] 1 AC 134, [2004] 4 All ER 587, at para 16.
[122]   *Ibid*, para 17.
[123]   *Sidaway*, n 94 above, at p 661.
[124]   [1993] 4 Med LR 151, at p 157.

doctor about the risk, then the doctor is required to give an honest answer'.[125] This seems the correct approach provided that it applies to questions regarding risks which would not objectively be regarded as material. Risks which would be regarded as material by a reasonable patient should be disclosed regardless of whether the patient asks about them. It is vital that these two points are taken together because otherwise there is a danger that the educated and articulate would be given a greater right to know than more compliant patients. The right to know must be the same for all patients regardless of whether they remember, and are able, to ask the correct questions. If a question is asked, however, a doctor should be honest in his reply.

(d)   Causation of Harm

Even if a doctor breaches his duty of care by failing to disclose a relevant risk, the patient will not be entitled to compensation unless injury has been caused by this negligent non-disclosure. English law on non-disclosure therefore rests entirely upon an outcome approach rather than a process approach. This seems inappropriate given that a patient has a right to the information necessary in order to make an autonomous choice, regardless of the outcome of the procedure. The requirement of causation can, therefore, appear to cause some injustice in its operation for it requires that a patient prove that he would not have undergone the treatment if he had known of the risks – ie but for the non-disclosure, the injury would not have been caused. For example, in *Smith v Barking, Havering and Brentwood Health Authority*[126] the patient suffered from a condition which would lead to paralysis within one year without an operation, but the operation itself held a 25 per cent risk of accelerating the paralysis. The patient was not told of this risk. Hutchinson J held that this was a negligent non-disclosure but that there was a strong possibility that the patient would have taken the risk anyway and so damages were restricted to the shock of discovering paralysis immediately after the operation without any prior warning. The test applied combined a subjective and objective test by asking whether a reasonable patient sharing this patient's characteristics would have declined the treatment if she had known of the risks. Despite the patient claiming that she would not have taken the risk, the judge held that she would have done so. Thus, even though a hugely significant risk (1 in 4) of an extremely serious outcome (paralysis) was wrongly withheld from the patient, she was not entitled to recompense for the paralysis nor for the violation of her rights inherent in such a cavalier attitude to her autonomy.

More recently, in the case of *Chester v Afshar*,[127] the House of Lords decided to take an innovative approach to causation. The facts of this case were that a

---

[125]   *Pearce*, n 118 above, p 120.
[126]   [1994] 5 Med LR 285.
[127]   See n 121 above.

patient required an operation for severe back pain. She was not warned of a small risk of nerve damage resulting in paralysis, which subsequently occurred leaving her in a worse position than before the operation. The non-disclosure was held to be negligent. The key question was causation. The patient did not deny that, even if she had known of the risk, she would still have had the operation at some time in the future, but she did claim that she would have postponed the operation and sought a second opinion. A majority of the House of Lords held that, although the traditional 'but for' test for causation was not satisfied (ie it could not be proved that but for the negligent non-disclosure the harm would not have occurred), policy reasons required that the patient recover damages in this case. Lord Steyn, adopting a very rights-based approach, also developed an unconvincing argument that causation was satisfied on the basis that but for the doctor's negligent failure to warn, the injury 'would not have occurred when it did and the chance of it occurring on a subsequent occasion was very small'.[128] This is a dubious argument. It suggests that because the small risk of injury materialised on the day of the operation, a similar operation on a different day would not have resulted in the injury. This is unconvincing statistical analysis, as Lord Bingham pointed out in his dissent: 'That injury would have been as liable to occur whenever the surgery was performed and whoever performed it'.[129] This is the meaning of a risk inherent in a procedure. It is similar to the chances of throwing a six with a dice: the chance does not decrease merely because your previous throw produced a six. The majority did not, sensibly, rely solely on this argument. Lord Steyn explained that he had stood back from the detailed arguments on causation and had arrived at the conclusion that:

> as a result of the surgeon's failure to warn the patient, she cannot be said to have given informed consent to the surgery in the full legal sense. Her right of autonomy and dignity can and ought to be vindicated by a narrow and modest departure from traditional causation principles.[130]

Lord Hope took the similar view that justice required the normal approach to causation to be modified:

> The function of the law is to enable rights to be vindicated and to provide remedies when duties have been breached. Unless this is done the duty is a hollow one. On policy grounds therefore I would hold that the test of causation is satisfied in this case. The injury was intimately involved with the duty to warn . . . So I would hold that it can be regarded as having been caused, in the legal sense, by the breach of that duty.[131]

---

[128]   *Ibid*, para 19.
[129]   *Ibid*, para 8.
[130]   *Ibid*, para 24.
[131]   *Ibid*, para 87.

As discussed in the previous chapter, this represents a transformation in the requirement of causation for negligence and, while it is encouraging to see such emphasis being placed upon the vindication of the rights of the patient, the majority judgments are ultimately unconvincing. Partly this is because, despite relying upon the idea of patients' rights, little analysis or even explanation of these rights and their implications is forthcoming. In addition, Lord Bingham, dissenting, makes a sound point when he argues that 'a claimant is not entitled to be compensated, and a defendant is not bound to compensate the claimant, for damage not caused by the negligence complained of'.[132] Certainly this had previously been an underlying principle of English law. Furthermore, despite the emphasis upon the patient being unable to give informed consent to the operation because of the doctor's failure to warn of risks,[133] this presumably does not apply if the risk does not materialise. Why? If the failure to warn is sufficient to justify an award of damages even though it did not, under previous English law, cause any harm, why does the risk need to materialise before a claim can be brought in negligence? Any negligent non-disclosure will equally violate the patient's rights, regardless of the outcome of the treatment. The lengths to which the Law Lords had to go in reworking or bypassing the law on causation in order to achieve the vindication of rights which they regarded as essential in this case suggests that negligence is not the appropriate cause of action for cases of this kind. The re-introduction of battery to the issue of non-disclosure would be one possible solution, but a more fitting alternative would be reliance upon the Convention rights under the HRA. Given the importance placed upon the vindication of patients' rights by the House of Lords in *Chester v Afshar*, an argument that an operation performed without informed consent was unlawful because it violated Article 8's protection of physical integrity seems a viable possibility, and it would have the advantage of not requiring the complete reformulating of the established law on negligence in order to ensure adequate protection for patient autonomy.

V. Conclusion

This chapter has sought to explain and analyse the fundamental principle of consent to medical treatment. It has argued that the need for consent represents an essential protection for patient autonomy. A number of problems with the current law have been identified. Perhaps the most significant is a tendency for both the law and the courts to protect the autonomy of the patient saying 'yes' to recommended treatment more fully than the autonomy of the patient who chooses, possibly for irrational reasons, to say 'no'. Other problems include a

---

[132] *Ibid*, para 9.
[133] See Lord Steyn, *ibid*, para 24.

reluctance to recognise and potentially check the undue pressure stemming from the doctor-patient relationship; the requirement in the *Re C* test (at least as originally conceived) that a patient must believe the information provided by the doctor in order to be regarded as competent; the possibility that a failure to fully inform a patient may result in him being regarded as incompetent even though the remedy lies entirely in the hands of the doctor; and the ineffectiveness of negligence as a remedy for the vindication of patient autonomy (and thus the need for fundamental reformulating of the traditional causation requirement). Despite these potential dangers, there is cause for optimism in relation to this area of English medical law. Senior judges in the Court of Appeal and House of Lords have recently recognised that patient autonomy must be the guiding light here and on the issues of competence (*Re B*), standard of care in respect of risk disclosure (*Pearce*) and causation of harm (*Chester v Afshar*) the courts have expressly emphasised the need for protection and vindication of patients' rights. Jones has recognised that this may justifiably cause some concern amongst the medical profession: 'a patient with rights is a lawsuit waiting to happen'. Jones continues by noting, however, that, 'On the other hand, a patient with no rights is a citizen who is stripped of his or her individuality and autonomy, as well as her clothes, as soon as she walks into the surgery or the hospital.'[134] That the higher courts no longer seem prepared to permit this to happen is an encouraging development in the law on consent to medical treatment.

Recommended Further Reading

G Dworkin, *The Theory and Practice of Autonomy* (Cambridge, Cambridge University Press, 1988).

M Gunn, 'The Meaning of Incapacity' (1994) 2 *Med L Rev* 8.

MA Jones, 'Informed Consent and Other Fairy Stories' (1999) 7 *Med L Rev* 103.

MA Jones and K Keywood, 'Assessing the Patient's Competence to Consent to Medical Treatment' (1996) 2 *Med Law Int* 107.

---

[134]   MA Jones, 'Informed Consent and Other Fairy Stories' (1999) 7 *Med L Rev* 103, at p 129.

5

Treating Incompetent Patients:
Beneficence, Welfare and Rights

In the previous chapter, we discovered that autonomy is central to current English medical law and that there is increasing judicial recognition of the importance of informed consent to medical treatment. For a significant category of patients, however, informed consent is unattainable, either because they lack consciousness, mental capacity or maturity. These incompetent patients may be temporarily, or even permanently, incapable of exercising an autonomous choice regarding healthcare and alternative means of authorising treatment must be adopted. This chapter will investigate who makes healthcare decisions in respect of incompetent patients and on what basis they do so. These issues will be considered with full regard to the requirements of both the patient's welfare and his or her human rights.

I. The Principle of Beneficence and
Conflicting Rights

The principle of beneficence refers to a moral obligation to act for the benefit of others.[1] It is one of the four ethical principles often regarded as underlying healthcare: autonomy, justice, non-maleficence and beneficence.[2] The human rights approach to medical law advocated in this book often prioritises the principle of individual autonomy of the patient. However, this principle cannot always provide the answer to healthcare dilemmas and this is particularly apparent in circumstances where the patient lacks competence to make his or her own treatment decisions. In this situation, beneficence stakes a claim for priority. It differs from non-maleficence in that it demands more from the healthcare professional: not merely refraining from causing harm but rather taking positive

---

[1] TL Beauchamp and JF Childress, *Principles of Biomedical Ethics*, 5th edn (Oxford, Oxford University Press, 2001), p 166.

[2] See Beauchamp and Childress, *ibid*, for detailed explanation and analysis of these principles.

steps to promote the welfare of the patient.[3] As such, it expresses medicine's primary rationale. The use of the principle of beneficence to justify medical interventions raises the possibility of paternalistic decision-making. Paternalism – so often contrasted with the competing concept of autonomy – is justified in respect of incompetent children in need of parental supervision. Its application to incompetent adults is perhaps more controversial but recognises the need of those adults for care analogous to beneficent parental guidance.[4] A paternalistic attitude towards a competent adult patient is unjustifiable for it inevitably detracts from the protection of that patient's autonomy which, as was discussed in the previous chapter, is in such circumstances paramount. Given the general acceptance of the role of beneficence in respect of incompetent patients, is there a danger that such paternalistic intervention may conflict with the patient's human rights?

A good starting point is the prohibition of degrading treatment in Article 3 ECHR. This right will have application to both competent and incompetent patients,[5] although it has been held in a domestic case that the patient must be aware of the degrading treatment which is being imposed in order to obtain the protection of Article 3.[6] Non-consensual treatment may amount to degrading treatment but will not do so if it is therapeutically necessary. This principle was established in the 1992 case of *Herczegfalvy v Austria*, which involved the forced-feeding and restraint of a mental patient.[7] The European Court of Human Rights held that this treatment did not amount to degrading treatment in violation of Article 3 and declared the general rule that 'a measure which is a therapeutic necessity cannot be regarded as inhuman or degrading'.[8] The Court emphasised, however, that it must 'satisfy itself that the medical necessity has been convincingly shown to exist'.[9] This provides some valuable protection for incompetent patients and this strict judicial oversight advocated by the Strasbourg Court stands in stark contrast to the light touch approach traditionally employed by the UK courts, as will be seen below.

Article 8 ECHR offers further protection for incompetent patients by means of the right to physical integrity included within the Article's broader right to

---

[3]   *Ibid*, p 165.

[4]   *Ibid*, p 177. As Beauchamp and Childress acknowledge, from this perspective, 'a healthcare professional is like a loving parent with dependent and often ignorant and fearful children' (p 178).

[5]   *Herczegfalvy v Austria* (1992) Series A, No 244, para 82: 'while it is for the medical authorities to decide, on the basis of the recognised rules of medical science, on the therapeutic methods to be used, if necessary by force, to preserve the physical and mental health of patients who are entirely incapable of deciding for themselves and for whom they are therefore responsible, such patients nevertheless remain under the protection of Article 3'.

[6]   *NHS Trust A v M; NHS Trust B v H* [2001] 1 All ER 801. This point is explained and criticised in chapter 11.

[7]   See n 5 above.

[8]   *Ibid*, para 82.

[9]   *Ibid*.

respect for private life.[10] The European Commission of Human Rights stated explicitly in *X v Austria* that a 'compulsory medical intervention, even if it is of minor importance, must be considered as an interference with this right'.[11] In this case, the complaint, concerning a compulsory blood test to determine paternity, was held to be manifestly ill-founded because the interference with Article 8(1) was justified by Article 8(2), specifically the protection of the rights of others. In another case, compulsory screening for tuberculosis was held to be capable of amounting to an interference with private life, but the complaint was again held to be inadmissible as the interference was justified as necessary to protect health in a democratic society.[12] Both of these cases illustrate that, although Article 8 protects a right of physical integrity, it does so subject to the other requirements of a democratic society, including the rights and freedoms of others and the protection of health and morals. Furthermore, both of these cases involved competent patients. While it is clear that the right to physical integrity offers protection to all individuals, regardless of their mental capacity,[13] an inability to offer consent will justify an infringement of physical integrity. This was clear in the *Herczegfalvy* case, mentioned above, where, in addition to the Article 3 complaint, a complaint under Article 8 was also dismissed. The Court held that there was a lack of evidence disproving that the applicant's psychiatric illness rendered him 'entirely incapable of taking decisions for himself'.[14] It is only in the absence of such evidence, however, that a non-consensual infringement with physical integrity will be compliant with Article 8. In principle, a patient whose mental capacity is the subject of dispute could argue that Article 8 had been infringed.

While an incompetent patient retains individual rights, including probably some element of autonomy and certainly a right to physical integrity, privacy and freedom from degrading treatment, the image of a stark conflict between a patient's rights and a patient's welfare can be misleading (as well as being ultimately unhelpful). This is because an incompetent patient may also possess a right (albeit limited) to receive beneficial treatment. Lacking ability to provide consent to necessary treatment, the incompetent patient is nevertheless entitled to not have his or her interest in good health ignored. A doctor's duty of care includes a duty to provide treatment which is in an incompetent patient's best interests. Such non-consensual treatment should not merely be regarded as a violation of the patient's right to be free of physical intrusions, but also the

---

[10]   *X and Y v Netherlands* (1985) Series A, No 91; 8 EHRR 235; *Costello-Roberts v United Kingdom* (1993) Series A, No 247.

[11]   (1980) 18 DR 154, at p 156.

[12]   *Acmanne v Belgium* (1984) 40 DR 251.

[13]   In *X and Y v Netherlands*, n 10 above, the failure of Dutch law to permit a complaint about the sexual assault of a 16 year old mentally handicapped girl within a care home was held to infringe Art 8.

[14]   *Herczegfalvy*, n 5 above, para. 86.

realisation of his or her right to receive beneficial treatment. Lord Jauncey recognised in the landmark case of *Re F* (discussed below):

> the importance of not erecting such legal barriers against the provision of medical treatment for incompetents that they are deprived of treatment which competent persons could reasonably expect to receive in similar circumstances. The law must not convert incompetents into second class citizens for the purposes of healthcare.[15]

This recognition of the importance of non-consensual interventions reminds us that this topic may be defined by a balancing of rights or interests rather than as a conflict between the protection of rights and the paternalistic protection of welfare.

II.   The Best Interests Test

(a)   Medical Best Interests

The issue of the imposition of non-consensual treatment on incompetent patients is now governed by the Mental Capacity Act 2005 but it has its roots in the common law. Perhaps surprisingly, the question of the legal basis for treating incompetent adults who are unable to provide consent did not arise in a judicial context until the late 1980s.[16] The landmark judgment of the House of Lords in the case of *Re F*[17] came in 1990 and set the legal foundations for the provision of treatment to incompetent adult patients. The case involved a 36 year old woman suffering from arrested mental development. She was a voluntary in-patient at a mental hospital and had formed a sexual relationship with a male patient, thus raising concerns amongst her carers about contraception. She was regarded as unable to cope with pregnancy, labour or delivery and, as other means of contraception were unsuitable, an application was made for the authorisation of a sterilisation operation. The court first acknowledged that it no longer had any inherent jurisdiction which would enable it to provide consent to the treatment

---

[15]   *Re F (Mental Patient: Sterilisation)* [1990] 2 AC 51, at p 83.

[16]   Brazier explains a possible reason for this: 'I suspect that until relatively recently no one gave much thought to the law governing treatment of such patients – they just went ahead on the paternalistic theory that 'doctors know best'. The rise in medical litigation and increased concern for patients' rights caused healthcare professionals understandable concern. Doctors and nurses not only feared litigation if they went ahead with unauthorised treatment, but also feared litigation if a patient suffered because they did nothing' (M Brazier, *Medicine, Patients and the Law*, 3rd edn (London, Penguin, 2003) at p 117).

[17]   *Re F*, n 15 above.

and instead the jurisdiction of relevance would be the court's declaratory jurisdiction – ie its ability to issue a declaration that the operation would be lawful in certain circumstances.[18]

The House of Lords focused its judgment upon the principle of necessity. It held that it is 'axiomatic that treatment which is necessary to preserve the life, health or well being of the patient may lawfully be given without consent'.[19] The Lords were willing to extend this principle, however, to cover treatment which may not be strictly necessary but is instead merely beneficial to the patients. Lord Bridge explained that:

> if a rigid criterion of necessity were to be applied to determine what is and what is not lawful in the treatment of the unconscious and the incompetent, many of those unfortunate enough to be deprived of the capacity to make or communicate rational decisions by accident, illness or unsoundness of mind might be deprived of treatment which it would be entirely beneficial for them to receive.[20]

This green light approach to the provision of beneficial treatment recalls Lord Jauncey's comments quoted in the previous section that barriers should not be erected against the provision of treatment to incompetent patients and reminds us that non-consensual treatment is not merely (if even) a potential violation of physical integrity rights but also (or rather) a potential realisation of rights to adequate care and medical attention.

Lord Goff further explains the varying degrees to which the necessity principle may extend depending upon the duration of incompetence. He states that where a patient is temporarily rendered unconscious in an accident, doctors should 'do no more than is reasonably required, in the best interests of the patient, before he recovers consciousness'.[21] For example, in *Williamson v East London & City Health Authority*,[22] a subcutaneous mastectomy performed while the patient was unconscious during an operation to remove and replace a leaking breast implant was held to be merely convenient rather than necessary and consent should have been sought before the procedure was performed.[23] However, where the incompetence is permanent or semi-permanent, for example because the patient suffers from a mental disorder, 'there is no point waiting to obtain the patient's consent'

---

[18] See Lord Bridge, *ibid*, p 65.

[19] *Ibid*, p 52.

[20] *Ibid*.

[21] *Ibid*, p 77.

[22] [1998] Lloyd's Rep Med 6.

[23] Two Canadian cases are widely cited to illustrate the distinction between necessity and convenience. In *Marshall v Curry* [1933] 3 DLR 260 the removal of a testicle during an operation for a hernia was held to be necessary for the patient's health, and possibly life, and it would have been unreasonable to delay the procedure. By contrast, in *Murray v McMurchy* [1949] 2 DLR 442 a sterilisation during a Caesarean section operation after it was discovered that another pregnancy would be hazardous, was held not to be necessary as there was no pressing need for the procedure at that time.

and more extensive beneficial treatment could be lawfully provided.[24] Thus, the treatment provided in the absence of consent does not need to satisfy a strict 'necessity' test but the legal authority for such treatment continues to derive from the necessity principle.[25] *Re F* held that doctors can lawfully treat incompetent adult patients provided that the proposed treatment is in their best interests. It was clarified by Lord Brandon that, in an oft-quoted comment, treatment will be in a patient's best interests 'if, but only if, it is carried out in order either to save their lives, or to ensure improvement or prevent deterioration in their physical or mental health'.[26]

The aspects of the *Re F* judgment discussed so far are relatively uncontroversial. The House of Lords courted controversy, however, by introducing the *Bolam* test into the issue. The *Bolam* test, discussed in Chapter 3, was developed as a means of assessing whether a doctor has met the requisite standard of care so as to avoid a finding of negligence. The House of Lords in *Re F* decided that the same test should be applied to the question of whether non-consensual treatment is in a patient's best interests. Lord Bridge explained that, if healthcare professionals have acted with due skill and care according to the *Bolam* test, they 'should be immune from liability in trespass, just as they are immune from liability in negligence'.[27] This means that, if a responsible body of medical opinion would regard a particular treatment as in the best interests of an incompetent patient, there will be no legal liability for its imposition. By contrast, the Court of Appeal, in its judgment in *Re F*, expressly rejected the application of the *Bolam* test to questions of best interests, considering it an insufficiently stringent test for this issue. As Neill LJ pointed out, 'to say that it is not negligence to carry out a particular form of treatment does not mean that that treatment is necessary'.[28] These sensible reservations were comprehensively rejected in the House of Lords where Lord Brandon emphasised that a more stringent test might result in some incompetent patients being 'deprived of the benefit of medical treatment which adults competent to give consent would enjoy'.[29]

The significance of the application of the *Bolam* standard to this question is compounded by the use of the declaratory jurisdiction to determine this, and similar, cases. Generally, court approval is not needed in order for an incompetent adult patient to be treated in his or her best interests and, therefore, the treatment of incompetent adults is determined solely on the basis of the views of a responsible body of medical opinion. The treatment in question in *Re F* – sterilisation – was, thankfully, treated as a special case due to its profound implications for the patient's reproductive autonomy[30] and the House of Lords

---

[24]   *Re F*, n 15 above, p 77.
[25]   *Ibid.*
[26]   *Ibid*, p 55.
[27]   *Ibid*, p 52.
[28]   *Ibid*, p 32.
[29]   *Ibid*, p 68.
[30]   See Chapter 8.

held that it would be good practice to obtain a court declaration of lawfulness before proceeding with such drastic and irreversible treatment. The legality of the treatment stems from the patient's best interests, however, and not from the declaration itself. The outcome of *Re F* was a declaration that the sterilisation operation would be lawful if performed in her best interests, and a legacy of prioritising an incompetent patient's medical best interests as judged by a responsible body of medical opinion. The legacy has been the subject of much criticism, often stemming, as Brazier notes, from 'a suspicion that the judgment benefited doctors rather more than patients'.[31]

The medical best interests test not only has application for incompetent adult patients as a consequence of *Re F*, but also applies in respect of minors who are unable to consent to treatment due to their age. This first became apparent in *Re B*[32] which involved a baby born with Down's Syndrome and also suffering from an intestinal blockage which would be fatal without an operation. The parents refused to consent to the operation as they regarded the additional complications as nature's way of allowing the Down's baby to die. Medical evidence made clear that without the operation the baby would die within days but with the operation it was possible that she may live a normal Down's lifespan of 20-30 years.[33] The child was made a ward of court and the Court of Appeal authorised the operation. In justifying this decision, Templeman LJ described the decision for the court as 'whether the life of this child is demonstrably going to be so awful that in effect the child must be condemned to die'.[34] Expanding upon this dilemma, Templeman LJ explained that:

> the choice which lies before the court is this: whether to allow an operation to take place which may result in the child living for 20 or 30 years as a mongoloid or whether (and I think this must be brutally the result) to terminate the life of a mongoloid child because she also has an intestinal complaint. Faced with that choice I have no doubt that it is the duty of this court to decide that the child must live.[35]

Re B makes clear, therefore, that in respect of a minor the medical best interests of the child patient will be the crucial factor. The wishes of the parents in this case, and the broader family interests of the child, were regarded as of lesser importance.

In the subsequent case of *Re J*,[36] the Court of Appeal clarified the issue of treating minors, while rejecting some of Templeman LJ's wording, quoted above. *Re J* involved a premature baby born at 27 weeks who was suffering from

---

[31]   Brazier, n 16 above, p 118.

[32]   *Re B (a minor)* [1990] 3 All ER 927.

[33]   *Ibid*, p 928.

[34]   *Ibid*, p 929. This wording was subsequently criticised in *Re J (a minor) (wardship: medical treatment)* where Taylor LJ regarded it as 'more emotive than accurate' ([1990] 3 All ER 930, at p 944).

[35]   *Ibid*.

[36]   *Re J*, n 34 above.

convulsions and breathing difficulties, as well as severe brain damage due to a shortage of oxygen and impaired blood supply at the time of birth. The most optimistic prognosis included paralysis of the arms and legs, blindness and deafness, an inability to sit up or hold head upright, unlikely to speak or have any intellectual abilities and a likelihood of feeling pain. The child was a ward of court and the question for the court was whether the child should be placed on a ventilator if he stopped breathing again. The Court of Appeal confirmed that this issue must be decided solely on the basis of the patient's best interests which must be determined by a balancing exercise performed by the doctors. The baby's quality of life was recognised as relevant to a determination of medical best interests.[37] The Court of Appeal concluded that it would not be in the baby's best interests to reventilate if his breathing should cease again. More recently in *Wyatt* the Court of Appeal has confirmed that best interests remains the only test for the determination of treatment of a severely ill baby.[38] The issue of intolerability of suffering was held not to be a supplementary test, or even a gloss on the best interests test, but merely a factor that may be relevant amongst others.[39] The end of life issues inherent in these decisions, and their implications for the patient's right to life, will be discussed further in Chapter 11 but for now it is important to appreciate that in respect of both minors and adults, the common law by 1990 had established that the key to the provision of treatment to incompetent patients was the patient's medical best interests, as determined by the medical professionals treating the patient.

(b)   Broader Social Interests

The initial focus upon solely medical best interests, and particularly its determination by means of the *Bolam* test, not only garnered academic criticism but also led to a re-evaluation of the test by the Court of Appeal in subsequent cases. *Re A*[40] is one of the first cases to reconsider the meaning of best interests. Like *Re F*, the case involved an application for a sterilisation operation upon a mentally disordered incompetent adult. However, a potentially significant difference between the two cases is that in *Re A* the patient was a 28 year old male. He suffered from Down's Syndrome and lived with his mother who made the application for a declaration that an operation to sterilise him by means of a vasectomy would be in A's best interests and lawful. The mother closely supervised her son but he was sexually aware and she was concerned that, once he moved into local authority care in the future, he may commence a sexual relationship which could result in a pregnancy. Butler-Sloss P held that a patient's best interests are not limited to his medical best interests but also encompass

---

[37]   *Ibid*, p 945.
[38]   *Wyatt v Portsmouth NHS Trust* [2005] 1 WLR 3995.
[39]   *Ibid.*
[40]   *Re A (Medical treatment: Male Sterilisation)* (2000) 53 BMLR 66.

emotional and other welfare issues. The judgment focuses upon the best interests of A and concludes that the proposed operation would not save A from the possibility of exploitation or help him cope with the emotional implications of any closer relationships, nor would it give him any greater freedom because he would still need to be closely supervised. It was held not to be in A's best interests to undergo the vasectomy. There is no doubt that A's gender is a crucial factor in this decision because, as a man, he would not have to endure any direct consequences from a pregnancy. Because of this, the proposed infringement upon his physical integrity is difficult to justify as in his own best interests, even though it may be a convenient step for his carers and potential female partners. In reaching their judgment in this case, the members of the Court of Appeal were particularly conscious of the imminent implementation of the Human Rights Act 1998 and Butler-Sloss acknowledged that 'the courts should be slow to take any step which might infringe the rights of those unable to speak for themselves'.[41]

A significant consequence of the inclusion of broader interests into consideration of a patient's best interests became apparent in *Re S*[42] when the limitations of the *Bolam* test were recognised. *Re S* again involved an application for a non-consensual sterilisation operation, this time, as in *Re F*, upon a female patient. The woman was 29 years old and suffering from severe learning disabilities. Her mother requested a declaration that a sterilisation and/or hysterectomy would be lawful. There were two reasons for the application: (1) a fear that S may become pregnant in the future if she were to live in a local authority home and be unsupervised, and that she would not be able to understand the concept of pregnancy or cope with a child; and (2) the therapeutic reason of preventing heavy menstrual bleeding which S does not understand and which causes her distress. At first instance, the judge authorised a hysterectomy despite hearing medical evidence that alternative, and less invasive, treatment such as a Mirena coil, would be preferable. This decision was strongly criticised by the Court of Appeal as being a disproportionate remedy for the problem to be solved:[43]

'the understandable concerns of a caring mother and the problems of dealing with S during her menstrual periods do not, on the facts of this case, tilt the balance towards major irreversible surgery for therapeutic reasons when they are unsupported by any gynaecological, psychological or other medical evidence'.[44]

There is a clear concern here that the application is being brought, at least partly, for the benefit of the carer rather than the patient and, while this may be understandable, it is vital that the court retain a focus upon the interests of the patient who is unable to speak for herself: 'The patient has a right, if she cannot

---

[41]   *Ibid*, p 11 of judgment.
[42]   *Re S (Adult Patient: Sterilisation)* [2000] 3 WLR 1288.
[43]   *Ibid*, p 1297.
[44]   *Ibid*, p 1296.

herself choose, not to have drastic surgery imposed upon her unless or until it has been demonstrated that it is in her best interests.'[45]

The Court of Appeal confirmed again in this case that an incompetent person's best interests extend beyond merely medical interests. It was held that a judicial decision on best interests will also incorporate 'broader ethical, social, moral and welfare considerations'.[46] Such considerations were recognised by the Court of Appeal as extending beyond the considerations set out in the *Bolam* case and, therefore, the relevance of the *Bolam* test to this issue was doubted. The judge at first instance had been satisfied that the medical experts did not regard a hysterectomy as outside the *Bolam* test. In other words, there was a responsible body of medical opinion which would support it. The Court of Appeal was adamant, however, that the proper question for the judge ought not to have been whether the proposed treatment was within the range of acceptable opinion among responsible practitioners but rather whether it was in the best interests of S.[47] The Court of Appeal was not convinced that a hysterectomy was currently in S's best interests and favoured the alternative, less invasive, treatment, at least initially. The rejection of the *Bolam* test as decisive on these issues, and the recognition of the relevance of ethical, social, moral and welfare, as well as medical, considerations, has transformed the best interests test into one which genuinely seeks to reconcile an incompetent patient's rights and welfare. However, it could also be regarded as opening the door to the inclusion of even broader interests, namely those of a third party.

(c)   The Interests of Others

The courts have always expressed clearly that the best interests in question when determining the treatment of an incompetent patient, adult or minor, are those of the patient alone. This is a vital protection for the patient's rights because the imposition of non-consensual treatment, and thus the interference with the patient's rights to physical integrity, can only be justified if necessary for the patient's other interests. We have just seen that these interests may be broad in scope. The courts have been reluctant, rightly so, to extend those relevant interests to those of other people, but unfortunately they have been tempted on occasion to do so. The first example is the case of *Re Y*.[48] This case involved a 25 year old woman with severe mental and physical disabilities (the defendant). Her sister (the plaintiff) was suffering from a pre-leukaemic bone marrow disorder and her only realistic prospect of recovery was a bone marrow transplant. Unrelated donors might be available but the transplant was more likely to be successful if a sibling donor was used. Unfortunately, the only sibling who was a

---

[45]   *Ibid*, p 1297.
[46]   *Ibid*, p 1299.
[47]   *Ibid*.
[48]   (1997) 2 WLR 557.

match was the one unable to consent or even understand the situation. Connell J recognised that the key issue was the best interests of the defendant and not those of the plaintiff. However, he was able to find an intriguing way around this apparent obstacle: 'The fact that such a process [the transplant] would obviously benefit the plaintiff is not relevant unless, as a result of the defendant helping the plaintiff in that way, the best interests of the defendant are served.'[49] The judge's reasoning was that, if the plaintiff died, the sisters' mother would be likely to suffer a deterioration in her own health and would need to look after the plaintiff's daughter and so would be less able to visit the defendant:

> In this situation, the defendant would clearly be harmed by the reduction in or loss of contact with her mother. Accordingly, it is to the benefit of the defendant that she should act as donor to her sister, because in this way her positive relationship with her mother is most likely to be prolonged. Further, if the transplant occurs, this is likely to improve the defendant's relationship with her mother who in her heart clearly wishes it to take place and also to improve her relationship with the plaintiff who will be eternally grateful to her.[50]

On this basis, Connell J authorised the bone marrow transplant to take place with the defendant as donor even though she could not consent, would gain no medical benefit and the only benefit to her would be the gratitude of her family (which she would be unable to appreciate due to her lack of mental capacity).

Not only was the potential benefit indirect and dubious, but the risks in the procedure were overlooked. Acting as donor in a bone marrow transplant is a serious procedure requiring a general anaesthetic and morphine to control subsequent pain. Why should the defendant be subjected to this pain, discomfort and risk when it is in no way necessary to her health? Far from being beneficial to her health, the procedure will be detrimental to her health. The judge emphasised, however, that the procedure, although not in the defendant's medical best interests, was in her emotional, psychological and social interests. The judge also placed great weight upon the fact that this was a 'particularly close family'[51] with the implication that this case is not a general precedent for an incompetent patient being forced to undergo serious medical procedures for the medical benefit of others. However, there is little evidence of this apparent unusual closeness. The defendant had lived in residential care since she was ten years old and, although she had formed warm relations with her mother from regular visits, she did not understand that the woman was her mother. The mother's visits were described as 'almost weekly' and the plaintiff visited much less frequently. In short, there was no evidence of a particularly close tie between the plaintiff and the defendant. Furthermore, the judge relied upon the mother's

---

[49] *Ibid*, p 559.
[50] *Ibid*, pp 561-62.
[51] *Ibid*, p 562.

belief that the defendant would consent to this procedure if she was able to do so. This is misleading, however, and not just because substituted judgment plays no part in English law. In different circumstances, a sister may indeed feel a moral obligation to act as a donor but the defendant's life was comprised of basic pleasures: would she really wish to consent to a distressing, painful and potentially risky procedure which she could not understand, for the benefit of a woman she did not recognise? The decision in this case is one of the most offensive to patient rights in recent years. It subjugates an incompetent person's interests to those of another person, despite the judge's denials that he was doing so. It is a precedent which has thankfully not been followed and it is highly unlikely that any judge would today sanction a procedure on an incompetent adult merely because it might improve her relationship with her family. There seems little doubt that this case would fall foul of the Convention rights. A non-consensual medical procedure for another's benefit is not a therapeutic necessity as required by *Herczegfalvy*[52] and is not something which should be tolerated within a democratic society.

Another example of the courts straying from consideration of a patient's own best interests is provided by the Court of Appeal judgment in *Re T (a minor-)(wardship: medical treatment)*.[53] This case involved a minor but it is no less important that the interests in question should be those of the minor patient rather than his family. The patient was an 18 month old baby suffering from a life-threatening liver defect. The unanimous medical prognosis was that he would not survive beyond the age of two to two and a half years without a liver transplant. However, his parents refused to consent to such a transplant. In investigating the best interests of the child, the Court of Appeal also felt compelled to have regard to the interests of the child's mother who would be caring for the child after the operation. The Court of Appeal went so far as to suggest that the interests of the mother and child were indivisible in this case: 'This mother and this child are one for the purpose of this unusual case and the decision of the court to consent to the operation jointly affects the mother and son and it also affects the father. The welfare of this child depends upon his mother.'[54] In particular, the court took into account the practical difficulties facing the mother if the operation were to go ahead and criticised the judge at first instance (ironically Connell J, the judge in *Re Y*) for not doing so. These practical considerations included her ability to cope with supporting the child in the face of her belief that the operation should not have taken place and the requirement to return to the United Kingdom from her current country of residence and to either leave her husband behind or force him to seek a new job in the UK.[55] Roch LJ also explained that the mother's views were relevant to the

---

[52] See n 5 above.
[53] [1997] 1 All ER 906.
[54] *Ibid*, pp 914-15, per Butler-Sloss LJ.
[55] *Ibid*.

determination of the issue, not just because as a parent she would have the best interests of her child at the forefront of her mind, but also because her objection to the treatment is of clinical relevance as it is likely to affect the clinical outcome for the child.[56]

The most unusual feature of this is that the Court of Appeal refused to authorise the operation even though the unanimous medical evidence regarded it as in the child's best interests, and the only way of saving his life. It is extremely rare for the courts to deviate from the recommendation of an incompetent patient's doctors. We saw above, for example, that in *Re B* the court was willing to authorise an operation against the wishes of the parents because the doctors regarded it as in the child's best interests. There are, perhaps, two explanations for the Court of Appeal's unusual approach in *Re T*. First, it should be noted that both parents were themselves healthcare professionals. Their opinions on the best course of treatment for their child may have carried greater weight than usual. Second, the parents' views seemed to be crucial even for the doctors. So, for example, one doctor gave evidence strongly recommending the operation – ie confirming that it was in the child's best interests – but added that he would not be prepared to perform the operation without the mother's consent.[57] In these circumstances, it is perhaps understandable that the Court of Appeal felt unwilling to authorise the operation against the parents' wishes. It is an unacceptable decision, however, because it totally ignores the rights of the child due to its preoccupation with the interests of the entire family.

The Court of Appeal did not attempt to reconcile their decision with the rights of the child and were unapologetic about this: 'It is not an occasion – even in an age preoccupied with "rights" – to talk of the rights of a child, or the rights of a parent, or the rights of the court . . . The sole yardstick must be the need to give effect to the demands of paramountcy for the welfare of the child.'[58] One might query when such an occasion would be if not when determining whether a terminally ill child is entitled to receive a life-saving transplant. The welfare of the child is indeed the paramount consideration. This is made clear in section 1(1) of the Children Act 1989 and is also implicit within the common law's focus upon a minor's best interests. But surely a child's welfare includes consideration of their fundamental human rights? As Davies has argued in response to *Re T*, 'the best interests of the child test would be more mature if it included respect for independent rights alongside consideration of the pain of the condition, the pain of the treatment and the prospects of its success'.[59] Davies describes the best interests test after *Re T* as 'rather empty'[60] and this is a good description of the

---

[56]   *Ibid*, p 919.

[57]   *Ibid*, p 910.

[58]   *Ibid*, pp 916-17, per Waite LJ.

[59]   M Davies, 'Selective Non-Treatment of the New-Born: In Whose Best Interests? In Whose Judgment?' [1998] 49 *NILQ* 82, at pp 91-92.

[60]   *Ibid*, p 82.

implications of *Re T*. Not only did the Court of Appeal expressly exclude consideration of the patient's rights from the best interests test but also, apparently, the medical interests of the patient, which were not in any way ambiguous or open to interpretation. The child would die within a year without the operation; the operation could restore the child's health. The operation was in the child's best interests, as well as indicated by his right to life. The only arguments against the operation were extraneous to the patient and should have been irrelevant. As with *Re Y*, *Re T* does not appear to have set a precedent for future cases, and it remains a blip in the usual environment of judicial support for medical opinion. However, it also serves as a warning of the precarious position of the rights of the incompetent patients and how easily they can be overlooked when, with all good intentions, the judiciary and the medical profession prioritise the interests of others.

(d)   Best Interests on a Statutory Footing

The Mental Capacity Act 2005 (MCA) represents long-awaited legislation on decision-making for incompetent persons. As Brazier succinctly notes, however, the best interests test 'survives the process of reform'[61] and, given the criticism of its operation at common law, this is perhaps surprising. The MCA will take precedence over the common law on issues of overlap. Therefore, once the Act comes into force in 2007, a person who, under the terms of section 2, lacks capacity will be treated according to the Act's provisions in relation to healthcare as well as other issues.[62] The common law is not directly repealed, however, and may still apply in some circumstances which fall outside the Act. Such circumstances include where there is no impairment or disturbance of the mind or brain, in which case the common law necessity defence would still be needed for emergency treatment.[63] The MCA also applies only to people aged 16 or over (section 2(5)) and therefore the treatment of minors under 16 will still be covered by the common law rules. It is also possible that the common law will be used for persons aged 16 to 18 because the courts' inherent jurisdiction over minors continues until the age of 18 and applications under this jurisdiction are likely to be more flexible than the MCA system.[64] Even where the common law is still used, however, the MCA is likely to serve as a guide.

Section 1 of the Act sets out the principles which should apply for the purposes of the Act. Bartlett notes that '[w]hat is striking about these principles is not how

---

[61]   Brazier, n 16 above, pp 130–31.

[62]   The test for capacity under the Act was discussed in the previous chapter. Here we are concerned only with the basis of decision-making for those individuals regarded as lacking capacity.

[63]   See P Bartlett, *Blackstone's Guide to the Mental Capacity Act 2005* (Oxford, Oxford University Press, 2005), pp 94–95.

[64]   *Ibid*, p 74.

much, but how little new they contain'[65] and he is correct, as evidenced, for example, through the assumption of capacity.[66] One of these principles is that '[a]n act done, or decision made, under this Act for or on behalf of a person who lacks capacity must be done, or made, in his best interests'.[67] The requirement of 'best interests' is then described in more detail in section 4 with a helpful set of criteria that was lacking in the common law's application of the best interests test. The section 4 criteria combine three different broad sets of factors: (1) protection of the patient's position, in the event that he is likely to regain capacity; (2) consideration of the wishes, feelings, values and beliefs that the patient had when competent or would have if competent now; and (3) consideration of the patient's current, incompetent, wishes and feelings and, linked to this, involvement of the patient in the decision-making process, notwithstanding his incapacity.[68] In other words, best interests under the MCA incorporate some protection for the incompetent patient's autonomy in the past, present and future. Past autonomy refers to the wishes or values which a previously competent patient may have had; present autonomy refers to any current wishes or values which the incompetent patient is able to express; future autonomy refers to the possibility that the currently incompetent patient will regain capacity in the future and be able to make his own autonomous choices again. The Act as a whole adopts the ethos that a person should be able to exercise autonomy to the greatest extent possible within the confines of his mental capacity. This is an approach which resonates with human rights protection because, as discussed in the previous chapter, individual autonomy is the foundation of human rights and, while a person lacking capacity may not have the ability to exercise full autonomous choice, they should be enabled, encouraged and assisted to exercise autonomy to the greatest extent possible. It must be recognised, however, that the effectiveness of this autonomy-enhancing approach will vary according to the nature and duration of the incapacity. Where an individual is rendered temporarily incapacitated by an accident, the preservation of past and future autonomy will be relatively straightforward. Where an individual is rendered permanently incapacitated by the development of a mental disorder, both past autonomy and some element of current autonomy may be retained with some effort on the part of the carers. But where an individual is permanently incapacitated by a severe mental disorder from birth, there will be no past wishes or present ability to engage with a decision-making process. The criteria in section 4 in this unfortunate situation begin to look rather idealistic.

Even though the inclusion of criteria in section 4 assists with the determination of a patient's best interests, by necessity the criteria remain extremely vague. It allows consideration of any factor which the patient would consider if

---

[65] *Ibid*, p 25.
[66] Section 1(2) MCA.
[67] Section 1(5) MCA.
[68] Bartlett, n 63 above, p 31.

competent.[69] This means that the best interests test under the MCA will be even broader than that developed at common law. It is not restricted to strictly medical best interests but will also incorporate consideration of broader social and ethical interests. Flexibility is important, and a distinguishing factor of the MCA, but it does not always sit easily with the procedural requirements of the ECHR. Bartlett has compared these two pieces of legislation:

> While both the ECHR and the MCA look to respect for the individual as a core value, they do so in quite different ways. The MCA is designed to provide a flexible regime, allowing carers to act in the best interests of the incapacitated person with minimal interference or red tape. The ECHR tends more to view procedural safeguards as inherent to the protection of rights.[70]

This is part of a larger problem of incorporating the rights of a person lacking the capacity to make autonomous choices into an autonomy-based human rights system. Bartlett argues that the 'process-based jurisprudence of the European Court of Human Rights works most convincingly when the rights subject is a competent individual, able to defend his or her rights'[71] and it is not immediately obvious how these procedural requirements can assist the mentally incapacitated. As argued above, however, core rights such as a right to physical integrity, a broader right to privacy, a right to be free from degrading treatment, and a right to life incorporating some positive obligations to preserve life and health, all offer essential protection to the individual already disadvantaged by a loss of mental capacity. The principle of beneficence which has found legal form in the best interests test is a sensible means of protecting the rights and interests of incompetent patients and its retention in the MCA is understandable. The key remains the interpretation of a patient's best interests by a third party whether that is by a doctor, a relative or a judge. It is, therefore, the crucial issue of who decides a patient's interests to which we will now turn.

III.   Who Decides?

(a)   Decision-making under the MCA

In respect of incompetent adult patients, it has long been established that the law does not permit proxy consent. If a patient is unable to provide consent to treatment, the doctors will provide treatment which is in that patient's best interests without the need to obtain consent from any third party (although in

---

[69]   Section 4(6).
[70]   Bartlett, n 63 above, p 18.
[71]   *Ibid*, p 82.

certain cases, including sterilisation and withdrawal of treatment, they should obtain a court declaration first). The MCA subtly changes the matter, however, because it is broadly conceived to apply to all decision-making for mentally incapacitated persons. Thus, it will not always be a doctor or healthcare professional treating a patient in his best interests. Indeed, the huge majority of decisions covered by the Act will be taken by relatives or carers of the incapacitated individual. Section 5 clarifies the legal position by providing a general defence for such person: any person who does an act in connection with the care or treatment of another will not incur liability provided that: (a) he has taken reasonable steps to establish whether the other person lacks capacity and reasonably believes that he does so; (b) he reasonably believes that the act is in the other person's best interests;[72] and (c) he performs the act without negligence.[73] While this provides welcome, and necessary, legal protection for carers, it also means that an individual may be deprived of his normal rights to autonomous choice and action, even though he does not actually lack mental capacity, provided only that the decision-maker has a reasonable belief in incapacity. Bartlett raises some valid concerns about this issue: 'The routine removal of rights under the general defence, without formal notice and without routine access to a juridical-style decision-maker may raise questions under Article 6 or 8.'[74] This raises once more the potential conflict between the flexibility valued by the MCA and the procedural guarantees valued by the Convention rights.

The MCA also provides two alternative means of decision-making for the mentally incapacitated, both of which involve the incompetent person to a much larger degree. First, advance directives are put on a statutory footing. As discussed in the previous chapter, a competent person can issue an advance refusal of treatment, even life-sustaining treatment, which will continue to bind his doctors once he loses competence.[75] The common law did not require any formalities in order for an advance directive to be binding, but the MCA requirements will now supersede the common law and are to be found in sections 24-26. An advance directive enables an individual to exercise autonomous choice to determine his future treatment and is thus the preferable means of determining treatment for an incompetent person. However, difficulties will arise if the circumstances change drastically subsequent to the making of the advance directive[76] and withdrawing treatment in line with a directive may also be problematic if the now incompetent wishes of the patient seem opposed to it. Second, the MCA introduces the concept of a 'Lasting Power of Attorney' (LPOA). This is reminiscent of the so-called 'Enduring Powers of Attorney' which could be registered with the Court of Protection under the Enduring Powers of Attorney Act 1985.

---

[72] Section 5(1) MCA.
[73] Section 5(3) MCA.
[74] Bartlett, n 63 above, p 81.
[75] *Re AK. (Medical Treatment: Consent)* [2001] 1 FLR 129.
[76] As happened in *Re T (Adult: Refusal of Medical Treatment)* [1992] 4 All ER 649.

However, these powers of attorney could only extend to matters of property and affairs; the MCA extends them to personal decisions.[77] A LPOA gives authority to an individual to make all decisions relating to an incompetent person's personal welfare, which would include questions of medical treatment. Therefore, there now exists a concept very similar to proxy consent for adults in relation to medical treatment. In line with the general ethos of the MCA, however, the current views and feelings of the incompetent patient must be taken into account by the person exercising a power of attorney and the patient must be involved so far as possible in the decision-making process.[78] The LPOA permits an individual to choose whom he trusts most to make decisions regarding his welfare but the potential for abuse is clear, and the ethical and legal requirement that any medical treatment must be in a patient's own best interests will continue to serve as vital protection for vulnerable incompetent patients.

(b)   Conflict Between Parents and Doctors

It was discovered above that medical treatment for minors must be in their best interests but what happens if the child's parents and his or her doctors disagree about this issue? The devastating implications of a serious disagreement between these two parties can be seen in *Glass v United Kingdom* when a dispute culminated in a physical fight over the child's seriously ill body.[79] The patient was a 12 year old boy who was severely physically and mentally disabled. His doctors regarded his condition as terminal and advised diamorphine to relieve his pain. The child's mother disagreed with the doctors' view that her son was dying and opposed the administration of diamorphine because of fears that this would amount to euthanasia. She was told by hospital authorities that she would be arrested if she sought to remove her son from the hospital. As the dispute worsened, other family members became involved and, believing that the patient was being euthanised, they sought to prevent entry to his hospital room. The hospital threatened to remove the family by force and a DNR order was placed in the child's medical notes without consulting his mother, although in response to the family's objections the diamorphine dose was halved. The family remained dissatisfied and subsequently a fight broke out between family members and doctors. The police were summoned and injuries were sustained by doctors, police and other patients. During this fight, the mother resuscitated her son. His condition subsequently improved and he was able to be discharged. The doctors' dire prognosis proved to be overly pessimistic and this serves as a much needed reminder that medical judgment is not infallible. As Judge Casadevall noted in his separate opinion in *Glass v United Kingdom*, 'the facts have shown – nearly six

---

[77]   Section 9(1).

[78]   Section 9(4).

[79]   ECHR 2004-II

years later and to date – that, in the particular circumstances of the present case, maternal instinct has had more weight than medical opinion'.[80]

The mother sought a number of legal and quasi-legal remedies for the treatment received by herself and her son. The GMC found the doctors not guilty of serious professional misconduct; the CPS decided not to bring criminal charges due to a lack of evidence; and an application for judicial review was rejected by Scott Baker J who regarded judicial review as too blunt an instrument for sensitive and ongoing problems of this type (a decision confirmed on appeal by the Court of Appeal).[81] An application to the European Court of Human Rights brought more success, however. It was held that the Article 8 rights of the son had been infringed by the disregarding of his mother's (and proxy's) views: 'the decision to impose treatment on the [patient] in defiance of [his mother's] objections gave rise to an interference with [his] right to respect for his private life, and in particular his right to physical integrity'.[82] Furthermore, it was emphasised that the Trust should have made an application to the courts to resolve this issue. Ideally, an application would have been made as soon as it was obvious that there was a disagreement between the family and the doctors. However, the Court emphasised that even once a crisis arose, the Trust could, and should, have made an emergency High Court application. Instead of doing so, 'the doctors and officials used the limited time available to them in order to try to impose their views on the second applicant'.[83] The irony of the Trust finding time to involve the police, but not the courts, was not lost on the European Court of Human Rights. It is clear, as a consequence of *Glass v UK*, that doctors should not impose treatment upon an incompetent child patient against the wishes of the parents, unless they have first sought court authorisation. To do so will amount to a violation of the child's Article 8 right to physical integrity. An NHS Trust will be regarded as a public authority and hence liability may ensue under the Human Rights Act 1998. The Trust can easily avoid liability, however, by involving the courts and, if they do so, previous case law suggests that the court will almost invariably[84] support the medical experts' view.

The courts are not always keen to become involved in disputes between parents and doctors. This point was noted in *Re A*,[85] the conjoined twins case, when the Court of Appeal was very reluctantly thrust into the limelight of a well-publicised disagreement between the twins' doctors, who advised an operation to separate the twins and thus save one (and only one) of their lives, and the parents, who were strongly opposed to any separation on religious grounds. The Court of Appeal recognised that, however reluctantly, it had a duty to determine the issue

---

[80] *Ibid*, para 2, separate opinion of Judge Casadevall.
[81] *R v Portsmouth Hospitals NHS Trust, ex p Glass* [1999] 2 FLR 905.
[82] *Glass v UK*, n 79 above, para 70.
[83] *Ibid*, para 81.
[84] *Re T* discussed above is a rare exception.
[85] *Re A (children)(conjoined twins: surgical separation)* [2000] 4 All ER 961.

in light of the dispute between the parents and the doctors: 'We do not ask for work but we have a duty to decide what parties with a proper interest ask us to decide ... Deciding disputed matters of life and death is surely and pre-eminently a matter for a court of law to judge. That is what courts are here for.'[86]

Another emotive example of judicial involvement in a dispute between parents and doctors can be seen in the *Wyatt* litigation. Charlotte Wyatt was born prematurely at 26 weeks. She suffered from chronic respiratory and kidney problems and severe brain damage. Her doctors believed that ventilation in the event of an infection which leads, or might lead, to a collapsed lung would not be in her best interests. This view was based on the doctors' belief that such ventilation might kill Charlotte or, if she survived, it would merely be a painful process which would bring no improvement to her condition.[87] A disagreement between Charlotte's parents and her doctors led the hospital to seek and obtain a court declaration that ventilation would not be in the patient's best interests. The parents subsequently applied for the discharge of the declarations on the basis that their daughter's condition had improved significantly. At the oral hearing in October 2004, when the declarations were issued, the medical evidence suggested that the chance of survival for twelve months was 5 per cent or less[88] and the judge concluded that there was a high probability that the baby would die during the winter. By March 2005, when the parents applied to discharge the declarations, this pessimistic diagnosis had proven to be in error and there was no doubt that some positive improvements in Charlotte's condition had occurred. The judge noted that she was no longer wholly unresponsive, nor in such discomfort as to require sedation. In other words, her condition was regarded as no longer 'intolerable' by the judge.[89] Nevertheless, the judge accepted the majority medical evidence that invasive methods would not be in the baby's best interests.[90] Permission to appeal on the best interests question was refused but an appeal on other issues only led to confirmation of the judge's approach. In particular, as noted above, the Court of Appeal confirmed Hedley J's approach that the concept of intolerability for the child should not be seen as a gloss on, much less a supplementary test to, best interests but is merely a valuable guide in the search for best interests.[91] The Court of Appeal did bring forward by one month the date of a scheduled judicial review of the declarations and this highlights the difficulty in ensuring that there is court involvement in issues such as this (as is required by *Glass v UK*): it is difficult for the court to keep appraised of changing circumstances in the patient's condition. In this sense, the courts are not the most appropriate forum for decision-making about life-sustaining treatment for

---

[86]   *Ibid*, at p 987, per Ward LJ.
[87]   *Wyatt*, n 38 above, para 13.
[88]   *Ibid*, para 27.
[89]   *Ibid*, para 32.
[90]   *Ibid*, para 37.
[91]   *Ibid*, para 76.

incompetent patients. However, the fact that in both *Glass* and *Wyatt* the medical evidence was unduly pessimistic and the family's more optimistic views proved correct reminds us that leaving decision-making entirely in the hands of the doctors will not always be wise and indeed, according to *Glass*, will violate the patient's rights. It remains difficult for the family's views to prevail in court, however, because they lack the medical expertise which, in a test of best interests, remains the key, although not the only relevant, factor.

Research by Bridgeman[92] into the evidence of parents to the Bristol Inquiry[93] helpfully illustrates the need for a balanced approach to the determination of a child's best interests. Bridgeman explains how parents viewed their decision-making task in practice:

> Parents did not assume that, from their position as adults, they knew what was best for their child. Decisions were difficult to make and reached with uncertainty. But best interests were determined in light of their involvement with the child and after careful evaluation following close observation. Respecting the child as an individual meant providing them with information to prepare them, but only to the level judged appropriate by the parent given their experience of and consideration of their child.[94]

Bridgeman concludes that the law 'should reflect the complexity of this process, ensuring that parents and professionals fulfil the responsibility to make decisions which respect the interests, needs and wants of the individual child whilst, when disputes come to court, respecting the particular expertise which parents have of their child'.[95] This is a useful reminder that parents have both rights and responsibilities in respect of their child and, while it is the parents' right to make decisions in respect of their child's medical treatment (and the child's right for the parent to do so), it is a right subject to the overriding parental responsibility to act in the interests of their child. That most parents will seek to do so does not necessarily make the determination of a child's best interests any more obvious but the parents have an invaluable contribution to make due to them probably knowing the child's needs, wishes and values better than anybody else.

(c)   Conflicts between Mature Minors and Parents or Doctors

While the parents are usually best placed to judge the interests of their child, when the child is more mature it is possible that the child could be capable of making his or her own decisions about medical treatment. The case of *Gillick v*

---

[92]   J Bridgeman, 'After Bristol: the Healthcare of Young Children and the Law' (2003) 23 *LS* 229.
[93]   See Chapter 3.
[94]   Bridgeman, n 92 above, p 236.
[95]   *Ibid.*

West Norfolk & Wisbech Area Health Authority[96] (discussed further in the following chapter) was a landmark judgment. The House of Lords held that a child under 16 could provide valid consent to treatment without the need to involve (or even inform) her parents. The test is one of competence: if the child has sufficient intelligence and understanding to be able to understand the treatment proposed then she will be classified as '*Gillick* competent' and may validly give consent on which the doctors can rely as legal authority for the provision of treatment. The case of *Gillick* involved contraceptive treatment and advice, issues which raise further ethical dilemmas (discussed further in the following chapter on confidentiality) but the concept of *Gillick* competence applies to any type of medical treatment. The *Gillick* decision seems to be one strongly in favour of individual autonomy. It adopts a functional approach to the issue of consent and holds that if a patient is mentally competent to make a decision regarding treatment then that decision should be respected regardless of the patient's age. Subsequent case law, however, has seriously restricted the ambit of the Gillick principle. This is most obvious in *Re R*.[97]

R was a 15 year old girl with a history of family problems whose mental health deteriorated while she was in voluntary care, culminating in her becoming suicidal and suffering hallucinations. The Court of Appeal obtained place of safety and interim care orders and placed R in an adolescent psychiatric unit. The unit sought permission to administer anti-psychotic drugs to R against her wishes. The local authority refused to give permission because R had been lucid at the time she refused consent but it initiated wardship proceedings and applied for leave for the unit to administer the treatment without consent. The Court of Appeal agreed with the judge's finding that R was not *Gillick* competent,[98] Lord Donaldson explained that 'even if she was capable on a good day of a sufficient degree of understanding to meet the *Gillick* criteria, her mental disability, to the cure or amelioration of which the proposed treatment was directed, was such that on other days she was not only '*Gillick* incompetent' but actually sectionable'.[99] This conclusion is hard to dispute and, although the case of *Re R* receives a great deal of academic criticism, it is not because of the *ratio* or outcome of the case. Instead, it is Lord Donaldson's *obiter* comments on the *Gillick* principle which have led to criticism. Lord Donaldson described consent as 'a key which unlocks a door' and, in his view, both the parents and the child possess such a key.[100] The consequences of this analogy is that a *Gillick* competent child can consent to treatment but, if he or she refuses to do so, consent can be provided by the parents (or the court) instead.[101] This means that a *Gillick* competent minor

---

96   [1986] AC 112.
97   *Re R (a minor)* [1991] 4 All ER 177.
98   *Ibid*, p 180.
99   *Ibid*, p 187.
100   *Ibid*, p 184.
101   *Ibid*, p 186.

cannot give a binding refusal of treatment: he or she can say 'yes' to treatment but cannot effectively say 'no'. This is surely illogical. The basis for the *Gillick* principle is autonomy. A minor's autonomy is not respected if his or her autonomous choice is restricted to an ability to say yes to treatment. Lord Donaldson, however, insisted that his interpretation of *Gillick* is consistent with that intended by the House of Lords: 'I do not understand Lord Scarman to be saying that, if a child was a '*Gillick* competent' . . . the parents ceased to have a right of determination, i.e. a veto.'[102] This attempt to distinguish a right of consent from a right of veto is unconvincing. As discussed at length in the previous chapter, the basis of consent is autonomous choice. The other members of the Court of Appeal in *Re R* did not join Lord Donaldson in this *obiter* discussion and indeed Staughton LJ expressly recognised a difference between Lord Scarman in *Gillick* and Lord Donaldson (even though Lord Donaldson denied such a difference).[103] Lord Donaldson did acknowledge that a refusal of treatment by a *Gillick* competent child is 'a very important factor in the doctor's decision whether or not to treat'[104] but, in his view, it is not conclusive and thus a competent patient can be treated against his or her express wishes, merely on the basis of age.

In *Re W*,[105] Lord Donaldson clarified his comments in *Re R* whilst also extending his restrictions upon the *Gillick* principle. W was a 16 year old suffering from anorexia nervosa. The local authority decided that it may need to give W medical treatment in the future without her consent and sought court approval for that, as well as for its plan to move W to a special eating disorder unit. Because W was aged 16, the Family Law Reform Act 1969 applied. Section 8(1) of this Act provides that the consent to treatment of a minor aged 16 or 17 'shall be as effective as it would be if he were of full age'. Lord Donaldson explained that, in his view, this provision 'is addressed to the legal purpose and legal effect of consent to treatment, namely to prevent such treatment constitut-ing in law a trespass to the person'.[106] In other words, the section protects doctors from legal repercussions rather than protecting mature minors from non-consensual interventions. This prioritisation of the needs of doctors can also be seen in Lord Donaldson's revised key analogy. Having said in *Re R* that consent is a 'key', Lord Donaldson now regretted that comparison 'because keys can lock as well as unlock' (ie followed through to its logical conclusion, a competent minor's use of her key to refuse consent should lock the door to treatment). In *Re W* he preferred to describe consent as a 'legal flak-jacket' which can protect doctors: 'Anyone who gives him a flak-jacket (i.e. consent) may take it back, but the doctor only needs one and so long as he continues to have one he has the legal right to

---

[102] *Ibid*, p 185.
[103] *Ibid*, p 189.
[104] *Ibid*, p 186.
[105] *Re W (a minor) (medical treatment: court's jurisdiction)* [1992] 4 All ER 627.
[106] *Ibid*, p 634.

proceed.'[107] The consequence of this approach is that section 8(1) is regarded by the Court of Appeal as enabling a 16 or 17 year old to provide valid consent (which protects a doctor from liability) but not enabling a valid refusal of treatment (because the parents can provide a flak jacket of consent to protect the doctors).

Thus, *Re R* and *Re W* conjoined have established that no patient under 18 years of age (even if mentally competent) can validly refuse medical treatment. Another way of expressing this point is that, in respect of refusal of treatment, all patients under 18 are regarded as incompetent and treated accordingly. This is objectionable on a number of grounds: it involves an assumption in favour of treatment; it destroys any possibility of a competent minor making an autonomous choice (the power to say yes is not a power to choose) and it prioritises the legal protection of the medical profession over the rights of the vulnerable patient. Furthermore, in neither *Re R* nor *Re W* was it necessary for the Court of Appeal to hold that it could overrule the refusal of a competent minor. In both cases, the Court of Appeal held that the minor was not *Gillick* competent. In *Re W*, Lord Donaldson explained that:

> it is a feature of anorexia nervosa that it is capable of destroying the ability to make an informed choice. It creates a compulsion to refuse treatment or only to accept treatment which is likely to be ineffective ... where the wishes of the minor are themselves something which the doctors reasonably consider need to be treated in the minor's own best interests, those wishes clearly have a much reduced significance.[108]

Despite some reservations about 'treating' the wishes of a patient rather than her condition, the outcome of *Re W*, like that of *Re R*, is far less objectionable than the reasoning of Lord Donaldson which has left a seemingly illogical precedent for other cases involving mature minors who are capable of understanding the proposed treatment and are not suffering from a mental disorder. It is perhaps not surprising that other judgments have invariably turned upon a lack of competence rather than a power to overrule a competent refusal.

The issue of a non-mentally disordered minor seeking to refuse medical treatment has most often arisen in relation to a young Jehovah's Witness's objection to blood transfusions. In *Re E*,[109] a 15 year old boy suffering from leukaemia refused a blood transfusion on the basis of his religious convictions as a Jehovah's Witness. The court held that he was unable to understand the full implications of his refusal and was therefore incompetent. The transfusion was authorised but subsequently, when E reached the age of 18, he refused consent again on the same basis and this refusal was upheld, in accordance with the established law, leading to his death. The finding of incompetence here is less

---

[107]   *Ibid*, p 635.
[108]   *Ibid*, p 637.
[109]   *Re E (a minor) (wardship: medical treatment)* [1993] 1 FLR 1097.

convincing with the benefit of hindsight. However, the fact that E's refusal endured beyond the age of majority does not necessarily mean that it was always a competent refusal. As Brazier and Bridge note: 'A life-long indoctrination bolstered by the convictions of his parents and church elders perhaps left little room for E to exercise free will.'[110] Two points can be made in response to this. First, it raises the possibility of a finding of undue influence. We saw in respect of adults that undue influence (including from a religiously committed parent) can vitiate a refusal of treatment.[111] In *Re E*, the judge did express some concern about the issue of religious influence and pressure. However, in order for this to be taken into account, there would have needed to be some evidence that E's uninfluenced wishes would have led to a consent to treatment rather than refusal and such evidence may have been lacking here. Second, the 'life long indoctrination' described by Brazier and Bridge did not suddenly cease on E's 18th birthday. Age is really nothing more than a distraction here. In *Re W*, Nolan LJ attempted to explain the significance of the seemingly arbitrary date of a patient's 18th birthday when he said that 'the present state of the law is that an individual who has reached the age of 18 is free to do with his life what he wishes, but it is the duty of the court to ensure so far as it can that children survive to attain that age'.[112] However, the *Gillick* decision implies that it is more important to attempt to ensure survival until the age of mental capacity to make one's own autonomous choices. This is far more logical and avoids the *Re E* situation of preserving life until an arbitrary date. Protecting a person's life until he reaches an age where he can make his own choices seems to carry far more weight than protecting it until an arbitrary date which serves no apparent purpose.

The question remains whether society would be willing to permit a 14 or 15 year old minor, even one who is regarded as satisfying the *Gillick* competence test, to refuse life-saving treatment on religious grounds.[113] Bridge argues that in *Re L*, where a 14 year old Jehovah's Witness had an advanced medical directive refusing blood which had been renewed only two months before her accident, 'the young person's religious beliefs, understanding and maturity were weighed alongside the prospect of an outcome which the majority of the community would deplore'.[114] The judge went through the process of making a determination on *Gillick* competence, eventually finding her not to be competent largely because she had not been given sufficient information about the likely consequences of

---

[110] M Brazier and C Bridge, 'Coercion or Caring: Analysing Adolescent Autonomy' (1996) 16 *LS* 84, at p 104.

[111] *Re T (Adult: Refusal of Medical Treatment)*, n 76 above.

[112] *Re W*, n 105 above, p 648.

[113] In *Re S (a minor) (medical treatment)* [1994] 2 FLR 1065, the minor patient was new to the Jehovah's Witness faith but had undergone long term medical treatment. She was, therefore, both less committed to her religious objection but more informed about the proposed treatment than E. Despite these subtle differences, the result was the same: she was held not to be *Gillick* competent.

[114] C Bridge, 'Religious Beliefs and Teenage Refusal of Medical Treatment' (1999) 62 *MLR* 585, at p 587.

her refusal, but he admitted that a finding of competence would not have changed his decision. On the basis of *Re R*, even if L had been *Gillick* competent she would not have been permitted to refuse a blood transfusion on religious grounds. The concept of *Gillick* competence is, therefore, a red herring in respect of refusal of treatment. If a minor is seeking to refuse life-saving treatment, it does not matter whether she is competent or not. If this is the law then, Bridge has argued, it may be preferable to say so clearly: 'The law should openly declare that welfare reigns when grave decisions with momentous outcomes are considered and recognise that adolescent autonomy is, inevitably, circumscribed.'[115] The prioritisation of welfare over autonomy in respect of minors is perhaps understandable but, unlike all other patients discussed in this chapter, mature minors may have the mental capacity to exercise their autonomy and, if so, then their rights to self-determination and physical integrity under Article 8 demand that it be respected by the law. The principle of beneficence, so appropriate to decisions in respect of incompetent patients, goes too far if it outweighs the autonomous choice of a competent patient. Hagger argues that the best way of demonstrating ethical decision-making in compliance with the Human Rights Act is 'if the views of everyone in the team, including the child and its significant others, are taken into account together with those of relevant experts where necessary'.[116] In a less than ideal world, where such consensus cannot be achieved, a choice has to be made between the protection of a minor's welfare or autonomy; between her health or free choice. The key to the choice must be the mental capacity of the minor, a commodity which is linked to, but not indivisible from, age.

IV. Conclusion

An incompetent patient retains a number of rights relevant to the healthcare context, including a right to physical integrity, a right to be free from degrading treatment and a right to life. The treatment of an incompetent patient must be performed with full regard to these rights. The treatment should be justified by the legal principle of therapeutic necessity and the ethical principle of beneficence. It must be genuinely in the best interests of the patient; the interests of others, including close family members, should be irrelevant to the matter. While the best interests test has been established for some time, the problems in its operation have arisen from the question of who decides whether treatment is in the patient's best interests. The original emphasis upon the medical experts' opinion has been somewhat reduced by the broadening of the relevant interests to include ethical, moral and social considerations, and the MCA's recognition

---

[115]   *Ibid*, p 594.
[116]   L Hagger, 'Some Implications of the Human Rights Act 1998 for the Medical Treatment of Children' (2003) 6 *Med L Int* 25, at p 40.

that on a day to day basis such decisions will be taken by relatives and/or carers. The greatest problems stem from disagreement: when two or more interested parties differ over the interests of the incompetent person. Where there is a dispute, the courts must be the arbiter, but the focus should always remain upon the interests of the patient. A lack of mental capacity (or a lack of age notwith-standing capacity) automatically places the patient in a vulnerable position and respect for his rights becomes vital if the patient is not to lose his dignity and welfare alongside his capacity. The most worrying cases cited in this chapter all arose because of a deliberate lack of focus upon the rights of the vulnerable and powerless incompetent patient. (*Re T*, *Re Y* and *Re E* are three examples.) Greater respect for human rights, rather than denials that they are relevant, will result in decisions more sensitive to the entirety of an incompetent person's interests. Neither the authorisation of non-beneficial treatment in *Re Y*, nor the denial of essential life-saving treatment in *Re T*, respected the rights of the incompetent patients, and such disregard for human rights in this context undermines all the good work in increasing rights' recognition for competent patients. The most vulnerable need the most protection for their welfare and the best means of ensuring this protection is through the conception and implementation methods of fundamental human rights.

Recommended Further Reading

TL Beauchamp and JF Childress, *Principles of Biomedical Ethics*, 5th edn (Oxford, Oxford University Press, 2001) Chapter 5.

AE Buchanan and DW Brock, *Deciding for Others: The Ethics of Surrogate Decision-Making* (Cambridge, Cambridge University Press, 1990) Chapter 2.

P Bartlett, *Blackstone's Guide to the Mental Capacity Act 2005* (Oxford, Oxford University Press, 2005).

M Davies, 'Selective Non-Treatment of the New-Born: In Whose Best Interests? In Whose Judgement? (1998) 49 *NILQ* 82.

M Brazier and C Bridge, 'Coercion or Caring: Analysing Adolescent Autonomy' (1996) 16 *LS* 84.

6

Medical Confidentiality And The Right To Privacy

The doctor-patient relationship is based upon trust. A patient expects that private information disclosed to a doctor will remain confidential. This chapter investigates the merits of such an expectation. We begin by considering the concept of a right to privacy, its protection in English law and its relevance in the medical context. Having established a right to medical confidentiality based upon the fundamental right to privacy, we then look at the numerous exceptions to the right which exist due to the need to balance an individual's privacy against competing societal needs, such as the prevention of crime, freedom of the press and parental responsibility for minors.

I. Rights to Privacy and Confidentiality in the Medical Context

(a) The Concept of a Right to Privacy

The concept of privacy is a vital aspect of the balance between individual and society, which so preoccupies human rights law and the constitution in general. At its broadest, privacy represents an individual's freedom from interference by public authorities. It is, therefore, an essential part of the individual's armoury against the state. It has roots in the concept of autonomy which requires individuals to be as free as possible from external forces so as to enable their actions to reflect as truly as possible their autonomous choices and intentions. As explained in Chapter 4, autonomy is the underlying concept of modern human rights law and therefore privacy occupies a central role in ensuring that individuals have the freedom from state interference to give their other rights (to life, liberty, freedom of expression and religion etc) meaning. Privacy also has roots in the foundational principle of dignity, as has been well explained by Feldman.[1]

The value of privacy has been recognised in international human rights law. Both the ECHR and the ICCPR protect a right to privacy in some form, but privacy is not a universal concept. The African Charter on Human and People's Rights does not include any protection for a right to privacy, suggesting perhaps that privacy is a predominantly Western concept. The idea of a distinction between a private sphere and a public sphere relies upon a certain concept of social organisation and government which is neither universal nor inevitable. In Western society, however, a concept of privacy is regarded as a fundamental right. Its precise meaning remains open for debate, however.

The question of how to conceptualise privacy divides the academic community. On the one side, there are those who regard privacy as an organising concept which encompasses many varied interests. This view embraces the autonomy roots of privacy. Feldman, for example, argues that it is important for privacy to be conceived at a high level of generality. In his view, 'privacy derives its weight and importance from its capacity to foster the conditions for a wide range of other aspects of human flourishing'.[2] This idea that the protection of our privacy enables us to 'flourish' in other ways reflects the autonomy based idea that privacy is a freedom from state interference. Some commentators have criticised such a broad conceptualisation of privacy, however, and argued that 'It has grown so large that it now threatens to devour itself.'[3] Wacks, for example, argues that a narrower conception would be preferable: 'Instead of pursuing the false god of 'privacy', attention should be paid to identifying what specific interests of the individual we think the law ought to protect.'[4] Wacks emphasises the need for protection of personal information and sees this as a more tangible value for protection than a generalised freedom from interference.

Whatever view of the concept of privacy is adopted, it is clear that the protection of personal information is a central aspect of privacy. While some commentators would restrict the legal protection of privacy to this core aspect, and others would view it as merely one element of a broader private sphere in which we should be protected from interference, it is clear that the protection of personal information is the least controversial aspect of a right to privacy. It is this aspect which is of vital significance to medical confidentiality but, before considering this specific context, it will be helpful first to consider the legal protection offered to privacy by English law.

---

[1]   D Feldman, 'Human Dignity as a Legal Value, Part 1' [1999] *PL* 682 and 'Human Dignity as a Legal Value, Part 2' [2000] *PL* 61.

[2]   D Feldman, 'Privacy-Related Rights and their Social Value' in P Birks, *Privacy and Loyalty* (Clarendon Press, Oxford, 1997), p 21.

[3]   R Wacks, *The Protection of Privacy* (London, Sweet & Maxwell, 1980), p 12.

[4]   R Wacks, *Personal Information* (Oxford, Clarendon Press, 1989), p 10.

(b)   The Protection of Privacy in English Law

The ECHR is a good starting point here as it protects privacy interests in a very broad Article 8. This provision states that 'Everyone has the right to respect for private and family life, home and correspondence.' The second paragraph of Article 8 makes clear that these rights can be limited provided that any limitations are prescribed by the law and necessary in a democratic society for a number of specified aims, including the rights and freedoms of others, the prevention of crime and the protection of health and morals. The emphasis on family and home in Article 8(1) signifies the drafters' preoccupation with the inviolability of the home after the horrors of the Second World War. However, the European Court of Human Rights has extended the scope of Article 8 beyond the home and has interpreted Article 8's privacy interests as relating to the personal sphere rather than the secret sphere.[5] At the core of Article 8's protection is the prevention of arbitrary interference by public authorities and the Court has been reluctant to present a comprehensive definition, regarding it as not 'possible or necessary to attempt an exhaustive definition of the notion of "private life".[6] It is clear, however, that a broad range of privacy interests are encompassed within Article 8's protection, including an individual's relations with others,[7] physical and moral integrity,[8] personal identity,[9] legal recognition of gender,[10] and sexuality,[11] as well as the more obvious aspects of personal information.[12] The wording of Article 8 – the 'right to respect' for private life rather than a mere right to non-interference with privacy – also means that the Article imposes some positive obligations upon the contracting states to foster the conditions which can ensure a respect for private life.[13] The permissible limitations have also been broadly interpreted, however, and the Court's application of a margin of appreciation, or measure of discretion, to the contracting states is perhaps more evident in Article 8 than any other Convention rights.

So, how has the United Kingdom sought to respect the right to private life? Traditionally, despite the old adage that an Englishman's home is his castle, there was no right to privacy in English law. The courts at times regretted this

---

[5]   See DJ Harris, M O Boyle and C Warbrick, *Law of the European Convention on Human Rights* (London, Butterworths, 1995), p 303.

[6]   *Niemietz v Germany* (1992) Series A, No 251 B; 16 EHRR 97, para 29.

[7]   *Ibid.*

[8]   *Costello-Roberts v United Kingdom* (1993) Series A, No 247.

[9]   *Burghartz v Switzerland* (1994) Series A, No 280 B; 18 EHRR 101.

[10]   *Goodwin v United Kingdom* (2002) 35 EHRR 18.

[11]   *Dudgeon v United Kingdom* (1981) Series A, No 45; *Smith v United Kingdom* (2000) 29 EHRR 493.

[12]   See, for example, *Leander v Sweden* (1987) Series A, No 116; 9 EHRR 433, which confirms that secret government files containing personal information amounted to an interference with Art 8(1).

[13]   This can sometimes come close to an appearance of horizontal effect as for example in *X and Y v Netherlands* (1985) Series A, No 91; 8 EHRR 235.

omission, as in *Kaye v Robertson*,[14] but insisted that it was for Parliament to legislate into existence a right to privacy and that, in the absence of a pre-existing cause of action in English common law, the courts were helpless to assist. However, while no right to privacy existed in the common law, a duty of confidence did find protection there. Stemming originally from confidential relationships such as marriages and business relations, a breach of the duty of confidence arose if a threefold test was satisfied: the information in question must have the necessary quality of confidence; the information must be imparted in circumstances importing an obligation of confidence; and there must be an unauthorised use of the information to the confider's detriment.[15] This was clearly distinct from a right to privacy as a stringent application of these requirements would only provide legal protection for personal information where the confider and the discloser of the information are in a relationship of confidence, such that implies an obligation of confidence. However, in the *Spycatcher* case in 1990, Lord Goff set out what may be regarded as a slightly broader test in which the focus has moved from the relationship of confidence to the nature of the information and the confidant's knowledge:

> a duty of confidence arises when confidential information comes to the knowledge of a person ... in circumstances where he has notice, or is held to have agreed, that the information is confidential, with the effect that it would be just in all the circumstances that he should be precluded from disclosing the information to others.[16]

On this basis, a private diary dropped in a public place and found by a passer-by would be protected by a duty of confidence.[17] This has led some commentators to argue that the rationale has moved from the protection of confidences to the protection of privacy[18] and that any distinction between a duty of confidence and a tort of privacy has vanished.

With the passage of the Human Rights Act 1998, this trend has become even more obvious. The first real signs of a reconciliation of Article 8 and the common law on confidence came in the 2001 case of *Douglas v Hello*[19] when, in a infamous case concerning the wedding photographs from the private wedding of Michael Douglas and Catherine Zeta Jones, Sedley LJ said that the law no longer needs to construct an artificial relationship of confidence in order to protect a person's privacy.[20] This was confirmed in *Venables v News Group Newspapers* when the President of the Family Division noted that a duty of confidence could arise

---

[14] [1991] FSR 62.

[15] *Coco v A N Clark* [1969] RPC 41.

[16] *A-G v Guardian Newspapers* [1990] 1 AC 109, at p 281.

[17] *Ibid*, p 282.

[18] See, for example, J Loughrey, 'Medical Information, Confidence and a Child's Right to Privacy' [2003] *LS* 510, at p 516.

[19] [2001] QB 967.

[20] *Ibid*, at p 1001.

independently of any relationship between the parties and, therefore, the court could restrain publication of personal information regardless of the circumstances in which it was obtained.[21]

These efforts to combine the protection offered by Article 8 and a duty of confidence have developed primarily because of the problem of horizontal effect. The HRA only prohibits the breach of Convention rights by a public authority. Confidential information is often misused not by a public authority but by the press, and therefore the HRA does not seem to be directly in issue. However, both the *Douglas* and *Venables* cases demonstrate that the courts will have regard to Article 8's protection of privacy even in a case between two private parties. This stems from section 6 HRA's categorisation of the courts themselves as public authorities bound by the Convention rights. There is no evidence to suggest that this merging of Article 8 and the common law duty of confidence is restricted to private law cases, however, and instead it seems to be the means by which all personal information is henceforth to be legally protected. The common law duty of confidence cannot now be disentangled from the fundamental right to respect for private life found in Article 8 but likewise Article 8's implementation in English law is fused to considerations of confidentiality which may conceivably prevent an expansive application of the right to privacy in respect of the disclosure of personal information.

The year 1998 was significant in terms of the legal protection of personal information not just because of the implications of the HRA but also because of the passage of the Data Protection Act (DPA). This important piece of legislation is extremely complex but actually adds little to the common law in the context of preventing disclosure of private data. This is because, although section 10 provides individuals with a right to prevent the use of personal data, this is only effective if the individual knows in advance about the nature of the proposed disclosure. Without this knowledge, the DPA cannot be used to prevent disclosure and subsequent to disclosure only breach of confidence provides a remedy.[22] Furthermore, the DPA requires that all processing of personal data must be performed 'fairly and lawfully'. The requirement of lawfulness includes a requirement that processing is not carried out in breach of a common law obligation of confidence.[23] There is no doubt, therefore, that the law on confidence still occupies a central role post-1998 despite the two legislative acts of that year.

---

[21] [2001] 1 All ER 908, at p 933.
[22] See J Loughrey, 'The Confidentiality of Medical Records: Informational Autonomy, Patient Privacy and the Law' (2005) 56 *NILQ* 293 at pp 295-96 for discussion of the limitations of the DPA in this context.
[23] *Ibid*, p 296. The Data Protection Act is based on eight principles of data protection. In addition to the requirement that data be fairly and lawfully processed, they comprise that the data be adequate, relevant and not excessive, accurate, secure and not kept for longer than necessary, plus that the data be processed for limited purposes and in accordance with the data subject's rights and not be transferred to other countries without adequate protection.

(c)   Confidentiality and Privacy in the Medical Context

The doctor-patient relationship has long been regarded as one of confidence. The Hippocratic Oath – the very foundation of medical ethics – contains the following principle: 'All that may come to my knowledge in the exercise of my profession or outside of my profession or in daily commerce with men, which ought not to be spread abroad, I will keep secret and will never reveal.' This reflects the fact that a doctor will be privy to private and sensitive information about a patient's physical and mental health (both now and in the past) as well as potentially broader social information about relationships, sexuality and lifestyle choices. The patient expects the information disclosed to a doctor to be kept confidential and to a large extent the law reflects this expectation. The fact that the unauthorised disclosure of medical information is a human rights issue has been clearly established by the European Court of Human Rights. In *Z v Finland*, for example, the disclosure of the applicant's identity and HIV status during her husband's criminal trial was held to be a clear interference with her right to respect for private life under Article 8.[24] The Court explained the importance of medical confidentiality in the context of Article 8: 'Respecting the confidentiality of health data is a vital principle in the legal systems of all the Contracting Parties to the Convention. It is crucial not only to respect the sense of privacy of a patient but also to preserve his or her confidence in the medical profession and the health services in general.'[25] On the facts of the case, the information about HIV status was recognised as particularly sensitive information,[26] but this had to be balanced against the legitimate aim under Article 8(2) of preventing crime and protecting the rights of others. Therefore, the court orders requiring the applicant's doctors to give evidence, as well as the seizure of the applicant's medical records and their inclusion in the investigation file, were held to be a proportionate interference with the applicant's private life and, therefore, satisfied the test of being necessary in a democratic society. However, there was held to be no justification for the naming of the applicant in the Court of Appeal judgment issued to the press, as the names could easily have been omitted in order to protect the applicant's confidentiality. Similarly, disclosure to the public of the confidential information even after a period of ten years was held to amount to a disproportionate interference with Article 8.

The balance between an individual's right to confidentiality in respect of medical data under Article 8(1) and broader societal interests listed in Article 8(2) can be a very fine one. In *MS v Sweden*, the applicant's claim for industrial injury compensation led to her medical records, including sensitive information about a termination of pregnancy, being forwarded to the social insurance office

---

[24]   (1997) 25 EHRR 371, para 71.
[25]   *Ibid*, para 95.
[26]   *Ibid*, para 96.

without her knowledge.[27] This disclosure of confidential information was held to be an interference with the applicant's Article 8(1) rights but was held to be justified under Article 8(2) on the grounds of protecting the economic well-being of the country, because the medical information may have been relevant to the granting of public funds.

The potential for protection of medical confidentiality under Article 8 is significant but the need for privacy has to be balanced against competing social needs. The incorporation of Article 8 into English law by means of the HRA has, as discussed above, led to an attempted judicial merging of Article 8's protection for private life with the common law's protection for confidence. The importance of medical confidentiality within that merged protection for personal informa-tion has been recognised by the English courts. For example, in *Campbell v Mirror Group Newspapers*, Baroness Hale recognised that, 'It has always been accepted that information about a person's health and treatment for ill-health is both private and confidential. This stems not only from the confidentiality of the doctor-patient relationship but from the nature of the information itself.'[28] These dual justifications clearly identify the reasoning behind the legal protection of medical confidentiality. It satisfies the traditional requirements of a duty of confidentiality: the information has the necessary quality of confidence and is imparted in circumstances importing an obligation of confidence, i.e. during a doctor-patient consultation. The new involvement of Article 8's right to respect for private life, and the confirmation of the value it places on medical confiden-tiality in cases such as *Z v Finland* (quoted by the House of Lords in *Campbell*), adds further weight to the law's protection of personal information disclosed to a doctor.

The law's protection of medical confidentiality is supplemented by the ethical guidelines imposed upon doctors to maintain their patients' confidentiality. The GMC guidance on confidentiality sets out the general principle that '[d]octors hold information about patients which is private and sensitive. This information must not be given to others unless the patient consents or you can justify the disclosure.'[29] As will be seen in the following section, there are many diverse reasons which may justify disclosure in the eyes of the law, and the GMC guidance contains detailed specifics about circumstances where disclosure may be both ethically and legally acceptable. It is the issue of exceptions to the duty of medical confidentiality to which we must now turn. While it is clear that a doctor owes a duty of confidentiality to his patients and that a breach of that duty will be an interference with the patient's right to respect for private life, competing societal interests will often justify both the breach of duty and the interference with a patient's rights.

---

[27] (1999) 28 EHRR 313.
[28] [2004] 2 All ER 995, at para 145.
[29] *Confidentiality: Protecting and Providing Information* (GMC, 2004).

II.   Exceptions to the Duty of Confidentiality: Balancing Privacy Against Other Public Interests

The legitimate exceptions to the duty of medical confidentiality are drawn both from the confidence case law on public interest and from Article 8(2)'s list of permissible limitations. There is considerable overlap between the substance of these. For example, the prevention of crime is a goal protected by both the common law and the ECHR. However, the procedure for balancing a conflicting interest with the core right to confidentiality differs significantly. For example, freedom of the press is both a public interest exception to the duty of confidentiality and a legitimate aim in Article 8(2) but there is a huge difference between balancing (a) the fundamental right of privacy with a public interest in a free press, and (b) the fundamental right of free speech with a limited duty of confidentiality.[30] The attempted judicial reconciliation of Article 8 and a duty of confidence means that either balancing exercise could be justified but may present starkly different conclusions. It is, therefore, necessary to understand, not just the substance of the interests that may conflict with medical confidentiality, but also the most appropriate means of balancing them with the patient's rights and expectation of confidence.

(a)   Disclosure with Consent

The most obvious exception to a doctor's duty of confidentiality is when confidential information is disclosed to others with the patient's consent. This exception is distinct from the others in that there is no question of balancing an individual right against a societal interest. Disclosure of confidential information with the confider's consent will not amount to a breach of confidence as there is no unauthorised disclosure. There are two particular issues which cloud the image of genuine consent to disclosure. First, medical records are routinely shared amongst a healthcare team. Confidential information is likely to be available not just to doctors but also to nurses, administrators, social workers and many others. Recent developments in information technology mean that even more people will now be privy to confidential patient information. For example, the computerised patient records at issue in *Ashworth Hospital Authority v Mirror Group Newspapers* could be accessed by over 200 people.[31] These records held confidential and personal information which was leaked to a national newspaper. Even without such an unauthorised disclosure, it is unlikely that genuine consent was obtained for the accessibility of confidential information to such a large

---

[30]   See G Phillipson, 'Transforming Breach of Confidence? Towards a Common Law Right of Privacy under the Human Rights Act' (2003) 66 *MLR* 726, at pp 748-58. This issue is considered in more detail below.

[31]   [2001] 1 WLR 515, at p 522.

number of people. There is a danger that an assumption of implied consent to circulation of information within a healthcare team may be inaccurate. It is vital, therefore, that the GMC's sensible advice on this issue is followed. The GMC guidance requires that patients be made aware that personal information about them will be shared within the healthcare team unless they object and that any such objection will be respected.[32] Controversy surrounds recent government plans to create a centralised medical records system for the NHS which would allow health professionals anywhere in the country to access confidential medical data.[33] An opt-out is available but only in relation to the 'Summary Care Record' (which will include all major illnesses, allergies and prescriptions for access in an emergency) and not in relation to the detailed medical records also to be stored on the system. In the absence of an opt-out, consent for the storage of personal data will merely be presumed. The details of the scheme are still being worked out (and campaigns to counter the threat to medical confidentiality are gaining support) but there is no doubt that the development of a centralised, computer-ised medical records system poses a huge threat to the privacy rights of all NHS patients.

The second, related, issue is whether a patient knows what personal informa-tion is recorded about him or her and thus might be shared with others. It is possible that consent to disclosure may be based on a misconception of what information is held. Therefore, the patient's right to know is inextricably linked with a right to confidentiality. A limited right to know what is recorded about one as a patient was first created in the Access to Medical Reports Act 1988, which gave a right to know in respect of reports written by doctors for insurance companies and employers. Two years later, the Access to Health Records Act 1990 extended the right to know to all information relating to physical or mental health of an individual who can be identified from that information (or from other information in the possession of the holder of the record) where the record has been made by or on behalf of a doctor or other healthcare professional, including a dentist, optician, pharmacist or nurse. Access to the record could be excluded, however, where the information, in the opinion of the holder, would be likely to cause serious harm to the physical or mental health of the patient or anyone else, or was provided by or relates to another individual who could be identified from the information and has not consented to the disclosure. Now, the Data Protection Act 1998 provides a more general right of access to personal data, with only the latter exception restricting access. The legal provisions exist, therefore, to enable access to one's own medical records prior to registering no objection to disclosure to a healthcare team. The difficulty, however, is that most patients would not be comfortable with, and indeed would not even consider, making an explicit request to view the information held about them before

[32] GMC guidance, n 29 above, para 10.
[33] See J Carvel, 'Ministers to Put Patients' Details on Central Database Despite Objections', *The Guardian*, 2 November 2006.

consenting to its disclosure. The danger still exists, therefore, that personal and sensitive information, and also potentially inaccurate information, may be widely circulated on the basis of an uninformed lack of explicit objection.

(b)   Public Safety

Perhaps the most obvious societal interest which may conflict with a patient's right to confidentiality is the prevention of crime. If a doctor receives confidential information that a patient poses a direct physical threat to another person, it may be proportionate to breach the duty of confidence. The leading case on this issue is *W v Egdell*,[34] decided long before the right to respect for private life became an essential consideration under the HRA. Nonetheless, the approach in this case is still likely to apply when Article 8 is taken into account because even fundamental human rights can be outweighed by a pressing social need. The case involved a patient, W, who was detained in a secure hospital for public safety after killing five people. W applied to a mental health review tribunal for either a discharge or a transfer with a view to future discharge. Dr Egdell was employed by W's solicitors to provide a medical report. When he met with W, Dr Egdell became concerned that the patient had been misdiagnosed as a paranoid schizophrenic and that he was actually suffering from paranoid psychosis. When W confessed to a long standing interest in explosives, the doctor became convinced that W remained a very serious threat to the public. His report strongly opposed any transfer from the secure hospital. On seeing the report, W withdrew his application, which meant that in the normal course of events, the doctor's concerns would not be disclosed to anyone. However, Dr Egdell sent his report to the medical director of the hospital who then forwarded it to the Secretary of State. W alleged that this action was in breach of Dr Egdell's duty of confidence. The Court of Appeal found for the doctor and held that he was entitled to take reasonable steps to communicate his concern about a danger to the public even if the relevant information was obtained in the course of a confidential relationship.[35] The Court of Appeal confirmed that a duty of confidence had arisen here, however, and they would not have sanctioned disclosure of the information to newspapers or as gossip to friends.[36] The disclosure was only permissible because it was to the appropriate authorities who could act to prevent a danger to the public. It is interesting to note that both medical confidentiality and public safety were regarded by the Court of Appeal to be public interests, which needed to be balanced against each other. In the circumstances of the case, greater weight was given to public safety because the information was highly relevant to W's

---

[34]   [1990] 1 All ER 833.
[35]   *Ibid*, pp 852-53, per Bingham LJ.
[36]   *Ibid*, p 848.

dangerousness to the public.[37] It appears that the extreme and urgent facts of this case – the very real threat to public safety – justified the disclosure of confidential information, and would also justify the infringement with W's right to respect for private life, but in less extreme cases a similar breach of confidence may not be condoned.

One difficult situation where the harm to the public may not be as clear cut is in respect of HIV status. As Boyd notes, HIV raises some new issues because it has 'potential not only to create a medical pandemic, but also to provoke social prejudice'.[38] The law on confidentiality remains unchanged, however, and a balance must still be struck between the patient's right to privacy and confidentiality and any tangible threat to a third party. The GMC guidance suggests that a doctor may breach the duty of confidence 'where the benefits to an individual or to society of the disclosure outweigh the public and patient's interest in keeping the information confidential' but emphasises that 'the possible harm (both to the patient, and the overall trust between doctors and patients)' must be weighed against the benefits likely to arise from disclosure.[39] It is vital that, before any such disclosure takes place, an effort is made to persuade the patient to disclose the information himself. Boyd takes the view that if the patient still refuses to disclose his HIV status to a sexual partner at risk of infection, and if that partner is not another patient of the doctor to whom he owes a duty of care, the most effective means of protecting everyone may be for the doctor to maintain confidentiality and seek to influence his patient to behave responsibly.[40] This recognises the particularly sensitive nature of HIV status, which was also recognised by the European Court of Human Rights in *Z v Finland*: 'In view of the highly intimate and sensitive nature of information concerning a person's HIV status, any State measures compelling communication or disclosure of such information without the consent of the patient call for the most careful scrutiny on the part of the Court, as for the safeguards designed to secure an effective protection.'[41] The need for close scrutiny of any breach of confidentiality will be particularly pressing if a person's HIV status is disclosed not to protect a specific individual but rather to facilitate public debate on the matter, as will be seen in the next case to be considered.

---

[37] *Ibid*, p 846, per Stephen Brown P.
[38] KM Boyd, 'HIV Infection and AIDS: The Ethics of Medical Confidentiality' (1992) 18 *J Med Eth* 173, at p 173.
[39] GMC guidance, n 29 above, para 22.
[40] Boyd, n 38 above, p 178.
[41] *Z v Finland*, n 24 above, para 96.

(c)   Freedom of the Press

In *X v Y*,[42] the names of two doctors being treated for AIDS was improperly disclosed to the press. The Health Authority sought an injunction to prevent publication. The court undertook a balancing exercise:

> On the one hand, there are public interests in having a free press and an informed public debate; on the other, it is in the public interest that actual or potential AIDS sufferers should be able to resort to hospitals without fear of this being revealed, that those owing duties of confidence in their employment should be loyal and should not disclose confidentiality matters and that, prima facie, no one should be allowed to use information extracted in breach of confidence from hospital records even if disclosure of the particular information may not give rise to immediately apparent harm.[43]

Thus, even if the doctors were not identified, they were regarded as having suffered a detriment due to the initial disclosure of their status.[44] In the circumstances, the legitimate public interest in the freedom of the press was regarded by the court as being 'substantially outweighed when measured against the public interests in relation to loyalty and confidentiality both generally and with particular reference to AIDS patients' hospital records'.[45] This focus upon a balancing of public interests is now outdated because, with the enactment of the HRA, there will now be a balancing of the Convention rights of privacy and free speech.

This can be seen in the more recent case of *Campbell v Mirror Group Newspapers*.[46] In this case, Naomi Campbell, the supermodel, brought a breach of confidence action in respect of the publication of details of her drug therapy and photographs of her leaving a clinic. The Daily Mirror had published stories revealing that the claimant was a drug addict, contrary to her earlier claims that she was not, that she was receiving treatment for her addiction, and details of that treatment with photographs of her leaving a Narcotics Anonymous meeting. The claimant accepted that there was a legitimate public interest in disclosing that she was a drug addict and thereby correcting a false impression given by her claims that she was not, and also in the fact that she was being treated for her addiction. However, she claimed damages for breach of confidence (as well as compensation under the DPA) for the additional details and photographs. The House of Lords, by a majority of 3 to 2, found in her favour. Lord Hope, in the majority, performed a balancing exercise in respect of Article 8 (the right to respect for private life) and Article 10 (the right to freedom of expression) and found that,

---

[42]   [1988] 2 All ER 648.
[43]   *Ibid*, p 660.
[44]   *Ibid*, pp 657-58.
[45]   *Ibid*, p 661.
[46]   [2004] 2 All ER 995.

without the publication of the photographs, the balance would have been even.[47] The photographs tipped the balance in favour of an Article 8 violation, however, and Lord Hope, together with Baroness Hale and Lord Carswell, found that the limitation of Ms Campbell's right to respect for private life was not proportionate in order to protect the freedom of the press.[48] It is worth noting that this emphasis on balancing Convention rights occurred in a case between two private parties: there was no public authority required to comply with these rights by the HRA. The House of Lords' judgment in *Campbell*, therefore, makes very clear that the Convention rights will be crucial in all cases and not just those involving a public authority.

Prior to the House of Lords judgment, there had been some criticism that the domestic courts were not genuinely balancing Articles 8 and 10 in such cases but rather seeing privacy interests as merely another public interest which must be proven to be a necessary and proportionate limitation to free speech.[49] This approach stems from the inherent value of free speech in the common law, as well as its central role in the ECHR, but the prioritisation of free speech can lead to a devaluing of the equally fundamental right to privacy. As Phillipson argued in 2003, 'the courts continue to exhibit this deep ambivalence towards the place and value of privacy in English law in their determination to treat the right to private life merely as a narrowly construed and grudgingly recognised exception to press freedom'.[50] Thankfully, the House of Lords in *Campbell* gave overdue recognition to the value of privacy by balancing it with freedom of the press and finding that the restriction on press freedom was proportionate to the need to protect Ms Campbell's right to respect for private life. *Campbell* is a turning point in legal recognition of privacy from press intrusion and it is interesting, and potentially significant, that it concerns confidentiality of medical treatment. There can be no doubt that medical confidentiality is at the very heart of an individual's right to privacy and only a particularly pressing societal interest will be sufficient to justify its restriction.

(d)   Parental Responsibility

The landmark case of *Gillick v West Norfolk and Wisbech Area Health Authority*[51] was the first to recognise that a minor has a right to medical confidentiality. The case concerned the legality of the provision of contraceptive advice and treatment to a minor under the age of 16 without her parents' knowledge or consent. The House of Lords held that such advice and treatment could be provided if the minor would understand it; could not be persuaded to inform her parents; was

---

[47]   *Ibid*, para 121.
[48]   *Ibid*, paras 122-24.
[49]   Phillipson, n 30 above, pp 748-58.
[50]   *Ibid*, p 758.
[51]   [1986] AC 112, [1985] 3 All ER 402.

likely to have intercourse with or without contraceptives; her physical or mental health was likely to suffer without the advice/treatment; and her best interests required it to be provided without parental consent.[52]

The *Gillick* case introduced the concept of *Gillick* competence, discussed in the previous chapter, where a minor has sufficient understanding and intelligence to enable her to fully understand the treatment proposed. The right to confidentiality exists independently of questions of competence, however. *Re C*[53] and *Re Z*[54] demonstrate that a duty of confidentiality is owed in respect of a very young child by both medical staff and the child's parents. Disclosure of information to parents of young children will be essential in order to enable the exercise of parental responsibility and the provision of authority for treatment. The principle of beneficence, discussed in the previous chapter, requires that necessary or beneficial medical treatment is provided to minors who are unable to authorise it themselves. Therefore, a fully informed parent able to provide proxy consent is essential. When the minor is more mature, however, and has acquired mental competency to consent, an informed parent may represent a threat. This is because cases such as *Re R* have determined that parental consent can overrule a *Gillick* competent minor's refusal of treatment.[55] Thus, in respect of mature minors, a breach of confidence may also result in infringement of bodily integrity.[56] It is vital, therefore, to regard an unauthorised disclosure of confidential information as a breach of the doctor's duty of confidence and a violation of the minor's right to privacy, which is only justified if the best interests of the minor require it.[57] As Loughrey notes, '[t]he tension between the welfare interests and the autonomy rights of the child, which is a recurring feature of child law, is also likely to form a part of the law of confidentiality when applied to children'.[58] In addition, the responsibility of parents for the health and moral welfare of their child should not be overlooked. This will be a particularly significant, and potentially problematic, factor when the treatment in question is contraceptive in nature or, especially, a termination of pregnancy.

Recently, the courts had the opportunity to consider the emotive issue of whether a doctor can perform a termination of pregnancy on a minor without her parents' knowledge or consent. *R (Axon) v Secretary of State for Health*[59] considered this very issue, together with the broader issue of the provision of contraceptive advice/treatment without parental involvement. It concerned the Department of Health's 2004 guidance, 'Best Practice Guidance for Doctors and Other Health Professionals on the Provision of Advice and Treatment to Young

---

[52] [1985] 3 All ER 402, at p 413.
[53] *Re C (a minor)(wardship: medical treatment)(No 2)* [1989] 2 All ER 791.
[54] *Re Z (a minor)(identification: restrictions or publication)* [1995] 4 All ER 961.
[55] *Re R (a minor)* [1991] 4 All ER 177.
[56] See Loughrey (2003), n 18 above, p 529.
[57] *Ibid*, p 530.
[58] *Ibid*, p 535.
[59] [2006] QB 539.

People under Sixteen on Contraception, Sexual and Reproductive Health'. This guidance emphasised that children under 16 have the same right to confidentiality as adults and recognised that doctors can provide both contraceptive advice/ treatment and a termination of pregnancy without informing the parents, provided that the child understands the treatment, and has been encouraged to involve a parent. Under the guidance, a child's right to confidentiality could only be breached where it is outweighed by a risk to the child's (or another's) health, safety or welfare. The claimant in *Axon*, the mother of a child who had undergone an abortion without her knowledge, argued in favour of a limitation on confidentiality based upon parental responsibility for the welfare of a child but the judge rejected such a limitation and emphasised the value of confidentiality in this context: 'the very basis and nature of the information which a doctor or a medical professional receives relating to the sexual and reproductive health of any patient of whatever age deserves the highest degree of confidentiality'.[60] The judge also emphasised both the need to encourage the use of contraceptives and to discourage unprotected teenage sex,[61] and the rights of children.[62] The judge referred to the United Nations Convention on the Rights of the Child which has been ratified by the United Kingdom and recognises the importance of a right to autonomy for the child.[63] The child's rights under Article 8 were also given special protection. The claimant argued that the case of *Gillick* needed to be reconsidered post-HRA in order to protect the Article 8 rights of parents – ie a right to respect for family life. However, it was held that a failure to notify parents of the provision of contraceptive advice or treatment to their child did not infringe Article 8(1) because of the importance of the right to confidentiality under Article 8[64] and the significance of the maturity and understanding of a child which will diminish parental rights.[65] Even if Article 8(1) had been infringed by the failure to inform the parents, it was held that the infringement would be justified under Article 8(2) as necessary in a democratic society for the protection of health and the rights of others. This recognition of (a) the key significance of the right to medical confidentiality under Article 8's broader right to respect for private life,[66] and (b) the dominance of a child's Article 8 rights

---

[60]   *Axon*, n 59 above, para 62.

[61]   The Court of Appeal decision in *Gillick* held that the provision of contraceptive treatment to a child under 16 without the consent of her parents would be unlawful. Between this decision in December 1984 and it being overruled by the House of Lords decision in October 1985, the number of children seeking advice or contraception fell from 1.7 per thousand to 1.2 per thousand (*Axon*, para 68). This appears to provide some evidence for the commonly held fear that a lack of confidentiality will deter children from seeking contraceptive advice and treatment.

[62]   *Axon*, n 59 above, paras 76-80.

[63]   Article 12: 'States Parties shall assure to the child who is capable of forming his or her own views the right to express those views freely in all matters affecting the child, the views of the child being given due weight in accordance with the age and maturity of the child.'

[64]   *Axon*, n 59 above, para 127.

[65]   *Ibid*, para 130.

[66]   *Ibid*, para 127.

over those of her parents[67] are two welcome confirmations that a mature minor's right to confidentiality will be enforced by English law. The principles at the core of *Gillick* not only endure post-HRA but are actually strengthened by it.

The only controversial aspect of *Axon* is the clear statement that abortion is to be treated in the same way as other sexual or contraceptive treatment, even though the judge recognised that this particular treatment raises more serious and complex issues.[68] It is arguable that parents should be notified of their child's termination of pregnancy in order that emotional support can be provided following this unique medical procedure. A termination of pregnancy is always prima facie a criminal act and so there is a distinguishing factor between it and other medical procedures. The emotional and health implications of a termination of pregnancy set it apart from other treatments and suggest that a limited exception to the child's right to confidentiality may be justified in this very special circumstance.

(e)   Anonymised Data for Research and Other Purposes

R v Department of Health, ex p Source Informatics Ltd[69] is an illuminating case on the issue of the disclosure of anonymised data and the nature of privacy interests more generally. Source Informatics was a database company seeking to obtain information about GPs' prescribing habits from pharmacists, which it then intended to sell to pharmaceutical companies for marketing purposes. The Department of Health advised GPs and pharmacists that participating in such a scheme would be a breach of confidence even if the information disclosed was anonymised. Source Informatics sought declaratory relief against this advice. At first instance, Latham J refused relief on the basis that a breach of confidence must be justified as being in the public interest and any such justification was absent here, but the Court of Appeal overturned this decision and shifted the basis of the duty of confidence from a public interest issue to a question of fairness of use. The Court of Appeal held that a duty of confidence rests on whether disclosure can occur without unfair treatment of the confider. The anonymisation of data prior to its disclosure was held to remove any possibility of unfair treatment of the patients and, therefore, there was held to be no breach of confidence. The key question for the Court of Appeal, which it was able to answer in the negative, was held to be: 'Would a reasonable pharmacist's conscience be troubled by the proposed use to be made of patients' prescriptions? Would he think that by entering Source's scheme he was breaking his customers' confidence, making unconscientious use of the information they provide?'[70]

---

[67]   *Ibid*, para 144.
[68]   *Ibid*, para 90.
[69]   [2000] 1 All ER 786.
[70]   *Ibid*, at p 796.

The Court of Appeal's judgment suggests that the concealment of the confider's personal identity is sufficient to secure protection of his or her privacy,[71] and this conclusion had been subject to much criticism:

> Arguably, the effect of *Source Informatics* is to reduce the individual's legal interest in his or her own information to no more than that of ensuring that anonymity is maintained. In so doing, other fundamental issues are ignored, including the role of consent in legitimising the uses of information, the concept of reasonable expectations of use and, ultimately, the importance of maintaining a prima facie respect for confidences.[72]

The assumption that privacy requires mere anonymity and that, once confidential information is anonymised, its original confider retains no further interests in the matter is shown to be a fallacy by Beyleveld and Histed who give the example of a patient who may object to the Source Informatics' scheme 'because he or she has deep personal ethical concerns about contributing to the profit making of large pharmaceutical manufacturers based on knowledge of those very manufacturers' lack of ethical concerns in other, less advanced, countries'.[73] Even in the absence of such specific ethical objections to the use to which the anonymised data will be put, there are broader interests retained in information disclosed under circumstances of confidence. As Beyleveld and Histed note, patients are in an inherently vulnerable position when they disclose personal information to health professionals and the Court of Appeal judgment in *Source Informatics* is insensitive to that vulnerability and shows little respect for patient autonomy.[74] It is in direct contrast to the indications in cases such as *Campbell* that a right to privacy, especially in the healthcare context, is of increasing importance in comparison with other societal interests. The need to breach medical confidentiality where there is a clear risk of serious physical harm to others is undeniable but the same is not true where the disclosure is merely for the purpose of selling confidential information to pharmaceutical companies.

An issue which breaches the gap between these two extremes is the disclosure of confidential information for medical research purposes. There is clearly a much stronger public interest justification here than in respect of commercial interests but the serious risk of physical harm, seemingly required by *Egdell*, will not be apparent here.[75] Perhaps the general benefits to society as a whole from efficient and informed medical research will be sufficient to justify a proportionate infringement with an individual's right to privacy but it is vital that the

---

[71]   *Ibid*, at p 797.

[72]   JK Mason, A. McCall Smith and G. Laurie, *Law and Medical Ethics*, 7th edn (Oxford, Oxford University Press, 2006), p 280.

[73]   D Beyleveld and E Histed, 'Betrayal of Confidence in the Court of Appeal' (2000) 4 *Med Law Int* 277, at p 295.

[74]   *Ibid*, p 303.

[75]   On this issue generally, see P Case, 'Confidence Matters: The Rise and Fall of Informational Autonomy in Medical Law' (2003) 11 *Med L Rev* 208.

presumption that information disclosed in the healthcare context is confidential remains the starting point for consideration of any unauthorised disclosures. This does not seem to be the case in respect of the Health and Social Care Act 2001 which empowers a government minister to make regulations enabling the bypassing of the general requirement of consent to disclosure. These regulations can either authorise or compel NHS bodies to disclose patient information[76] where necessary for medical purposes of improving patient care or in the public interest. Although there are safeguards in place,[77] these are insufficient as demonstrated by the Health Service (Control of Patient Information) Regulations 2002. These regulations permit, inter alia, the disclosure of otherwise confidential patient information where processing is 'with a view to diagnosing communicable diseases and other risks to public health'.[78] As Case explains, the latter may potentially provide justification for access to information concerning alcohol, tobacco, obesity or genetic tests,[79] and furthermore the regulations extend access to anyone employed by a government department or other public authority in communicable disease surveillance.[80] Such ominous legislation suggests that a patient's right to confidentiality and privacy remains in an extremely precarious position, vulnerable not only to the legitimate needs of public health and safety but also potentially to the whims of political and commercial curiosity.

III. Conclusion

The issue of medical confidentiality is one of the most obvious candidates for a human rights conceptualisation. The right to privacy and the duty of confidence have become entwined in English law, particularly post-HRA. This brings both advantages and disadvantages. On the positive side, a right to the protection of personal information can be relied upon by patients not just against public authorities, such as the NHS, but also against private parties, such as the press. On the other hand, Article 8 ECHR seems to have restricted application in respect of personal information in domestic law due to the continued relevance of duties of confidence. The House of Lords judgment in *Campbell* provided a welcome recognition that a right to privacy in respect of medical treatment is a

---

[76]   Section 60 Health and Social Care Act 2001.

[77]   The regulations must be approved by both Houses of Parliament; there must be no reasonably practicable alternative to the use of confidential information, having regard to cost and available technology (s 60(3)); and the views of the Patient Information Advisory Group (PIAG) must be taken into account (s 61).

[78]   Health Service (Control of Patient Information) Regulations 2002, regs 2(1) and 3(1).

[79]   Case, n 75 above, p 231.

[80]   Regulation 3(3)(c).

weighty value that will not be easily overturned. However, the lingering impression left from an investigation of this topic of medical law is that a patient's privacy rights are under threat from a number of directions. Examples include the widespread release of personal information within a healthcare team, especially using modern information technology; the law's failure to recognise a continued privacy interest in confidential data once it is anonymised; the Regulations that allow public authorities to gather confidential information about patients that would otherwise be protected; and the plans for a centralised database of patients' medical records. Judicial acceptance of the relevance of human rights law to the issue of confidential medical information is of limited value unless privacy is given its true status as a fundamental human right which can only be restricted if other pressing social needs make such an infringement into a patient's private life genuinely necessary within a democratic society.

Recommended Further Reading

DJ Feldman, *Civil Liberties and Human Rights in England and Wales*, 2nd edn (Oxford, Oxford University Press, 2002) Chapter 9.

J Loughrey, 'Medical Information, Confidence and a Child's Right to Privacy' [2003] *LS* 510.

D Beyleveld and E Histed, 'Betrayal of Confidence in the Court of Appeal' (2000) 4 *Med Law Int* 277.

P Case, 'Confidence Matters: The Rise and Fall of Informational Autonomy in Medical Law' (2003) 11 *Med L Rev* 208.

7

Property Rights in the Body

Throughout this book, we are concerned with the law on medical treatment and the role human rights play in that relationship. Before proceeding further into particular categories of treatment, namely those specifically located at the beginning and end of life, it will be constructive here to investigate the status of our bodies and the question of whether we hold property, as well as personal, rights in them. The chapter will be divided into three parts. The first part will investigate the theory of self-ownership and the role of rights. The second part will consider the role of property rights in respect of human material taken from living persons, and the final part of the chapter will turn to the emotive issue of property rights in the dead body and its parts.

I. The Theory of Self-Ownership and the Role of Rights

The concept of property rights in our own bodies, or 'self-ownership', has a long and disputed history. Both Locke and Kant developed an idea of self-ownership, although the interpretation of this aspect of their works varies. Locke famously wrote that: 'Though the earth and all inferior creatures be common to all men, yet every man has a property in his own person: this nobody has the right to but himself. The labour of his body and the work of his hands we may say are properly his.'[1] The significance of this theory was recently recognised by Brooke LJ in *Re A (children: conjoined twins)* when he claimed that it 'underpins much of the moral dialogue in this area'.[2] It would be misleading, however, to place too much weight in Locke's argument that 'every man has a property in his own body' without recognising the context of this argument. As Morgan recognises, 'the context defines and constricts the claim' and, in Morgan's view, the claim by

---

[1] J Locke, 'An Essay Concerning the True Original Extent and End of Civil Government' (2nd treatise, 1690, para 27) in Locke's *Two Treatises of Government* (ed P Laslett (Cambridge, Cambridge University Press, 1988).
[2] [2000] 4 All ER 961.

Locke was 'less a metaphysical statement declaring self-ownership, more a political statement denying ownership by another . . . . My body and my life are my property in the limited sense that they are not yours.'[3] This illustrates one of the primary purposes of a theory of self-ownership: to prevent ownership of our bodies by anyone other than ourselves. However, the theory goes too far because a denial of any right to own a body would suffice to prevent the justification of slavery. Indeed, it may be a smaller step from self-ownership to ownership by someone else than from a lack of property in the body to ownership by another.

The concept of self-ownership entails recognition of the dualistic theory of mind: the concept that the mind and the body are distinct. As Naffine explains, 'Self-ownership is usually not intended to denote the entire person reflexively owning the entire person . . . Rather there is presumed to be an internal division of the person, two different and distinct parts which represent the owner and the owned.'[4] Naffine raises a further concern about the concept of self-ownership, namely that women surrender access to their bodies both to men, during heterosexual intercourse,[5] and to their unborn children, during pregnancy. As Naffine argues, '[f]or women to exclude others from their physical beings would mean the end of life'.[6] Self-ownership for women, therefore, cannot imply absolute exclusionary rights over the property of the female body. Perhaps this problem can be at least partly rectified by further clarification of the meaning of self-ownership. Property rights take two distinct forms: rights of ownership and rights of possession. The former implies complete dominion over the property, whereas the latter implies only a lesser interest.[7] It is possessory rights which seem more appropriate to explain and govern the relationship between our minds and our bodies, for whether we philosophically own our bodies or not, there is little doubt that we possess them. And it is, therefore, entirely logical that we should have first claim over the use to which they are put. This role of property rights in facilitating individual autonomy is important and serves as a justification for property rights in our own bodies.[8] A complicating factor arises,

---

[3]   D Morgan, 'Where Do I Own My Body? And Why?' in D Morgan, *Issues in Medical Law and Ethics* (2001, Cavendish, London), p 86.

[4]   N Naffine, 'The Legal Structure of Self-Ownership: Or the Self-Possessed Man and the Woman Possessed' (1998) 25 *JLS* 193, at p 201. We will see in Chapter 11 that English law recognises that the mind and body are distinct through the concept of Brain Stem Death, the application of which means that a person is regarded as legally and clinically dead when the brain is irreversibly destroyed, even if the body continues to function.

[5]   'At the end of the day, it is women who are possessed in the act of sex and men who take possession . . . The 'natural' heterosexual form of sex is one which allows man to retain property in his own body, while appropriating the body of a woman' (Naffine, *ibid*, p 207, 208).

[6]   Naffine, *ibid*, p 204.

[7]   See A Grubb, ' "I, Me, Mine": Bodies, Parts and Property' (1998) 3 *Med Law Int* 299, at p 301. As Grubb notes, English property law is generally concerned with protecting the rights of the possessor of property and is only concerned with ownership where it serves as a trump in disputes with other less entitled possessors.

[8]   See K Mason and G Laurie, 'Consent or Property? Dealing with the Body and its Parts in the Shadow of Bristol and Alder Hey' (2001) 64 *MLR* 711, at p 727: 'property rights can bolster the respect

however, in respect of property rights in the body after death. Individual autonomy can only be expressed, and is only of value to the individual, prior to death. After death, the question arises whether our bodies, or parts of them, can be the subject of other people's property interests.

Traditionally, the English law has been adamant that there is no property in a corpse.[9] Matthews explains that this is partly due to religious sentiment, partly due to public health concerns requiring the prompt disposal of bodies, and partly due to the lack of medical justification for permitting access to dead bodies.[10] All three of these reasons have been the subject of change over the last century, however: society has become more secular; public health concerns have been lessened; and, most significantly, the potential societal benefits of the medical use of human tissue has increased. As Matthews concludes, 'all the societal pressures which a century ago pointed *away* from lawfully possessing and using human tissue now point *towards* it. The non-property solutions of yesterday are inadequate to the task of today.'[11]

Perhaps the lingering concern about the appropriateness of property in the body relates to a fear of commercialisation of the human body. While it is not inevitable that commerce will flow from a classification of the body as property, the instinctive revulsion many of us feel at such a development highlights the primacy of human dignity as a legal and moral value. Mason and Laurie argue that the traditional justification for the no-property rule was an intuitive belief that some degree of human dignity remains in the body after death.[12] The concept of human dignity is one (but not the only) underlying value in modern human rights law. It is particularly vital in the context of a right to be free of inhuman or degrading treatment (protected in Article 3 ECHR) but can also have application in the context of the right to respect for private and family life and the right to be free of discriminatory treatment.[13] The concept lacks clarity, however, and, as Feldman's articles on this topic recognise, it is 'a highly complex concept'[14] which is 'culturally and contextually specific . . . and dependent as much on the viewpoint of the observer as on the aspirations of the protagonists'.[15]

Human Dignity has particular relevance in the field of bioethics and its central role is recognised in the European Convention on Human Rights and Biomedicine when the Preamble includes an acknowledgement that the contracting

---

that each of us deserves and which can be demonstrated, in part, through the rigid application of the doctrine of informed consent'. For further argument on this point, see the section below on property in living persons.

[9]   See further below.

[10]   P Matthews, 'The Man of Property' (1995) 3 *Med L Rev* 251, at p 255.

[11]   Matthews, *ibid*, p 256.

[12]   Mason and Laurie, n. 8 above, p 714. Mason and Laurie also point out the irony that the no-property rule means that a corpse cannot be stolen (p 715).

[13]   See D Feldman, 'Human Dignity as a Legal Value – Part I' [1999] *PL* 682, at pp 688-96.

[14]   D Feldman, 'Human Dignity as a Legal Value – Part II' [2000] *PL* 61, at p 75.

[15]   Feldman, *ibid*, p 76.

parties are 'conscious that the misuse of biology and medicine may lead to acts endangering human dignity'. This concern is reflected in many of the provisions of the Convention including, of prime relevance on this topic, Article 21 which states that the 'human body and its parts shall not, as such, give rise to financial gain'. The Explanatory Report acknowledges that this Article 'applies the principle of human dignity'.[16] This reflects the concern that commercial dealing in human material will have a negative impact upon human dignity. It is a complex matter, however, because it is possible that laws denying self-ownership may also violate human dignity by restraining an individual's autonomous choices of how to use (or even abuse) his own body, and its parts. This is most likely to arise in respect of a living person wishing, for example, to offer his kidney either for profit or altruism, but it may also arise in respect of the wishes of a deceased person. If some sense of human dignity does endure after death, as the restrictions on the use of a dead body and its parts implies, then disregard of the wishes of the deceased may also conflict with this important value. To use a dead body in a way contrary to the wishes of the person when alive may amount to a violation of human dignity. This will only be true; however, if dignity survives after death and, as we shall see below, the inevitable disintegration of the body belies this proposition.

So far we have encountered a number of aspects of the property in the body issue. It may be helpful to unpick these. First, there is the philosophical issue of self-ownership: do we 'own' our own bodies? Second, if we do not own our own bodies, can others own parts of it? Thirdly, after death, do we retain an element of human dignity which will restrain the use of cadavers and body parts? Finally, underlying these issues are two influences of the modern world: human rights to dignity and autonomy, and the medical use of human tissue for transplantation, research, teaching or other purposes. The remainder of this chapter will investigate the conflict between individual rights and societal benefits in the context of the debate about property rights in the body and its parts, both living and dead. We will investigate which of the following rhetorical propositions are most accurate: (1) 'It is a commonly felt connection that all that is "I" is also "Mine" and somehow belongs to "Me".'[17]; or (2) 'In the deepest sense, my body is nobody's body, not even mine.'[18] Most importantly, we will consider the respective implications of these two views on the individual right to human dignity and the societal interest in preserving life.

---

[16]   Explanatory report, para 131.
[17]   Grubb, n 7 above, p 302.
[18]   Morgan, n 3 above, p 86.

II.   Property Rights in Human Material taken from Living Persons

A good starting point in consideration of whether there are property rights in human material taken from a living person is the infamous US case of *Moore v Regents of the University of California*[19] which establishes the curious point that the one person who is least likely to own such material is the person from whom it is taken. Mr Moore suffered from hairy cell leukaemia and as a result had his spleen removed. His doctors subsequently discovered that cells from his spleen had unusual beneficial properties and they developed a cell line based on this without Moore's knowledge or consent. They then obtained a patent for the cell line and eventually sold it to a drug company for 15 million dollars. Moore, whose removed spleen had provided the human cells necessary for this techno-logical advance, received none of this substantial profit. He brought a claim before the Californian Supreme Court which found that there had been a breach of fiduciary duty and a lack of informed consent due to his lack of knowledge and consent, but it firmly denied that Moore had any property rights in respect of his cells. One major reason for this decision was that such property rights would potentially hinder medical research. It is an extremely unsatisfactory decision, however. As Skene points out a cell line 'consists of living cells that can be reproduced indefinitely . . . Although preserved in an artificial medium, each cell contains Mr Moore's DNA. Yet the court found that Mr Moore did not own them . . . He could not get them back nor require that they must be destroyed.'[20] In this context, the denial of self-ownership seems unjust and raises concerns about a lack of autonomous control over the information specific to our own bodies. The dissenting judge, Mosk J, perhaps goes too far when he compares today's biotechnology industry with slavery,[21] but the commercial use of human material unique to an individual, while that individual is excluded from the transaction, presents a strong argument in favour of a legal recognition of some property-type interest in our own bodies.

Following the organ retention scandals at Alder Hey and Bristol hospitals and the inquiries into them in 2001 (discussed below), a new wide-ranging piece of legislation was introduced to regulate the use of all human tissue. The Human Tissue Act 2004 attracts most attention in the context of the use of organs from deceased persons (and this aspect of the Act will be discussed below) but it also regulates all use of 'relevant material' from living persons, defined as material which consists of or includes human cells, other than hair and nails, gametes and

---

[19]   (1990) 793 P 2d 479.
[20]   L Skene, 'Proprietary Rights in Human Bodies, Body Parts and Tissue: Regulatory Context and Proposals for New Laws' (2002) 22 *LS* 102, at p 107.
[21]   Mosk J claimed that the spectre of slavery 'haunts the laboratories and boardrooms of today's biotechnological research-industrial complex' (n 19 above).

embryos outside the human body.[22] In respect of these exceptions, English case law suggests that regenerative body material, such as hair,[23] blood,[24] and urine[25] can be the subject of property and the Human Fertilisation and Embryology Act 1990 sets out a detailed regulatory system for human gametes and embryos. The key in this regulatory system is the need for consent. If one of the gamete providers withdraws his or her consent, the gametes or embryos will be destroyed.[26] There is no express development of property rights but the control exercised over the gametes/embryos by their providers implies a quasi-property interest, somewhat complicated by questions of whether an embryo is a human life worthy of protection in its own right. Furthermore, an interesting case in Jersey dealt with the issue of fetal material.[27] The authorities sought to obtain fetal tissue from an aborted fetus in order to bring a prosecution against the sexual partner of an underage mother. The mother refused to release the fetal tissue to the police and the Jersey Royal Court accepted that she had a property-type interest in the fetal material. However, the Jersey Royal Court, and subsequently the Jersey Court of Appeal, overrode her refusal because of the conflicting public interest in the investigation and prosecution of crime.

In respect of other human material from living donors, the Human Tissue Act 2004 requires the consent of the source of the human material when that material is used for any of a number of specified purposes, including transplantation.[28] Section 33 regards the use of organs from living donors for transplantation purposes as unlawful without a licence but a licence may be granted, even if the donor is unrelated, provided there has been no financial reward. More broadly, the Act prohibits all commercial dealings in human material for transplantation purposes, regardless of whether the donor is living or deceased. This prohibition is set out in section 32 of the Act. This section imposes a no-trade rule for 'controlled material', meaning that such material cannot be supplied or offered for supply in return for a reward.[29] Controlled material is defined as any material consisting of or including human cells (except gametes, embryos and material which is the subject of property because of an application of human skill) which is, or is intended to be, removed from a human body and which is intended to be used for the purpose of transplantation.[30] This emphasises the point made in the

---

[22]   Section 53 Human Tissue Act 2004.

[23]   *R v Herbert* (1961) 25 JCL 163.

[24]   *R v Rothery* (1976) 63 Cr App R 231.

[25]   *R v Welsh* [1974] RTR 478.

[26]   *Evans v Amicus Healthcare* [2004] 3 All ER 1025.

[27]   *In the Matter of X* [2005] JCA050.

[28]   Section 3(2) requires consent of living persons. The full list of purposes requiring consent are found in Schedule 1, Part 1: (1) anatomical examination; (2) determining the cause of death; (3) establishing after a person's death the efficacy of a drug or treatment administered; (4) obtaining scientific or medical information which may be relevant; (5) public display; (6) research; (7) transplantation.

[29]   Section 32(1).

[30]   Section 32(8).

previous section that it is primarily the commercialisation of human tissue which is often perceived to be objectionable, rather than its use or the adoption of a property lens through which to view it. As Matthews succinctly explains: 'It is not turning tissue into things that people are afraid of, it is turning people into commodities.'[31]

While the categorisation of human organs as a commercial commodity is distasteful, this must be placed in the context of a severe organ shortage. This has led some commentators to argue in favour of the establishment of an ethical market in human organs from living donors.[32] There is no doubt that safeguards would need to be in place to ensure against exploitation. Erin and Harris propose the establishment of a single purchaser system (for example, the NHS) within a confined marketplace (for example, the UK) as a means of accomplishing this. As they point out, there is 'a lot of hypocrisy about the ethics of buying and selling organs or indeed other body products and services – for example, surrogacy and gametes. What it usually means is that everyone is paid but the donor.'[33] Erin and Harris seek to justify a market in human organs on the basis of the pressing need for an increase in the supply of organs for transplant: a societal interest, perhaps, in preserving life. However, there is an alternative means of justifying such a market, proposed by Savulescu, which focuses more on the right of an individual to sell parts of his or her body.[34] This could be regarded as a specific, albeit controversial, aspect of the widely accepted right to autonomy.

Skene also proposes a personal autonomy right to choose whether to permit one's own human tissue to be used for teaching or research purposes.[35] He makes this suggestion in the context of rejecting the idea of any proprietary interest in our own bodies, although he does accept the concept of others, such as a hospital or research institute, subsequently acquiring proprietary rights in extracted tissue, including rights of possession, control, use and commercial exploitation.[36] The use of autonomy as an ethical justification for the retention of control over the use to which our bodies are put is entirely logical. It has the advantages of retaining the focus on the individual involved, and his or her rights of bodily integrity. The emphasis on autonomy can be enhanced, however, by the recognition of ownership rights.

The ECHRB, in line with its emphasis on the preservation of human dignity, prohibits the use of the human body and its parts for financial gain,[37] and prioritises the need for consent to the storage and use of extracted body parts.[38]

---

[31]   Matthews, n 10 above, p 273.
[32]   See, for example, CA Erin and J Harris, 'An Ethical Market in Human Organs' (2003) 29 *J Med Eth* 137.
[33]   Erin and Harris, *ibid*, p 137.
[34]   J Savulescu, 'Is the Sale of Body Parts Wrong?' (2003) 29 *J Med Eth* 138.
[35]   Skene, n 20 above, pp 117-18.
[36]   Skene, *ibid*, p 125.
[37]   Article 21 ECHRB.
[38]   Article 22 ECHRB.

The prohibition on financial gain is broader than that found in the Human Tissue Act 2004 which relates only to material used for transplant. Article 19 of the ECHRB discourages the removal of organs or tissue from living donors for transplantation purposes by requiring that this only occur if there is no suitable organ or tissue available from a deceased person and no other alternative therapeutic method of comparable effectiveness.[39] The Additional Protocol on Transplantation of Organs and Tissues of Human Origin develops these points. It identifies its object in Article 1 as being to 'protect the dignity and identity of everyone and guarantee, without discrimination, respect for his or her integrity and other rights and fundamental freedoms with regard to transplantation of organs and tissue of human origin'. It requires that organ removal from a living donor only be carried out if either the donor has a close personal relationship with the recipient or there is approval by an appropriate independent body.[40] The prohibition of financial gain is further explained, with exceptions being made for compensation of living donors for loss of earnings and justifiable expenses, and advertising with a view to offering or seeking financial gain being expressly prohibited. Both the ECHRB and the Additional Protocol on Transplants reveal the role human rights can play in this context. The protection of human dignity is a fundamental goal of human rights protection and the commercial or exploitative use of human tissue can undermine the dignity of both the individual concerned and humanity in general. Both the Convention and the Protocol avoid specificity on the application of rights to the issue, however, and instead prioritise the protection of underlying principles such as human dignity and autonomy by requiring informed consent and prohibiting financial gain. That individual human rights are engaged by the use of human material from living donors is clear, but the role of human rights law in governing the area remains in a very embryonic and uncertain stage. It seems likely, however, that autonomy or dignity based personal rights will be emphasised rather than property based rights such as possession and ownership. Perhaps the best solution will prove to be a combination of the two.

The best way of deciding whether we should accept the idea of self-ownership is to look at the benefits and dangers which such a concept would introduce. There is little doubt that acceptance of ownership rights in human bodies raises the danger of commercialisation which may pose a threat to the vital ethical principle of dignity of the human person. However, there is no reason why the danger of commercialisation could not be countered by the imposition of limitations upon the powers of use and/or disposal held by the owner of a body or a body part. There are already many legal restrictions upon the use to which we can put our own bodies. For example, laws in place in respect of the inability

---

[39] Article 20 provides additional protection for persons lacking capacity to consent, whose tissue should only be used in exceptional circumstances. Note the English case of *In Re Y* [1997] 2 WLR 557, discussed in the previous chapter, demonstrates the need for this type of protection.

[40] Article 10 Additional Protocol on Transplants.

to grant valid consent to harmful activities, public decency laws and age limits for legal intercourse, all suggest that the possession of our bodies does not carry with it complete freedom of use. A further restriction on commercial use does not preclude self-ownership and provides essential protection for the dignity of the individual and the human race in general. So, self-ownership is not ruled out by the threat of dangerous consequences but are there sufficient benefits to justify it? Existing law ensures that individuals have the right of autonomous choice over the use of their bodies. For example, medical treatment without valid consent is, as we have seen, an unlawful battery (with necessary exceptions for those unable to consent). Any touching of another's body can amount to a battery and the criminal law imposes harsh penalties for the imposition of bodily harm or death. We are all free to use our bodies as we wish, subject to the restrictions in place to protect others and the core values of society (such as human dignity and protection of the vulnerable). What would self-ownership add to this? The potential benefits are marginal but the wider acceptance of property rights into the laws on dealing with human material would add a new dimension of protection to the autonomy based freedom we enjoy today. While there would be few practical implications from owning our own living bodies (other than to enhance our rights to autonomy and bodily integrity), the real benefits would come with the ability to control what happens to human material taken from our living bodies. As Price notes, 'whilst infringement of personal rights may generate entitlements to compensation for, or an injunction to prevent, improper storage or use, they do not provide rights to possess, retrieve/recover or more broadly control' human material.[41] While sale may be prohibited (to prevent commercialisation), gift would be permitted, theft prohibited and conditions upon use and ownership enforceable.

III.   Property Rights and Dead Bodies

(a)   The No Property Rule and Its Exceptions

There is a clear, unambiguous and well-established legal rule governing the role of property in respect of dead bodies: there is no property in a corpse or any part of it. Despite the lack of clear authority for the origin of this ancient rule, it continues to be cited and applied by modern day courts in the UK (and elsewhere). The lack of property in the corpse means that the rights of the deceased's relatives, for example to respect for family life and freedom of conscience and religion, become more crucial as the only means of protecting their wishes. Family life would include the process of mourning and freedom of

---

[41]   D Price, 'The Human Tissue Act 2004' (2005) 68 *MLR* 798, at pp 820-21.

religion may include the protection of beliefs about the appropriate disposal of the body. Neither right is absolute, however, and both will need to be balanced against conflicting societal interests such as public health, public order and even the protection of the rights of others.

Public health concerns have traditionally led to the imposition of a legal duty to dispose of a dead body. The practicalities of doing this would seem, at first glance, to imply a right to (at least) possess the body in order to arrange disposal. In 1996, the Court of Appeal had the opportunity to consider the relationship between such a limited right of possession and the general no-property rule. The case of *Dobson v North Tyneside Health Authority*[42] concerned the body of a woman who died of brain tumours. At the post-mortem the brain was removed and preserved. It was not returned with the body for burial. Subsequently, the brain was delivered to the hospital and disposed of without a histological examination of the tumours. The deceased's family were claiming negligence against the hospital for an initial failure to diagnose her condition and they needed to examine the tumours in order to establish negligence. The family brought an action claiming that the deceased's brain was property to which they were entitled to possession. The Court of Appeal rejected this claim. The court held that there is no right to possession of a corpse or any part of it. The court held that the duty to inter the body is held by the executors of the will or administrators of the estate and there is, therefore, no legal right to possession of the corpse by the next of kin. Even if there is, the Court of Appeal held that it would be limited to a right to possess in order to dispose of the body.[43] There is no enduring right to possession after disposal of the body.

The very limited exception to the no-property rule which exists in respect of interment of a dead body (and which is limited to the executor/administrator) does not present any substantial challenge to the general rule. However, there is another potentially much more significant exception to the no-property rule which originally derives from an Australian decision of 1908. In *Doodeward v Spence*, Griffiths CJ laid out the following rule:

> a human body, or a portion of a human body, is capable by law of becoming the subject of property. It is not necessary to give an exhaustive enumeration of the circumstances under which such a right may be acquired, but I entertain no doubt that, when a person has by the lawful exercise of work or skill so dealt with a human body or part of a human body in his lawful possession that it has acquired some attributes differentiating it from a mere corpse awaiting burial, he acquires a right to retain possession of it.[44]

In *Dobson*, the Court of Appeal declined to regard the fixing of the brain in paraffin as a sufficient 'exercise of work or skill' to enable the acquisition of

---

[42] [1996] 4 All ER 474.
[43] *Ibid*, p 600.
[44] (1908) 6 CLR 406, at p 414.

property in the brain. However, in *R v Kelly* in 1998,[45] the Court of Appeal not only applied the *Doodeward* exception but also potentially expanded it. *R v Kelly* involved a junior technician employed by the Royal College of Surgeons who removed numerous body parts from the College's stores and gave them to an artist who made casts of them for exhibition at an art gallery. The body parts taken included three human heads, parts of a brain, six arms and ten legs or feet. Some were subsequently found buried in a field; others were found stored in a basement. The technician and the artist were prosecuted for theft and claimed as a form of defence that there is no property in a corpse (and thus the statutory requirements for theft were not satisfied). The Court of Appeal considered the ancient no-property rule and, although recognising that its historical origins are questionable, it accepted that 'it has now been the common law for 150 years at least that neither a corpse nor parts of a corpse are in themselves and without more capable of being property protected by rights'.[46] However, the Court of Appeal also considered the *Doodeward* exception and approved its application in this case. It was held that the dissection and/or preservation techniques employed by the College for teaching or exhibition purposes had caused the College to acquire property rights over these body parts. Their removal without authorisation was, therefore, theft.

This judicial acceptance of the *Doodeward* exception signifies a substantial intrusion into the no-property rule. However, the Court of Appeal went further by proposing a potentially far more wide-ranging exception which might undermine the rule in its entirety. Rose LJ said: 'the common law does not stand still. It may be that if, on some future occasion, the question arises, the courts will hold that human body parts are capable of being property ... even without the acquisition of different attributes, if they have a use or significance beyond their mere existence.'[47] Rose LJ then proceeds to give a few examples of such a use or significance: use in an organ transplant operation; for the extraction of DNA; or as an exhibit in a trial.[48] The difficulty with this proposed exception to the no-property rule is that there will be little point in removing a body part from a dead body *unless* it is of some use or significance. As Grubb argues, the *Kelly* exception would 're-write the "no property" rule itself such that it became: there is 'no property' in corpses (excluding excised body parts) ... The exception would now prove a new, and more limited, rule ...'[49] Such a rewriting of the no-property rule – in effect to exclude body parts – is particularly problematic given the recent and controversial retention of organs and body parts after post-mortems and without consent. The fact that the retained tissue was thought, at least at some point, to have a use or significance justifying its retention has

---

[45]   [1998] 3 All ER 741.
[46]   *Ibid*, p 630, per Rose LJ.
[47]   *Ibid*, p 631.
[48]   *Ibid*.
[49]   Grubb, n 7 above, p 312.

done little to alleviate the emotional distress felt by relatives whose loved one's body was unknowingly incomplete at the time of burial.

(b) Organ Retention Scandals

Scandals at both Alder Hey Hospital in Liverpool and Bristol Royal Infirmary revealed to a shocked public that the retention of organs and body parts after post-mortems was a routine practice. The fact that the deceased were mainly children and that their parents had not given informed consent to the retention led to public inquiries.[50] It soon became apparent that the problem was larger than just these two hospitals and the Government's Chief Medical Officer revealed that more than 54,300 organs, body parts, stillborn children and fetuses were held by hospitals across England.[51] The lack of consent issue was perpetuated by the (mis)use of the word 'tissue'. Many of the recently bereaved parents gave consent for tissue to be removed and retained at the post-mortem. Almost invariably they understood 'tissue' in its colloquial sense of a small tissue sample, perhaps preserved on a slide. When the word tissue was used by doctors when seeking consent, however, they meant it in its technical definition of any part of the human body, including major organs and body parts. There is no doubt that the consent given by parents for tissue retention was uninformed. Whatever the medical meaning of the word tissue, it was nothing other than misleading to use it in conversations with grieving relatives and (even more so) on official consent forms.[52] The distinction between major organs and small tissue samples is revealed by the instinctive compulsion felt by many of the parents to hold additional burials to reunite the extracted organs with the bodies of their deceased children. Many of the parents were extremely distressed by the thought that their child was buried incomplete.

The issues raised by the Alder Hey and Bristol scandals were considered judicially in *AB v Leeds Teaching Hospital*.[53] This case revealed that at Leeds also, organs and body parts of deceased children were retained by the hospital after the post-mortem. The parents of these children claimed damages against the hospital for psychiatric injury. The facts of the case undoubtedly make harrowing reading: one couple, despite specifically requesting that all organs be returned with the

---

[50] The inquiries led to a series of reports: the Redfern Report ('The Royal Liverpool Children's Inquiry Report' (2001) in respect of Alder Hey); the Kennedy Report ('The Inquiry into the Management of Care of Children receiving Complex Heart Surgery at the Royal Bristol Infirmary, Interim Report' (2000)); and the McLean Report ('Independent Review Group on Retention of Organs at Post-mortems, Final Report' (2001) in respect of similar issues in Scotland).

[51] Chief Medical Officer, 'Report of a Census of Organs and Tissues Retained by Pathology Services in England' (2001) available at www.doh.gov.uk/organcensus/index.htm.

[52] Skene makes the point that the Reports of the Inquiries into these scandals fall into a similar trap. For example, the Bristol Report avoids using 'tissue' as an umbrella term but still groups together disparate things so 'human material' is defined as including organs and tissue. Would it be more appropriate to distinguish between organs and small tissue samples? (See Skene, n 20 above, p 113.)

[53] [2005] QB 506.

body for burial when consenting to a post-mortem, discovered many years later that their child's brain, heart, lungs and spinal cord had been retained by the hospital.[54] Again, the parents had thought that the use of the word 'tissue' in the post-mortem consent forms referred to small samples of tissue, rather than major organs.[55] The court's judgment is long and complex but there are three main points of general importance. First, the court held that consent to carry out a post-mortem necessarily includes consent to all the proper procedures involved in a post-mortem, including the removal and retention of organs for diagnostic purposes.[56] It was crucial here that the retention was solely for diagnostic purposes rather than for research, as at Alder Hey. The court emphasised that the doctors at Leeds had all acted in good faith.[57] Retention for research raises the possibility of selfish motives and/or a conflict of interests which is not existent in respect of retention for diagnostic purposes. As a consequences of the court's decision that removal of organs is included in consent to a post-mortem, it was held that the removal of organs in the cases before it was lawful 'and the right of the parents to possess them, based on a duty to bury, does not arise'.[58] This is a clear authority that relatives of the deceased, even parents of a minor, do not have any legal right to obtain possession of all parts of the deceased's body before burial. While they are entitled to return of the body, it was held that this could not realistically mean every part of the body when a post-mortem has been performed.

The second major point decided by the court was that the hospital was able to obtain property rights over the retained organs. The court established this by applying the *Doodeward* exception. It was held that, because 'to dissect and fix an organ from a child's body requires work and a great deal of skill', the pathologists had acquired a possessory right over the organs and were entitled to dispose of them.[59] This seems a natural application of the *Doodeward* requirement of the exercise of work or skill but it must be noted that the decision in *AB* is inconsistent with the view in *Dobson* that fixing a brain in paraffin was not a sufficient exercise of work or skill to enable the acquisition of possessory rights by the pathologist.

So far the decision of the court in *AB* seems to be weighted against the parents. However, the final important point decided by the court was that the doctors owed the parents a duty of care when obtaining consent for a post-mortem. This duty existed despite the fact that the parents were not the patients of the doctors. The duty of care was held to include a duty to give the parents an explanation of the purpose of the post-mortem and details of what it involves, including alerting

---

[54] *Ibid*, para 5.
[55] *Ibid*, para 39.
[56] *Ibid*, para 126.
[57] *Ibid*, para 115.
[58] *Ibid*, para 157.
[59] *Ibid*, para 148.

them to the possibility that organs may be retained.[60] The court accepted that there may be an exception to this general duty to inform if it would be unnecessarily distressing for the parents to know the details[61] but it was held that this must be assessed on individual circumstances and not amount to a blanket practice.[62] In this case, the court held that the doctors obtaining consent for the post-mortem had breached their duty of care and some compensation was available where the breach caused genuine psychiatric injury to the parents.

At the end of the lengthy judgment in *AB*, there is a brief tagged-on mention of the Human Rights Act 1998 in which it is held, on the basis of hypothetical agreed facts, that the use of a brain for research purposes without consent will engage the family's Article 8(1) rights.[63] There is no analysis, however, and the judgment as a whole lacks any recognition of the key role of human rights in situations of conflict such as this. There is little doubt that the retention of organs and body parts without consent engages the Article 8 and 9 rights of loved ones. The right to respect for family life and to freedom of religion and conscience must both include religious observances in relation to a relative's dead body. The devastation caused to families who subsequently discovered that they had been denied the ability to bury their relative in a complete state has the potential to amount to an infringement of the family's rights in respect of the process of bereavement. However, neither Article 8 nor Article 9 are absolute and competing societal interests may come into play. The *AB* case concerned the removal of organs for diagnostic purposes. Such a justification may be regarded as sufficient to satisfy the 'necessary in a democratic society' requirement of Articles 8(2) and 9(2). The legitimate aim of protecting public health would be applicable here. However, retention of organs for undefined research purposes, as at Alder Hey and Bristol, may fail the proportionality test, especially when the stockpile of organs at those hospitals was never in fact put to beneficial use.

One difficulty underlying this subject is the applicability of the law on informed consent. On the one hand, a failure to obtain consent from relations for the removal and retention of organs may engage their Convention rights to the extent that it undermines their ability to observe religious conventions. On the other hand, it is unclear exactly what role consent can play when it relates to the body of another (deceased) individual. As Harris explains (and as we have seen in Chapter 4), consent usually protects and facilitates autonomy and/or bodily integrity. It therefore has no role to play in respect of dead bodies:

> Autonomy involves the capacity to make choices, it involves acts of the will, and the dead have no capacities – they have no will, no preferences, wants nor desires, the dead cannot be autonomous and so cannot have their autonomy violated. Equally, the dead

---

[60]   *Ibid*, para 206.
[61]   *Ibid*, para 231.
[62]   *Ibid*, para 238.
[63]   *Ibid*, para 298.

cannot have their bodily integrity violated, for violation consists not simply in a breach of bodily integrity, but in a breach of bodily integrity that is not consented to.[64]

It could be argued that on this issue we are concerned with the autonomous choices of the deceased's relatives rather than the deceased himself and that, therefore, Harris's rejection of the application of autonomy is not dispositive. However, in English law, as we have seen in Chapter 5, a human being can only provide consent for interventions on another human being if the latter lacks capacity and where the consent of the relatives represents a reasonable interpretation of the latter's best interests.[65] This becomes problematic once the latter is deceased: does a dead person have interests of any kind? There can certainly be no enduring interest in preserving the physical integrity of a dead body for, as Harris graphically points out, this is quite impossible to achieve: 'No dead body remains intact; the worms . . . or the fire and eventually the dust claims it. It is disintegrated, dispersed and may end as the bung in a beer barrel or the mortar in a wall. The alternatives are not burial intact or disintegration. There is simply no alternative which does not involve disintegration.'[66]

One unfortunate consequence of the Alder Hey and Bristol scandals was the prioritisation of a family's interest in ensuring the bodies of their loved ones were intact prior to burial. This 'quite absurd, if understandable, preoccupation with reverence and respect for bodily tissue'[67] overlooks the loss of tissue in other contexts which we do not mourn: on toilet paper, bandages, sanitary towels and in blood.[68] The perceived need to reunite retained tissue or organs with the remainder of the body is born of emotional distress and compounded by the regrettable lack of information given to relatives at the time of retention. We should be sympathetic but whether we should allow the law to prioritise these issues, when the shortage of organs for transplant is posing a direct threat to the lives of many in the same society, is an arguable issue.[69] This is exactly what happened as a result of the public scandals on retention of organs, however, as the government wasted no time in announcing that it would change the law to prevent similar events from happening again in the future. Circumventing the twin problems of the inappropriateness of 'consent' to treatment of a dead body and the inaccuracy of the illusion of preserving the physical integrity of a corpse, the government introduced a new Human Tissue Act which prioritises the need for informed consent before organs or tissue are taken from a dead body.

[64] J Harris, 'Law and Regulation of Retained Organs: The Ethical issues' (2002) 22 *LS* 527, at pp 531-32.
[65] Harris, *ibid*, p 528.
[66] Harris, *ibid*, p 547.
[67] Harris, *ibid*, p 546.
[68] *Ibid.*
[69] Two opposing views are strongly and convincingly argued by Harris (*ibid*) and Brazier (M Brazier, 'Retained Organs: Ethics and Humanity' (2002) 22 *LS* 50).

(c)   The Human Tissue Act 2004

The pre-existing legislation, the Human Tissue Act 1961, was the subject of much criticism, and not only because it was the relevant legislation in place when the organ retention scandals occurred. The problems inherent in the 1961 Act included an ambiguous concept of the 'person lawfully in possession of the body'. This person was entitled under section 1(1) and (2) to authorise the removal and use of parts of a dead body for therapeutic, educational or research purposes. The only additional requirement was that either the removal and use had been requested by the deceased[70] or there was no reason to believe that the deceased or surviving relatives objected.[71] The 'person lawfully in possession' was, therefore, given a crucial role in the 1961 Act but there was no certainty as to who qualified as this person. Conceivably it could have been either the executor (who, as we have seen, has a limited right of possession of the body for burial purposes) or the hospital (who, if the deceased has died in hospital, has actual possession of the body). The latter seems to have been the most widely accepted view but such ambiguity in respect of a crucial aspect of the Act was undesirable. Further instances of ambiguity could also be found in the 1961 Act, such as the requirement that there be 'such reasonable enquiry as may be practicable' in the context of ruling out potential objections from surviving relatives, and indeed the scope of 'relative' itself.[72] Another major problem in respect of the 1961 Act, which particularly came to light in the organ retention scandals, was that there were no penalties imposed under the Act for non-compliance with the statutory requirements.

As a direct response to the organ retention scandals at Bristol and Alder Hey, the government introduced the Human Tissue Act 2004. Originally the government had intended to introduce only a short Bill rectifying the twin problems of the lack of informed consent from relatives and the lack of penalties for non-compliance. However, it subsequently chose to introduce a more wide-ranging reform of the human tissue laws.[73] A Human Tissue Authority is established and a licensing system put in place, comparable in many ways to the regulatory system under the Human Fertilisation and Embryology Act 1990.[74] Consent lies at the heart of the 2004 Act. The storage or use of dead bodies or 'relevant material' from the deceased requires consent if done for any of a number of specified purposes. These purposes include anatomical examination, determining the cause of death, public display, medical research, transplantation

---

[70]   Section 1(1).

[71]   Section 1(2).

[72]   Generally on the problems with the 1961 Act, see D Price, 'From Cosmos and Damian to Van Velzen: The Human Tissue Saga Continues' (2003) 11 *Med L Rev* 1.

[73]   See Price, *ibid*, pp 2-3.

[74]   See Chapter 8. The Human Tissue Authority and the Human Fertilisation and Embryology Authority are eventually to be merged to create a new body, the Regulatory Authority for Tissue and Embryos (RATE) as part of the government's rationalisation of regulatory agencies.

and education or training.[75] 'Relevant material' is defined broadly as human cells.[76] The consent required for that broad range of activities can be provided either by means of (a) the consent of the deceased; (b) the consent of a person nominated by the deceased;[77] or (c) the consent of a person in a 'qualifying relationship' to the deceased.[78] The latter are listed, in hierarchical order, as spouse or partner; parent or child; brother or sister; grandparent or grandchild; niece or nephew; stepfather or stepmother; half-brother or half-sister; and friend of longstanding. The consent must be sought from the relative ranked highest in the list, raising concerns about whether the ranking system is equally fitting for all families. In addition, it is not clear what the legal position will be if there is disagreement between relatives: while a relative of a lesser or the same rank cannot veto a consent, it is unclear if they can provide consent to overrule a refusal to consent from a relative of higher rank. Previously a veto from any surviving relative would have been sufficient in law.[79] The role of the relatives of the deceased is undoubtedly increased in the 2004 Act notwithstanding doubts expressed by many commentators about the applicability of 'consent' by a relative to the issue. As a response to the organ retention scandals, it is unconvincing,[80] and as a broader piece of reform with such a wide scope, including organs for transplantation, it threatens 'to throw the baby out with the bathwater'.[81] It is ironic that, in the midst of an organ shortage, this recent reform has further restricted the availability of organs with apparent disregard for the medical needs of society.

(d)   Shortage of Organs for Transplant

The shortage of organs for transplant is a serious issue which demands a serious response. During the passage of the Human Tissue Bill, the BMA proposed an

[75]   Schedule 1 Human Tissue Act 2004. In addition to the purposes listed in Sch 1, Part 1 which require consent regardless of whether the material is taken from a living or deceased person, Sch 1, Part 2 lists further purposes which require consent only if the material is from a deceased person, such as clinical audit, education or training and public health monitoring.

[76]   Section 53. The definition, which also applies to human material from living persons, excludes hair and nails of a living person, gametes and embryos outside the human body.

[77]   Where the deceased is a minor, the consent of a person with parental responsibility for the child replaces this option (s 2(7)).

[78]   Donation of the whole body for anatomical examination or public display requires explicit consent from the deceased (s 3(3)).

[79]   Price makes the point, however, that, even pre-2004, the position in practice required positive consent: 'The essential elements of the statute with respect to cadaveric donation will generally do no more than embed existing transplant practice in legislation. The central actors in the transplant process, notably transplant co-ordinators have adopted an explicit consent policy for many years, despite the actual wording of the 1961 Act' (Price (2005), n 41 above, at p 812).

[80]   Ironically, coroners' post-mortems (those required by the law) are exempted from the Act even though the events of Bristol and Alder Hey mainly involved retention after coroners' post-mortems. The crucial distinction between the retention of major organs and small tissue samples, which seems at the root of the scandals, is also ignored.

[81]   Price (2003), n 72 above, p 46.

'opting out' or 'presumed consent' system which was rejected by the government. The current system for organ transplants can best be described as an 'opting in' system in that the positive consent of the deceased will authorise the removal of organs for transplantation (or other) purposes. As we have seen, it goes slightly further than this because, even in the absence of consent by the deceased, a relative or nominated person can provide sufficient authorisation. An opting out system would entail an assumption that all deceased persons agree to the use of their organs after death <u>unless</u> they have previously registered an objection. Therefore, a person can opt out of the system but, if he fails to do so, then he is presumed to have consented. Presumed consent is always problematic because, if consent is an expression of autonomous choice, a presumption cannot create it. It is particularly problematic in this context as there will be a large proportion of society who fail to choose one way or the other due to a widespread discomfort in confronting issues of mortality. The illusion that a failure to register an objection is implicit consent cannot hold in such circumstances. Perhaps it is the illusion which needs to be disregarded, however, for it serves little purpose other than to ease our consciences. A failure to object to the use of one's organs after death does not imply consent, but neither does it imply objection. In the absence of an indication either way, it could be argued that we do a disservice to humanity by presuming a lack of altruism:

> if any presumption is made in the absence of an advanced directive or a clear autonomous expression of will, it should not be that the deceased would have wished to frustrate altruistic or beneficial purposes; it should rather be a presumption in favour of their good character that they would have wished to promote such purposes.[82]

To some limited extent the Human Tissue Act 2004 permits (as did the 1961 Act before it) the removal and use of organs without the deceased's consent and this is probably almost always done due to the willingness of relatives to presume altruistic intent into the deceased's failure to express an opinion on the use of his organs. However, under the Human Tissue Act 2004, the relatives retain a decisive veto. It is possible that the use of organs without the consent of either the deceased person or his or her relatives may engage the rights of the relatives to respect for family life and/or respect for religious beliefs (if the reluctance to allow organ removal is due to religious sentiment). However, the rights rarely taken into account here are the rights of those dying while on a transplant waiting list. While we have seen the difficulties of implying a positive right to treatment under the Human Rights Act, in this context we are looking only at whether the legitimate aims of the protection of the rights of others and the

---

[82] Harris, n 64 above, p 541. Brazier criticises Harris for postulating 'a society in which cold rationality drives all human actions' (Brazier, n 69 above, p 551). It could be countered that, while rationality, cold or otherwise, does not always drive human behaviour, it, rather than emotion, should indeed drive the law.

protection of health will necessitate a restriction on the rights of grieving relatives. Striking a balance between the conflicting rights and interests of those in need of a transplant and those who must come to terms with losing a loved one, as well as with respecting the autonomous wishes and values of the deceased when alive, is no easy task. That the HTA 2004 fails to strike an appropriate balance is clear, however. A preoccupation with consent where it is not appropriate (ie in the hands of relatives), the omission of any attempt to confront the organ shortage problem, and the illusion of enabling a family to bury their loved one intact, have led to an unsatisfactory Act that misleads relatives, ignores those in need of transplants and continues to conflate a number of distinct issues by applying the same rules to starkly different types of human material with potentially different beneficial purposes.

IV. Conclusion

This chapter has looked at the way in which law and philosophy seeks to protect human bodies and extracted human material. At its heart has been the challenging question of whether we should own our own bodies. It was proposed above that self-ownership may bring some benefits in respect of the laws dealing with living bodies. In theory self-ownership could also have the advantage of securing an ability to choose how our bodies are disposed of after death, as we do with our other property. However, this would need to be balanced against the pressing need, discussed above, to protect the health of society by utilising viable organs for transplant. This book emphasises the role human rights can and should play in the law and ethics of medical treatment. The human rights discussed all have autonomy at their core and this must remain the fundamental guiding principle for these topics but, in the field of the status of the human body, the introduction of a self-ownership dimension to work alongside, and perhaps give greater meaning to, autonomy is to be recommended. The evolution of property rights in body parts or human tissue from other persons demonstrates that property is not an entirely inappropriate framework here, and ownership of our own bodies would return the ownership to where it belongs: the individual whose autonomous choice controls the actions and survival of the body. Once autonomous choice is no longer possible, theories of property should yield to the more pressing societal need of the preservation of the lives of others.

Recommended further reading

D Price, 'From Cosmos and Damian to Van Velzen: The Human Tissue Saga Continues' (2003) 11 *Med L Rev* 1.

D Price, 'The Human Tissue Act 2004' (2005) 68 *MLR* 798.

K Mason and G Laurie, 'Consent or Property? Dealing with the Body and its Parts in the Shadow of Bristol and Alder Hey' (2001) 64 *MLR* 711.

J Harris, 'Law and Regulation of Retained Organs: The Ethical issues' (2002) 22 *LS* 527.

D Morgan, *Issues in Medical Law and Ethics* (2001, Cavendish, London), Chapter 6.

N Naffine, 'The Legal Structure of Self-Ownership: Or the Self-Possessed Man and the Woman Possessed' (1998) 25 *JLS* 193.

8

Medically Assisted Conception and a Right to Reproduce?

New technology in respect of medically assisted conception has meant that infertility in a woman or her partner is no longer a bar to conceiving children, nor is being single, gay, post-menopausal or a virgin. At the same time, we are living in a human rights age. When this trend collides with the contemporary emphasis upon individual rights, discussed throughout this book, we may encounter calls for a right to reproduce: a right to have a child protected in law and made possible by new technology. Today, an infertile man or woman has a number of options, depending upon the nature of the infertility, including:[1] assisted insemination, either by a partner or donor (AID); in vitro fertilisation (IVF, where an embryo is created outside the womb, using either the woman's own eggs or donated eggs); Gamete Intra-Fallopian Transfer (GIFT, where eggs and sperm are injected into a woman's fallopian tubes to fertilise there); and Intra-Cytoplasmic Sperm Injection (ICSI, a form of IVF where a single sperm is injected into an egg). It should also be noted that surrogacy arrangements can be used in conjunction with IVF or AID and may add further moral and legal complexity to the issue. These medical advances have brought with them complex moral issues. The Human Fertilisation and Embryology Act 1990, which sought to offer a legal response to some of these issues, is currently under review.[2]

---

[1] The scientific advances which have made such ideas possible are not completely new. The first so-called 'test tube baby' – a child conceived outside the womb – was born in 1978 and the use of donor insemination has existed since the 19th century.

[2] After widespread consultation, the government issued a White Paper in December 2006 entitled 'Review of the Human Fertilisation and Embryology Act: Proposals for Revised Legislation (including the Establishment of the Regulatory Authority for Tissue and Embryos)' (Cm 6989, 2006). Where relevant, proposed changes in this document will be noted throughout this chapter but the bulk of the discussion relies upon the existing legislation. This is justified given that, despite a number of proposals for reform of the 1990 Act, the white paper makes clear that the core principles of the Act will remain unchanged: 'The Government has concluded that the foundations of the current law remain sound, and provide an effective and appropriate model of regulation' (para 1.8). The most significant proposed change for the purposes of this chapter is in relation to assigning parentage and will be referred to in that section. Furthermore, the white paper refers to the previously announced commitment to replace the Human Fertilisation and Embryology Authority and the Human Tissue Authority with a new body called the Regulatory Authority for Tissue and Embryos (RATE).

The fifteen years since its creation have seen both further medical advances in this field, including pre-implantation genetic diagnosis (which enables the selection of embryos for implantation based upon genetic traits) and even the possibility of cloning, and also the evolution of society's moral views on issues such as family, infertility and technology. It is not surprising then that the Act is under review nor that it has been described as 'a temporary marshalling of arguments, a transitory marker in continued moral reflection'.[3] The growth in human rights protection is a key factor for consideration when the laws governing assisted conception are reviewed. This chapter considers whether a right to reproduce is a meaningful, viable and necessary development in modern English medical law.

I. The Origins of a Right to Reproduce

The idea of a right to reproduce derives from a number of diverse sources. First, a number of commentators have asserted the concept of procreative autonomy or liberty.[4] Ronald Dworkin, for example, identifies procreative autonomy – a freedom to make choices about reproduction – as a vital aspect of the concept of human dignity which is a feature of all democratic societies.[5] Dworkin was primarily using this idea to assist with analysis of the abortion debate but John Harris and John Robertson have both developed theories of procreative autonomy and liberty respectively which apply also to medically assisted conception. There is some theoretical dispute as to whether such autonomy or liberty should be limited to a negative right to be free from state interference with choices to procreate or to avoid procreation,[6] or whether it should extend to some positive right of access to medically assisted conception. We will return to this issue later. What is clear is that any concept of procreative autonomy/liberty would not entail absolute freedom to procreate but would instead be a presumptive primacy subject only to restrictions to prevent substantial harm to others.[7]

Second, the domestic courts have occasionally recognised a common law right to reproduce. This was first apparent within the context of non-consensual sterilisations of the mentally incompetent. For example, in *Re D (a minor)*, Heilbron J recognised that a 'sterilisation is an operation which involves the

---

[3] RG Lee and D Morgan, *Human Fertilisation and Embryology: Regulating the Reproductive Revolution* (London, Blackstone Press, 2001), p 24.

[4] See R Dworkin, *Life's Dominion: An Argument about Abortion and Euthanasia* (London, HarperCollins, 1993); J Harris, 'Rights and Reproductive Choice' in J Harris and S Holm (eds), *The Future of Human Reproduction: Ethics, Choice, and Regulation* (Oxford, Clarendon Press, 1998); JA Robertson, *Children of Choice: Freedom and the New Reproductive Technologies* (Princeton, Princeton University Press, 1994).

[5] Dworkin, *ibid*, pp 166-67.

[6] Robertson, n 3 above, p 23.

[7] *Ibid*, p 35.

deprivation of a basic human rights, namely the right of a woman to reproduce'.[8] Subsequently, Lord Hailsham in the House of Lords approved this idea but, significantly, rejected its application to the mentally incompetent woman in the case before him: 'To talk of the "basic right" to reproduce of an individual who is not capable of knowing the causal connection between intercourse and child-birth, the nature of pregnancy, what is involved in delivery, unable to form maternal instincts or to care for a child appears to me wholly to part company with reality'.[9] This view presents some difficulties. If there is a right to reproduce protected at law, it must be available to all. The exclusion of a class of persons in this way is unacceptable. On the other hand, it is perfectly acceptable to recognise limitations to the right. In the case of the mentally incompetent, a conflicting interest in preventing harm to the patient, and perhaps even a conflicting right to treatment, may come into play. Indeed, what Lord Hailsham's restriction on the right to reproduce in this context fails to appreciate is that non-consensual sterilisation will prima facie amount to a violation of the patient's right to physical integrity and will require independent justification regardless of the application of the controversial right to reproduce.

Third, Article 12 of the European Convention of Human Rights explicitly protects a right to marry and found a family. A number of points should be noted in respect of this, however. First, it is not an absolute right. Indeed the exceptions to it are potentially the most wide-ranging of any of the convention rights. Article 12 merely states that the right is subject to 'the national law governing the exercise of this right'. This is, perhaps, not quite as unhelpful as it at first appears because the European Court of Human Rights has previously ruled that there is a minimum standard which must not be infringed by the state. For example, in *Rees v United Kingdom*, the Court held that any limitations on the right 'must not restrict or reduce the right in such a way or to such an extent that the very essence of the right is impaired'.[10] Furthermore, the prohibition of discrimination in Article 14 means that the right to found a family must be secured 'without discrimination on any grounds such as sex, race, colour, language, religion, political or other opinion, national or social origin, association with a national minority, property, birth or other status'. This requirement of non-discrimination in the enjoyment of relevant convention rights is an issue we will return to later. It is sufficient here to acknowledge that while laws may be introduced to govern the right to found a family, they must not threaten the essence of the right nor may they be discriminatory on any grounds.

The second point to note in respect of Article 12 is that it links the right to found a family with the right to marry. This has led Baroness Hale to regard the

---

[8]   [1976] 1 All ER 326 at 332.
[9]   *Re B (a minor) (wardship: sterilisation)* [1987] 2 All ER 206 at p 213.
[10]   (1986) Series A, No 106, para 50.

right to marry and found a family as 'one right, not two'[11] and this did seem to be the favoured approach of the European Court of Human Rights until recently.[12] However it means both that the right to found a family is restricted to those who are married and, perhaps more of a problem, that the right to marry is restricted to those who are able to found a family.[13] The 2002 case of *Goodwin v United Kingdom*[14] made a considerable advance in this area when the Court found a violation of Article 12's right to marry in respect of the United Kingdom's prohibition on marriage between a man and a male to female transsexual. Thus, by recognising that a right to marry may be disassociated from the question of founding a family, the Court may have opened the door to freeing the right to found a family from marriage. What remains clear, however, is that the wording of Article 12 restricts both rights (assuming there are two) to 'men and women of marriageable age'. The Court upheld the importance of this principle in *Goodwin* despite recognising that the issue of gender cannot nowadays always be decided solely with reference to biological criteria. So it is clear that Article 12 offers no protection other than to a man and a woman of marriageable age. It is not obvious from the text of Article 12, however, nor is it inevitable that either the domestic courts or the European Court of Human Rights would require, that such a couple be married before they seek to assert their limited right to found a family. Uniquely, however, Article 12 does appear to be a right for couples rather than individuals. This connects well with the choice of wording in Article 12: a right to found a family rather than merely to reproduce. It appears that it is the institution of the 'family' (however one may define that), rather than an individual's freedom to reproduce, which is the basis of Article 12's protection.

The gaps in protection apparent within Article 12 are compensated for by the additional protection offered by Article 8. This provision of the ECHR protects an individual's 'right to respect for private and family life'. Reproduction clearly falls within the category of 'private' matters which may find some protection in Article 8, although it should be noted that in an abortion case the European Commission of Human Rights has held that pregnancy is not solely a private matter.[15] Nevertheless, it is clear that reproduction is so central to our personal identity that it forms a core interest in our private lives. Article 8(2) declares that 'there shall be no interference by a public authority with the exercise of this right'. There are exceptions however and a public authority is permitted to interfere with the right to respect for private life if such interference is in accordance with the law and necessary in a democratic society for a number of specified aims.

---

[11]   B Hale, *From the Test Tube to the Coffin: Choice and Regulation in Private Life* (London, Sweet and Maxwell, 1996), p 8.

[12]   See DJ Feldman, *Civil Liberties and Human Rights in England and Wales*, 2nd edn (Oxford, Oxford University Press, 2002), pp 728-29.

[13]   Thus excluding transsexuals. See, for example, *Rees v United Kingdom* (1986) Series A, No 106; *Sheffield and Horsham v United Kingdom* (1998) Reports V.

[14]   (2002) 35 EHRR 18.

[15]   *Bruggemann and Scheuten v Germany* (1977) 10 DR 100.

Therefore, within this Article there is an explicit balancing of individual (private) rights with societal (public) interests. Included within the specified aims which may justify an interference with this right are three of particular relevance to this discussion. First, the rights and freedoms of others is specified as a legitimate aim. This will include, for example, the rights of the donor of genetic material. It is doubtful, however, that it would include the potential child. While some protection for an unborn child under the convention has not yet been ruled out,[16] it seems likely that a potential person must at least exist before it can be offered any protection.[17] Second, Article 8(2) controversially includes the protection of morals as a legitimate aim for interference with an individual's private life. This may have implications for non-traditional family units and also for any particularly controversial treatments, for example human cloning, which it could be argued were contrary to public morality. Third, Article 8(2) permits the economic well-being of the country to serve as a justification for interference. It has never been entirely clear what this might entail but the existence of finite resources within a health care system may legitimise restrictions upon access to assisted conception techniques. Article 8(2) imposes a negative obligation upon the state not to interfere with the right (subject to limitations just mentioned) but in addition Article 8(1) has been interpreted as imposing a positive obligation upon the state by virtue of the requirement of respect for private life.[18] This may be of significance in the context of arguments that the state should positively assist (by means of facilities and funding) rather than merely not interfere with a reproduction. So, the ECHR, and thus the HRA, provides potential for the development of a strong right to reproduce in the terms of Articles 8, 12 and 14.

Further protection within Europe might be thought to derive from the European Convention on Human Rights and Biomedicine (ECHRB). Although not legally binding, this international agreement often offers more specific protection for rights within the medical law field. Unusually for this document, however, its only contribution to the issue of assisted conception is negative. Article 14 ECHRB declares that medically assisted procreation techniques should not be used for the purpose of sex selection. Nowhere in the Convention is there any suggestion of a right to reproduce.[19] The preamble does remind us, however, of 'the need to respect the human being both as an individual and as a member of the human species' and warns that 'the misuse of biology and medicine may lead

---

[16]   *Vo v France* (2005) 10 EHRR 12.

[17]   When considering the legitimate aims of an interference with Art 10 in *Open Door Counselling and Dublin Well Woman Centre v Ireland*, the Court accepted the protection of the unborn in the Irish Constitution as amounting to the legitimate aim of the protection of morals and used this conclusion to avoid answering the question of whether the 'protection of others' extends to the unborn ((1992) Series A, No 246; 15 EHRR 244, at para 63).

[18]   See, for example, *Marckx v Belgium* (1979) Series A, No 31; 2 EHRR 330; *X and Y v Netherlands* (1985) Series A, No 91; 8 EHRR 235.

[19]   There is also protection for the embryo in Art 18, including a total prohibition on the creation of human embryos for research purposes, and a prohibition in Art 21 on financial gain from the human body: 'The human body and its parts shall not, as such, give rise to financial gain.'

to acts endangering human dignity . . .'. As we will see, these concerns may have some relevance to certain assisted conception techniques.

II.   Access to Treatment: A Right to Reproduce in Practice?

The Human Fertilisation and Embryology Act which governs this area does not exclude any person or category of persons from procreating by means of assisted conception. (Nor does the Code of Practice.) However, the allocation of finite resources under the NHS means that public funding for assisted conception treatment is often very limited, leaving many people with no choice but to self-fund the treatment. For those who lack the financial resources to afford such expensive treatment, the lack of public funding in effect excludes them from treatment. An upper age limit is one common criterion for NHS funding. The limit is usually set at 35, and when an attempt to challenge this policy by means of judicial review was made in 1994 it was held to be neither illegal nor irrational for a health authority to take into account the age of the woman seeking treatment when providing IVF treatment on an extremely limited budget.[20] Other common criteria for funding include the existence of a stable relationship, no existing children and a limit of three cycles of treatment.[21]

The first question which we should address is, therefore, whether a right to reproduce includes a right to receive free treatment designed to assist reproduction. This is an aspect of a broader question of whether a patient is ever able to claim a right to any particular treatment. Traditionally, as we saw in Chapter 2, the English courts have rejected any such right to treatment and declined to become involved in treatment decisions which are based upon the allocation of finite resources.[22] They have, however, been willing to criticise a blanket policy against funding certain treatments.[23] Each case should, therefore, be decided on its merits although it is entirely acceptable to accord some treatments lower funding priority than others. Assisted conception treatment such as IVF is likely to be given a lower priority by NHS Trusts than, for example, cancer treatment. This is appropriate and no court would regard this as a violation of an

---

[20]   *R v Sheffield Health Authority, ex p Seale* (1994) 25 BMLR 1. In respect of age, a survey of clinics revealed that while only 5% said they would refuse treatment to any woman over 40, 89% would refuse treatment to any woman over 50 (D Savas and S Treece, 'Fertility Clinics: One Code of Practice?' (1998) 3 *Med Law Int* 243, at p 250).

[21]   See E Jackson, *Regulating Reproduction: Law, Technology and Autonomy* (Oxford, Hart Publishing, 2001), p 198.

[22]   See *R v Secretary of State for Health, ex p Walker* (1987) 3 BMLR 32; *R v Cambridge Health Authority, ex p B* [1995] 2 All ER 129.

[23]   See *R v North West Lancashire Health Authority, ex p A* [1999] Lloyd's Rep Med 399. The treatment in question in this case was gender reassignment surgery for transsexuals. See Chapter 2 for further discussion.

individual's right to reproduce.[24] Nevertheless, an individual may be entitled under the protection offered by a right to reproduce to expect fair treatment in the allocation of funded treatment and, more generally, in access to self-funded treatment.[25] A number of conflicting interests may arise in the context of assisted conception, however, and these may potentially restrict an individual's access to treatment. The nature of these conflicting interests will now be considered.

(a) Conflicting Interests I: Welfare of the Child

While no one is excluded from treatment under the statutory terms, section 13(5) of the 1990 Act requires account to be taken of the welfare of any child born as a result of the treatment, including, controversially, the need of that child for a father. (It is proposed that the latter requirement will be removed when the 1990 Act is revised.)[26] The dice are thus loaded in favour of heterosexual couples. This is borne out in a survey of clinics by Savas and Treece in which over 50 per cent of the clinics replying to the survey (both NHS and private) admitted that they would not provide treatment for a single woman and similarly over 50 per cent would not provide treatment for a homosexual couple.[27] Both of these exclusions may enable arguments to be raised on the basis of discriminatory access to treatment essential to a person's right to reproduce.[28] Certainly the denial of access to treatment on the grounds of sexuality does prima facie appear to be discrimination contrary to Article 14 of the ECHR.[29] What must be remembered,

[24] As Douglas notes, the state is not obliged to provide assisted conception for all the infertile because, after all, 'we do not assume that the state should find suitable partners for single fertile people' (G Douglas, *Law, Fertility and Reproduction* (London, Sweet & Maxwell, 1991), p 21.

[25] See Hale: 'The state cannot have a duty to supply a service on demand. Would-be parents may, however, be entitled to expect fair treatment from those who allocate what the state does supply or who regulate what others will supply either voluntarily or for reward' (Hale, n 11 above, pp 8–9). Certainly, blatant discrimination will be illegal. See *R v Ethical Committee of St Mary's Hospital (Manchester) ex p H*, in which Schiemann J held that an exclusion of, for example, all Jews from IVF treatment may well be illegal, although the refusal of treatment for a woman based on her previous convictions for prostitution was held not to be unreasonable ([1988] 1 FLR 512).

[26] The government White Paper (n. 2 above) proposes the retention of a welfare of the child requirement (para 2.23) but proposes the removal of the reference to the need of that child for a father (para 2.26). At the time of writing there remains the prospect of much heated debate before this amendment becomes law.

[27] Savas and Treece, n 20 above, p 250.

[28] In Australia, the South Australian Supreme Court held in 1996 that the restriction of IVF to married couples discriminated against single women on the grounds of marital status: *Pearce v South Australia Health Commission* (1996) 66 SASR 486.

[29] See McLean: 'whilst the state may have no general duty to facilitate reproduction through technology or the supply of a partner, once facilities are provided – for example, through IVF and surrogacy programmes – to deny access on grounds of sexuality is to infringe the right on a discriminatory basis' (S McLean, 'The Right to Reproduce' in T Campbell, D Goldberg, S McLean and T Mullen (eds), *Human Rights: From Rhetoric to Reality* (Oxford, Basil Blackwell, 1986), p 111).

however, is that a right to reproduce is not absolute (under any of its guises) and so the individual's right needs to be balanced against any pertinent conflicting interests.

Section 13(5) of the 1990 Act is designed to protect the welfare of the unborn child, clearly a vital aspect of the legal regulation of assisted conception, although one which some commentators have argued discriminates against infertile people because those who conceive naturally are not required to prove they will be good parents before giving birth.[30] And even if they were required to do so, could we agree upon which characteristics would be desirable for parents? We may in fact find that it is environmental factors such as poverty, poor housing, and badly funded local schools which are more detrimental to a child's welfare than the characteristics, and especially the sexuality and marital status, of the potential parents.[31] The bottom line is that even if society wished to license potential parents before they were permitted to conceive, this is not viable, and so we are forced to wait for a threat to a child's welfare to arise after birth before the law and state can intervene to protect the child.[32] The availability of medically assisted conception means that a pre-conception licensing system is possible in this context. Thus, even if self-funding is not a problem, treatment may be denied on the basis of a perceived danger to the welfare of the potential child. Emily Jackson is very critical of this dual approach, arguing that 'the law purports to restrict access to infertility treatment [merely] because it can' and that 'the ease with which certain people's freedom can be restricted does not, without more, justify such restrictions'.[33] It should be added that such infringement of individual freedom has the potential to be unlawful when it amounts to a violation of a right to reproduce derived from the convention rights. It is also worth remembering that, where there are concerns about the welfare of the future child, the only alternative to the child being born into that situation is for the child not to be born at all. Whether no existence is ever preferable to an existence is a difficult question which the courts have grappled with in different contexts.[34] Certainly a life free of pain and severe disability can surely not be regarded as worse for that individual than never being born, even if the family situation is not ideal? Thus the welfare of the future child is a concept based upon a misconception of the options open to the parties.[35]

---

[30] See Harris: 'If we are serious that people demonstrate their adequacy as parents *in advance* of being permitted to procreate, then we should license all parents. Since we are evidently not serious about this, we should not discriminate against those who need assistance with procreation' (Harris, n 3 above, p 7).

[31] See Harris: 'One of the most reliable predictors of bad outcomes for children is poverty, but no one has yet suggested that the poor should not be permitted to reproduce' (*ibid*, p 15).

[32] Although harm caused to the child before birth may have postnatal legal implications: *D (a minor) v Berkshire County Council* [1987] AC 317. See Chapter 10.

[33] Jackson, n 21 above, p 196.

[34] See Chapters 10 (wrongful birth cases) and 11 (withdrawing life-sustaining treatment).

[35] The Human Fertilisation and Embryology Authority has recently reviewed the topic of the welfare of the child and has changed its guidance to clinics. The most important change is the HFEA's

(b) Conflicting Interests II: Consent of Gamete Donors

The right to reproduce is not absolute, however, as a sufficiently strong conflicting interest may outweigh it, and a good example of this is the fact that all adult parties must give valid, written consent to their participation in the treatment process. This means, for example, that the gamete providers retain a veto over the use and storage of their genetic material. Given that proprietary rights in the embryo have been consistently denied, such control seems curious. Furthermore, the high priority given to the consent of the potential father here is out of all proportion with the father's normal powerless position. As Harris notes, 'men are notorious for leaving their gametes behind in all sorts of places, some of which may well result in the creation of life . . .[and] we normally accept that they have no say in the outcome one way or another'.[36] The father cannot normally prevent a woman giving birth to his child even if, subsequent to the conception, he rescinds his consent, but he can prevent the use of his sperm if the procreation is to be medically assisted.

This point was before the Court of Appeal in the recent case of *Evans v Amicus Healthcare*,[37] a case which goes to the heart of the debate about a right to reproduce. The situation in this case was that Natalie Evans and her partner Howard Johnston sought to conceive by means of IVF. Tragically it was discovered that Ms Evans had a cancerous tumour in both ovaries. She needed to have an operation to remove the tumours after which she would be forever unable to conceive a child. Before the operation, however, the clinic was able to harvest, and fertilise with Mr Johnston's sperm, eleven eggs resulting in the creation of six embryos which were then frozen for future implantation. The relevant consent forms were signed by both parties. Subsequently the couple split up and Mr Johnston withdrew his consent for the use and storage of the embryos. As these embryos were the only way in which Ms Evans would ever have a child of her own, she challenged the clinic's refusal to continue the treatment on the basis that this was a violation of her right to respect for private life. The Court of Appeal accepted that an interference with this right had occurred (and thus has provided authority for the earlier proposition that Article 8 incorporates a form of a right to reproduce). However, the more difficult issue before the court was whether this interference was justified under Article 8(2). The conflicting interest in question here was the right of Mr Johnston. As mentioned earlier, Article 8(2) envisages a balancing of conflicting rights, if appropriate, and the question for

---

conclusion that there should be a presumption to provide treatment to all who request it, unless there is evidence that the child to be born would face a risk of serious medical, physical or psychological harm. This is a welcome interpretation of s 13(5) which focuses on preventing a child being born into an abusive environment. Whether this guidance will have the intended effect in practice remains to be seen ('Tomorrow's Children: Report of the Policy Review of Welfare of the Child Assessments in Licensed Assisted Conception Clinics' (2005) (available at the HFEA website: www.hfea.gov.uk).

[36] Harris, n 3 above, p 18.

[37] [2004] 3 All ER 1025.

the Court of Appeal was, therefore, whether the interference with Ms Evans' rights was disproportionate to the aim of protecting Mr Johnston's rights. The Court of Appeal held that it was not disproportionate and so there was no violation of Article 8. The argument that a potential father is given more rights – and correspondingly the potential mother less rights – in this context was held not to amount to discrimination on the basis of infertility. As Arden LJ explained, 'in a world in which many people have come to accept a woman's right of choice as to whether she should have a child or not, the genetic father should have the equivalent right – a right greater than that conferred by nature'.[38]

The UK's approach to these ethically difficult issues was approved by the European Court of Human Rights in *Evans v United Kingdom*.[39] The Court, sitting as a Chamber,[40] confirmed that Article 8 incorporates 'the right to respect for both the decisions to become and not to become a parent'.[41] The Court granted a wide margin of appreciation (or measure of discretion) to the UK because it recognised that there is no international consensus with regard to the regulation of IVF treatment[42] and that it 'gives rise to sensitive moral and ethical issues against a background of fast-moving medical and scientific developments'.[43] The UK had sought to regulate this area by means of a detailed piece of legislation and the Court found that the balance struck within it was within the state's margin of appreciation.[44] It did note, however, that a different balance could legitimately have been struck by Parliament (such as making the consent of the male donor irrevocable or by drawing the line at the point of creation of the embryo)[45] but the Court concluded that:

> in adopting in the 1990 Act a clear and principled rule, which was explained to the parties to IVF treatment and clearly set out in the forms they both signed, whereby the consent of either party might be withdrawn at any stage up to the point of implantation of an embryo, the United Kingdom did not exceed the margin of appreciation afforded to it or upset the fair balance required under Article 8 of the Convention.[46]

Clearly this case raises some complex and morally difficult issues. On the one hand it presents a scenario where the right to reproduce is at its most important. Natalie Evans, through no fault of her own, has only this one chance to give birth to a child genetically her own and she is being prevented from doing so by the court's protection for the wishes of her ex-partner. It is easy to perceive an

---

[38]   *Ibid*, para 89.
[39]   (2006) 43 EHRR 21.
[40]   The case has been referred to a Grand Chamber whose decision is still pending at the time of writing.
[41]   *Evans*, n. 39 above, para 57.
[42]   *Ibid*, para 61.
[43]   *Ibid*, para 62.
[44]   *Ibid*, para 68.
[45]   *Ibid*.
[46]   *Ibid*, para 69.

injustice. However, it may also be argued that the right decision was reached in this case. The contrast with a father's inability to prevent a child being born as a result of natural conception is far too simplistic. The reason that the father has no comparable right of withdrawing consent in that situation is that it would require an invasion of the bodily integrity of the woman in the form of an abortion. It is not that the father is not entitled to an equal say in respect of his unborn child, it is merely the fact that the child resides within the mother's body which prioritises her rights and choices over those of the father. In the assisted conception scenario, there is no longer this imbalance between the two potential parents. Therefore, we can, and should, give equal priority to the wishes of the mother and father. In the *Evans* case, the courts had to choose between two conflicting rights and, by upholding the fundamental principle of consent to medical treatment, made the right decision in a very difficult situation.

The value placed upon the need for consent in the 1990 Act can also be seen via the *Blood* case.[47] In this case, Dianne Blood was seeking to use her dead husband's sperm in order to conceive. The problem was that the sperm had been taken when the husband was already in a coma and so, even though it was acknowledged that the couple had previously been trying to conceive, there was no written consent from the husband. The case was decided, strangely, on the basis of EC trade law because, while the sperm could not be used in the UK in the absence of consent, the HFEA had acted unlawfully by failing to consider whether EC law required Mrs Blood to be free to export it for use in another country. Article 59 of the Treaty of Rome creates a right to receive medical treatment in another EU country. This is not an absolute right but it was a relevant consideration which the HFEA should have considered before refusing to permit it. In addition, the HFEA was held to be wrong in taking into account that allowing export would create an undesirable precedent. The Court of Appeal held this was not so because the storage of sperm without consent remains illegal and so the issue will not arise in future cases. It is difficult to see why this should be so, however, given that there were no sanctions in this case for the illegal storing and taking of the sperm. Again this is a case central to the debate about the right to reproduce. Indeed if it was decided today, the key issue would surely be Articles 8 and 12.[48] And yet there seems little consistency between the upholding of Mrs Blood's rights and the overriding of Ms Evans' rights. Is the distinction merely that Mr Johnston was actively refusing consent while Mr Blood was, by necessity, silent on the matter? Or was the fact that the Bloods were married and seeking to start a family contrasted favourably with Ms Evans' position, thus surreptitiously promoting a more traditional concept of the family? Is there a sufficient distinction between the facts of these two cases to justify the upholding of the consent requirement in one case and its bypassing in the other?

---

[47] *R v Human Fertilisation and Embryology Authority, ex p Blood* [1997] 2 All ER 687.
[48] As Feldman notes at p 733, n. 12 above.

(c)   Conflicting Interests III: Parties to a Surrogacy Arrangement

Thus far we have considered two potentially conflicting interests to that of an individual who wishes to assert her right to reproduce: the welfare of the potential child; and the rights of the gamete donors. A third potentially conflicting interest is the rights and interests of other parties to a surrogacy arrangement. Surrogacy was defined by the Warnock Committee as the situation where one woman carries a child for another with the intention that the child should be handed over after birth.[49] Such arrangements have existed for centuries but the recent development of medically assisted conception techniques has added a further dimension as surrogacy can now be combined with artificial insemination by the commissioning father or with IVF where the commissioning couple are the genetic parents and the surrogate mother merely carries the embryo to term. Surrogacy in all its forms creates potentially conflicting interests. On the one side is the right to reproductive autonomy of the couple who seek to commission a surrogate (perhaps because the woman is unable to carry a child and this is the only way for them to have a child genetically their own). On the other side, the welfare of the child, the interests of the surrogate mother, and a societal interest in non-commercialisation of reproduction may require limitation of the commissioning couple's freedom to reproduce by means of surrogacy.

It is the latter interest, that of non-commercialisation, which has been the main concern of English law in recent decades. The Warnock Report identified the use of a woman's uterus for financial profit as one of the problems inherent in surrogacy arrangements.[50] John Harris has sensibly queried why the uterus should be treated differently to other parts of our bodies: 'We most of us use our hands and our brains for profit. Hair, blood and other tissue is often donated or sold, what is so special about the uterus?'[51] Nevertheless, the birth of 'Baby Cotton' to a surrogate mother in 1985 led to a parliamentary response in the Surrogacy Arrangements Act 1985. While this Act does not prohibit all surrogacy arrangements, it does prohibit commercial surrogacy arrangements and advertising.[52] The emphasis in the Act is on preventing third parties and organisations from profiting from surrogacy arrangements. It does not prohibit the involvement of non-profit making organisations nor does it prevent the surrogate herself from profiting from the arrangement. Mason makes a comparison with the law's approach to prostitution: 'As an analogy, we may not *like* prostitution but we do not regard it as criminal activity; the criminal context of prostitution lies in exploiting a woman for the financial gain of another. Moral suspicion of

---

[49]   'Report of the Committee of Inquiry into Human Fertilisation and Embryology' (1984), para 8.1.

[50]   *Ibid*, para 8.10–8.12.

[51]   J Harris, *The Value of Life: An Introduction to Medical Ethics* (London, Routledge, 1985), p 144.

[52]   The recent White Paper proposes that the revised legislation will 'clarify the extent to which not-for-profit organisations may undertake activities for the facilitation of surrogacy arrangements, including advertising their services' (n 2 above, para 2.64).

financial involvement in reproduction is greatest when advantage accrues to parties who are uninvolved in the biological sense...'[53] The recent Brazier Review of surrogacy proposes going a step further, however, by prohibiting payment to the surrogate beyond genuine expenses.[54] Freeman is highly critical of this recommendation, arguing convincingly that a lack of remuneration will force commissioning parents to deal with 'shady agencies on the margins of the underworld ... as the supply of legitimate surrogates ... dries up'.[55] We might wonder why the law should seek to restrict a couple's freedom to reproduce by means of paying a surrogate when it makes no attempt to prevent a couple paying for IVF treatment. Medical professionals are paid for their role in assisting reproduction; why should a woman who is willing to undergo the physically and emotionally draining task of carrying a child for nine months and then giving birth not be similarly recompensed?

A second interest which may conflict with a couple's freedom to reproduce by means of surrogacy is the need to protect the rights and interests of the surrogate mother. In particular, the question arises as to what happens if the surrogate changes her mind after birth and wishes to raise the child herself. The Human Fertilisation and Embryology Act 1990 inserted a new Section 1A into the Surrogacy Arrangements Act 1985. This declares that 'No surrogacy arrangement is enforceable by or against any of the persons making it.' Therefore, a commissioning couple could not seek to enforce an agreement through the courts and the surrogate mother, as the gestational mother, will be granted the full protection of the law as the legal mother.[56] Even if all parties are agreed that the surrogacy arrangement should be enforced, the law will not recognise it and the commissioning couple will not acquire parental responsibility unless either they go through a formal adoption procedure or they acquire a 'parental order' under section 30 of the 1990 Act. This requires that the surrogate mother (and her husband or partner if he is regarded in law as the father) consents[57] and that no money other than reasonable expenses has been paid to her by the commissioning couple (unless the payment was authorised by a court).[58] In addition, the child must be genetically related to at least one of the commissioning couple[59]

---

[53] JK Mason, *Medico-Legal Aspects of Reproduction and Parenthood*, 2nd edn (Aldershot, Dartmouth Publishing, 1998), p 255.

[54] 'Surrogacy: Review for Health Ministers of Current Arrangements for Payment and Regulation' (Cm 4068, 1998). Brazier also recommends the introduction of a regulatory body and registration of non-profit making agencies.

[55] M Freeman, 'Does Surrogacy have a Future after Brazier?' (1999) 7 *Med L Rev* 1, at p 8. Freeman also queries whether payment to surrogates is really a problem given that the Brazier Report acknowledges that only 3% of cases involve payments in excess of £10,000 (*ibid*, para 5.6) and the average payment, when a payment is made (meaning that the overall average is much lower), is only £3,800 (*ibid*, para 1.31).

[56] Section 27 (1) HFEA. See the section below on assigning parentage.

[57] Section 30(5). A six week cooling-off period is required after birth before such consent can be given.

[58] Section 30(7).

[59] Section 30(1)(b).

and the child must be residing with the commissioning couple.[60] This last requirement is curious as it requires that the child be living with people who have no legal responsibility for him. Of course, it also leads to a strong presumption in favour of granting the parental order because it would rarely be in the child's interests to remove him from his home environment.[61] Nevertheless, the child's interests do form a third potentially conflicting interest with the rights to reproduce of both the commissioning couple and the surrogate.

The Brazier Report was clear that the welfare of the child must be paramount.[62] The difficulty is that it may be easy to manipulate this principle. For example, a newly born baby's welfare will surely almost always be served by remaining with the parents to whom he has bonded since birth. In addition, the paramountcy of the welfare of the child will be difficult to reconcile with the existing law's emphasis upon regarding the gestational mother as having a mother's trump card in determining the child's future. As Jackson has described, 'protecting the surrogate's right to keep the child to whom she has given birth appears to be a non-negotiable part of the British regulatory scheme'[63] and this appears so even if it is inconsistent with preserving the child's interests. Thus it can be seen that the surrogate mother's rights in respect of reproductive autonomy are preserved under the current law on surrogacy arrangements: such arrangements are not enforceable in the courts; she is regarded as the legal mother in all circumstances and for ever after; and must give formal consent to a 'parental order' in favour of the commissioning (and even genetic) parents. The commissioning couple's freedom to reproduce by means of surrogacy is much more restricted: they cannot acquire parental responsibility without the surrogate's consent and their freedom to select a surrogate is limited by the legal prohibition on commercial arrangements. The need to ensure that the rights of all parties to a surrogacy arrangement are protected inevitably means that the right to reproduce for a couple seeking IVF plus surrogacy will be more restricted than for a couple seeking merely IVF. The surrogate mother's rights cannot be ignored. But the current law goes so far in protecting the traditional gestational mother's dominant position that it overlooks the rights of the genetic parents who seek to reproduce by means of a surrogacy arrangement.

Furthermore, the law only tolerates a surrogacy arrangement involving medically assisted conception techniques where 'the commissioning mother is unable for physical or other medical reasons to carry a child or where her health may be impaired by doing so'.[64] Thus surrogacy in conjunction with medically assisted conception will not be an option unless there is a serious medical reason for it.

---

[60]   Section 30(3).
[61]   See Jackson, n 21 above, p 275.
[62]   See n 54 above.
[63]   Jackson, n 21 above, p 266.
[64]   Code of Practice, 6th edn, para 3.17. The BMA also regards surrogacy as only acceptable as a 'last resort' ('Changing Conceptions of Motherhood: A Report on Surrogacy' (BMA, 1995)).

There seems no convincing reason why surrogacy should be available as a last resort for medical reasons but not for other social reasons, for example to assist a homosexual couple to reproduce. This further restriction on the rights of couples seeking to reproduce via surrogacy suggests that the current law on surrogacy is inconsistent with the right to reproduce and, while changes may be introduced in response to the Brazier Review, these are unlikely to deal with this underlying human rights concern.

(d)   Conflicting Interests IV: Interests of Society

Perhaps the most common interest said to conflict with reproduction by means of assisted conception is the interest of society in protecting 'natural' reproduction and prohibiting anything considered to be 'unnatural'. Thus when new technology permits us to select the sex of an embryo before implantation, or produce an embryo by means of a cloning technique, or enable a post-menopausal or non-sexually active woman to give birth, the law may impose restrictions upon an individual's freedom to utilise this technology in order to reproduce. Hale identified the perceived problem in respect of so-called 'designer babies' when she wrote of 'the interest which we all have in supporting the essential randomness of nature'.[65] However, this is not a convincing argument. All medical treatment seeks to counteract the randomness of nature and yet in other fields we are largely happy to allow the randomness, for example of death, to be overcome by medical advances. Why should the field of assisted conception be so different? It may be that we feel this goes to the heart of our humanity and the respect which is owed to the human species but if an individual's freedom is to be infringed it must be to prevent a real harm occurring, as for example, when another individual's rights or freedoms are at stake.[66] Mere distaste or unease at a procedure should not be sufficient to override an individual's legitimate interest in exercising his or her right to reproduce.

III.   Assigning Parentage: Giving Legal Recognition to the Right to Reproduce?

The right to reproduce is perhaps of most obvious relevance to issues of access to treatment, but the question of assigning parentage to a child born as a result of medically assisted reproduction may also produce implications for this right.

---

[65]   Hale, n 11 above, p 44.
[66]   See Robertson: 'without a clear showing of substantial harm to the tangible interests of others, speculation or mere moral objections alone should not override the moral right of infertile couples to use these techniques to form families' (Robertson, n 3 above, p 35).

Robertson has described one of the effects of advanced technology in the area of reproduction as 'the decomposition of the usually unified aspects of reproduction into separate genetic, gestational, and social strands'.[67] In other words, parentage is no longer the simple recognition of biological fact that it used to be. To some extent, changes in society and the family have had a similar effect: remarriage, adoption, complex family relationships which have dislodged the familiar marriage with 2.4 children. Crucially, however, these deviances from the traditional norm are reactive: a marriage breaks down; or a child is abandoned, and thus a new arrangement is sought. The novelty of the complexity brought to parenthood by medically assisted conception is that of an intentional creation. A child is created whose genetic parents are not, and never could have been, the same as his gestational parent, who may again be distinct from his social parent. The 1990 Act makes very clear provision for assigning parentage in the newly complex circumstances of assisted reproduction but its provisions are not without controversy.[68]

(a)   Identifying the Mother

The 1990 Act declares that the carrying or gestational mother is always to be regarded as the legal mother.[69] This is so even if another woman has the claim of being the genetic mother, and also applies even if the pregnancy is the subject of a surrogacy arrangement. Thus neither the genetic nor the social/commissioning mother is necessarily regarded as the mother by the law. This could be regarded as an infringement of their right to reproduce. The law gives some protection to the commissioning mother in a surrogacy arrangement by providing an easier and more fitting alternative to the adoption route via Section 30.[70] If this 'mother' has no genetic or gestational ties to the child, greater protection in law is probably not justified. The Court of Appeal held in *Re R*, for example, that 'where there is neither a genetic link nor a personal relationship of a family nature, there is no family life to respect' under Article 8.[71] Of course if there is a personal relationship, such as would exist if the child resides with the commissioning mother, this may establish a familial relationship (although not necessarily a reproductive one) which deserves respect.

---

[67]   Robertson, n 3 above, p 120.

[68]   The recent White Paper (n 2 above) proposes revisions to the legal parentage provisions of the 1990 Act 'to enable a greater range of persons to be recognised as parents following assisted reproduction. This will involve introducing parenthood provisions for civil partners and other same-sex couples in line with those for married and unmarried couples respectively' (para 2.69). As the details of these proposed changes are not yet known, this section only states the law as it currently exists.

[69]   Section 27(1).

[70]   See above for details of parental orders under Section 30.

[71]   *Re R (parental responsibility: IVF baby)* [2003] 2 All ER 131, at para 78.

In respect of a genetic mother the situation is far more difficult. Why does the law regard the gestational mother as more deserving of the label of 'mother', and the authority which comes with it, than the genetic mother? Is it not the latter who has actually 'reproduced' in a crude genetic sense, and is it not a violation of her right to do so if she gains no legal recognition of this genetic fact? Of course, as we have seen, the right to reproduce is not absolute and a balance should certainly be struck with the interests of the other relevant parties, including, on the question of parentage, those of the child who will, in this context, already be born. However, legal recognition of a change in status such as becoming a genetic parent will be an important value to be weighed in the balance.[72] The overriding priority given to the gestational mother harps back to a simpler age when a woman could only give birth to her own child. Times have changed and the law should recognise this.[73]

(b) Identifying the Father

If the position in respect of assigning motherhood is controversial, it is far more so in respect of fatherhood. There is unmistakable irony in the fact that the 1990 Act stresses the need of the child for a father, in section 13(5), and yet legislates to create legally fatherless children. This occurs because, again, genetic parentage is not prioritised in law. Instead, if the gestational mother is married, her husband will be regarded as the legal father, regardless of genetic heritage, unless he can prove that he did not consent to the reproductive treatment.[74] If the gestational mother is unmarried, her partner will also be regarded as the father if the couple were being 'treated together'.[75] If the husband or partner is not, under these provisions, able to be regarded as the father, then the child has no father under the law. Not only is this inconsistent with the professed welfare need of that child for a father, but it could also be inconsistent with the genetic father's right to reproduce. In the past it could have been said that he might wish to preserve

---

[72] In *Goodwin v United Kingdom* (2002) 35 EHRR 18, the European Court of Human Rights acknowledged that the denial of legal recognition for a change in status (in that case, it was a change in gender) could amount to an infringement of Art 8.

[73] Wallbank suggests that there should be a move towards 'child sharing' involving both the genetic and gestational mother. See J Wallbank, 'Too Many Mothers? Surrogacy, Kinship and the Welfare of the Child' (2002) 10 *Med L Rev* 271.

[74] Section 28(2). In *Leeds Teaching Hospital v A* [2003] EWCA 259, a husband was held not to be the legal father when another man's sperm was mistakenly injected into his wife's eggs rather than his own. In a rather harsh judgment, Dame Butler-Sloss P held that the presumption of paternity had been displaced by DNA testing and there was no consent from the husband for the mistaken use of donor sperm. An infringement of Art 8(1) was identified but held to be proportionate under Art 8(2) due to the existence of remedies such as adoption.

[75] Section 28(3). In *Re R (a child)* [2003] 2 All ER 131, the Court of Appeal held that this provision must be interpreted narrowly in order to require that the embryo be placed in the mother at a time when the treatment services are being provided for the man and woman together. In this case, where the couple had split prior to the implantation of the embryo, the man was not the legal father under s 28(3).

anonymity and thus his right to privacy would take precedence (although if he chose to relinquish his privacy, the possibility of legal recognition of his genetic contribution may have been desirable). Now anonymity for donors has been removed.[76] This means that the genetic father has no claim to privacy, and the child will be able to find out his identity. Why, then, should the law prohibit him being regarded as the father of the child? This query also applies if another man's name is put on the birth certificate as the father (i.e. the husband or partner of the gestational mother). By requiring the consenting husband to be treated in law as the father for all purposes,[77] the Act presumably requires such registration on the birth certificate but this can be criticised as inconsistent with the genetic facts. As Mason has argued, 'the inevitable conclusion is that Parliament has deliberately authorised the falsification of a legal document'.[78] When the genetic father is known, has no right of anonymity, and is traceable by the child, why does the law refuse to recognise this as a claim to fatherhood? Of course, in many cases the genetic father will not wish to be regarded as the legal father, especially given the financial as well as moral obligations which go with this status, but if a genetic father does wish, for whatever reason, to be given legal recognition of that status, would not a failure to do so violate his right to reproduce?

Perhaps Gillian Douglas has the answer when she emphasises the social role of parents over and above the mere fact of procreation.[79] This is reflected in a right to found a family more than in the commonly termed right to reproduce. Perhaps the mere fact of genetic linkage should not engage the right unless there is an intention to raise the child – ie to voluntarily undertake the social role of parent. However, while it does appear reasonable to emphasise the importance of the social parents, it should be noted that, as discussed above, in respect of motherhood, it is the gestational mother who is given all legal recognition, rights and responsibilities, even if she had no intention of raising the child. If the law wishes to prioritise the physical role of carrying the child for nine months, over the emotional role of caring for a child for at least 18 years, should not the genetic role of creating the child also play a part in the law's recognition of increasingly complex reproductive techniques?

---

[76]   Human Fertilisation and Embryology Authority (Disclosure of Donor Information) Regulations 2004 (SI 2004/1511).

[77]   Section 29(1).

[78]   Mason, n 53 above, p218.

[79]   Douglas, n 24 above, p 20.

IV. A Right to Reproduce a Healthy Child? Selection of Embryos

One final issue on a potential right to reproduce is whether it could include a more specific right to have a child with particular characteristics. The obvious, and most sympathetic, example is that of a healthy child. Could we interpret the right to reproduce to mean the right to reproduce a healthy child and if so should technological advances be used to achieve that goal? If this is accepted, however, the door is open to specifying other characteristics such as sex selection[80] and even finding a matching tissue type in order to provide a donor for an existing child. It is this latter example which has been before the courts in this country. In *R (on the application of Quintavalle) v Human Fertilisation and Embryology Authority (the Hashmi case)*,[81] a couple sought pre-implantation genetic diagnosis (PGD) on embryos in order to ensure that the child was born free of a blood disorder suffered by their three year old son, Zain, but they also sought tissue typing in order to select the embryos which would provide a blood match for Zain and enable him to have a much needed transplant. The HFEA agreed to the procedure but an interest group, CORE, brought a legal challenge. The case reached the House of Lords, which allowed the treatment to proceed. The key issue before the House was whether the procedure was 'designed to secure that embryos are in a suitable condition to be placed in a woman or to determine whether embryos are suitable for that purpose'.[82] By adopting a very broad interpretation of 'suitability', the House of Lords found that the treatment was designed for those purposes. This case is often contrasted with the case of the Whittakers, whose application for a similar procedure was refused by the HFEA because the disease in question was not hereditary. Thus while the Hashmi's child had a 1 in 4 chance of being born with the same disease as the existing child, the Whittaker's child had the same chance as amongst the population as a whole, ie 1 in 5-7 million. The HFEA therefore decided that the sole purpose of PGD for the Whittakers would be to select a donor for their existing child, rather than to select a healthy embryo. Could the refusal of the Whittakers' application be an infringement of their right to reproduce as it was the only means by which they wished to reproduce? This would surely be stretching the right too far, not because of any concerns about the welfare of the future child born as a donor for a sibling (because, as explained above, the only alternative for that child is not to be born and we surely cannot regard its life as so bad as to be worse than never being born), nor because such selection of embryos is unnatural and that society's interests in preventing designer babies should justify a limitation on the

---

[80] Sex selection is not directly mentioned in the current legislation but the government White Paper recommends the prohibition of sex selection for non-medical reasons (n 2 above, para 2.47).
[81] [2005] 2 All ER 555.
[82] Section 1(1)(d) Sch 2.

right to reproduce. The mere distaste for a new procedure should never justify restricting an individual's freedom to pursue it. The rejection of the applicability of the right to reproduce here is, instead, simply because the right is not in issue. The rejection of an application to enable PGD does not prevent a couple reproducing. A couple seeking a specific type of embryo – one who can act as a life-saving donor for an existing child – may have a legitimate interest in rejecting other means of reproducing, but there can be no right to reproduce at stake. The same is true if the parents wish to select the gender, eye colour or any other trait of their future child. We may allow them to do so but, if we do not, they cannot claim a violation of the right to reproduce because the core of their reproductive freedom was never violated.

V. Conclusion

To conclude, this chapter has argued that a right to reproduce should be acknowledged as reproduction is a core personal interest which goes to the heart of who we are, both as individuals and also as a race.[83] We live in a human rights age when individual freedom is protected in law. It is clear that the right to respect for private life, the right to respect for family life and the right to found a family are all brought into domestic law through the Human Rights Act 1998 and meet there proclamations of a common law right to reproduce and, more generally, a long, and not entirely unsuccessful, tradition of personal liberty and freedom. It cannot be denied that we owe some legal respect to an individual's freedom to make reproductive choices. What exactly this entails is more complex, of course, but it may be argued that restrictions on access are not justifiable, either by reference to the welfare of a future child or by reference to the morality of society (if such a thing even exists). However, the interests of other parties to the reproductive process must be balanced against an individual's right to reproduce. Thus, for example, the withdrawal of consent by one party may override another's freedom to continue treatment and the protection of the rights of a surrogate mother may restrict a commissioning couple's ability to enforce a surrogacy arrangement. In addition, the right to reproduce cannot entail a right to publicly funded treatment for this is not an economically viable possibility, nor is it consistent with the continued reluctance of the courts to intervene substantially in issues of resource allocation, discussed in Chapter 2. The only proviso to this rejection of a right to publicly funded treatment is that treatment must be provided free of discrimination so that a class of persons should not be excluded by means of a blanket policy without scope for individual assessment. Both the prohibition on discrimination in the ECHR and the

---

[83]　Richard Dawkins writes of the 'selfish gene' and the genetic imperative to reproduce. See, for example, *The Selfish Gene*, 3rd edn (Oxford, Oxford University Press, 2006).

traditional grounds for judicial review require this. Furthermore, the current laws on assigning parentage take insufficient account of an individual's right to reproduce by sticking rigidly to old-fashioned ideas of the gestational mother and her husband as legal parents, regardless of the circumstances of the reproductive process. Finally, a right to reproduce cannot incorporate a right to produce a particular type of child, however admirable the parents' motives in wishing to do so.

It may be that a right to reproduce sounds wrong to us: a symptom of a world too obsessed with rights, and dominated by frightening technological advances which threaten the very nature of the human species. What it really amounts to, however, is a freedom to make reproductive choices without interference from the state, and subject only to the need to balance the interests of other parties to the reproductive process. Such freedom is inherent in our democratic society, implicit in the ECHR and thus the HRA, and vital if men and women are to be given the respect in their private lives that free citizens in a modern society deserve.

Recommended Further Reading

J Harris, 'Rights and Reproductive Choice' in J Harris and S Holm (eds), *The Future of Human Reproduction: Ethics, Choice, and Regulation* (Oxford, Clarendon Press, 1998).

JA Robertson, *Children of Choice: Freedom and the New Reproductive Technologies* (Princeton, Princeton University Press, 1994), Chapter 2.

E Jackson, *Regulating Reproduction: Law, Technology and Autonomy* (Oxford, Hart Publishing, 2001), Chapters 5 and 6.

M Freeman, 'Does Surrogacy have a Future after Brazier?' (1999) 7 *Med L Rev* 1

9

Termination of Pregnancy: A Conflict of Rights

An abortion, or termination of pregnancy (the terms will be used interchangeably here), is a medical procedure unlike all others. A conflict of interests between mother and fetus is almost inevitable, while there may also potentially be a conflict of interests between the mother and father and between the mother and her doctor. This chapter addresses this issue by considering in turn the interests of the fetus, mother, father and medical professional. Does a fetus have a right to life? Does a pregnant woman have a right to an abortion? Does the father have any legal rights in the matter? And does a doctor have a primary duty to the woman, the fetus or to his or her own conscience? There are few definitive answers in this chapter – the questions have long posed moral dilemmas beyond the ability of the law to answer – but sometimes asking the right questions can be a worthwhile task in itself and one which may bring us closer to a reasoned response to the eternal moral complexity of abortion.

I. The Fetus

(a) A Right to Life for the Fetus?

As we have seen in previous chapters, Article 2 ECHR protects the right to life. It declares that '[e]veryone's right to life shall be protected by law'. No further guidance is provided in the text, however, as to whether 'everyone' includes a fetus or is limited to persons already born. The significance of this question to the abortion debate is profound. In *Paton v United Kingdom* in 1980[1], the European Commission of Human Rights had to consider this issue when a British father sought to prevent the abortion of his unborn child. The Commission noted that

[1] (1980) 3 EHRR 408.

most uses of the term 'everyone' in the Convention can only apply postnatally[2] and that the remainder of Article 2, with its limitations of everyone's right to life in respect of the death penalty and law enforcement, suggests that Article 2 protects persons already born.[3] The Commission excluded the possibility that Article 2 recognises an absolute right to life for the fetus. It held that such an interpretation of Article 2 would be contrary to the object and purpose of the Convention because it would require the prohibition of abortion even when the mother's life is at risk. The mother, as an already existing person, is entitled to the full protection of the right to life subject only to the express limitations in Article 2. An absolute right to life for the fetus would add an additional implied limitation to the mother's right to life which would be contrary to the object and purpose of the Convention. The Commission was not willing, however, to rule out the possibility that the fetus may be entitled to some limited protection under Article 2. It held that this issue did not have to be decided on the facts of the case before it because the abortion in question had occurred at an early stage in the pregnancy (ten weeks) and was performed on the basis of protecting the life or health of the mother which would amount to an implied limitation on any limited right to life a fetus might enjoy under Article 2. Thus the Commission declared the complaint inadmissible as manifestly ill-founded because either the fetus has no protection under Article 2 or the death of the fetus in this case fell within an implied limitation to the fetus's right to life. The *Paton* decision therefore left open the question of whether Article 2 extends any protection of the right to life to an unborn entity.

An opportunity for the European Court of Human Rights to reconsider this difficult issue was eagerly awaited and finally, in 2004, a prime opportunity presented itself. *Vo v France*[4] concerned a case of mistaken identity in a French hospital. Thi-Nho Vo, the applicant, attended Lyons General Hospital for a medical examination during her sixth month of pregnancy. At the same time, another Vietnamese woman, Thi Thanh Van Vo, was scheduled to have a coil removed at the same hospital. The applicant, who did not speak French, answered the doctor's call of 'Mrs Vo' and the doctor then sought to remove a coil without carrying out the medical examination which would have revealed her pregnancy. In the course of the procedure, the amniotic sac was pierced, causing the loss of a substantial amount of amniotic fluid. As a result, a few days later the applicant's pregnancy was terminated on health grounds. She lodged a criminal complaint against the doctor for the death of her child but the French courts held that a fetus could not be the victim of homicide. Mrs Vo therefore complained under the ECHR of a violation of Article 2 due to the lack of protection for an unborn child under the French criminal law.

---

[2]   *Ibid*, para 7. Other uses of 'everyone' include Arts 1, 5, 6, 8-11 and 13.
[3]   *Ibid*, para 8.
[4]   *Vo v France* (2005) 10 EHRR 12.

The European Court of Human Rights found no violation of Article 2 but refused to decide whether the fetus has any protection under Article 2. The crucial part of the judgment is in paragraph 85 in which two conclusions are reached which enable the Court to evade the core issue. First, the Court concludes that it would be neither desirable nor possible to answer in the abstract whether an unborn child is given protection under Article 2. Second, the Court concludes that it is also unnecessary to decide the issue on the facts of the case before it because, even if this fetus does have a right to life, it was not violated by the French laws. The basis for this second argument is that a criminal sanction for unintentional homicides is not essential under Article 2. Other legal options such as negligence were held to be sufficient to satisfy the requirements of this Article. The difficulty with the Court's approach in *Vo* is that it seeks to discuss the requirements of a right to life for the fetus before deciding whether such a right even exists under Article 2. To assert, as the Court does, that even if the fetus has a right to life, it is not violated, assumes that the boundaries and implied limitations of such a right have been determined and yet the Court's refusal to decide whether such a right even exists prevented this. Without any guidance as to the substance of a right to life for the fetus, it is hard to understand how the Court could conclude that French law was compatible with it.

The Court's approach was not unanimous. In fact, although there was officially a 14 to 3 majority for the decision that Article 2 had not been violated, a total of 9 judges expressed an opinion on the key question of whether Article 2's protection encompasses the fetus. The three officially dissenting judges all regarded Article 2 as extending protection to the fetus and concluded that Article 2 had been violated.[5] One other judge agreed that a fetus has a right to life but held that it had not been violated on the facts of the case.[6] Five other judges wrote a separate opinion in which they concluded that the fetus does not have any protection under the right to life.[7] In the view of these five judges, Article 2 was inapplicable to this case. This leaves only 8 out of the 17 judges on the Court who did not express an opinion on whether Article 2 encompasses protection for the life of the fetus.[8] In the view of many, refusal to express an opinion on one of the pressing legal, medical and moral issues of the day was an unacceptable abdication of judicial responsibility. It cannot be denied that it is a difficult ethical issue with potentially wide-ranging political implications across Europe, but the text of Article 2 is ripe for interpretation and the Court should not evade that task. As Judge Costa queried in his separate opinion:

Does the present inability of ethics to reach a consensus on what is a person and who is entitled to the right to life prevent the law from defining these terms? I think not. It is

---

[5] Judges Ress, Mularoni and Straznicka.
[6] Judge Costa.
[7] Judges Rozakis, Caflisch, Fischbach, Lorenzen and Thomassen.
[8] Judges Wildhaber, Bratza, Jungwiert, Hedigan, Baka, Traja, Ugrekhelidze, Hajiyev.

the task of lawyers, and in particular judges, especially human rights judges, to identify the notions ... that correspond to the words or expressions in the relevant legal instruments.[9]

In other words, what prevents the Court defining the term 'everyone' in Article 2 as it seeks to define other terms in the Convention?

The nine judges who did express an opinion were unanimous in perceiving an underlying decision in the judgment of the Court. Judge Costa, concluding that the fetus is included in Article 2, said '[h]ad Article 2 been considered to be entirely inapplicable, there would have been no point ... in examining the question of fetal protection and the possible violation of Article 2 ...'.[10] This perception of the Court's decision as amounting to a belief that the fetus is included in Article 2 is shared by those judges who took the opposite view. Judge Rozakis (joined by four other judges) recognised that 'reliance on the procedural guarantees of Article 2 to determine whether or not there has been a violation presupposes the prima facie applicability of that Article'.[11] Thus, even though the *Vo* decision may be criticised as an abdication of judicial responsibility, it is possible to identify a willingness to concede the applicability of Article 2 to the fetus. Given this, it is even harder to conceive why the Court was not willing to investigate and declare the nature of the protection offered to a fetus by Article 2. If ever the Court is to do so, it will never face a better opportunity than the case of *Vo* because, unusually, the interests of the fetus were not in conflict with the interests of the mother. Indeed, the mother was seeking to assert the rights of her deceased, unborn, child. Therefore, a rare opportunity to determine the extent of Article 2's protection for the fetus in isolation from the complicating factor of limiting the rights of the mother presented itself. That the Court declined to take advantage of this does not bode well for future determination of the issue.

(b)   The Ethical Background to the Right to Life Debate

The European Court of Human Rights's reluctance to conclusively determine the nature and extent of the Convention's protection for the fetus reflects the depth of ethical disagreement on the issue of when life begins and should thus be protected. It may be that there are two distinct ethical questions here: when does human life begin? And when does a fetus become a 'person' entitled to full protection of the law? Many ethical views conflate these two questions, searching for a single point in time when the fetus is indisputably entitled to legal protection. There is no agreement upon what stage in human development should be chosen as this crucial moment. Conception, implantation, viability and

---

[9]   Para 7 of Judge Costa's Separate Opinion.
[10]   *Ibid*, para 10.
[11]   Separate Opinion of Judge Rozakis (joined by Judges Caflisch, Fischbach, Lorenzen and Thomassen.)

birth all have individual merits but choosing any one of these will be an arbitrary decision. As Glover explains, the development of human life is a continuous and steady progress during which a zygote gradually becomes a baby. Any boundary between a person and non-(or pre-)person is man-made: 'To ask "When does one start to be a person?" is like asking 'when does middle age begin?' Conventional lines for social or legal purposes could always be drawn, but we would be mistaken if we took the shadows cast by these lines for boundaries in biological reality.'[12]

In this context, it is not surprising that the European Court of Human Rights has been reluctant to impose a view on this issue across Europe. If a conventional line is drawn, conception is the earliest candidate for the location of such a line. Many people believe, often for religious reasons, that life begins at conception and that all human life should be protected from that initial stage. If such a view were legally accepted, it would mean that not only abortion, but also some contraceptive methods, would have to be prohibited. The contraceptive pill, for example, not only works to prevent fertilisation but also changes the womb lining to make it reject fertilised eggs and thus prevent implantation. Is this murder? If so, we should, as Mason has noted, also regard each menstrual period as a potential for mourning as 'untold numbers of zygotes are lost daily on a worldwide basis'.[13] The inappropriateness, not to mention the futility, of seeking to legally protect all human life from conception, particularly when such protection will inevitably involve legal restraints upon the mother's freedom, is what leads many to reject this early starting point for legal protection. A slightly later starting point – implantation of the fertilised egg onto the womb – suffers from similar criticisms although it is to some extent the starting point for legal protection of the fetus in the UK due to the criminal offence of procuring a miscarriage.[14]

A more realistic point at which an unborn life is entitled to protection is that of viability. Once a fetus is capable of being born alive and has the potential to survive independently of its mother's body, there is a strong argument that the issue is no longer one internal to the mother but rather one which the state and its laws should regulate. If the fetus has a good chance of a life outside the mother's womb it should not at that stage be destroyed within the mother, especially if there is no good reason to do so. As convincing as this argument is, viability remains an incomplete solution to the problem because it is a shifting boundary dependent upon the state of modern technology and its availability to a particular fetus. As Glover argues, there 'seems to be something absurd about a moving boundary, so that we might say "last year this fetus would not have been a person at this stage, but since they re-equipped the intensive care unit, it is one".

---

[12] J Glover, *Causing Death and Saving Lives* (London, Penguin, 1977) at p 127.
[13] JK Mason, *Medico-Legal Aspects of Reproduction and Parenthood*, 2nd edn (Aldershot, Dartmouth Publishing, 1998), pp 109-10.
[14] This issue is discussed further below.

This just does not seem to be the morally significant boundary people are looking for.'[15] This leads us on to birth: a clear, certain and unambiguous point in time which also has the advantage of avoiding all issues of a conflict of interests with another human being within whose body the fetus resides. So, birth is the most obvious answer to when life begins and deserves legal protection but we must query whether we would really be happy to permit a fully developed fetus to be arbitrarily destroyed the day before its birth? Whether or not a fetus is legally regarded as a person, there is undoubtedly a human life at stake here, which should be valued by society and its laws.

Dworkin perhaps offers the most convincing analysis of the value of human life and in doing so suggests a reconciliation of the pro-life versus pro-choice dichotomy which has long dominated the abortion debate. Dworkin identifies two different types of objections to abortion: (1) derivative objections, which are derived from the idea that a fetus has rights and interests; and (2) detached objections, where the fetus is not necessarily regarded as having any rights or interests but abortion is opposed because it disregards and insults the intrinsic value in human life.[16] He argues that, while pro-life rhetoric is based on a derivative objection, this merely disguises the true objections to abortion:

> The disagreement that actually divides people is a markedly less polar disagreement about how best to respect a fundamental idea we almost all share in some form i.e. that individual human life is sacred. Almost everyone who opposes abortion really objects to it, as they might realise after reflection, on the detached rather than derivative ground. They believe that a fetus is a living, growing human creature and that it is intrinsically a bad thing, a kind of cosmic shame, when human life at any stage is deliberately extinguished.[17]

If this view is accepted, it bypasses the problematic, ethical question of whether a fetus has rights and emphasises instead that a fetus is a valuable human life and that decisions about its survival must be taken responsibly and in full recognition of the gravity of the decision. On this basis, the dispute between pro-life and pro-choice is not about irreconcilable views on the moral status of the fetus but rather in what circumstances avoidable premature death is an unacceptable frustration of the biological investment in life,[18] and in what circumstances it can be justified in order to avoid further frustration of the human investment in life (such as the mother's investment or the child's own investment in its life if born to a short life of pain and suffering).[19] We can all agree that human life is sacred,

---

[15]   Glover, n 12 above, p 125.

[16]   R Dworkin, *Life's Dominion: An Argument about Abortion and Euthanasia* (London, HarperCollins, 1993), p 11.

[17]   *Ibid*, p 13.

[18]   *Ibid*, p 90.

[19]   *Ibid*, pp 90-96.

and that decisions about it must be taken responsibly, without necessarily agreeing on when, if ever, it is justifiable to cut short that life.

(c)   The Fetus in English Law

We must now turn to the question of whether English law ensures adequate respect is given to a fetus's human life. First, it must be noted that the English courts have consistently denied any legal status to the fetus. In *Paton v British Pregnancy Advisory Service Trustees*, the domestic case which led to *Paton v United Kingdom*, Sir George Baker P categorically denied that a fetus has any rights or interests until born. He held that the fetus 'cannot, in English law . . . have a right of its own at least until it's born and has a separate existence from its mother'.[20] No English court has ever denied this statement even though, perhaps because, it has been acknowledged that a fetus is a 'unique organism'. This was stated in the 1997 case of *A-G's Reference (No 3 of 1994)*.[21] This is a criminal law case involving the stabbing of a pregnant woman which caused her unborn child to be injured, born prematurely, and subsequently die. The question for the court was whether the defendant had committed murder or manslaughter by deliberately inflicting an unlawful injury on a mother carrying a child in utero where the child was subsequently born alive and then died from the injuries inflicted in utero. The Court of Appeal viewed the fetus as a part of the mother and therefore held that the actus reus and mens rea for murder and manslaughter could exist in such a case: 'the fetus is taken to be a part of the mother until it has an existence independent of the mother. Thus an intention to cause serious bodily injury to the fetus is an intention to cause serious bodily injury to a part of the mother just as an intention to injure her arm or leg would be so viewed'.[22] This controversial view of the fetus as merely a part of the mother, of no greater moral significance perhaps than her arm or leg, was categorically rejected by the House of Lords: 'The mother and the fetus were two distinct organisms living symbiotically, not a single organism with two aspects. The mother's leg was part of the mother; the fetus was not'.[23] The House of Lords rejected the application of murder to facts such as those of this case because, although a transfer of intent from the intended to the actual victim is possible, this case would require a double transfer: from mother to fetus then from fetus to child. Such a double transfer was unacceptable. However, the House of Lords was able to find criminal liability for the death of the child on the facts of the case by using the offence of manslaughter by unlawful act where the issue of transferred intent need not arise.

[20]   [1979] 1 QB 276, at 279.
[21]   [1997] 3 All ER 936.
[22]   [1996] 2 All ER 10, at 18 (Lord Taylor CJ).
[23]   [1997] 3 All ER 936, at p 429 (Lord Mustill).

What are the broader implications of the categorisation of the fetus as a 'unique organism'? While some commentators are concerned about its implications for maternal liability for fetal harm,[24] it does appropriately recognise that the fetus both is, and is not, a part of the mother. Perhaps the best explanation of the nature of the fetus and its physical relationship with its mother comes from the feminist writer, Catherine Mackinnon: 'More than a body part but less than a person, where it is, is largely what it is. From the standpoint of the pregnant woman, it is both me and not me. It "is" the pregnant woman in the sense that it is in her and of her and is hers more than anyone's. It "is not" her in the sense that she is not all that is there.'[25] While recognising that the fetus is more than just a part of the woman who is carrying it, this quotation simultaneously emphasises that the carrying woman must be a crucial factor in any attempt to define the nature of the fetus and the protection it deserves: 'where it is, is largely what it is'.

As explained above, the English law's view of the fetus is that it is not entitled to any rights before birth but that it is an organism distinct from its mother. The latter factor may explain why, despite the fetus lacking legal rights and interests, it is protected by the criminal law from destruction whether by the mother or a third party. Section 58 of the Offences Against the Person Act 1861 contains the criminal offence of procuring a miscarriage. This action is prohibited whether initiated by the pregnant woman herself or by a third party, including a doctor, and by whatever means it is performed. There is, therefore, a legal prohibition on terminating a pregnancy, which remains in force today. It is a clear indication that the fetus, as a unique human life, will be protected by the law even if not yet a person or entitled to any legal rights or interests. The Abortion Act 1967 (amended in 1990) now creates a legal defence to the offence of procuring a miscarriage if one of four grounds for a termination are satisfied. This will be discussed in much greater detail below. It is significant to note here, however, that, despite the widespread availability of legal abortion in the UK today, a termination of pregnancy remains prima facie a criminal offence. It is a clear message that, even if tolerated by the criminal law, abortion is assumed to be morally wrong and to be discouraged.

In recent times, the 1861 offence has caused most interest in the context of very early abortions. The topical question, which came before the court in *R (on the application of Smeaton) v Secretary of State for Health*,[26] is whether the effect of the morning after pill amounts to procuring a miscarriage and therefore is a criminal offence under the 1861 Offences Against the Person Act unless taken in accordance with the requirements of the 1967 Abortion Act. This issue relates back to the question, discussed above, of from when exactly human life should be

---

[24]   See S Fovargue and J Miola, 'Policing Pregnancy: Implications of the *Attorney-General's Reference (No. 3 of 1994)* (1998) 6 *Med L Rev* 265.

[25]   CA Mackinnon, 'Reflections on Sex Equality under Law' (1991) 100 *Yale LJ* 1281, at 1316, quoted in Dworkin, n 16 above, pp 54-55.

[26]   [2002] 2 FLR 146.

legally protected. The morning after pill serves to prevent implantation of a fertilised egg. If fertilisation has already occurred, does the prevention of implantation amount to a miscarriage? Munby J held that it did not do so. In reaching this conclusion, he investigated the meaning of 'miscarriage' in 1861 when the offence was created and doubted whether it was then regarded as including the prevention of implantation. Furthermore, even if the 1861 definition of miscarriage did include the prevention of implantation, Munby J held that an updating construction should be applied to the words of the statute so that it does not mean this today. Among other factors, the judge seems to have been swayed by the practical consequences of a finding that preventing implantation is prima facie a criminal offence. Not only would this criminalise the morning after pill, but also the normal contraceptive pill which not only prevents fertilisation but can also prevent implantation of an already fertilised egg.[27] This is perhaps the least convincing part of Munby J's judgment. The fact that many people commit a criminal offence on a daily basis does not usually mean that the offence ceases to exist, although it may not be enforced stridently.[28] Munby J is on much firmer ground when he holds that a 'miscarriage' assumes carriage, which requires some type of physical attachment to the woman's body.[29] Furthermore, his conclusion is consistent with the statutory approach in the 1990 Human Fertilisation and Embryology Act in which a woman is not treated as carrying a child until the embryo has become implanted. In the modern world of cutting-edge technology, this is an essential approach to the issue. Problems ensue in this context if a woman is regarded as pregnant before implantation because it is now possible to create an embryo outside the woman's body.[30] It is only at the point of implantation that a pregnancy becomes truly established and the current law adopts the sound approach of protecting the implanted fetus from this point in time. There are limits to the protection, however, because, as we have seen, the fetus has no legal rights and interests until born and, even though the criminal law prohibits the destruction of a fetus, it currently provides a broad legal defence to the crime which frequently absolves the mother and her doctors of any legal

---

[27] 'There would in my judgment be something very seriously wrong, indeed grievously wrong with our system – by which I mean not just our legal system but the entire system by which our polity is governed – if a judge in 2002 were to be compelled by a statute 141 years old to hold that what thousands, hundreds of thousands, indeed millions, of ordinary honest, decent, law abiding citizens have been doing day in day out for so many years is and always has been criminal. I am glad to be spared so unattractive a duty' (*ibid*, para 394).

[28] Speeding is one obvious example of a criminal offence widely committed and the recent more strident attempts to enforce speed limits through speed cameras have met with widespread public criticism and cynicism, perhaps because it is perceived as a violation of an unspoken rule that such offences will not be the subject of strict enforcement.

[29] Some commentators take a very different view. See, for example, J Keown, '"Morning After" Pills, "Miscarriage" and Muddle' (2005) 25 *LS* 296.

[30] See E Jackson, *Regulating Reproduction: Law, Technology and Autonomy* (Oxford, Hart Publishing, 2001), p 88 for discussion of this point.

liability for procuring a miscarriage. It is therefore the issue of the mother's rights in respect of the fetus to which we must now turn.

II. The Mother

(a)   A Right to Choose for the Mother?

The concept of reproductive autonomy, introduced in the previous chapter, also has application in respect of a right *not* to reproduce. Indeed, this is the context in which the idea was first formed and has widest acceptance. Some legal jurisdictions have acknowledged that the idea of reproductive autonomy encompasses a right to an abortion or, less emotively, a 'right to choose'.[31] The Canadian Supreme Court has stated that '[f]orcing a woman, by threat of criminal sanction, to carry a fetus to term unless she meets certain criteria unrelated to her own priorities and aspirations, is a profound interference with a woman's body and thus a violation of security of the person'.[32] This was held to be contrary to the Canadian Charter of Rights and Freedoms and specifically its protection of a right to security of the person.[33]

More famously, the United States also protects, at a constitutional level, a woman's right to an abortion. In the landmark case of *Roe v Wade*,[34] the US Supreme Court interpreted the constitutional right to privacy as including a right to an abortion. It is only an absolute right, however, during the first trimester. During the second trimester it may be regulated by a state in order to protect the woman's own health and, significantly, during the third trimester restrictions may be introduced in order to protect the fetus. This decision has formed the backdrop to a political and often violent conflict between pro-life and pro-choice camps which, in Dworkin's words, 'is tearing America apart'.[35] Despite this, and the appointment of Justices onto the Supreme Court principally because they promised to vote down *Roe*, the core principles of this case endure. Subsequent

---

[31]   Fox criticises the language of choice as unproductive. She argues that most women who have an abortion do not see this as a choice but rather as their only viable option. (Preferred choices might include not conceiving or giving birth to a healthy child.) (M Fox, 'A Woman's Right to Choose? A Feminist Critique' in J Harris and S Holm (eds), *The Future of Human Reproduction: Ethics, Choice, and Regulation* (Oxford, Clarendon Press, 1998), p 82.) Fox also notes that in the polarised discourse between pro-life and pro-choice 'the moral high ground is implicitly conceded to the 'pro-life' camp' (p 95) because it seemingly pits a woman's convenience against an unborn child's life (p 98).

[32]   *R v Morgentaler* [1988] 1 SCR 30, Dickson CJ at p 56.

[33]   Section 7 Canadian Charter of Rights and Freedoms: 'Everyone has the right to life, liberty and security of the person and the right not to be deprived thereof except in accordance with the principles of fundamental justice.'

[34]   93 S Ct 705 (1973).

[35]   Dworkin, n 16 above, p 4.

cases such as *Planned Parenthood of Southeastern Pennsylvania v Casey*[36] have introduced amended tests. For example, the key question now is whether restrictions on access to abortion amount to an undue burden, but a woman's right to an abortion remains a constitutional entitlement under the US Constitution.

It is not only pro-life campaigners who are dismayed by this, some feminists also reject the use of privacy as a mechanism for protecting reproductive autonomy. They argue that defining abortion as a private matter brings two detrimental consequences for women. First, it suggests that sex is a private matter about which the government has no right of intervention, and thus the abuse of women in the bedroom is implicitly sanctioned.[37] This is not a convincing concern, however, because it is the personal autonomy in respect of decisions about abortion which falls within the category of private matters, rather than the territorial location of conception.[38] If free choice about sexual and reproductive issues is constitutionally protected, the woman need not fear that the law will not intervene if her choices are overborne in the bedroom. Second, feminists are concerned that the categorisation of abortion as a private matter means that the state need only allow it but need not help to finance it.[39] There is some merit in this concern. As Robertson has argued, a constitutional right to abortion is only of utility to those women who can afford to pay to exercise their right to choose: 'Those who have the means and knowledge to exercise their rights are well protected. Those who lack the means have the right in name only'.[40] Public funding of abortion, or the lack of it, is one significant restraint upon reproductive autonomy and, as Jackson has noted, the gulf between legality and access is particularly wide in the US where abortion 'is both a constitutionally protected right, and widely unavailable'.[41] This should serve to remind us that access to medical treatment always depends just as much on the availability of resources as on an enforceable right to self-determination.[42] The feminist concern about a lack of access to abortion services is entirely justified, although whether this problem would be lessened by the use of a means other than a constitutional right to privacy to protect abortion is less certain.

Within Europe there has been continued resistance to the categorisation of abortion as a private matter falling within an individual's right to respect for private life.[43] The European Commission of Human Rights considered this issue

---

[36] (1992) 112 S Ct 2791.

[37] See Dworkin, n 16 above, p 52 for discussion of this feminist objection.

[38] See also Dworkin, n 16 above, pp 53-54.

[39] *Ibid*, p 52.

[40] JA Robertson, *Children of Choice: Freedom and the New Reproductive Technologies* (Princeton, Princeton University Press, 1994), p 47.

[41] Jackson, n 30 above, p 87.

[42] See Chapter 2.

[43] Article 8 ECHR.

in the 1977 case of *Bruggemann and Scheuten v Germany*.[44] This case concerned a change in the criminal law on abortion in the Federal Republic of Germany. Previously, abortion was legal up to 12 weeks' gestation without requiring any reason but this was held by the German Federal Constitutional Court to violate the constitutional obligation to protect the unborn child. Thus the 15th Criminal Law Reform Act, which entered into force in 1976, maintained that abortion is always a criminal offence, albeit one with broadly drafted exceptions. The applicants complained that this change in the law amounted to an interference with their right to respect for private life in that abortion was no longer available on demand in the first 12 weeks of pregnancy. The Commission rejected this argument, holding that 'pregnancy cannot be said to pertain uniquely to the sphere of private life'.[45] In the Commission's view, not every regulation of abortion amounts to an interference with the right to respect for private life of the mother. Judge Fawcett, dissenting, makes the sound point that the Commission's reasoning is illogical. Once it is accepted that Article 8(1) does cover pregnancy and its termination, any limits imposed must be justified under Article 8(2). Fawcett argued that the limitation on abortion in Germany was not 'necessary in a democratic society' for any of the legitimate aims specified in Article 8(2). This is arguable: the protection of health or morals, or the protection of the rights and freedoms of others, could perhaps justify limitations upon the availability of abortion, or at least it may be within a state's margin of appreciation (area of discretion) to regard these as justifiable limitations. However, the Commission's opinion fails to address these issues and, since no similar case has reached the Commission or Court, we are left with the unsatisfactory position that pregnancy is to be regarded under the ECHR as an aspect of, but not solely of, a woman's private life, and therefore a choice to terminate it cannot be an enforceable right under Article 8.

(b)   The Mother's Rights in English Law

(i)   Taking Account of Maternal Interests

As was described in the previous section, abortion, or 'procuring a miscarriage', is a criminal offence in the United Kingdom. The first legal recognition of the possible existence and significance of the mother's conflicting interests came in 1929 with the Infant Life (Preservation) Act. In order to close the lacuna of the killing of a child during the process of birth, which was neither a miscarriage nor the homicide of a human being with an independent existence, this Act created an additional criminal offence of causing the death of a child capable of being born alive and included a defence if the act was done in good faith to preserve the

---

[44]   (1977) 10 *DR* 100.
[45]   *Ibid*, para 59.

life of the mother. Ten years later, in *R v Bourne*,[46] MacNaghten J, in a direction to the jury, extended this defence to the offence of procuring a miscarriage and in doing so expanded its interpretation. The case of *Bourne* was a criminal trial of a doctor charged with the offence of procuring a miscarriage. He had performed an abortion upon a 15 year old girl who was pregnant after being raped. The doctor made no attempt to do so secretly and sought to test the law. The outcome was unexpected. MacNaghten J made two intellectual leaps in his direction to the jury. First, he used the term 'unlawfully' in the 1861 offence to incorporate the defence of preserving the life of the mother from the 1929 Act. Second, he held that 'life depends upon health' and thus the preserving life defence includes an abortion done with the purpose of preserving the physical or mental health of the mother. On the basis of this direction, the jury acquitted Bourne. The law was left in a state of uncertainty, however. A judge and jury had recognised the relevance of maternal interests in a decision to perform a termination of pregnancy, but there remained no statutory recognition that abortion was anything other than a criminal offence. Finally, in the 1967 Abortion Act, this changed.

The pressures for an Abortion Act stemmed from two parliamentary concerns. First, there was the fact that abortion, like prostitution, is not susceptible to removal by legislation. As the Home Secretary, Roy Jenkins, pointed out in 1966:

> the existing law on abortion is uncertain and is also, perhaps more importantly, harsh and archaic and . . . is in urgent need of reform . . . How can anyone believe otherwise when perhaps as many as 100,000 illegal operations per year take place, that the present law has shown itself quite unable to deal with the problem? . . . [T]he law is consistently flouted by those who have the means to do so . . .[47]

Many of these illegal abortions were being performed by backstreet abortionists and posed a danger to the health of the woman forced to choose this option. In addition, the 1967 legislation stemmed from a second concern which was to protect medical autonomy and discretion and to remove the fear of prosecution from doctors.[48] Thus, it has been argued that the Abortion Act was not a lessening of state control over the relationship between a woman and her unborn child, but rather 'a shift in the modalities of control' from the criminal law to the medical profession.[49] This is because the Abortion Act 1967 (both in its original form and as amended in 1990) provides a defence to the 1861 offence of

---

[46] [1939] 1 KB 687.

[47] HC Debs, Vol 732, col 1141-142, 22 July 1966.

[48] S Sheldon, *Beyond Control: Medical Power and Abortion Law* (London, Pluto Press, 1997), pp 17-19.

[49] *Ibid*, p 31. See also p 148: 'The Act represents a shift from a legal regulation based on criminal prohibition, to one based on a decentralised network of medical control over women. This is not to deny that the 1967 Act represented a gain for women, but rather to note that it simultaneously grounded a particular modality of power over them'.

procuring a miscarriage only if two doctors certify in good faith that one of a number of specified grounds for the abortion exist. These grounds were slightly amended in 1990 (and will be discussed below) but the emphasis on doctors as gate-keepers to a legal abortion remains. This leads to an interesting contradiction. On the one hand, access to legal abortion is now relatively easy. The grounds specified in the Abortion Act have been interpreted broadly by the medical profession, so much so that Mason has argued that 'it is difficult to see how it is possible now to perform an unlawful abortion in Great Britain provided the administrative conditions of the Act and its associated regulations are observed'.[50] On the other hand, in the absence of any positive right to an abortion, the woman remains entirely in the hands of the doctors. In particular, this means that an abortion on the NHS is dependent upon a referral by the woman's GP. Failing that, the woman will need to use her initiative to find a doctor sympathetic to her needs.[51] The involvement of medical discretion in access to legal abortion arose because the legal grounds for abortion in the Abortion Act focus upon the mental and physical health of the mother and her unborn child. It is now time to consider these grounds in detail.

(ii)   The Legal Grounds for Abortion

The current grounds for abortion are to be found in section 1(1) Abortion Act 1967 as amended by the Human Fertilisation and Embryology Act 1990:

> . . . if two registered medical practitioners are of the opinion, formed in good faith –
>
> (a)   that the pregnancy has not exceeded its twenty-fourth week and that the continuance of the pregnancy would involve risk, greater than if the pregnancy were terminated, of injury to the physical or mental health of the pregnant woman or any existing children of her family; or
> (b)   that the termination is necessary to prevent grave permanent injury to the physical or mental health of the pregnant woman; or
> (c)   that the continuance of the pregnancy would involve risk to the life of the pregnant woman, greater than if the pregnancy were terminated; or
> (d)   that there is a substantial risk that if the child were born it would suffer from such physical or mental abnormalities as to be seriously handicapped.[52]

Grounds (b) and (c) are the least controversial, and raise the fewest issues, and so we will consider these first. They permit a termination of pregnancy if it is necessary to prevent either grave, permanent injury to the physical or mental health of the woman or a risk to the life of the woman greater than if the

---

[50]   Mason, n 13 above, p 117.
[51]   Sheldon, n 48 above, p 59.
[52]   Note that in emergencies only one doctor need certify the grounds for abortion: 'where he is of the opinion, formed in good faith, that the termination is immediately necessary to save the life or to prevent grave permanent injury to the physical or mental health of the pregnant woman' (s 1(4)).

pregnancy is terminated. In other words, the mother's right to life and health are clearly prioritised here by the legal protection of those rights at the expense of protection for the fetus. The risk to life or health must be certified as existing by two doctors acting in good faith, and it is unlikely to be sufficient to rely upon statistical evidence that all abortions in the first trimester carry a smaller risk to life than continuation of the pregnancy to full term. There is no time limit in respect of grounds (b) or (c) and therefore they serve as legal justifications for a termination of pregnancy at any time during the pregnancy. Even a viable fetus is not legally entitled to be preserved at the cost of its mother's life or health. Prior to the 1990 amendments, the Abortion Act as originally drafted did include an implicit time limit because it only provided a defence to the criminal offence of procuring a miscarriage. The offence of causing the death of a child capable of being born alive could not be avoided by a doctor's certificate under the original Abortion Act and thus the Act's defences only applied before fetal viability. In the context of what are now grounds (b) and (c), this was not hugely significant because, as explained above, the offence of child destruction included a statutory defence of acting in good faith to save the life of the mother and *Bourne* widened the scope of this on the basis that 'life depends upon health'. Thus, abortions on these grounds were probably legally permissible anyway, even if performed at a late stage in the pregnancy. Furthermore, in practice, the use of grounds (b) and (c) for late abortions is very rare because in such cases it is the pregnancy (which is causing a threat to the mother's health or life), rather than the child, that is unwanted. Therefore, late terminations of pregnancy under these grounds are, in effect, induced labour through Caesarean section, performed with the hope of fetal survival.

The huge majority of abortions take place much earlier in the pregnancy under ground (a). This permits a legal abortion if continuance of the pregnancy would involve risk, greater than if the pregnancy were terminated, of injury to the physical or mental health of the pregnant woman or any existing children of her family. There is no requirement under this ground for the risk to health to be grave or permanent and indeed it has been interpreted so broadly by the medical profession that it is commonly termed the 'social ground' for abortion. It is important to note, however, that, even under this most easily satisfied ground, it remains the woman's health, rather than her freedom of choice, which justifies the termination of pregnancy. Even though legal abortion is widely available under this ground, the need to convince two doctors of a health reason for terminating the pregnancy, even if merely in the sense of a likelihood of mild depression if forced to continue an unwanted pregnancy, means that the woman's right to autonomy over her body remains unprotected at law and vulnerable to interpretation, and perhaps prejudice, by her doctors. The only exception in ground (a) to the requirement of health implications for the woman is the mention of the 'existing children of her family'. A threat to the physical or mental health of these existing children is also a legal justification for abortion under section 1(1)(a) and is perhaps the most curious ground of all.

It should also be noted, in respect of ground (a), that there is a time limit of 24 weeks specified in section 1(1)(a). This broad, 'social' ground does not, therefore, authorise an abortion at the late stages of pregnancy. Twenty four weeks is an increasingly controversial time limit because, with the state of modern technology, there is no doubt that a child born at 24 weeks today will be capable of surviving. Thus, the broadest ground for abortion permits the destruction of viable fetuses and there is growing political concern about this. Such concern has the effect of obscuring the fact that at no stage during the pregnancy, even during the first trimester, does the woman have any right under English law to exercise her autonomy in a way which will destroy her fetus unless she has a medical need to do so. It is clear, therefore, that the central feature of section 1(1) Abortion Act (amended) is that the woman's health justifies termination of the fetus's life but the mere exercise of her autonomy does not.

The final ground for abortion is the most problematic because it sanctions an abortion on the basis of the fetus's, rather than the mother's, health. The requirement in section 1(1)(d) is that there be a substantial risk that if the child were born it would suffer from such physical or mental abnormalities as to be seriously handicapped. Neither 'substantial risk' nor 'serious handicap' is defined in the statute, deliberately so.[53] The lack of statutory guidance to the medical profession seems to have led to a discrepancy between public and professional understanding of the seriousness of a handicap. When it was discovered in 2003 that doctors had performed a legal termination of pregnancy for reason of fetal abnormality on a fetus with a cleft lip and palate, there was widespread public unease, although the doctors were not prosecuted and the police and CPS were not liable for judicial review for the failure to prosecute.[54] At the very least, some degree of consistency amongst the medical profession across the country is essential and professional guidelines may serve that purpose as effectively as statutory rules. The requirement of a 'substantial risk' is also so vague that the Royal College of Obstetricians and Gynaecologists has recognised that 'there is room for lawyers to argue about what risks are substantial' although the College has also concluded that the risk must be more than 'a mere possibility' but need not be 'more likely than not'.[55]

The ambiguity in the terms of ground (d) are not helped by uncertainty as to the purpose of the ground: is it designed to prevent distress and emotional or economic burdens to the parents of a child who if born will suffer from a serious handicap?; or is it designed in the fetus's own interests to prevent the pain and

---

[53]   In the parliamentary debates on the 1990 amendments, the then Lord Chancellor, Lord Mackay of Clashfern, addressed the issue of a definition of these terms and concluded that 'It is surely impossible to take an absolutely certain view of these cases. It is a matter of opinion, and the requirement is that the opinion should be formed in good faith' (HL Debs, Vol 522, col 1098).

[54]   *R (application of Jepson) v Chief Constable of West Mercia* (1 December 2003, unreported). For discussion, see 'Does a Cleft Palate Justify an Abortion? Curate Wins Right to Challenge Doctors' *The Guardian,* 2 December 2003.

[55]   *Termination of Pregnancy for Fetal Abnormality* (RCOG, 1996), para 3.2.1.

suffering which may accompany a serious handicap? Morgan prefers the latter view, arguing that ground (d) is 'primarily a fetal interests ground and not a parental interests ground, nor [and this now almost goes without saying] a state (eugenic) interest provision'.[56] The justification for this view is that the mother's interests are adequately served by the other grounds in section 1, ie through the harm to mental health or existing children grounds. However, Morgan's view carries with it the difficulty that, if a termination of pregnancy for fetal abnormality is in the fetal interest, surely it should be compulsory once a substantial risk of a serious handicap has been identified? The fact that this is not the case strongly suggests that, even under the fetal handicap ground, a termination of pregnancy is lawful in order to protect the interests of the mother rather than the fetus. Furthermore, the Court of Appeal's recognition in the conjoined twins case of *Re A*[57] that even a life consisting of only a few months of pain and suffering was preferable to non-existence does not fit easily with the proposition that the destruction of fetuses because there is a 'substantial' risk that they will suffer 'serious' handicap is in the fetus's own interests.[58]

The message sent out by the current law on abortion unambiguously elevates the woman's health interests over those of her unborn child. However, there is also a clear signal that a woman's right to bodily autonomy is restricted in this context. A termination of pregnancy is treated differently from other medical procedures in that it remains a prima facie criminal offence. Until this changes, the most common surgical operation for women of reproductive age[59] will remain rooted in the legal illusion of a threat to the woman's or fetus's health, rather than an aspect of the woman's right to self-determination and reproductive autonomy.

III. The Father

The legal issue of abortion is dominated by the maternal-fetal conflict but there is inevitably a third party with a moral interest in the continuation or termination of the pregnancy: the father. The scientific fact that the father has contributed half of the genetic material which comprises the fetus, and the moral responsibility which goes with that, is (as we have seen in the previous chapter) legally recognised in the context of medically assisted conception. The mother and father are given equal rights over an embryo created outside the body. Even in an emotive situation such as the mother being unable to conceive again due to

---

[56] D Morgan, 'Abortion: The Unexamined Ground' [1990] *Crim LR* 687 at p 692.

[57] *Re A (Children) (Conjoined Twins: Surgical Separation)* [2000] 4 All ER 961.

[58] See S Sheldon and S Wilkinson, 'Termination of Pregnancy for Reason of Fetal Disability: Are There Grounds for a Special Exception in Law?' (2001) 9 *Med L Rev* 85, at p 91.

[59] Jackson, n 30 above, p 72.

cancer, the father is given a legally enforceable right to determine the future of the embryo, requiring its destruction if his consent for its use and storage is withdrawn.[60] This principle of equal control over the embryo stands in stark contrast to the legal position once the embryo is implanted into the mother's womb. Upon this event, the father immediately loses all legal rights over his child until it is born, when the rights and responsibilities resume. The justification is clear: any intervention by the father to preserve or destroy the fetus now requires an infringement of the mother's right to bodily integrity and/or autonomy. While outside the body, the rights in respect of the embryo can, and should, be equal, but once inside the mother, her interests must prevail over those of the father. The possibility of a father withdrawing consent for the continued existence of the fetus created from his sperm and requiring its immediate destruction by means of a termination of pregnancy against the wishes of the mother reveals the impossibility of the mother and father having equal rights over the fetus: a termination of pregnancy should never be forced upon an unwilling woman. On the other hand, what if the father wishes the fetus to survive but the mother has chosen to have an abortion? Should the father have any say in this situation? If he expresses a willingness to raise the child himself, with no financial or emotional contribution from the mother, is it really too much to require the woman not to destroy the fetus before viability?

The closest that any court has come to recognising fathers' rights in respect of abortion is the Canadian case of *Tremblay v Daigle*[61] in which the Quebec Court of Appeal granted a father an interlocutory injunction to prevent an abortion but this was struck down by the Supreme Court of Canada. The Supreme Court noted the lack of any substantive rights on which the injunction could be founded and held that the 'lack of a legal basis is fatal to the argument about 'fathers' rights'.[62] English law is extremely clear and unambiguous on this issue: the father has no legal rights in the context of abortion. In *Paton v British Pregnancy Advisory Service Trustees*,[63] the father seeking to prevent his partner's abortion argued not only on behalf of the fetus (discussed above) but also in his own right as father, but the court was equally unconvinced by this latter argument. Sir George Baker P merely emphasised that the Abortion Act contains no provision for spousal permission or consultation and thus, provided that the abortion was lawful under the terms of the Act (and this was a matter more for the medical profession than the courts), the father cannot stop the abortion by means of an injunction.[64] When the European Commission of Human Rights

---

[60] See *Evans v Amicus Healthcare* [2004] 3 All ER 1025. The European Court of Human Rights has confirmed that the English approach is consistent with the ECHR: *Evans v United Kingdom* (2006) 43 EHRR 21.

[61] (1989) 62 DLR (4th) 634.

[62] *Ibid*, p 665.

[63] See n 20 above.

[64] *Ibid*, p 280. A further attempt by a father to prevent his ex-partner's abortion in *C v S* [1987] 1 All ER 1230 also failed. Here the father sought to argue that a fetus of 18-21 weeks was capable of

considered the case, it concluded that the father's lack of involvement in the decision to abort his fetus may fall within Article 8's protection of the right to respect for his private and family life but interference with this right was justified under Article 8(2) as necessary in a democratic society for the protection of the rights of another person, namely the mother.[65] This seems to be a logical approach to the question: determination of the future of a fetus is a matter which falls within the private life of both the mother and the father (although, as discussed above, it may not be solely a private matter as the state may have a legitimate interest in the fate of the fetus). However, a balance must be struck between two potentially conflicting interests and in this balance it is the mother's interests which must prevail given that any decision about the fate of the fetus will have an impact upon her bodily integrity.

IV. The Medical Professionals

The Abortion Act gives medical professionals the key role in determining the legality of an abortion. This role brings with it grave responsibility. Performing a termination of pregnancy is always a criminal offence under the 1861 Offences Against the Person Act, punishable by up to life imprisonment. Only if the correct administrative procedures are followed and the good faith requirement satisfied will the doctor performing this medical procedure be relieved of criminal liability. As the Abortion Act defences specify legal protection only when the termination of pregnancy is performed by a 'registered medical practitioner', there was initially some doubt over the protection for nursing staff who often play crucial roles in the procedure. The Royal College of Nursing queried whether nurses could potentially be found criminally liable for procuring a miscarriage due to the emphasis upon doctors in the Abortion Act defence but the House of Lords clarified the issue in *Royal College of Nursing of the UK v Department of Health*.[66] It was held that an abortion is a team effort and all participants will be absolved of criminal liability if an Abortion Act defence exists, provided that the procedure is initiated and overseen by a registered medical practitioner.

In practice, the chances of any prosecution are slim. Only one case has been brought against a doctor under the Abortion Act 1967, *R v Smith*,[67] and here the prosecution and conviction was based upon the lack of good faith. The doctor in this case had failed to make any genuine medical assessment of the woman

being born alive and thus an abortion would be unlawful under the Infant Life (Preservation) Act 1929 (to which the Abortion Act defences did not apply pre-1990). The court rejected this argument, holding that the fetus was not yet capable of being born alive because it was incapable of breathing, and the father therefore had no right to prevent the lawful termination.

[65] *Paton v United Kingdom*, n 1 above.

[66] [1981] 1 All ER 545.

[67] [1973] 1 WLR 1510.

seeking an abortion and this, coupled with other actions characteristic of a lack of good faith such as a failure to inform the patient of the need for a second opinion and excessive fees, led the court to convict him of unlawfully procuring a miscarriage. The case indicates the limits of medical discretion, namely that 'to authorise abortion for no more reason than a woman's desire to have one was indeed an abuse'.[68] But this 'abuse' can easily be avoided. If Dr Smith had conducted an examination of the patient and certified that the termination of pregnancy was necessary for her mental or physical health, a conviction, or even prosecution, would have been extremely unlikely. Does this mean that the crucial exercise of medical discretion under the Abortion Act is merely a legal fiction? The breadth of the legal grounds and the ease with which they can be satisfied suggests that doctors do little more than give a medical stamp of approval to decisions already taken by the mother. However, the role of the doctor can be vital, not only in acting as a gatekeeper to treatment, but also in creating a presumption in favour of abortion. This may occur, for example, when prenatal testing is offered for a condition for which there is no plausible treatment.[69] In some situations, doctors have dual roles as advisors on the implications of a complex diagnosis and as the gatekeeper to abortion services.[70] Their role under the Abortion Act is, therefore, both complex and ambiguous.

The legality of terminations of pregnancy at very late stages in pregnancy, especially on the basis of fetal handicap, leads to the disturbing possibility that a fetus may show signs of life following the procedure. This is not as rare an event as might be imagined.[71] As the defence in the Abortion Act has no application after the child is born alive, a doctor may face legal liability for any subsequent death. The doctor is vulnerable to both criminal and civil liability. Criminal liability may arise because the death of a child born alive following an abortion is likely to satisfy the actus reus of murder (death being caused by the procedure or the fact of prematurity) and the issue will then hinge upon whether an intention to kill a fetus can be transferred (on the basis of the transferred malice concept considered in *A-G's Reference (No 3 of 1994)*[72]) to the child born alive.[73] Civil liability for wrongful birth[74] could arise if the doctor's failure to ensure death in utero amounts to a breach of his duty of care but it may be difficult to establish the causation of damage unless the mother and/or father can prove psychiatric suffering from witnessing the birth of a live child following a termination of

---

[68]   Sheldon, n 48 above, p 84.

[69]   See Jackson, n 30 above, p 97.

[70]   *Ibid*, p 106.

[71]   During the period 1995-2002, 104 live births occurred following a termination of pregnancy for fetal abnormality within the West Midlands region (E Wicks, M Wyldes and M Kilby, 'Late Terminations of Pregnancy for Fetal Abnormality: Medical and Legal Perspectives' (2004) 12 *Med L Rev* 285, at pp 285-86).

[72]   See n 21 above.

[73]   See Wicks, Wyldes and Kilby, n 71 above, pp 298-301.

[74]   This cause of action is discussed in Chapter 10 below.

pregnancy for fetal abnormality. Prosecution of a doctor for circumstances surrounding a live birth from a termination of pregnancy are unlikely, and a conviction even more so, but the mere possibility of criminal, as well as civil, liability reminds us that doctors performing terminations of pregnancy are in an ambiguous and vulnerable legal position.

In addition, the moral sensitivity of abortion means that a conscience clause was required in the Abortion Act to enable doctors, and others involved in the treatment, to be free to abstain from performing this controversial medical procedure.[75] Under Section 4, a conscientious objection is permitted although not, understandably, in an emergency situation. If a doctor does have a conscientious objection to abortion, there must surely be an ethical obligation to make a timely referral to a colleague. Indeed in *Barr v Matthews* Alliot J suggested that this may be a legal as well as an ethical obligation: 'once a termination of pregnancy is recognised as an option, the doctor invoking the conscientious objection clause should refer the patient to a colleague at once'.[76] The existence of a conscientious objection clause reminds us, however, that the medical professional has been given an important, and morally burdensome, task under the British abortion laws. Even though they lack the intimate connection with the pregnancy which so dominates the interests of the mother, father and fetus, the medical professionals involved in a termination of pregnancy have legitimate interests in avoiding criminal liability, in acting in their patient's (ie the mother's) best interests and in remaining true to their own consciences. It will at times be a hard balance to strike.

V. Conclusion

It might appear that a rights-based perspective is ultimately of limited utility to the issue of termination of pregnancy. The notoriously controversial issue of whether a fetus has a right to life remains undecided. The European Court of Human Rights has desperately avoided addressing the question and English law, although purporting to deny all rights and legal status to the fetus, remains rather ambiguous due to the continued criminalisation of abortion. (The case law on non-consensual Caesarean section operations, discussed in the following chapter, provides further evidence of such ambiguity.) The rights of the mother in this context are also somewhat uncertain. In all other circumstances, a woman has a right to self-determination in respect of her bodily integrity. Does this necessarily

---

[75] The conscience clause only applies if an individual will actually be participating in the procedure. Thus, in *Janaway v Salford Area Health Authority* [1988] 3 All ER 1079, the House of Lords confirmed that a typist who claimed she was unfairly dismissed following her refusal to type a letter referring a patient for an abortion was not legally entitled to rely upon a conscientious objection under the Abortion Act.

[76] (1999) 52 BMLR 217, at 227.

mean that any legal restriction upon access to abortion services is an infringement of that right? Even if we do not grant the fetus any legally enforceable rights pre-birth, the nature of a termination of pregnancy and its resulting destruction of human life must necessitate responsible decision making in this context. Furthermore, to view the abortion debate as merely a conflict between the rights of the fetus and the rights of the mother drastically oversimplifies the matter: for example, what about the father's interests? Or the state's interest in protecting human life? Or the fetal interest in not suffering once born? The maternal-fetal conflict approach also fails to provide a solution. A pregnant woman will in practice almost always feel a responsibility towards the unborn child inside her. If she nevertheless decides that a termination of pregnancy is the correct or necessary choice for her and/or the unborn child, she should at least do so, and be required by the law to do so, in full knowledge that a termination of pregnancy is more than a mere exercise of her individual autonomy. Its consequences for the unborn child, the potential father, the medical professionals involved in the procedure, and indeed for human society in general, are profound. A termination of pregnancy should never be regarded as merely another medical procedure, akin to the removal of a tooth or a tumour, but it does remain a medical procedure performed upon an individual woman and therefore it must be she who ultimately decides whether to undergo the procedure or not. That is one fundamental right which is vital to the topic of abortion and should never be overlooked as our knowledge and understanding of (and thus empathy for) the fetus increases through improvements in medical technology.

Recommended Further Reading

R Dworkin, *Life's Dominion: An Argument about Abortion and Euthanasia* (London, HarperCollins, 1993), Chapters 1-3.

E Jackson, *Regulating Reproduction: Law, Technology and Autonomy* (Oxford, Hart Publishing, 2001), Chapter 3.

S Sheldon, *Beyond Control: Medical Power and Abortion Law* (London, Pluto Press, 1997).

S Sheldon and S Wilkinson, 'Termination of Pregnancy for Reason of Fetal Disability: Are There Grounds for a Special Exception in Law?' (2001) 9 *Med L Rev* 85.

E Wicks, M Wyldes and M Kilby, 'Late Terminations of Pregnancy for Fetal Abnormality: Medical and Legal Perspectives' (2004) 12 *Med L Rev* 285.

10

Pregnancy and Freedom of Choice

The previous two chapters have discussed issues of reproductive autonomy in the two most common and significant contexts: termination of pregnancy and medically assisted conception. Beyond these two extreme reproductive choices, however, there is a plethora of other legal and moral issues in relation to pregnancy which impact upon the principle of reproductive autonomy. The freedom of a pregnant woman to make her own choices, whether about medical treatment or behavioural habits such as smoking or drug-taking, potentially impinges upon the welfare of her unborn child, thus raising the question of whether pregnancy imposes some restraints upon autonomy for the good of the fetus. In addition, the actions of medical professionals in performing sterilisation operations or pre-natal screening, or advising as to sterility or fetal health, have the potential to limit the spectrum of autonomous choices about reproduction open to a woman. Therefore, this chapter considers these diverse issues against the backdrop of a right to autonomy for the pregnant woman and on the basis of an assumption, drawn from the analysis in Chapter 9, that a fetus has no rights under English law until born alive.

I. Refusal of Medical Treatment During Pregnancy

(a) Freedom of Choice and the Pregnant Woman

The fundamental importance of the principle of autonomy in the healthcare context was established in Chapter 4. It is an essential ethical principle which has found legal identity in both international human rights law (for example, Article 8 ECHR) and domestic common law. In *Re T*, Lord Donaldson MR confirmed that:

> An adult patient who . . . suffers from no mental incapacity has an absolute right to choose whether to consent to medical treatment, to refuse it or to choose one rather than another of the treatments being offered . . . This right of choice is not limited to

decisions which others might regard as sensible. It exists notwithstanding that the reasons for making the choice are rational, irrational, unknown or even non-existent.[1]

Provided that the competency test is satisfied – not always a straightforward task –the patient has an absolute right under English law to refuse any form of medical treatment without the need for justification of his or her decision. A pregnancy undoubtedly adds complexity to the matter, however. Improvements in medical technology mean that the fetus is increasingly viewed as a patient itself. Therefore, a doctor may feel that he has a professional duty towards two patients, rather than just one, and the unilateral medical decisions of the pregnant woman, which will inevitably impact, possibly unfavourably, on the fetus, may not garner the respect given to the decisions of other competent patients. The potential exclusion of the pregnant woman from the general right to autonomy in medical decisions was recognised in *Re T*. The quotation above from Lord Donaldson in this case has one important point omitted. He added that there is one 'possible qualification' to the general right to refuse treatment and this is where 'the choice may lead to the death of a viable foetus'.[2]

It is worth re-iterating at this point the fact that a fetus has no legal rights or interests in English law until it is born and, as we saw in the previous chapter, a termination of pregnancy is legal at any stage in the pregnancy, even after viability, if the mother's life or health is at grave, permanent risk or if there is a substantial risk that the fetus will be seriously handicapped. Does this mean that Lord Donaldson's 'possible qualification' is inconsistent with other areas of English law? It should be noted that abortion always remains a prima facie criminal offence and after viability a defence only exists if the health of the mother is at serious risk. Thus, to permit, for example, a woman in labour to validly refuse a Caesarean section delivery, which is essential in order for the child to be born alive, for a trivial reason such as a wish to avoid an abdominal scar, would seem contrary to the strict limits on abortion at this late stage of pregnancy. This argument is less convincing, however, when it is noted that a Caesarean section is a major operation with a risk of death to the mother estimated to be four times higher than that of a natural delivery.[3] Even in abortion law it is clearly established that a viable fetus does not have the right to be saved at the cost of the mother's health or life. The fact that the fetus does not appear to have a right to life (subject to the European Court of Human Rights eventually deciding otherwise) but that, once born alive, the child is entitled to the full and equal protection of the law, only adds further to the moral

---

[1]   *Re T (adult: refusal of treatment)* [1992] 4 All ER 649 at 652-53.
[2]   *Ibid.*
[3]   R Scott, *Rights, Duties and the Body: Law and Ethics of the Maternal-Fetal Conflict* (Oxford, Hart Publishing, 2002), p xxvl.

complexity of this situation because, as Wells notes, 'there is no simple line between being at full-term in a pregnancy and being the mother of a new-born baby'.[4]

In the United States, there originally appeared to be a judicial willingness to limit the pregnant woman's autonomy in order to protect her unborn child. Thus, in *Jefferson v Griffin Spalding County Hospital Authority*[5] in 1981, the court granted temporary custody of a 39 week old fetus to the county department, giving it authority to consent to a surgical delivery without the woman's consent. The woman had been told that there was a 99% chance of a stillbirth without the operation but had refused consent on religious grounds. The court justified its decision as follows: 'the intrusion involved into the life of Jessie May Jefferson . . . is outweighed by the duty of the state to protect a living unborn human being from meeting his or her death before being given the opportunity to live'.[6] This prioritisation of fetal interests over those of its mother suggests that the pregnant woman lacks the legal protection given to all other competent adults:

> the enormous disparity between compulsory major surgery in this domain and the rejection everywhere else of far lesser intrusions strongly suggests that these unparalleled burdens that pregnant woman are forced to bear constitute invidious discrimination, despite the state's benevolent motive.[7]

Compulsory intervention in this context, as elsewhere, is based upon the premise that the doctors know best, and so the reality that Jessie May Jefferson eventually gave birth naturally to a healthy baby undermines such intervention even further. Even more objectionable than a non-consensual Caesarean section is an unnecessary, non-consensual Caesarean section.

Nevertheless, the US courts persevered for a time with compulsory intervention, the most tragic example of which is undoubtedly *Re AC*.[8] This case involved a pregnant woman of 26 weeks gestation who was dying of cancer and had only days to live. It was universally agreed that a Caesarean section operation would hasten Angela Carder's death, as well as resulting in a very premature baby with little chance of surviving, and she refused consent to the operation. Following an emergency hearing at the hospital, a judge ordered the operation to go ahead against the wishes of the dying patient, and her distressed family. The child died within hours of the operation and the mother died two days later. The tragic circumstances of this particular non-consensual Caesarean section delivery led to widespread public outcry and following the intervention of numerous interest

---

[4] C Wells, 'On the Outside Looking In: Perspectives on Enforced Caesarians' in S Sheldon and M Thomson (eds) *Feminist Perspectives on Health Care Law* (London, Cavendish, 1998), p 254.

[5] 247 Ga 86; 274 5E 2d 457.

[6] *Ibid* at p 460.

[7] N Rhoden, 'The Judge in the Delivery Room: The Emergence of Court-Ordered Caesareans' (1986) 74 *Cal L Rev* 1951, at p 1988.

[8] 573 A 2d 611 (DC, 1987), 573 A 2d 1235 (DC, 1990).

groups, the decision was eventually overturned on appeal years after the death of Angela Carder. Notwithstanding this appeal decision, the first instance decision was used as authority in the first UK case to authorise a non-consensual Caesarean section delivery.

This arose in the 1992 emergency hearing in *Re S*.[9] The pregnant woman in this case, supported by her husband, refused consent to a Caesarean section on religious grounds as a 'born again Christian'. Her doctors were of the view that this refusal would lead to the death of both the mother and her unborn child. Against this emotive background, Sir Stephen Brown issued a declaration authorising the operation without consent within 48 minutes of the application coming to the notice of the court. His only authority for doing so was Lord Donaldson's obiter statement in *Re T* and the first instance decision in *Re AC* which had subsequently, and apparently without the knowledge of Sir Stephen Brown, been overruled on appeal.[10] In the US, a woman's right to refuse a Caesarean section has been upheld,[11] although the question of a right to refuse less invasive procedures has been left open.[12] In the UK, following the *Re S* decision, there was great concern that a pregnant woman was indeed an exception to the general requirement of patient autonomy. By 1998, however, the Court of Appeal had reasserted the importance of patient autonomy for all patients even those responsible for another life besides their own.

In *St George's Healthcare NHS Trust v S*,[13] a woman of 36 weeks' gestation was diagnosed with pre-eclampsia and advised of the immediate need of admission to hospital for an induced delivery. The woman refused consent to this as she wanted her baby to be born naturally. She was then compulsorily admitted to Springfield hospital under section 2 of the Mental Health Act 1983 for assessment (ie 'sectioned') and subsequently transferred to St George's Hospital for a Caesarean section delivery. A court application was made *ex parte* on behalf of the hospital and Hogg J granted a declaration dispensing with the need for S's consent. The Caesarean section was performed without the woman's consent. A week later, her section 2 assessment was terminated and S immediately discharged herself against medical advice. At no point during this compulsory detention under the Mental Health Act was any treatment provided for a mental

---

[9]   *Re S (adult: refusal of medical treatment)* [1992] 4 All ER 671.

[10]   The judicial reliance upon *Re AC* as authority in favour of the authorisation of a non-consensual Caesarean section is generally regarded as a mistake. However, the matter is a little more complicated than it may at first appear because the Appeal Court in *Re AC* restricted its judgment to the facts of the case before it – ie one in which only the fetus's health requires the operation and where the operation will shorten the life of the mother. The *Re S* type of case, in which the health interests of the mother and fetus are not in conflict, was expressly left open (573 A 2d 1252). Therefore, as Scott explains, the reliance upon *Re AC* in *Re S* may have been in line with the letter, if not the spirit, of the American case (Scott, n 3 above, p 123).

[11]   *Baby Boy Doe* 632 NE 2d 326, Appeal Court of Illinois.

[12]   A blood transfusion, however, has been regarded as an invasive procedure and thus one which could be validly refused by the pregnant woman (*Re Fetus Brown* (1997) 294 Ill App 3d 159).

[13]   [1998] 3 WLR 936.

disorder and, indeed, there seemed little evidence for a mental disorder other than an apparently irrational refusal of consent to a Caesarean section. At the court hearing there were a litany of errors: there was no discussion of whether the woman in question was competent to make decisions herself; the judge was told that S had been in labour for 24 hours and that lives were imminently at risk, neither of which was true; and neither S nor the solicitor she had previously consulted were informed of the hearing. Hogg J said, 'if the mother wishes to appeal this case it means that it has worked'[14] which seems to indicate a clear disregard of the importance of individual autonomy and an unjustified prioritisation of the sanctity of life in all circumstances which is at odds with other aspects of English medical law.[15] On appeal, the Court of Appeal strongly and unambiguously declared that S's autonomous choice should have been respected:

> In our judgment while pregnancy increases the personal responsibilities of a woman it does not diminish her entitlement to decide whether or not to undergo medical treatment ... She is entitled not to be forced to submit to an invasion of her body against her will, whether her own life or that of her unborn child depends on it.[16]

The Court of Appeal recognised that this approach may necessitate the protection of an irrational and/or morally erroneous choice by the pregnant woman but this is an inevitable legacy of the principle of autonomy: all choices must be respected, even those which are objectively wrong. Thus, the Court of Appeal said that the pregnant woman's right to refuse 'is not reduced or diminished merely because her decision to exercise it may appear morally repugnant'[17] and an interference with that right is not lawful even when the motive for the interference 'is readily understandable, and indeed to many would appear commendable'.[18] If this approach results in unnecessary deaths, the justification remains that, in the words of Nancy Rhoden, 'it is far better that some tragic private wrongs transpire than that state-imposed coercion of pregnant women become part of our legal landscape'.[19]

A similarly strong affirmation of the right to autonomy of a pregnant woman was apparent in the earlier Court of Appeal judgment of *Re MB*.[20] In this Court of Appeal judgment, however, the rhetoric of autonomous choice was somewhat

---

[14]   *Ibid*, p 948.
[15]   *Re B (adult: refusal of medical treatment)* [2002] 2 All ER 449 suggests that self-determination can take priority over sanctity of life considerations, while *Airedale NHS Trust v Bland* [1993] 1 All ER 821 also asserts that the sanctity of life is not absolute.
[16]   *St George's*, n 13 above, p 957 (per Judge LJ).
[17]   *Ibid.*
[18]   *Ibid*, p 953.
[19]   Rhoden, n 7 above, p 1953.
[20]   'The law is, in our judgment, clear that a competent woman who has the capacity to decide may, for religious reasons, other reasons, or for no reasons at all, chose not to have medical intervention, even though ... the consequence may be the death or serious handicap of the child she bears or her own death' ([1997] 8 *Med LR* 217.)

undermined by the reality of a finding of incompetence and the authorisation of compulsory intervention. In the context of the pregnant patient, even more than in respect of other patients, the spectre of competency casts a dark shadow upon freedom of choice in healthcare decisions.

(b)   Competency during Pregnancy

There were seven English cases on the question of non-consensual Caesarean sections between *Re S* 1992 and *St. George's* in 1998 and in six of these cases the mental competency of the pregnant woman was in issue. The only exception was the very first case, *Re S*, where it seems to have been assumed that the pregnant woman was fully competent. In this case, however, as we have seen, the judge was prepared to authorise the treatment without a finding of incompetence. In all subsequent cases, the judicial justification for compulsory treatment was that the woman was incapable of making a competent decision herself. This does not mean that the women in question were necessarily suffering from an established mental disorder, although in one case, *Tameside & Glossop Acute Services Unit v CH*,[21] this was the situation. In this case, Wall J was willing to define a Caesarean section as routine treatment for a mental disorder which could be authorised under section 63 of the Mental Health Act 1983 without consent and which could be imposed using force if necessary. This very broad interpretation of medical treatment 'for a mental disorder' is consistent with other case law which has established, for example, that the force-feeding of an anorexic patient also falls within this category.[22] It is particularly objectionable, however, not only because of the misuse of the mental health legislation, but also because it was an unnecessary application of this compulsory treatment power as the woman was clearly incompetent and could have been treated under the common law power of necessity.[23]

In the remaining non-consensual Caesarean section cases the pregnant woman was not suffering from a pre-existing mental disorder and thus the only doubt about competency arose from the apparently irrational refusal of consent to an objectively necessary form of delivery. For example, in *Rochdale Healthcare NHS Trust v C*,[24] the pregnant woman declared that she would rather die than repeat her previous experience of a Caesarean section under epidural anaesthetic. C's obstetrician confirmed that her mental capacity was not in doubt and she was fully competent. This did not prevent Johnson J, during a two minute *ex parte* hearing, taking the opposite view and holding C to be mentally incompetent. His reasons for doing so were that C was 'in the throes of labour with all that is

---

[21]   [1996] 1 FLR 762.
[22]   *Riverside Mental Health Trust v Fox* [1994] 1 FLR 614.
[23]   *Re F (mental patient: sterilisation)* [1990] 2 AC 1.
[24]   [1997] 1 FCR 274.

involved in terms of pain and emotional stress'.[25] She was regarded as failing to satisfy the third aspect of the *Re C* competency test: weighing the information about the proposed treatment in the balance in order to arrive at a choice.[26] Johnson J held that C could not appropriately balance her fear of another operation against her own death and the death of her unborn child. This approach raises two difficulties. First, there seems to be an assumption that a woman 'in the throes of labour' will inevitably lack competence. This generalisation has potential to discriminate against the pregnant woman. Second, this use of the third aspect of the *Re C* test potentially opens the door for judicial consideration of fetal interests if there is a requirement that the woman must weigh all information in the balance, including the impact of her decision on the fetus.[27] When C said she would 'rather die' than endure an operation of which she had previous experience, it could be argued that she had proved her ability to weigh the issues in the balance and that she had decided that death was her preferred option. This is, without doubt, a strange, probably irrational, and certainly selfish, conclusion to have reached but, as we saw in Chapter 4, a refusal of treatment does not need to be rational, well-considered or sensible in order for English law to respect it.[28] *Rochdale* suggests, however, that for a pregnant woman, particularly one in labour, a refusal of treatment would need to be objectively rational in order to be upheld. The only explanation for this distinction is that the law, almost surreptitiously, protects the fetus at this very late stage in the pregnancy. The failure to acknowledge that this is the case leaves the law with a worrying discrepancy between rhetoric and reality. The right to respect for private life in Article 8 ECHR, incorporated into domestic law in the Human Rights Act 1998, requires the protection of self-determination and bodily integrity in the healthcare context, as in all others, and the European Court of Human Rights has emphasised that the Convention 'is intended to guarantee not rights that are theoretical or illusory but rights that are practical and effective'.[29] Therefore, a rhetorical right to refuse medical treatment which is impossible for a pregnant woman to enforce in practice may not be sufficient protection for her freedom of choice under the ECHR.

Before leaving the *Rochdale* case, it should be noted that during the time of the hearing, the woman actually changed her mind and consented to the Caesarean section. Whether this was an entirely voluntary re-evaluation of the situation or was a response to the medical pressure upon her to undergo the operation is open to question. It is certainly interesting that once she had agreed to the

---

[25]   *Ibid.*

[26]   *Re C (adult: refusal of medical treatment)* [1994] 1 WLR 290. See Chapter 4 for discussion of the *Re C* test.

[27]   Scott, n 3 above, p 161.

[28]   See, for example, Lord Donaldson MR in *Re T*: 'This right of choice is not limited to decisions which others might regard as sensible. It exists notwithstanding that the reasons for making the choice are rational, irrational, unknown or even non-existent' (n. 1 above, pp 652-53).

[29]   *Airey v Ireland* (1979-80) 2 EHRR 305 at para 24. This point is made by Scott, n 3 above, p 231.

operation her consent was considered to be a valid exercise of her autonomy and the doubts about her competency faded from sight. The same development occurred in respect of the *St. George's* case when, just before the operation was performed non-consensually under the court declaration, S was asked once more if she consented. If S was indeed incompetent, as the judge's issuing of the declaration seems to suggest, it would be futile for medical staff to seek her consent to the procedure. The fact that they did so clearly re-iterates that these pregnant women were being found to be incapable of making a choice merely because of the choice which they had made. This is contrary to the English law on consent, as well as to the ECHR's protection of self-determination.

The application of the competency requirement in the pregnancy context was reconsidered in the 1997 Court of Appeal judgment in *Re MB*. This case involved a fetus in a breech position who faced a 50% chance of death without a Caesarean section delivery. The mother, MB, agreed to undergo a Caesarean section but suffered from a needle phobia and therefore refused to allow the administering of anaesthesia by means of an injection. An alternative means of administering anaesthesia, by mask, was also refused due to the increased medical risks in this method. Emergency hearings were held before Hollis J and, later in the same evening, the Court of Appeal. As mentioned above, the Court of Appeal gave a judgment strongly in support of the autonomy of the pregnant woman. However, the court also held that on the evidence MB was temporarily incompetent due to her needle phobia which was rendering her incapable of making a decision in respect of the operation. Butler-Sloss LJ recognised that 'fear of an operation may be a rational reason for refusal to undergo it. Fear may also, however, paralyse the will and thus destroy the capacity to make a decision'.[30] The mention of rationality of fear here is open to the same criticism raised above in relation to the *Rochdale* case, namely that rationality has no part to play in determining competency under English law. Nevertheless, the Court of Appeal's decision was focused upon MB's capacity to make a decision and it is at least arguable that this capacity was diminished due to her phobia. This has led some commentators to argue that the Court of Appeal's decision actually upheld the patient's autonomy by enabling her to achieve her autonomous wish to undergo the operation which had been compromised by her phobia of needles.[31] As the Court of Appeal recognised, 'it was never a case of her wanting natural childbirth. She wanted the surgical procedure to be over and done with'.[32] Michalowski takes issue with this argument that MB in effect wished to consent to the Caesarean section and notes that she only wished to consent to the Caesarean section provided that the

---

[30]   [1997] 8 Med LR 217.
[31]   See Scott, n 3 above, p 155.
[32]   [1997] 8 Med LR 217 at 221.

procedure did not involve needles.[33] A court order authorising the procedure with the use of an injection could not in any sense be viewed as the realisation of MB's autonomous choice.

A finding of incompetency is not the end of the issue, however, because as we discovered in Chapter 5, an incompetent patient can only be provided with treatment which is in his or her best interests. In some of the non-consensual Caesarean section cases this presents no difficulty as the woman's life is at imminent risk without the operation.[34] In some cases, however, such as *Re MB*, the woman's life is not at risk from a natural delivery and it is only the unborn child who requires the Caesarean section. How can the treatment be lawfully imposed on the incompetent mother in this situation? In *Re MB*, Butler-Sloss LJ held that '[i]t must be in the best interests of a woman carrying a full-term child whom she wants to be born alive and healthy that such a result should if possible be achieved'.[35] The Court of Appeal's approach here was supported by the psychiatric evidence which identified a risk of long term psychiatric damage if the child were born handicapped or died and which also failed to identify any risk of lasting harm from compulsory treatment.[36] Michalowski criticises the Court of Appeal's consideration of this issue as being 'far too superficial'.[37] There was no adequate discussion of the risks that this compulsory treatment would impose upon MB: risks of anaesthesia; the inherent risks of a Caesarean section delivery; and the effect of a forced injection on a patient with a needle phobia. Even if these risks were considered to be minimal, and therefore it could not be established that the procedure would be against the interests of the woman, the Caesarean section can only be regarded as positively in the best interest of MB if the interests of her unborn child are also taken into account. English law does not usually permit compulsory treatment of one patient for another's benefit. The one exception to this rule is the case of *In Re Y* which, as was discussed in Chapter 5, authorised the imposition of a serious medical procedure on an incompetent woman for the benefit of her sister.[38] This case is open to significant criticism for its disregard of the medical interests of the vulnerable incompetent patient, and its application to the *Re MB* context would be even more dubious given that the other 'patient' is a fetus with no legal rights or interests in English law. The apparent discrepancy in the law in respect of protection of the fetus, evident in the previous chapter in the context of the criminalisation of abortion, is again manifest here: the law clearly says that a fetus has no legal interests until birth and yet many judges will intervene to protect the fetus from an irrational decision by

---

[33] S Michalowski, 'Court-Authorised Caesarean Section: The End of a Trend?' (1999) 62 *MLR* 115, at p 119.

[34] As, for example, in *Re S*, n 9 above, and *St George's*, n 13 above.

[35] *Re MB*, n 30 above.

[36] *Ibid.*

[37] Michalowski, n 33 above, p 121.

[38] (1997) 2 WLR 557.

its mother, even if this means compulsorily imposing a major operation upon the mother which carries significant risk, and no medical benefit, to her.

The current law on non-consensual Caesarean section operations is that a competent woman has an absolute right to refuse such treatment even if the refusal will cause the death of her viable fetus. The requirement of competency is a significant hurdle, however, and it remains extremely unlikely that a pregnant woman will be able to prove that she is competent if she is perceived as making the irrational, and above all selfish, choice of refusing an operation necessary to save the life of her child. The judicial willingness to intervene in these unfortunate situations raises the question of whether other selfish choices by a pregnant woman which will or may result in harm to her unborn child should also be prohibited in the interests of the future child.

II. Preventing Pre-natal Harm

(a) Harming the Fetus

A pregnant woman will usually feel a significant moral obligation towards her unborn child and will strive to protect it from all harm. Yet the most serious risk of harm to the fetus comes from its mother herself: smoking, drinking and drug-taking have all been proven to harm the fetus, while a pregnant woman is now directed towards a healthy diet as well for fears that an unhealthy one may not provide the optimum growing conditions for the fetus. In addition, any harm to the mother is also likely to harm the fetus inside her. Thus, a road traffic accident, for example, could be fatal to her child whether the mother or a third party is the driver at fault. To what extent are these issues correctly regarded as legal questions? We have already established that a woman retains her right to autonomy upon becoming pregnant. She can, provided that she is declared competent, refuse medical treatment necessary for her child's survival. Up to 24 weeks, she can terminate the pregnancy for minor 'health' reasons. The fetus has no legal rights or interests until born. In these circumstances, does the law have any role to play in preventing a pregnant woman from smoking or drinking alcohol, or in punishing her for causing the death of her child due to negligence?

In the United States, a number of prosecutions have been brought against pregnant woman for harming their fetus. For example, in 1986 Pamela Rae Stewart was prosecuted in San Diego after she gave birth to a severely brain damaged child who died within a month of birth. The child was found to have traces of marijuana and amphetamines in his urine and it was discovered that the woman had ignored all of her doctor's warnings. The doctor had advised her during her ninth month of pregnancy that, due to the identification of a complication in her pregnancy, she should take medication, refrain from sexual intercourse and illegal drugs, and go immediately to a hospital if she began bleeding. She ignored all aspects of this advice, taking amphetamines, having sexual intercourse and not seeking medical attention for seven to eight hours after a bleed. She was charged under a California law which required parents to furnish necessary food, clothing, shelter and medical attention to their children, but the case against her was dismissed prior to trial on the ground that the relevant statute did not apply to pre-natal conduct.[39] A similar conclusion was eventually reached in a Florida prosecution in 1992. In *State v Johnson*,[40] a woman was prosecuted for using cocaine daily throughout her pregnancy, including on the day of the birth. She was (rather innovatively) charged with the delivery of drugs to a minor, a serious felony, based on the passage of drugs through the umbilical cord in the minutes after birth before it was severed. She was convicted and sentenced to one year in a rehabilitation programme and fourteen years probation but this was eventually reversed by the Florida Supreme Court because, again, the relevant statute was held not to be intended to apply in such circumstances.[41] This conclusion is vulnerable to subsequent legislative intent, however, and a number of US states have now expanded their definition of child abuse to include fetal drug exposure.[42] For example, following the dismissal of the case under Californian law, mentioned above, new legislation was immediately introduced to extend the statute in question to apply in such circumstances.[43]

In the United Kingdom, there has been no comparable legislative intent to protect the fetus from its mother's harmful acts and the judicial approach has re-affirmed that the fetus has no legal rights or interests until born. In *Re F (in utero)*,[44] a local authority was concerned about the welfare of an unborn child whose mother suffered from severe mental disturbance and occasional drug abuse. In particular, she had faced previous problems due to living what was described as a nomadic existence. A previous child had been made a ward of court and the mother's access terminated. The local authority asked a court to exercise its wardship jurisdiction upon the fetus in order to protect it from its mother (even though the mother's location was, at the time of the court hearing, unknown and therefore it was not entirely clear how the fetus could be protected even if it was to be made a ward of court). May LJ recognised that '[u]ntil the child is actually born there must necessarily be an inherent incompatibility

---

[39]   See JA Robertson, *Children of Choice: Freedom and the New Reproductive Technologies* (Princeton, Princeton University Press, 1994), pp 182-83 for more detail.

[40]   578 So. 2d 419 (Fla 1991).

[41]   *Johnson v Florida* 602 So. 2d 1288 (Fla 1992). See Robertson, n 39 above, p 183 for more details.

[42]   Robertson, n 39 above.

[43]   California Penal Code, s 270 states that 'A child conceived but not yet born is to be deemed as an existing person insofar as this section is conceived.'

[44]   [1988] 2 All ER 193.

between any projected exercise of wardship jurisdiction and the rights and welfare of the mother'.[45] The Court of Appeal thus declined to intervene before birth on pragmatic grounds:

> The court cannot care for a child, or order that others do so, until the child is born; only the mother can. The orders sought by the local authority are not by their nature such as the court can make in caring for the child; they are orders which seek directly to control the life of both mother and child.[46]

To prove this final point, Balcombe LJ referred to the decision of the European Commission of Human Rights in *Paton v United Kingdom* when it recognised that '[t]he 'life' of the foetus is intimately connected with, and cannot be regarded in isolation from, the life of the pregnant woman'.[47] This recognition ensures that, at least in this context, English law has a consistent approach to its treatment of the fetus. It is not regarded as a person in its own right until birth and therefore pre-birth it is devoid of independent rights.

(b)   Harming the Future Child

The issue of preventing pre-natal harm to the fetus can be distinguished from the debates in the abortion context as to whether the fetus has any rights. The distinction is that, while abortion is concerned with the killing of a fetus, preventing pre-natal harm is concerned with the harming of a future person. It could be argued, therefore, that the moral and legal status of the fetus is irrelevant to this issue.[48] The pregnant woman is causing harm to a future living person who will, upon birth, be entitled to the full protection of the law. When it is a person other than the mother who is causing the harm, English law permits the child, once born, to recover damages for the pre-natal harm. It regards the potential relationship between the causer of harm and the fetus as crystallising at birth so that the causer of harm is liable then, but not before, for injuries caused in utero. The explanation for this approach was provided in *Burton v Islington Health Authority*: 'in law and in logic, no damage can have been caused to the plaintiff before the plaintiff existed. The damage was suffered by the plaintiff at the moment that, in law, the plaintiff achieved personality and inherited the damaged body for which the defendants were responsible.'[49]

The mother is an exception to this general rule that pre-natal claims crystallise upon birth. The Congenital Disabilities (Civil Liability) Act 1976, passed in response to the thalidomide scandal, provides that a child has a cause of action if

---

[45]   *Ibid*, at p 194

[46]   *Ibid*, at p 201 (Balcombe LJ).

[47]   *Ibid*.

[48]   See S Bewley, 'Restricting the Freedom of Pregnant Women' in DL Dickenson (ed), *Ethical Issues in Maternal-Fetal Medicine* (Oxford, Oxford University Press, 2002), p 133.

[49]   [1993] QB 204, at p 214, per Phillips J.

born alive with a disease or abnormality caused by a negligent act, provided that the said act would be actionable by the child's mother or father. (In other words, there is no cause of action unless there is a duty of care owed to the child's parents.) The mother is immune from liability for injuries to the fetus, except if the injuries result from her negligent driving.[50] The inclusion of this one exception to the general maternal immunity may, at first glance, seem curious but it is explainable by the compulsory motor insurance which will ensure that an insurance company, rather than the mother, actually compensates the child for its injuries. It may be queried, however, whether the existence of an insurance policy is a sufficient reason, or indeed necessary requirement, for the imposition of civil liability, particularly when such liability infringes upon a pregnant woman's freedom of choice and her right to respect for a private life under Article 8 ECHR. Even if the existence of an insurance policy were to be regarded as a sufficient reason to impose liability on a pregnant woman, there remains no logical reason to restrict this to circumstances of negligent driving as it is possible that a pregnant woman may have cover for all tort liability under a home insurance policy.

This situation arose in the American case of *Grodin v Grodin*.[51] In this case a child had suffered tooth discolouration due to his mother taking tetracycline during pregnancy. The child sued his mother's doctor for a failure to administer a pregnancy test and thus remove his mother from this medication. However, during the discovery stage, the doctor claimed that he had warned the mother to stop taking the medication. The child's lawyer then advised the child to sue his mother as well in order to prevent the possibility of a jury ascribing the injury solely to the mother and refusing damages. The mother was insured against tort liability by a homeowner's policy and therefore she would benefit from an insurance company compensating her child for his injury.[52] This reveals a further reason for preventing the imposition of civil liability for a mother causing pre-natal harm to her child: in the absence of an insurance policy she will in effect be paying compensation to herself; in the presence of an insurance policy, she will be being paid for her own wrongful act. This bizarre situation is the legacy of a child's relationship with its mother. We have already seen that before birth the life of the fetus and the pregnant woman are inextricably linked but

---

[50]   Congenital Disabilities (Civil Liability) Act 1976, s 2: 'A woman driving a motor vehicle when she knows (or ought reasonably to know) herself to be pregnant is to be regarded as being under the same duty to take care for the safety of her unborn child as the law imposes on her with respect to the safety of other people . . '. The Law Commission's 'Report on Injuries to Unborn Children', which led to the enactment of this statute, explains the reason for this approach: 'the child whose pre-natal injury was caused by his own mother's negligence should not be singled out as the one class of blameless victims of negligent road accidents to be unentitled to compensation'. (Law Com No 60, 1974, para 60).

[51]   Mich App 301 NW 2d 869 (1981).

[52]   See B Steinbock, *Life Before Birth: The Moral and Legal Status of Embryos and Fetuses* (Oxford, Oxford University Press, 1992), pp 96-98 for more details of this interesting case.

even after birth there is likely to continue to be a close, familial relationship between the mother and child, ie between the person who caused harm and the person who suffered it.

One potential intervention which circumvents this situation was apparent in *D (a minor) v Berkshire County Council*.[53] In this case, a child was taken away from its mother and placed in care due to the mother's drug use during the pregnancy. The child was born prematurely and suffering from drug dependency. The House of Lords was willing to apply section 1(2)(a) of the Children and Young Persons Act 1969 to conduct pre-birth. This provision permits the imposition of a care order if a child's 'proper development is being avoidably prevented or neglected or his health is being avoidably impaired or neglected or he is being ill-treated'. The House of Lords regarded it as essential that this statutory provision be given a broad and liberal construction which gives full effect to its purpose of protecting children.[54] As there was nothing in this provision to expressly exclude the taking into account of conduct pre-birth, it was held that the statutory purpose was best furthered by taking this into account.[55] This House of Lords decision makes clear that, even though a fetus has no legal rights and interests until born, and even though an abortion is in practice easily available during the first six months of pregnancy, and even though there is no criminal or civil liability for a pregnant woman causing harm to her unborn child, her conduct during the nine months of pregnancy may be held against her in future decisions about the welfare of her child. The solution in this case could be regarded as the worst of all possible worlds: the harm to the fetus, and thus the future child, was not prevented plus the child was separated from its mother after birth once the harm had ceased. There can be no doubt that removing the child after birth is a punishment for the mother rather than a means of protecting the child. (If future harm is suspected, the reasons for the removal are different and the action is more justifiable.)

It has to be assumed that there is an important distinction here between illegal activities which cause harm to a fetus and legal activities which do so. If the harm is caused by illegal drug taking or negligent driving, then it could be argued that some punishment is due, but if the harm is caused by smoking tobacco or drinking alcohol, to punish the pregnant woman would be to discriminate against her in respect of her freedom to enjoy legal activities solely on the basis of her pregnancy. In addition, smoking is harmful not just to a fetus but also potentially to all living persons in the vicinity of a smoker. There is an argument that it should be illegal (and, indeed, it is increasingly restricted in public places) but if it is not, then it cannot be justifiable to punish a woman for exercising her legal freedom to smoke during pregnancy, even though to do so is morally

---

[53]   [1987] AC 317.

[54]   Lord Brandon, *ibid*, at p 347.

[55]   Lord Goff took a slightly different approach by taking into account not only the past conduct but also the future risk to a child from living with parents who are drug addicts (*ibid*, p 350).

objectionable. Seymour has argued, however, that 'it is not self-evident that . . . smoking by a pregnant woman represents an expression of autonomy that the state should necessarily respect'.[56] This is an unconvincing argument because, for autonomy to have value, it must protect all choices, even those which are objectively wrong or selfish choices. (We encountered this argument in Chapter 4 in relation to consent to medical treatment.) There may be conflicting societal interests which outweigh a particular exercise of autonomy but it is hard to identify such an interest in relation to a lawful activity which may harm an entity with no legal rights.[57]

Seymour also makes a broader point, however, when he recognises that by drinking alcohol or smoking or taking illegal drugs, 'a woman may not be proclaiming her autonomy; she may be simply living her life. Any analysis that overlooks the fact that this life has been partly determined by social, economic, and cultural conditions is deficient.'[58] This introduces a vital aspect of the topic of pre-natal harm which has been overlooked so far: it is rarely the pregnant woman's autonomous choice to harm her fetus. As Jackson argues, an assumption that the failure to adopt a healthy lifestyle during pregnancy can be attributed to moral failure and personal inadequacy is flawed. Such an assumption suggests that 'all pregnant women are equally willing or able to adopt some optimum prenatal lifestyle . . . [and] also tends to obscure the close correlation between socio-economic class and high-risk conduct, such as smoking or the use of illegal drugs'.[59] The mother's socio-economic class will also, of course, impact upon the future child's welfare once born and Jackson argues that her poverty will represent a more statistically significant risk than her failure to adhere to health promotion advice.[60]

Thus, while not forgetting the significant role played by the mother, whose life, as the European Commission of Human Rights has noted, is intimately connected with that of her unborn child, it is unreasonable to place an absolute legal obligation upon her to protect her child while ignoring her own legal interests. Miller makes a sound point when she argues that we 'cannot hope to protect the fetus by laws that punish the mother'[61] and it is undoubtedly true that the law

---

[56] J Seymour, *Childbirth and the Law* (Oxford, Oxford University Press, 2000), p 225.

[57] It is interesting to note that the law does not – but perhaps should – seek to prevent a mother smoking in the presence of her young children even though they may also be harmed by secondary smoke, have equally little choice but to inhale it, have legal rights and interests which may come into play, and even though the harm could be prevented by smoking in a separate room rather than by the mother being forced to give up entirely. Should a mother's moral obligation to protect her child really require a greater limitation upon her freedom before the child is born? (See Bewley, n 48 above, p 134).

[58] Seymour, n 56 above, p 227.

[59] E Jackson, *Regulating Reproduction: Law, Technology and Autonomy* (Oxford, Hart Publishing, 2001), p 156.

[60] *Ibid*, p 159.

[61] L Miller, 'Two Patients or One? Problems of Consent in Obstetrics' (1993) 1 *Med Law Int* 97, at p 99.

'should play no part in pitting the fetus against its mother'.[62] The fetus needs its mother to do her best to protect it but it also needs society to protect both it, and its mother, from harm:

> it is clear that responsibility for fetal harm is so deeply shared with men, with public institutions, and with social structures, that it makes little sense to try to tease out individual from collective responsibility for fetal harm. How are we to separate poor nutrition from drug use from lead paint from poverty from genetics from chronic violence and abuse as causes of fetal harm?[63]

If society is serious about preventing fetal harm, all of these factors need to be addressed. Singling out the mother for her morally objectionable but legally permissible actions may ultimately be self-defeating. The mother is, after all, usually the fetus's closest ally.

III. Wrongful Conception and Birth: Financial Recompense for an Unwanted Pregnancy?

The previous two chapters illustrated different aspects of reproductive autonomy: the use of medical assistance to conceive and the option of terminating an unwanted pregnancy. This concept of choice in reproductive issues has been developed in this chapter with focus upon a pregnant woman's freedom to act in a manner potentially harmful to her unborn child. There is one important remaining aspect of freedom of choice in reproduction which will now be discussed and this relates to an unwanted pregnancy which results from a doctor's negligence. In such a situation, the pregnant woman has had her reproductive autonomy infringed by the 'harm' of a pregnancy she did not choose and would not have had to endure but for the doctor's negligence. The situation can arise in two distinct ways: (1) any pregnancy may be unwanted (usually termed 'wrongful conception'); or (2) a particular pregnancy, for example of a fetus suffering from abnormalities, might be unwanted (usually termed 'wrongful birth').[64]

---

[62]   *Ibid*, p 109.
[63]   C Daniels, 'Fathers, Mothers and Fetal Harm' in LM Morgan and MW Michaels (eds), *Fetal Subjects: Feminist Positions* (Philadelphia, Pennsylvania University Press, 1999), pp 83-84.
[64]   The terms are emotive and unhelpful but widely used.

(a)   The Nature of Wrongful Conception and Wrongful Birth Claims

The first of these categories, wrongful conception, arises where a woman or her partner sought sterilisation but the sterilisation failed due to negligence or the patient was negligently told that the sterilisation had achieved permanent sterility when it had not, thus leading the couple to rely upon the operation rather than other birth control methods as contraception. Recovery of damages will only be available if the usual requirements for negligence are satisfied. If a woman becomes pregnant due to a negligently performed sterilisation operation or a negligent failure to warn of a risk of natural reversal of a sterilisation, she still has the option of terminating the pregnancy. Indeed, an unwanted pregnancy (due to the woman's or her partner's reckless act rather than a doctor's negligence) is a common phenomenon and many will result in an abortion at an early stage during the pregnancy on the grounds of risk to the mother's mental health if the unwanted pregnancy is continued. Through the termination of pregnancy the woman's autonomy in reproductive matters is reasserted. If a woman with an unwanted pregnancy due to a doctor's negligence decides not to terminate the pregnancy, does this relieve the doctor of liability as an intervening act? Park J at first instance in *Emeh v Kensington & Chelsea & Westminster Area Health Authority* suggested that it did do so but the Court of Appeal disagreed. Slade LJ said that 'save in the most exceptional circumstances, I cannot think it right that the court should ever declare it unreasonable for a woman to decline to have an abortion'.[65] This was confirmed in even stronger terms by Lord Steyn in *McFarlane v Tayside Health Board*: 'I cannot conceive of any circumstances in which the autonomous decision of the parents not to resort to even a lawful abortion could be questioned.'[66] This must be the correct approach. A termination of pregnancy remains prima facie a criminal offence. Even if a legal defence does conceivably exist (and a pregnant woman could never judge this for herself as the defence relies upon a good faith certification by two doctors), a termination will always be a difficult choice for a woman and she should not be denied damages from the negligent doctor who put her in this position merely because she chooses not to abort. The pregnant woman may perceive a huge moral distinction between using contraception to prevent a pregnancy and terminating a pregnancy once a fetus is in existence. Declining to terminate the pregnancy will not necessarily mean it is any less unwanted. In addition, if a woman or a couple had relied upon false assurances of permanent sterility or a negligently performed sterilisation, the pregnancy is likely to be discovered at a later stage than usual and thus the options for a legal abortion may be limited, and certainly its moral ambiguity will have increased.

---

[65]   [1984] 3 All ER 1044 at 1053.
[66]   [1999] 3 WLR 1301 at 1317.

Given the legal irrelevance of an unrealised possibility of terminating an unwanted pregnancy, it is perhaps curious that wrongful birth actions, where a particular pregnancy is unwanted, revolve around the denial of a possibility to terminate the pregnancy. In this context, the pregnant woman will be complaining about being denied the opportunity to terminate the pregnancy by not being accurately informed about the health of her unborn child. Advances in medical technology enable pre-natal screening and diagnosis which has two potentially distinct consequences: as discussed in the previous sections, the fetus is personified and potentially becomes a second patient, but also the pregnant woman is provided with greater information about the state of her pregnancy and the health of her fetus, enabling a more informed exercise of her reproductive autonomy. A pre-natal diagnosis of severe mental or physical fetal abnormalities may lead to a decision to terminate the pregnancy.[67] If a negligent diagnosis is made, however, the pregnant woman's ability to make an autonomous choice is restricted by the lack of accurate information available to her.[68] Scott accurately explains the vital connection between reproductive autonomy and wrongful birth actions: 'Morally speaking, given that parents are entitled to choose whether to reproduce, arguably they should also be able to choose to avoid reproduction under certain conditions, for instance because of what caring for a severely disabled child may entail.'[69] The practical effect of this moral justification, however, is that a woman could recover damages for being deprived of the information which would have led to her terminating the pregnancy. Failure to terminate results in a child with abnormalities (which are not themselves due to anyone's negligence): is this a 'harm' for which there should be compensation available? If we admit the moral ambiguity of this question, how much more ambiguous is the recovery of damages for the birth of a completely healthy child in wrongful conception cases? Is the birth of a child ever a harm?

(b)   Is a Child Always a Blessing? Reasons for Denying Compensation for an Unwanted Pregnancy

In the 1983 case of *Udale v Bloomsbury Health Authority*,[70] the trial judge decided that the birth of a child is always a benefit; never a detriment. The case concerned a negligently performed sterilisation operation which did not prevent a subsequent pregnancy. Damages were sought for the pain and suffering of the unwanted pregnancy, loss of earnings and the costs of raising the child until the

---

[67]   Pre-natal screening and diagnosis may conversely restrict reproductive autonomy because, as discussed in Chapter 9, screening for an abnormality for which there is no treatment creates an assumption in favour of abortion.

[68]   It is also worth noting that most pregnant women's freedom of choice in respect of their pregnancy will be limited to the pre-natal screening available in an under-resourced NHS.

[69]   R Scott, 'Pre-natal Screening, Autonomy and Reasons: The Relationship between the Law on Abortion and Wrongful Birth' (2003) 11 *Med L Rev* 265, at pp 300-01.

[70]   [1983] 2 All ER 522.

age of 16. Jupp J refused this final head of damage on policy grounds. He was worried about the impact on family life if an unplanned child should learn that it was so unwanted that its parents gained damages for his or her upkeep, and also that awarding damages in such a situation might encourage doctors to recommend abortions as a means of avoiding negligence claims. Most significantly of all, Jupp J could not disregard his moral instinct that the birth of a child is always a positive event: 'it has been the assumption of our culture for time immemorial that a child coming into the world . . . is a blessing and an occasion for rejoicing'.[71] The fact that this couple, by positively seeking sterilisation, did not regard the birth of another child to them as an occasion for rejoicing was completely ignored in Jupp J's rhetoric of the positivity of birth.

Subsequent cases took a different view. Thus, in *Emeh v Kensington & Chelsea & Westminster Area Health Authority*, the Court of Appeal made clear that there were no sufficient policy reasons to prevent the recovery of damages if a birth results from a doctor's negligence.[72] Jackson has argued, however, that this was less of a rejection of the *Udale* reasoning than is sometimes assumed: 'the judgment in *Emeh* was not so much a robust rejection of the "all children are a blessing" argument, but reflected instead the Court's concern that if damages are unavailable, people might be encouraged to have late abortions'.[73] This reveals the ambiguity of judicial reasoning in respect of wrongful conception. In *Udale*, the judge regarded an award of damages as an incentive for doctors to encourage abortions as a means of avoiding liability, while in *Emeh* the court took the view that declining to award damages might encourage women who are pregnant as a result of negligence to seek a late abortion in the knowledge that they will gain no financial assistance in raising the child. Which of these opposing views is most likely to materialise is pure conjecture but the *Emeh* reasoning, by implicitly acknowledging that a child may be a costly legacy of negligence, as well as a blessing, is to be preferred.[74] The *Emeh* approach was followed in a number of cases,[75] but was overturned by the House of Lords in the landmark case of *McFarlane v Tayside Health Board*,[76] which revived the policy-based obstacles to recovery in wrongful conception cases and left a legacy of inconsistent rules and exceptions in which respect for both reproductive autonomy and the sanctity of the life of the child are lost.

---

[71] *Ibid*, at p 530.

[72] *Emeh*, n 65 above.

[73] Jackson, n 59 above, p 32.

[74] At first instance in *Emeh*, Peter Pain J noted that he could understand the reason for querying how the birth of a baby could possibly give rise to an action in damages: 'But every baby has a belly to be filled and a body to be clothed. The law relating to damage is concerned with reparation in monetary terms and this is what is needed for the maintenance of a baby' ([1984] 2 All ER 513 at 526).

[75] *Thake v Maurice* [1986] QB 644; *Gold v Haringey Health Authority* [1988] 1 QB 481.

[76] [2000] 2 AC 59.

Mr McFarlane was negligently informed that he no longer needed to take contraceptive precautions following a vasectomy. Two years later his wife became pregnant and gave birth to a healthy child. The House of Lords held that there could be no recovery of damages for the costs of raising this healthy child, although damages were awarded for the pain, suffering and inconvenience of the pregnancy and childbirth. The reasoning of the five Law Lords was unhelpfully diverse but the majority categorised the costs of raising a healthy child as a pure economic loss which, under the law of torts, requires the satisfaction of a three stage test: foreseeable loss; a relationship of sufficient proximity; and a require-ment that the imposition of a duty of care is fair, just and reasonable.[77] It was the third stage of this test which proved crucial to most Law Lords in *McFarlane* as they held that it would not be fair, just and reasonable in the circumstances to require the payment of the upbringing costs. The vagueness of a fair, just and reasonable test enabled Lord Steyn to refer to 'the traveller on the Underground' for a gut reaction. Lord Steyn held that instinctively such a member of the public 'would consider that the law of tort has no business to provide legal remedies consequent upon the birth of a healthy child, which all of us regard as a valuable and good thing'.[78] Thus, the 'child is a blessing' argument is resurrected and once more little attention is paid to the fact that the autonomous choice of the McFarlanes was to seek permanent sterility precisely because they did not regard the birth of a child to them as 'a valuable and good thing'. Lord Millett countered this very point by explaining that 'if the law regards an event as beneficial, plaintiffs cannot make it a matter for compensation merely by saying that it is an event they did not want to happen'.[79] However, as Jackson notes, 'this must surely be wrong. Where a patient has decided to have an operation in order to irrevocably remove the possibility of conception, it seems perverse to argue that they should regard the failure of this surgery as a blessing.'[80]

In addition to the 'child is a blessing' line of argument, and perhaps linked to it, is a question of limited resources. Although not expressly relied upon, it is clear that the potential size of the award and its impact upon Tayside Health Board's other pressing healthcare priorities were significant factors. Indeed, it is undeni-able that limited NHS funds could be put to better use than excessive awards of damages for the birth of a healthy child. However, this is really an argument against the system of medical negligence in its entirety and, as noted in Chapter 3, alternative means of vindicating the rights of patients may be preferable.

---

[77] *Caparo v Dickman* [1990] 2 AC 605.
[78] [2000] 2 AC 59 at 82.
[79] *Ibid*, at p 114.
[80] Jackson, n 59 above, pp 35–36.

(c)   The Post-McFarlane Fudge

The House of Lords' decision in *McFarlane* seemed to make clear that damages would not be recovered for the cost of raising a child in a wrongful conception claim, and strongly suggested that wrongful birth claims would also be so restricted, but subsequent cases have chipped away at the *McFarlane* precedent. Hoyano explains that:

> The confusion generated by the divergent lines of reasoning adopted by the five Law Lords has permitted trial judges and the Court of Appeal elbow room to undercut *McFarlane*, a case with which it would seem they are clearly unhappy. The reasoning in these cases shows how far negligence law has come adrift of principle.[81]

The first decision to take advantage of this 'elbow room' was that of Newman J in *Rand v East Dorset Health Authority*.[82] The case involved a negligent omission to inform Mr and Mrs Rand of the results of a scan which disclosed the likelihood that their child would be born with Down's Syndrome. The judge was convinced that, if this knowledge had been made available to the couple, Mrs Rand would have terminated the pregnancy. The judge held that the House of Lords in *McFarlane* had not precluded the award of compensation for the cost of raising a disabled child and, therefore, in this wrongful birth case, upbringing costs directly related to the disability were recoverable. Similarly in *Parkinson v St James & Seacroft University Hospital NHS Trust*,[83] the Court of Appeal expressly disapplied *McFarlane* to all cases involving special costs associated with raising disabled children. This particular case involved the birth of a disabled child following a negligently performed sterilisation operation. The disability was not caused by the negligence but, nevertheless, the Court of Appeal was willing to award damages for the costs of raising this child which were in excess of normal child-raising costs.

It is difficult to understand the justification for the development of the law in this context. *McFarlane* establishes that a healthy child born as a result of negligence is not a detriment for which compensation should be available but *Parkinson* makes clear that the extra costs of raising a disabled child are recoverable, regardless of whether the disability is caused by the negligence. The infringement of the mother's autonomy is identical in both cases: her freedom of choice about whether to become (or remain) pregnant is restricted due to another person's negligence. The *Parkinson* decision leaves the law suggesting that an infringement of reproductive autonomy is fine provided that the result is a healthy child but if, by sheer luck, that unwanted child is disabled, then compensation for raising the child will be available. The disability in a wrongful

---

[81]   LCH Hoyano, 'Misconceptions about Wrongful Conception' (2002) 65 *MLR* 883, at p 892.
[82]   (2000) 56 BMLR 39.
[83]   [2001] 3 All ER 97.

conception case is not due to negligence and its relevance to the recover of damages is dubious. It is a characteristic of the child born as a result of the unwanted pregnancy and nothing more.

The peculiarity of this aspect of the law seemed to continue in the Court of Appeal decision in *Rees v Darlington Memorial Hospital NHS Trust*.[84] In this case, the mother who conceived after a negligently performed sterilisation operation was herself suffering from a severe visual disability. The Court of Appeal used this disability to distinguish the case from *McFarlane* and awarded damages for the extra costs involved in a disabled mother raising a healthy child. Fortunately the House of Lords soon reversed this decision and restored a little more consistency to the law by denying that a disabled mother amounted to an exception to the *McFarlane* principle.[85] However, the House of Lords also decided in this case that a 'conventional award' of £15,000 should be paid to the claimant, in addition to the compensation for pain and suffering during pregnancy. Lord Millett explained that this was:

> not for the birth of the child, but for the denial of an important aspect of their [the parents'] personal autonomy, viz the right to limit the size of their family. This is an important aspect of human dignity, which is increasingly being regarded as an important human right which should be protected by law. The loss of this right is not an abstract or theoretical one . . . [T]he parents have lost the opportunity to live their lives in the way that they wished and planned to do. The loss of this opportunity, whether characterised as a right or a freedom, is a proper subject for compensation by way of damages.[86]

This seems a fitting note on which to conclude the topic of freedom of choice in pregnancy. It is not only decisions reached by the mother during pregnancy which raise the question of autonomy but also the need of individuals not to have their reproductive choices compromised by negligent actions, omissions or statements. In today's world of birth control, termination of pregnancy and assisted conception, available choices in the reproductive sphere are diverse and when that freedom of choice is restricted by a doctor's negligence the law must, at the very least, recognise that a harm has been caused to the parents, even if they have been 'blessed' with a child for whom they will subsequently love and care.

IV. Conclusion

A pregnant woman is entitled to exactly the same legal protection of her autonomy as any other competent adult. The moral expectation that she will

---

[84]   [2002] 2 All ER 177.
[85]   [2003] 4 All ER 987.
[86]   *Ibid*, at para 123.

make decisions responsibly, paying full regard to the interests of her unborn child, almost always mirrors her actual intentions. Ultimately, however, her freedom of choice includes a freedom to act in a way harmful to the fetus and the law will intervene here at its own peril. The risks of harm to a fetus by its mother's action are often unquantifiable, while the mother's harmful choices can rarely be seen in a vacuum removed from her position in society. Perhaps most significantly, it is hard to see where the law's intervention would end if it were to engage with pre-natal harm by the mother: if smoking and alcohol are harmful to the fetus, what about certain foods or sport or work or stress? There is no doubt that the most morally difficult issue in this chapter is the refusal of treatment in late pregnancy where it is extremely difficult to disregard the interests of the full-term child, minutes away from gaining the full protection of the law, and where the mother's decision to refuse treatment often appears irrational and selfish. However, if a pregnant woman is entitled to legal protection for her autonomous choices, the protection must apply to all choices, even those which we know will result in the death of her child. English case law declares this principle loudly and clearly but also allows issues of competency to undermine the principle. Finally, if the pregnant woman's autonomy is to be respected, her choices must not be constrained by negligent actions or statements. Reproductive autonomy – established in Chapter 8 as deriving from a mixture of Convention rights, common law principles and academic theory – therefore requires not only the protection of a choice of whether to procreate or not, but also the choice of how to behave once a pregnancy is established and the provision of both competent medical care and accurate information about fertility and fetal health.

Recommended Further Reading

R Scott, *Rights, Duties and the Body: Law and Ethics of the Maternal-Fetal Conflict* (Oxford, Hart Publishing, 2002), Chapter 3.

E Jackson, *Regulating Reproduction: Law, Technology and Autonomy* (Oxford, Hart Publishing, 2001), Chapter 4.

S Michalowski, 'Court-Authorised Caesarean Section: The End of a Trend?' (1999) 62 *MLR* 115.

LCH Hoyano, 'Misconceptions about Wrongful Conception' (2002) 65 *MLR* 883.

11

The Right to Life at the End of Life

The final part of this book concentrates upon some of the most morally controversial and ethically challenging issues in medical law: those located at the end of life. The following chapter will focus on whether there is a 'right to die' but first in this chapter we will consider the application, relevance and value of a right to life in the context of end of life decisions. We will begin by looking at the nature of the right to life, its boundaries and the significance of the underlying ethical principle of the sanctity of human life. Then we will look in some depth at the case of *Airedale NHS Trust v Bland*,[1] perhaps the landmark case in English medical law. In particular, we will consider the human rights implications of the principles stemming from *Bland*, before considering the implications of conflicting rights to life in the conjoined twins case. The questions underlying this chapter are whether the right to life has equal value regardless of the length and quality of a person's life, and whether its protection by law necessitates the continued provision of life-sustaining treatment regardless of its benefit to the individual.

I. The Right to Life in Context

(a) The Right to Life in Article 2 ECHR

We have encountered the right to life a number of times previously in this book. It is often regarded as the most fundamental of all human rights, partly because without it the other rights are meaningless, but also because it gives legal protection to the important ethical principle of the sanctity of human life. The European Convention on Human Rights was the first international human rights treaty to protect the right to life in any detailed manner,[2] and it is no coincidence that it was drafted in the post-war period when memories of the Nazis' disregard

---

[1] [1993] 1 All ER 831.
[2] The Universal Declaration of Human Rights 1948 declared only that 'Everyone has the right to life, liberty and the security of person' and is, anyway, not legally binding. During the drafting of the

for the value of human life in the concentration camps of World War Two were still fresh. Article 2 ECHR declares that 'Everyone's right to life shall be protected by law. No one shall be deprived of his life intentionally …' The Article then proceeds to outline some exceptions to this right related to the imposition of the death penalty and the use of lethal force in law enforcement, but none of these are directly of relevance to the medico-legal issues which are our focus. They do, however, illustrate the first of three interesting points to note from the text of Article 2, namely that the right is not absolute. It is, perhaps, surprising that this most fundamental right includes permissible limitation, whereas by contrast Article 3's prohibition on torture and inhuman or degrading treatment or punishment does not, but the Convention sends out a clear message that, where human life is preserved, it must be treated with the respect and dignity owing to it. The second point to note in respect of Article 2 is that it does not create a right to life: it does not declare that 'everyone has a right to life' in the same manner in which it declares in Article 10 that 'everyone has a right to freedom of expression'. Rather, it recognises the pre-existence of the right to life and requires that it be 'protected by law'. This suggests that the right to life exists independently of attempts to express it in writing in international conventions. Third, the text of Article 2 relies greatly upon the meaning of 'intentionally'. Only an intentional deprivation of life is prohibited under the Article, although this is itself a much broader prohibition than exists in the International Covenant on Civil and Political Rights, where only 'arbitrary' deprivations of life are prohibited in Article 6. It seems clear that a deprivation of life could be intentional, but not arbitrary, and thus the Article 2 wording encompasses a tighter prohibition on the taking of life than other comparable international human rights treaties.

Article 2 has been interpreted by the European Court of Human Rights as imposing three distinct obligations upon contracting states: (a) a duty to refrain from unlawful killing; (b) a duty to investigate suspicious deaths; and (c) in some circumstances, a positive obligation to take steps to prevent the avoidable loss of life.[3] It is the first and last obligation with which we are concerned here. The first obligation is clear from the wording of Article 2: any intentional deprivation of life by the state or its agents (which does not fall within one of the exceptions) is prohibited. The positive obligation to preserve life, on the other hand, is derived from the Court's judgment in *Osman v United Kingdom*[4] where it stated that Article 2 'enjoins the state not only to refrain from the intentional and unlawful taking of life, but also to take appropriate steps to safeguard the lives of those

---

ECHR, the right to life was not included in the Council of Europe's Consultative Assembly's first draft but was later added in the form in which Art 2 exists today, largely based upon the UK's insistence for narrowly defined rights and limitations. See E Wicks, 'The UK Government's Perceptions of the European Convention on Human Rights at the Time of Entry' [2000] *PL* 438, at p 439.

[3] See C Ovey and RCA White, *The European Convention on Human Rights*, 4th edn (Oxford, Oxford University Press, 2006), Chapter 4.

[4] (2000) 29 EHRR 245.

within its jurisdiction'.[5] This positive obligation was held to apply only where there is a real and immediate risk to life, and it was acknowledged that a state must balance resources and that the positive obligation under Article 2 should not be interpreted to impose 'an impossible or disproportionate burden' on the authorities.[6] We saw in the context of the right to treatment, discussed in Chapter 2, that the shortage of resources in the NHS makes it difficult to assert a right to receive medical treatment under Article 2, especially when it is an expensive treatment with a limited chance of success. Now, in this penultimate chapter, we are concerned solely with life-sustaining medical treatment and thus the potential significance of Article 2 increases. It is now time to consider the role of the right to life at the very end of a person's life and, specifically, what characterises the 'life' that should be preserved.

(b)   The Boundaries of the Right to Life: Defining Death

Despite the fundamental nature of the right to life, its boundaries remain one of the most problematic and controversial elements of human rights law. There is a lack of consensus about both the beginning and the end of life which seriously undermines the implementation of the right. In Chapter 9, we looked in some depth at the emotive question of when 'life', and therefore the legal protection of the right to life, begins. Now, we must focus on when life ends, for only after finding a workable answer to this can we fully comprehend the application of the right to life at the end of life.

It is tempting to assume that there is a clear boundary between life and death but death, like birth, is a process. Individual cells in the body cease to function at different times depending on their sensitivity to a lack of oxygen. In addition, modern technology means that a person who would once have been regarded as dead can now be revived. Death occurs when tissue is deprived of oxygen ('tissue anoxia') and thus destroyed. This can occur either because respiration has ceased or because the heart has ceased beating. The former results in a failure to harvest oxygen; the latter in a failure to distribute oxygen to the tissues. Traditionally, therefore, death – tissue anoxia – was synonymous with cardiorespiratory failure: the heart stopped beating and/or breathing ceased. Countless movies have ended with such a death scene. In the modern day, however, cardiorespiratory failure has lost the guarantee of permanence: medical technology means both that a heart can be restarted and that breathing can be assisted by an artificial ventilator. Cardiorespiratory failure no longer inevitably signifies death. However, in the time it takes to restart cardiorespiratory function, some tissue will be damaged and the tissue most sensitive to oxygen deficiency is the brain. The possibility exists, therefore, for a dead brain to be trapped in a revived body. The fears of this

---

[5]   *Ibid*, para 115.
[6]   *Ibid*, para 116.

macabre state of being have led to an acceptance of the concept of 'brain death'. This means that a person may no longer be living despite continuing cardiorespiratory function. The concept of brain death has been further defined as 'brain stem death' (BSD) because the brain stem is the part of the brain least affected by oxygen deficiency. If the brain stem is dead, then so is the rest of the brain. The brain stem controls basic functions, including breathing and sleeping. A person whose brain stem is still functioning but whose higher brain has been irreversibly damaged may be breathing independently but will have no awareness or consciousness of the world around him. Such a person is described as being in persistent vegetative state (PVS) and, as we shall see, this condition poses considerable ethical and legal dilemmas. Is such a patient really still alive or has the person already left the body?

Some commentators have argued that it is our higher brain functions which render us human and the irreversible loss of these brings our life to a close. Such an argument is based upon the principle of dualism: that the mind and body are distinct. There appears to be some merit in this if we consider a hypothetical brain transplant.[7] The living person presumably travels with the brain into a new body while the old body can be treated as an empty shell. McMahan takes this view and regards patients in PVS as already dead, due to the loss of their higher brain functions, even though their organism, or body, lives on. He argues that this organism should be treated as a dead body because 'a mere organism does not have interests and cannot itself be benefited or harmed. To end its life is no more objectionable than it is to kill a plant, provided that what is done does not contravene the posthumous interests of, or manifest disrespect for, the person who once animated the organism'.[8] The difficulty with this view is that the 'organism' of the 'dead' PVS patient closely resembles a living person including, most problematically, by continuing to breathe without artificial assistance. How could we bury a breathing corpse?

English law avoids these ethical problems by accepting the BSD definition of death, thus requiring the irreversible destruction of the whole brain, and not merely its higher functions, before regarding a person as dead.[9] Even though this avoids problematic ethical dilemmas in the context of a breathing corpse, it merely shifts the ethical problems to the context of treatment decisions at the end of life. If a PVS patient is still alive, he has a right to life under Article 2. Does this

---

[7]   See J McMahan, 'Brain Death, Cortical Death and Persistent Vegetative State' in H Kuhse and P Singer, *Companion to Bioethics* (Oxford, Blackwell, 1998), p 254.

[8]   *Ibid*, p 258.

[9]   *Re A* (1992) 3 Med LR 303. This case involved a young boy taken to hospital with head injuries which suggested a non-accidental injury. He was placed on a ventilator but subsequently declared BSD. His parents wanted him to be maintained on the ventilator to enable their own experts to examine him in the light of potential legal proceedings. The court refused, however, holding that the boy was legally dead. The doctors would not be acting unlawfully by disconnecting the ventilator. This judicial acceptance of BSD as legal death was confirmed in *Airedale NHS Trust v Bland*: 'In the eyes of the medical world and of the law a person is not clinically dead so long as the brain stem retains its function' (n 1 above, p 859, per Lord Keith).

mean that his life, such as it is, must be preserved indefinitely, for example by the provision of artificial feeding? What about by more extraordinary means, such as a heart transplant, if these become necessary? These issues had to be decided by the House of Lords in the 1992 case of *Airedale NHS Trust v Bland*, which will be considered in depth below. Before this, however, it will be useful to consider why, and to what extent, 'life' is a state worthy of protection. Do we have a right to life because life in itself is sacred? Or because of the use to which we can put our lives? Is an irreversibly unconscious life as valuable as a conscious one? Or do we need some degree of awareness in order for our lives to be of value?

(c)   The Sanctity of Human Life

The principle of the sanctity of life is the subject of much debate in the academic literature. Instinctively, it seems a valuable guiding principle in end of life issues, as well as other contexts, but upon closer scrutiny it loses some of its appeal.[10] The *Bland* case had the sanctity of life principle at its core (should life be preserved at all costs?) but only Lord Hoffmann in the Court of Appeal really analysed the principle's foundations. He noted both the religious origin of the concept and its more recent secular application:

> We have a strong feeling that there is an intrinsic value in human life, irrespective of whether it is valuable to the person concerned or indeed to anyone else. Those who adhere to religious faiths which believe in the sanctity of all God's creation and in particular that human life was created in the image of God himself will have no difficulty with the concept of the intrinsic value of human life. But even those without any religious belief think in the same way.[11]

This secular belief in the sanctity of human life is given voice in modern human rights because human rights are based upon the concept that all humans are equal and are entitled to protection of their life, dignity, liberty and freedom. The concept of human rights treats all humans as valuable and worthy of respect and therefore goes a long way towards promoting the idea of human life being sacred.

Despite the judicial recognition of the principle of sanctity of life, the *Bland* judgment, and subsequent cases, have recognised that it cannot be an absolute principle: self-determination and dignity of the person are both potentially conflicting principles which may outweigh it. Singer has argued that British law

---

[10] As Singer succinctly explains, 'We all like the notion of the intrinsic worth of human life. We accept such a noble idea without much critical scrutiny, as long as it does not restrict us from doing what we really think is important. Then one day we find it making us do things that are manifestly pointless, or likely to lead to disaster. So we take a better look at the fine phrases we so readily accepted. And start to wonder why we ever believed them in the first place. Then we drop them' (P Singer, *Rethinking Life and Death: The Collapse of our Traditional Ethics* (Oxford, Oxford University Pres, 1995), p 57).

[11]   *Bland*, n 1 above, p 851.

has 'abandoned the idea that life itself is a benefit to the person living it, irrespective of its quality'.[12] He interprets the law as holding that 'for life to be a benefit to the person living it, that person must at a minimum, have some capacity for awareness or conscious experience'.[13] This view suggests that life is instrumentally, but not intrinsically, of value. It is important in order that we can achieve other potentially valuable things. But, the argument goes, there is nothing of value in an irreversibly comatose life.[14] An alternative view is proposed by Finnis who stresses that human life is not a merely instrumental good and that a person's 'inability to participate in any other basic human good does not nullify their participation in the good, the benefit, of human life'.[15]

Another commentator who favours the view of human life as an intrinsic good is John Keown, whose views have been especially influential in the context of end of life decisions. As a Christian ethicist, Keown strongly supports the sanctity of life, but he helpfully outlines three different approaches to the issue of the valuation of human life.[16] First, there is the 'vitalism' approach. This regards human life as an absolute moral value and considers it always to be wrong to either shorten life or fail to lengthen it, regardless of considerations of pain, suffering, or expense. Keown sensibly notes that this approach is 'as ethically untenable as its attempt to maintain life indefinitely is physically impossible'.[17] Second, Keown outlines the 'sanctity of life' approach. This holds that we ought never to intentionally kill an innocent human being. It asserts that human life is not only an instrumental good but also a basic good. There is an absolute prohibition on taking life, although this approach does not regard life as an absolute good and therefore there is no moral obligation to preserve life by imposing treatment which is not worthwhile 'either because it offers no reasonable hope of benefit or because, even though it does, the expected benefit would be outweighed by burdens which the treatment would impose, such as excessive pain'.[18] This approach is the one most in sync with Article 2's protection for the right to life. As we have seen, Article 2 prohibits the intentional deprivation of life and imposes some limited positive obligations upon the state to preserve life. This approach to the value of life has also received judicial approval by Ward LJ in *Re A (children)(conjoined twins: surgical separation)* where he quoted Keown's definition of sanctity of life with approval and confirmed that 'each life has inherent value in itself and the right to life, being universal, is equal for all of us. The sanctity of life doctrine does, however, acknowledge that it may be proper to withhold or withdraw treatment'.[19] The third and final approach to the valuation

---

[12] Singer, n 10 above, p 68.
[13] *Ibid.*
[14] See J Glover, *Causing Death and Saving Lives* (London, Penguin, 1977), p 51.
[15] J Finnis, 'Bland – Crossing the Rubicon?' (1993) 109 *LQR* 329, at p 334.
[16] J Keown, 'Restoring Moral and Intellectual Shape to the Law after Bland' (1997) 113 *LQR* 481.
[17] Keown, *ibid*, p 482.
[18] *Ibid*, p 485.
[19] [2000] 4 All ER 961, at p 1000.

of human life outlined by Keown is the 'quality of life'. This approach assesses the worthwhileness of the patient's life (rather than the proposed treatment) and regards certain lives as not worth living and therefore susceptible to intentional termination. Keown rightly criticises this approach for denying 'the ineliminable value of each patient' and for engaging in potentially discriminatory judgments.[20] It certainly poses problems for a right to life based upon the inherent equality of all human lives.

II. The *Bland* Principles

Having now set the scene, it is time to consider the landmark case of *Airedale NHS Trust v Bland* and its implication for a right to life based upon the sanctity of life. Anthony Bland was 17 years old when he suffered severe brain damage during the Hillsborough football stadium disaster. He was diagnosed as being in a persistent vegetative state (PVS). This means, as mentioned above, that his higher brain (or cortex) had been destroyed due to oxygen deprivation but his brain stem was still functioning. Bland could breath without assistance but had no awareness of his surroundings. Three years after the disaster, the hospital treating him, with his family's support, sought a court declaration that it would be lawful to discontinue all life-sustaining treatment, including artificial hydration and nutrition (ANH). In all, nine judges gave judgments in this case: Stephen Brown P at first instance; Sir Thomas Bingham MR, Butler-Sloss LJ and Hoffmann LJ in the Court of Appeal; and Lords Keith, Goff, Lowry, Browne-Wilkinson and Mustill in the House of Lords. All nine agreed that the declaration should be granted and that Anthony Bland should be allowed to die. The reasoning differs drastically, however, especially between the Court of Appeal and the House of Lords. The House of Lords judgment has set an important precedent in medical law, indeed it is perhaps the single most significant judgment so far in English medical law. All nine of the judgments in the three courts stray over diverse topics in medical law from euthanasia to treating incompetent patients to the provision of consent. As Sir Thomas Bingham MR noted, the case 'raises moral, legal and ethical questions of a profound and fundamental nature, questions literally of life and death'.[21] The first profound question was whether Anthony Bland was alive at all.

---

[20]   Keown, n 16 above, p 487.
[21]   *Bland,* n 1 above, p 835.

(a) Was Bland still alive?

In the previous section we encountered some arguments that a patient with no higher brain function – no consciousness or awareness – is really no longer a living person. However, all nine judges in *Bland* asserted that the patient was still alive and thus accepted the brain stem death diagnosis as the legal definition of death. Lord Browne-Wilkinson, for example, stated unambiguously that '[h]is brain stem is alive and so is he . . .'[22] and Lord Goff said 'I start with the simple fact that, in law, Anthony is still alive.'[23] However, Lord Goff proceeds to raise a doubt about this conclusion which was also apparent in many of the other judgments. He continued: 'It is true that his condition is such that it can be described as a living death; but he is nevertheless still alive.'[24] He then outlines the reason for the introduction of the BSD concept – 'because, as a result of developments in modern medical technology, doctors no longer associate death exclusively with breathing and heartbeat' – but this is a misleading diversion because on the traditional cardiorespiratory definition of death, Bland is also still alive. Indeed it is even more self-evident on that basis, because he is clearly still breathing. Lord Goff's comments only serve to cloud the issue and seemingly raise some doubt about whether Bland is truly still alive or, as Lord Goff put it, in a 'living death'. Hoffmann LJ in the Court of Appeal also fell into this same trap and confusingly stated that 'the very concept of having a life has no meaning in relation to Anthony Bland. He is alive but has no life at all.'[25] Even if Hoffmann LJ is correct that the concept of 'life' has no meaning for the patient himself, it has great meaning for the law. A patient who is alive must be treated in his best interests or in line with his competently expressed wishes; he has a right to life which includes some degree of positive obligation on the part of the state to preserve life; and he has the gamut of other rights and interests accorded to living persons on the basis of their humanity. A dead body has no such rights or interests. There may be moral and legal restrictions upon how we treat a dead body but the idea of fundamental human rights or autonomy have no meaning in this context. So, the question of whether Bland is alive or dead is crucial and while the courts treated him as if he were alive, suggestions that he 'has no life' or is in a 'living death' are extremely unhelpful.

Perhaps the underlying reason for such doubts is explained by Lord Browne-Wilkinson when he pondered the meaning of 'life' in the modern age and whether the principle of sanctity of life applies to a patient in a condition such as Bland's:

---

[22] *Ibid*, p 878.
[23] *Ibid*, p 865.
[24] *Ibid*.
[25] *Ibid*, p 853. At other points in his judgment, Hoffmann LJ repeated this theme: 'the stark reality is that Anthony Bland is not living a life at all' (p 855); 'His body is alive but he has no life ...' (p 850).

What is meant now by 'life' in the moral precept which requires respect for the sanctity of human life? If the quality of life of a person such as Anthony Bland is non-existent since he is unaware of anything that happens to him, has he a right to be sustained in that state of living death and are his family and medical attendants under a duty to maintain it?[26]

This quotation helpfully introduces many of the issues in the *Bland* case: sanctity of life, quality of life, the right to life and duties of care. In the context of whether Anthony Bland was alive and, if so, whether his life is sacred, the quotation raises the element of doubt which seemed to have been in many of the judges' minds. A number of judges referred to the ethical principle of the sanctity of life, but they mainly noted it in order to explain that it is not absolute and that other conflicting principles may overrule it. For example, in the Court of Appeal, Butler-Sloss LJ identified two exceptions to the sanctity of life which already existed in English law: the principle of self-determination; and the *Re J* situation of extreme pain and suffering.[27] Neither of these exceptions apply in the *Bland* case as the patient is unable either to express his wishes or to feel pain. However, Butler-Sloss LJ argued that other factors apply in the *Bland* situation: 'He has the right to be respected. Consequently he has a right to avoid unnecessary humiliation and degrading invasion of his body for no good purpose.'[28] This appears to be an argument that the right to dignity of the person outweighs sanctity of life in certain situations.[29] There is much merit in this argument but it should be acknowledged that it could be used to open the door to euthanasia. Deciding what is most in need of, and worthy of, protection for a living but comatose patient is a difficult task: is it the right to life or the right to dignity which should prevail? Are they necessarily inconsistent with each other? Having decided that Anthony Bland was alive (albeit with a few misgivings), and being open to the possibility that the important principle of sanctity of life did not necessarily require unending preservation of a comatose state, the judges had to turn their minds to the crux of the case: what was in Bland's best interests?

(b)   Bland's Best Interests

As Anthony Bland was a living, but comatose, patient, the decision about how to treat him had to be decided in line with the law on treating incompetent patients. In the US, a substituted judgement test is applied to determine what the incompetent patient would have chosen if he was competent to make a choice. Thus, in the case of Nancy Cruzan, a PVS patient sustained by ANH, the key

---

[26]   *Ibid*, p 878.

[27]   *Ibid*, p 846; *Re J (a minor)* [1990] 3 All ER 930.

[28]   *Ibid*, p 848.

[29]   Hoffmann LJ also regarded sanctity of life as 'only one of a cluster of ethical principles which we apply to decisions about how we should live' and expressly referred to respect for dignity of the individual as one of the other principles (p 851).

question for the US courts was whether there was clear and convincing evidence that she would have wanted the feeding tube removed.[30] The Missouri Supreme Court failed to find such evidence and held that in its absence the state had an interest in preserving the patient's life, an approach accepted as constitutional by the US Supreme Court. When subsequently, and somewhat conveniently, friends recalled a clearly expressed wish not to be sustained in such a state, a second application for removal of ANH succeeded. In the UK, as we discussed at length in Chapter 5, the decisive factor, both at common law and now in the Mental Capacity Act 2005, is not the patient's assumed wishes but rather the patient's best interests as judged by his doctors. Prior to the case of *Bland*, the UK courts had already applied the best interests test to determine the appropriateness of withdrawal of life-sustaining treatment in the context of severely disabled infants. As was seen in Chapter 5, in *Re J (a minor)*[31] the Court of Appeal held that it would not be in a baby's best interests to reventilate if his breathing ceased because of his very poor quality of life.

When the judges in *Bland* sought to assess the patient's best interests, they were keen to clarify that it was not a question of whether death would be in his best interests. As Lord Goff explained 'the question is not whether it is in the best interests of the patient that he should die. The question is whether it is in the best interests of the patient that his life should be prolonged by the continuance of this form of medical treatment or care.'[32] The difficulty faced by the judges in answering this question was the inclination of many of them that Bland no longer had any interests of any kind. Lord Keith explained the difficulty of ascribing any interests to Anthony Bland:

> In the case of a permanently insensate being, who if continuing to live would never experience the slightest actual discomfort, it is difficult, if not impossible, to make any relevant comparison between continued existence and the absence of it. It is, however, perhaps permissible to say that to an individual with no cognitive capacity whatever, and no prospect of ever recovering any such capacity in this world, it must be a matter of complete indifference whether he lives or dies.[33]

Lord Mustill also concluded that Bland had 'no interests of any kind',[34] including in being kept alive and, therefore, the justification for the non-consensual treatment regime had vanished.

Keown has strongly criticised this approach, claiming that to assert that Bland has no interests is misleading: 'Would it not have been contrary to his interests to use him as, for example, a sideboard?'[35] Such a vivid picture is unnecessary as it is

---

[30]   *Cruzan v Director, Missouri Department of Health* (1990) 110 S Ct.
[31]   See n 27 above.
[32]   *Bland*, n 1 above, p 869.
[33]   *Ibid*, pp 860-61.
[34]   *Ibid*, p 894.
[35]   Keown, n 16 above, p 494.

clear from a human rights perspective that Anthony Bland retained interests, and indeed rights, in how he was treated despite losing his competence and consciousness. The strongest criticism that can be made of the *Bland* judgments is that they regard the patient as being bereft of interests. This probably stems from the belief that Bland is existing in 'a twilight world',[36] neither fully alive nor fully dead, but in a 'living death' with 'no life at all'.[37] However, Bland was alive. He had a variety of potentially conflicting interests which should have been unpicked and balanced. This was especially important because of the extremely vulnerable position which he was in, where there was no possibility of him being able to defend his own interests. Bland also had a plethora of rights, including a right to life and to dignity (or, in the words of the ECHR, a right to be free from inhuman or degrading treatment). These rights seemed to conflict in Bland's case and a reconciliation of them should have been sought. Instead, Bland is regarded as having no interest in being alive or in dying; in being subjected to futile treatment or in being deprived of food and water. He was not treated as a living person and neither his best interests nor his fundamental rights were properly assessed.

In determining that continued treatment was not in the patient's best interests, the judges encountered further problems in respect of the means for assessing this. The Court of Appeal judgments appear to be confused on the issue of whether the question of best interests should be determined on an objective or subjective basis, and the House of Lords on whether it is a decision for the doctors or the courts. In the Court of Appeal, Sir Thomas Bingham MR made the following confusing statement: 'Looking at the matter as objectively as I can, and doing my best to look at the matter through Mr Bland's eyes and not my own, I cannot conceive what benefit his continued existence could be thought to give him.'[38] How one can be both objective and look at the matter through one person's eyes is not clear. There are elements here of both a best interests test and a substituted judgment test. Bingham's lack of clarity continues when he lists the factors of relevance to, in his words, 'an objective assessment of Mr Bland's best interests, viewed through his eyes'. He holds that weight should be given:

> to the constant invasions and humiliations to which his inert body is subject; to the desire he would naturally have to be remembered as a cheerful, carefree, gregarious teenager and not an object of pity; to the prolonged ordeal imposed on all members of his family, but particularly on his parents; even, perhaps, if altruism still lives, to a belief that finite resources are better devoted to enhancing life than simply averting death.[39]

All of these are legitimate considerations but they are not all aspects of Anthony Bland's best interests. Neither the ordeal for others nor the issue of resources are

---

[36]   *Bland*, n 1 above, per Butler-Sloss LJ, at p 842.
[37]   See above.
[38]   *Bland*, n 1 above, p 839.
[39]   *Ibid*, p 840.

elements of the patient's interests, whereas the preservation of life should surely feature as one of his interests, even if it is ultimately outweighed by other factors.

The House of Lords did not have such difficulty with the objective nature of best interests but they encountered a different source of division in the application of the best interests test. Lords Keith, Goff, Lowry and Browne-Wilkinson all held that Bland's best interests should be determined by his doctors on the basis of the *Bolam* test.[40] This is a further controversial aspect of the case because the extension of *Bolam* into issues far removed from the standard of care for negligence leaves it looking increasingly like an inappropriate abdication of judicial responsibility. Both Keown and Finnis argue that the application of *Bolam* in *Bland* was unsound,[41] and even some of the other judges had doubts. In the Court of Appeal, the *Bolam* test was not relied upon. Butler-Sloss LJ expressly doubted its application, recognising that it 'may not by itself be an adequate basis for this grave decision' because the 'best interests of an incompetent patient in the present circumstances encompasses wider considerations, including some degree of monitoring of the medical decision'.[42] Hoffmann LJ summed up the issue by holding that 'the medical profession will no doubt have views which are entitled to great respect, but I would expect medical ethics to be formed by the law rather than the reverse'.[43] In the House of Lords, Lord Mustill also doubted the application of the *Bolam* standard by recognising that 'the decision is ethical, not medical, and there is no reason in logic why on such a decision the opinions of doctors should be decisive'.[44] Nevertheless, despite these convincing concerns about the extension of medical discretion, the majority of the Lords held that the *Bolam* test applied and, therefore, decisions about withdrawing life-sustaining treatment will now be decided on the basis of what a responsible body of medical opinion regard as in the patient's best interests, irrespective of whether there are other opposing bodies of opinion.

(c)   Is Artificial Feeding a Form of Medical Treatment?

The decision that continuing to administer life-sustaining treatment was no longer in Bland's best interests raises a further concern. Bland was breathing independently and therefore the only 'treatment' being administered was artificial nutrition and hydration (ANH) – ie food and water administered through a nasogastric tube – as well as a catheter, enemas and antibiotics to fight infection. Withdrawing treatment from Bland meant depriving him of food and water. Arguments have been raised that this does not amount to medical treatment but

---

[40]   Lord Keith, p 861; Lord Goff, p 871; Lord Lowry, p 876; and Lord Browne-Wilkinson, p 883. The *Bolam* test is discussed in Chapter 3 in its proper context of the standard of care in negligence.
[41]   Finnis, n 15 above, p 334; Keown, n 16 above, pp 495-96.
[42]   *Bland*, n 1 above, p 845.
[43]   *Ibid*, p 858.
[44]   *Ibid*, p 895.

is rather an element of basic care comparable to providing shelter and warmth, which ought not to be withdrawn from any living patient. All of the judges in the *Bland* case dismissed this argument and held that artificial feeding is medical treatment and therefore can be withdrawn if it is no longer justified as in the patient's best interests. Keown succinctly explains the difficulty with this conclusion: 'The question in such a case is why the pouring of food down the tube constitutes medical treatment. What is it supposed to be treating?'[45] Sir Thomas Bingham MR attempted to explain why tube feeding differs from other means of feeding, claiming that the insertion of the tube requires skill and knowledge, the tube is invasive, and the mechanical pumping of food through the tube is an unnatural process.[46] The point remains, however, that the provision of food for an incompetent patient is a basic expectation within an affluent society, rather than an extraordinary means of preserving life, and is far more likely to fall within a state's positive obligations to preserve the life of its citizens. Finnis has argued that:

> to desist from providing at least food and basic hygiene to invalids whose death is not imminent, and to whom the processes involved are no significant burden, seems to be either (1) to intend and bring about their death as a means, e.g. to saving the other costs involved in their continued existence, or (2) to make a choice (however hidden by benign sentiments and palliative accompaniments) to cease providing care for them. And in an affluent society . . . the latter is willy-nilly a choice to deny the personhood of those invalids by breaking off human solidarity with them at its root.[47]

It was argued above that patients such as Bland do remain persons, with rights and interests. The denial of basic care such as food and water from a patient who otherwise requires no medical intervention to support life can be regarded as a distinctly different issue to a decision that medical treatment is no longer in a patient's best interests. The judges' reluctance to rely upon this distinction in *Bland* may be criticised as leading to further confusion.

(d)   Is Withdrawing Treatment an Act or an Omission (and does it matter)?

Regardless of whether feeding is regarded as medical treatment or basic humanitarian care, many people feel uncomfortable with the withdrawal of it as a means of causing death. If, the argument goes, Anthony Bland would be better off dead, he should be killed quickly and painlessly by means of a lethal injection rather than be allowed to die slowly from dehydration. The fact that Bland is entirely

---

[45]   Keown, n 16 above, p 491.
[46]   *Bland*, n 1 above, p 836. To be fair, this viewpoint was overwhelmingly supported by the medical evidence presented in the case.
[47]   Finnis, n 15 above, p 335.

unaware of his death and is not suffering does not entirely remove the instinctive revulsion of this manner of death in a modern NHS hospital. And the blame is usually laid at the feet of the act/omission distinction. Assuming the requisite intention, an act which causes death – such as a lethal injection – will amount to murder, whereas an omission which causes death, even if the intention is the same, is not culpable. This distinction is at the foundation of English criminal law. There is an important exception, however, if the perpetrator owes a duty of care to the victim. Therefore, in the normal circumstances, a doctor depriving an incompetent patient of food and water with the intent to cause his death would be liable for murder. But in the case of *Bland* the courts had held that continued treatment – ie food and water – was no longer in the patient's best interests. Therefore, there was no duty to treat him. An omission to treat causing death would not subject the doctors to criminal liability. This assumes, however, that withdrawing treatment is an omission rather than an act, and this is arguable. If, for example, the treatment in question is artificial ventilation, how can pressing a button to cease the ventilation be regarded as an omission to act? The same is true of ANH where a positive act is needed in order to stop the feeding. The House of Lords in *Bland* were not prepared to decipher such fine distinctions between acts and omissions to act. Instead, the Lords compared the withdrawal of treatment with the withholding of treatment: switching off a ventilator being no different from failing to ventilate in the first place.[48]

Despite the Law Lords' reliance upon an act/omission distinction and categorisation of withdrawing treatment as an omission, there were a number of misgivings. Lord Browne-Wilkinson, having held that the removal of the nasogastric tube was an omission which was not culpable if there was no duty to treat, expressed his concerns about the consequences of that conclusion:

> the conclusion I have reached will appear to some to be almost irrational. How can it be lawful to allow a patient to die slowly, though painlessly, over a period of weeks from lack of food but unlawful to produce his immediate death by a lethal injection, thereby saving his family from yet another ordeal to add to the tragedy that has already struck them? I find it difficult to find a moral answer to that question. But it is undoubtedly the law . . .[49]

This assumption that the law was clear and left the House of Lords with little choice was repeated by Lord Mustill who recognised the ethical difficulties inherent in the act/omission distinction:

> however much the terminology may differ the ethical status of the two courses of action is for all relevant purposes indistinguishable. By dismissing this appeal I fear that your

---

[48]   See, for example, Lord Goff at pp 867-68 and Lord Browne-Wilkinson at p 882.
[49]   *Ibid*, p 884.

Lordships' House may only emphasise the distortions of a legal structure which is already both morally and intellectually misshapen. Still, the law is there and we must take it as it stands.[50]

This 'misshapen' criticism has been picked up by many commentators. Finnis, for example, argues that '[w]hat is misshapen and indefensible is a law that treats as criminal a harmful "act" while treating as lawful (and indeed compulsory) an "omission" with the very same intent, by one who has a duty to care for the person injured'.[51] This is a helpful way of looking at the dilemma because it stops short of dismissing an act/omission distinction in its entirety. Despite its controversial nature, it is arguable that there is a moral, and therefore should be a legal, distinction between an act causing death and an omission causing death. Throwing a person in a river to drown may be regarded as morally worse than failing to jump in to save him, even if there is malicious intent in both cases. Both may be morally blameworthy but to take a positive step to bring about a person's death deserves greater blame than to fail to prevent the death.[52] So, the act/omission distinction may have some merit but it seems inappropriate in situations where the perpetrator owes, or has owed, a moral and legal duty of care to the victim. Even though it was decided in *Bland* that continuing treatment was no longer in his best interests, the doctors and hospital could be regarded as continuing to owe a duty of care to their patient which distinguishes their position from that of a stranger failing to jump into a river to save a drowning man. The hospital would not have been entitled, for example, to abandon Anthony Bland on the pavement outside the hospital. A duty of care still existed even if the duty to treat had ceased.

The Court of Appeal judgments in *Bland* were far preferable to that of the House of Lords on the issue of an act/omission distinction. Hoffmann LJ explained that the act/omission distinction was not crucial to the case but, instead, the important distinction was between (a) either an act or an omission which allows an existing cause to operate, and (b) the introduction of an external agency of death.[53] The difficulty here is with the assumption that death from lack of food and water is death from an 'existing cause'. Hoffmann LJ recognised this difficulty and noted that if someone allows a child or invalid in his care to starve to death, we do not say that nature took its course but, rather, that a wicked crime has been committed. However, Hoffmann LJ asserted that a duty to provide care 'ceases when such treatment can serve no humane purpose' whereas the prohibition on violating the person, by introducing an external agent, is absolute.[54] This approach would have resulted in the same morally challenging solution of a

---

[50] *Ibid*, p 885.

[51] Finnis, n 15 above, p 333.

[52] The famous and influential article by Rachels takes a different view: J Rachels, 'Active and Passive Euthanasia' (1975) 292 *New England Journal of Medicine* 78.

[53] *Bland*, n 1 above, p 855. Butler-Sloss LJ made a similar point at p 849.

[54] *Ibid*, p 856.

patient starving to death slowly rather than being eased quickly on his way, but it would have avoided the logically problematic reliance upon the act/omission distinction adopted by the House of Lords, and to that extent would have been far preferable.

(e)   Conclusion: The *Bland* Principles

We have devoted a great deal of attention to the *Bland* case because of the landmark nature of the judgments and the huge impact it has had on other cases. Having examined the main issues of the case and assessed the criticisms of the judges' conclusions upon them, three main principles stemming from the case can be identified:

(1)   Withdrawing treatment is an omission rather than an act;
(2)   Doctors will face no liability for this omission if the treatment is regarded by a responsible body of medical opinion as no longer in the patient's best interests;
(3)   The provision of nutrition and hydration through a nasogastric tube is a form of medical treatment, not an element of basic care, and is therefore indistinguishable in legal terms from any other form of life-sustaining treatment.

These important, but somewhat unsatisfactory, conclusions have been applied in subsequent cases. The trend apparent from within them is that the principles of *Bland* can be applied without the strict requirements emphasised in that case, as we will now see.

III.   The *Bland* Principles in Practice

(a)   The Beginning of a Slippery Slope?

All nine judges involved in the *Bland* case took great care to consider the legal and moral intricacies of Bland's situation. Subsequent cases have tended to be more of a rush to judgment, with the withdrawal of life-sustaining treatment author-ised without due consideration of the issues; where there is disagreement within the family; or even where there is no firm diagnosis of PVS. The first signs of a relaxation of the strict approach in *Bland* came in *Frenchay Healthcare NHS Trust v S* in 1994.[55] The patient at issue here had been diagnosed as in PVS for two and a half years as a result of a drug overdose. The patient's gastrostomy tube became

---

[55]   [1994] 2 All ER 403.

dislodged and the hospital sought a declaration that it would be lawful not to replace the tube. The time pressures of this emergency application meant that the case was heard and decided quickly without adequate time for reflection. The court granted the declaration even though the medical evidence of PVS was not as strong as in *Bland*. There was no need for this application to be time-pressured. The feeding tube could easily have been replaced and an application made in due course to withdraw it. This would have encouraged a more reasoned decision with no disadvantage to the unconscious and unaware patient. Where issues of the right to life are in play, a presumption in favour of preserving life would seem appropriate. The replacement of the tube would have preserved life until a court had the time and expert evidence to fully consider whether the state's duty to preserve life continued to apply in this situation.

The case of *Re G*[56] in 1995 involved the unfortunate complicating factor of a dispute within the patient's family. The wife favoured withdrawing treatment but the mother was opposed to it. This disagreement did not unduly delay the court's decision because the medical evidence of the patient's doctors recommended withdrawal and therefore the mother's objections were overruled. The case demonstrates the sound principle (discussed in Chapter 5) that it is the best interests of the patient, rather than the wishes of relatives, which determine the patient's future treatment. Of greater concern is a trend in the case law to authorise the withdrawal of ANH where the PVS diagnosis is ambiguous or even entirely absent. In *Re D*,[57] the patient had suffered severe brain damage from a head injury. As in *Frenchay*, her feeding tube had become dislodged, but in this case medical opinion did not regard the patient as in PVS because, even though she was totally unaware, one of the diagnostic criteria for PVS had not been satisfied. Nevertheless, the President of the Family Division held that the patient was in PVS and granted the declaration sought. Similarly, in *Re H (adult: incompetence)*,[58] the patient did not satisfy the diagnostic criteria for PVS but was severely brain damaged and unaware. Sir Stephen Brown P held that 'a precise label is not of significant importance' and granted the declaration. Thus, even when doctors are unable to diagnose a patient as in PVS the courts may still regard it as in the patient's best interests to withdraw food and water. The slippery slope continued in *Re G (adult incompetent: withdrawal of treatment)*[59] in 2001. In this case, a patient suffering serious brain damage had been kept alive by means of ANH for nine months until a court granted a declaration permitting the withdrawal of this artificial assistance. The patient was not in PVS.

In 2004, in *W v Healthcare NHS Trust v KH*,[60] the Court of Appeal finally stopped the descent down the slippery slope of withdrawing ANH by holding

[56] [1995] 3 Med LR 80.
[57] (1997) 38 BMLR 1.
[58] (1997) 38 BMLR 11.
[59] (2001) 65 BMLR 6.
[60] [2005] 1 WLR 834.

that a patient who had suffered from multiple sclerosis for thirty years, and had required artificial feeding for five years, should continue to be fed. It was undeniable that the patient had a poor quality of life but a vital distinguishing factor with the other cases discussed here is that the patient was conscious and sentient, despite being disorientated, barely able to speak and unable to recognise anybody.[61] Although the patient had previously, when competent, expressed her wish not to be kept alive by machines, she had not, understandably, addressed the issue of whether she would prefer a slow death by starvation or to remain alive in a relatively comfortable condition.[62] As she would be aware of her death by starvation, the life-sustaining treatment continued to provide a benefit and, as the first instance judge explained, 'starvation would be even less dignified than the death which she will face in due course if kept artificially alive for more weeks or months or possibly years'.[63] The 'heavy burden' placed on those 'who are advocating a course which would lead inevitably to the cessation of a human life' had not here been discharged.[64] This is a welcome recognition that the life of an incompetent patient continues to deserve active protection at the very least until it is no longer of any benefit to the patient.

(b)   Duty to Provide ANH to Competent Patients

The apparent judicial willingness to approve the withdrawal of ANH from patients suffering severe brain damage inevitably caused concern amongst some patients. Leslie Burke suffered from a degenerative brain condition which would require ANH at a later stage. He argued that the GMC guidelines which permitted withdrawal of such treatment were inconsistent with a patient's human rights, specifically Articles 2, 3 and 8. This argument was based upon his concern that withdrawal of ANH was possible even if the patient wished to remain alive. As Gurnham explains, this could be regarded as a logical viewpoint: 'It is not altogether unreasonable to interpret these guidelines, as Burke did, as stipulating that the actual views of the patient concerning the quality of his own life were simply part of the evidence taken into consideration by the doctor in forming his professional judgment.'[65]

At first instance in *R (Burke) v The General Medical Council*[66] Munby J issued declarations that a competent patient's wishes (or advance directive) that he wants ANH is determinative of his best interests and withdrawal would, in those circumstances, be a violation of Articles 3 and 8. Munby J held that the 'personal

---

[61]   *Ibid*, para 2.
[62]   *Ibid*, para 20.
[63]   *Ibid*, para 27.
[64]   *Ibid*, para 30 (per Brooke LJ).
[65]   D Gurnham. 'Losing the Wood for the Trees: *Burke* and the Court of Appeal' (2006) 14 *Med L Rev* 253, at p 254.
[66]   [2005] QB 424.

autonomy protected by Article 8 means that in principle it is for the competent patient, and not his doctor, to decide what treatment *should* or *should not* be given in order to achieve what *the patient* believes conduces to his dignity and in order to avoid what *the patient* would find distressing'.[67] This came perilously close to a right to treatment and, as discussed at length in Chapter 2, the Court of Appeal disagreed strongly with such a right and overruled Munby J's lengthy judgment. In the Court of Appeal the clear view was taken that 'Mr Burke's fears are addressed by the law as it currently stands.'[68] The Court explained that the provision of ANH is part of the hospital's duty of care – the 'duty to take such steps as are reasonable to keep the patient alive'[69] – and that in respect of a competent patient expressing a wish to remain alive, the duty of care will require ANH to continue: 'Indeed, it seems to us that for a doctor deliberately to interrupt life-prolonging treatment in the face of a competent patient's expressed wish to be kept alive, with the intention of thereby terminating the patient's life, would leave the doctor with no answer to a charge of murder.'[70] The Court of Appeal's strong belief that the interests of patients such as Mr Burke in remaining alive are adequately served by existing English law will serve as some reassurance to competent patients, but the more challenging ethical and legal question remains whether an incompetent patient in an inevitably comatose state has any enforceable right to life which would preclude the withdrawal of artificial feeding. The question of a reconciliation between the principles stemming from *Bland* and the rights introduced into English law by the Human Rights Act 1998 will now be addressed.

(c)   The Bland Principles in a Human Rights Age

When the Human Rights Act came into force in 2000, it introduced, inter alia, the right to life and the right to be free from inhuman and degrading treatment into domestic law. These two rights applied to every living person within the UK jurisdiction. Bland was a living person. The House of Lords confirmed that he was still alive even though he had lost any higher brain function, and in *NHS Trust A v M; NHS Trust B v H*[71] in 2001, Dame Butler-Sloss, the President of the Family Division, confirmed that a patient in PVS is entitled to the full protection of Article 2's right to life.[72] So, how can the withdrawal of essential life-sustaining treatment such as ANH be consistent with the state's duty to protect the right to life of all persons, including those in PVS? And, why isn't the withdrawal of food and water from a comatose patient, causing him to starve to death, regarded as

---

[67]   *Ibid*, para 178.
[68]   [2005] 3 WLR 1132, at para 23.
[69]   *Ibid*, para 32.
[70]   *Ibid*, para 34, per Lord Phillips MR giving the judgment of the Court.
[71]   [2001] 2 WLR 942.
[72]   *Ibid*, para 17.

degrading treatment by the state? Dame Butler-Sloss recognised in the *NHS Trusts* case that there was a need to reconsider the *Bland* principles in the light of the Human Rights Act[73] and she also acknowledged that, due to the HRA, she was no longer necessarily bound by the House of Lords' decision in *Bland*.[74]

The case involved two patients diagnosed as in a PVS condition. Mrs M had been in PVS for three years and with ANH would be able to survive in this condition for years more. By contrast, Mrs H had only been in PVS for nine months and her feeding tube had become blocked. Invasive methods were needed to rectify this situation and so the court application was an emergency one in respect of this patient. Both NHS Trusts sought declarations that it would be lawful to withdraw ANH from these patients and both were supported by the patients' families. Dame Butler-Sloss considered in some detail whether Article 2 was consistent with the withdrawal of ANH from a patient in PVS. She divided the issue into two parts reflecting the two aspects of Article 2: a negative and a positive obligation. First, she queried whether an omission to provide life-sustaining treatment was an 'intentional deprivation of life', which is prohibited in Article 2. She regarded this phrase as requiring a deliberate act, as opposed to an omission:

> A responsible decision by a medical team not to provide treatment at the initial stage could not amount to intentional deprivation of life by the state. Such a decision based on clinical judgment is an omission to act. The death of the patient is the result of the illness or injury from which he suffered and that cannot be described as a deprivation.[75]

There has been some criticism of this reliance upon the act/omission distinction in respect of the negative obligation on the state to avoid intentional deprivations of life. For example, Maclean argues that both acts and omissions are capable of 'depriving' someone of his life, although he concedes that the omitted act would need to be one that would have been efficacious if performed, and the actor would need to be both capable of performing the act and under an obligation to do so.[76] With these provisos, it is certainly possible to regard a deliberate omission to act as depriving a person of his or her life, and as such, Butler-Sloss's eagerness to discount the relevance of the NHS Trusts' negative obligation to PVS patients under Article 2 is problematic. Nevertheless, Butler-Sloss did proceed to consider the other obligation under Article 2, namely the positive obligation to preserve life.

In *Osman v United Kingdom*,[77] the European Court of Human Rights had held that public authorities (the police in that case) must do all that is reasonable to avoid a real and immediate risk to life. This obligation was discussed at length in

---

[73]   *Ibid*, para 14.
[74]   *Ibid*, para 18.
[75]   *Ibid*, para 30.
[76]   A Maclean, 'Crossing the Rubicon on the Human Rights Ferry' (2001) 64 *MLR* 775, at p 780.
[77]   (2000) 29 EHRR 245.

Chapter 2 and it was noted there that it could in certain situations require the continuation of life-sustaining medical treatment. However, Dame Butler-Sloss sought to superimpose the domestic best interests test (discussed in Chapter 5) onto the requirements of Article 2:

> Article 2 . . . imposes a positive obligation to give life-sustaining treatment in circumstances where, according to responsible medical opinion, such treatment is in the best interests of the patient but does not impose an absolute obligation to treat if such treatment would be futile. This approach is entirely in accord with the principles laid down in *Bland's* case . . .[78]

The *NHS Trusts* case therefore holds that a state's (and an NHS Trust's) positive obligation to preserve life is discharged if a decision to withdraw life-sustaining treatment is taken in the patient's best interests and supported by a responsible body of medical opinion. Indeed, Butler-Sloss even went so far as to claim that the UK set a higher standard than that required by the ECHR because of the requirement of judicial oversight.[79] This overlooks the fact that the best interests test is not evident in the text of Article 2 and has never been expressly read into it by the Strasbourg institutions. Article 2 does not say that everyone's right to life must be protected by law until the continuation of that life is no longer in the person's own interests, and indeed such a restriction on the right to life would imply the rejection of the sanctity of life principle by its assumption that death is sometimes preferable to life. The difficult ethical issues inherent in the sanctity of life principle were discussed above. It is sufficient here to note that Butler-Sloss's judgment can be criticised for its abject failure to grapple with the question of whether Article 2 seeks to uphold the sanctity of life in a relatively strict form or whether it admits the idea that life has mainly instrumental value. This latter argument has some support from the location of Article 2 in a convention primarily concerned with upholding an individual's right to self-determination and freedoms within a democratic society. Butler-Sloss, however, fails to make this argument, or even acknowledge the question, and therefore the *NHS Trusts* case's reconciliation of the *Bland* principles with Article 2 is entirely unconvincing. As Maclean notes, this is largely because of the superficial approach of Butler-Sloss's judgment: 'in trying to fit the convention into the framework of the common law, Dame Butler-Sloss P has skimmed the surface of the problems surrounding the use of futility and has missed a valuable opportunity to improve the coherence and consistency of the law in this area'.[80]

The judge also considered briefly the relevance of Article 3 to this issue. The argument here is that a treatment decision which knowingly causes a patient to

---

[78] *NHS Trusts* case, n 71 above, para 37.
[79] *Ibid*, p 38.
[80] Maclean, n 76 above, pp 786–87.

starve to death could amount to the imposition of degrading treatment, prohibited under Article 3. However, Butler-Sloss controversially held that Article 3 requires the victim to be aware of the inhuman or degrading treatment or, at least, to be in a state of physical or mental suffering.[81] A PVS patient could not rely upon the protection of Article 3. This conclusion is clearly open to criticism because there is no case law under the ECHR requiring that a victim of an Article 3 violation must be aware of the degradation and it is easy to envisage situations where a person is unaware of degrading treatment. If a PVS patient were raped or left in unsanitary conditions or in some other way treated without the respect owed to a human being, would there be no violation of the patient's rights? Even if a person has no enduring interest in life, dignity is a value attaching to all human beings and worthy of protection under human rights law. The *NHS Trusts* case is, therefore, unsatisfactory in its reasoning in respect of both Articles 2 and 3. The conclusion that the *Bland* principles present no human rights difficulties is overly simplistic and fails to adequately investigate the complex dilemmas presented by a patient whose life no longer has any, or much, value.

IV. Equal Rights to Life: The Conjoined Twins Case

The conjoined twins case in 2000 added another complicating factor to the determination of the value of life by forcing a court to choose between two conflicting rights to life. *Re A (children)(conjoined twins: surgical separation)*[82] was an immensely difficult case involving many apparently irreconcilable ethical dilemmas. It concerned a pair of conjoined twins, called Jodie and Mary by the court. The weaker twin, Mary, had a poorly developed brain, an abnormal heart and scarcely any functional lung tissue. The only reason she survived after birth was because her sister Jodie's heart was pumping blood through both of their bodies. The difficulty was that the extra effort required for this task by Jodie's heart would undoubtedly soon lead to Jodie suffering heart failure. When this happened, probably within three to six months, both twins would die. An operation to separate the twins would save Jodie's life but would simultaneously and inevitably cause Mary's death. It was a terrible dilemma for everyone concerned. The twins' parents were opposed to the separation on religious grounds. When the case reached the Court of Appeal, Ward LJ admitted that the Court was merely 'choosing the lesser of two evils'.[83] It could save one life by taking another, or it could condemn both twins to die within a few months.

It is immediately obvious that the right to life underlies this dilemma. All three Court of Appeal judges confirmed the importance of the right to life and the fact

---

[81]   *NHS Trusts* case, n 71 above, para 49.
[82]   [2000] 4 All ER 961.
[83]   *Ibid*, at p 1006.

that each life is of equal value: 'What the sanctity of life doctrine compels me to accept is that each life has inherent value in itself and the right to life, being universal, is equal for all of us . . . Given the international conventions protecting "the right to life" . . . I conclude that it is impermissible to deny that every life has an equal inherent value.'[84] This strong statement that all lives, and thus all rights to life, are equal meant that Mary's severely disabled and inevitably short-lived life was equally as important as Jodie's potentially normal life. The majority of the Court of Appeal was adamant that Mary's life had 'its own ineliminable value',[85] even though it was filled with pain and suffering. The court, therefore, seemed to adopt an intrinsic view of the value of life, holding that 'life is worthwhile in itself, whatever the diminution in one's capacity to enjoy it'.[86] As a consequence of the adoption of this view, both Ward LJ and Brooke LJ were forced to admit that the proposed separation would not be in Mary's best interests. It would inevitably end her life and, even though that would put an end to her suffering, would not be in her interests. Robert Walker LJ dissented on this point and, agreeing with the judge at first instance, held that 'to prolong Mary's life for a few months would confer no benefit on her but would be to her disadvantage'.[87] This view was not accepted by the majority, however, who continued to see benefit in the mere fact of prolonged life.

This left the majority in the difficult position of choosing between the path in Jodie's best interests (the separation operation) and that in Mary's best interests (no separation). Given that the Court of Appeal had already acknowledged that both twins had an equal right to life, some fudging of the issue was to be expected. Ward LJ explained that '[t]he universality of *the right* to life demands that the right to life be treated as equal. The intrinsic value of their human life is equal. So the right of each goes into the scales and the scales remain in balance.'[88] He continued, however, by holding that the worthwhile-ness of the treatment, and not their lives, could be compared, and this comparison would include considerations of their respective qualities of life. It would be, Ward LJ argued, 'impossible not to put in the scales of each child the manner in which they are individually able to exercise their right to life'.[89] So, Ward LJ is seeking to distinguish between a comparison of the value of the twins' respective lives, which would be inappropriate given that each has an equal right to life, and a comparison of the way in which they can respectively exercise their right to life. With the operation, Jodie could potentially live a relatively normal life; without the operation, Mary has at most six months of a very poor quality of life to enjoy. It is easy to accept the conclusion that the scales come down heavily in Jodie's

84   *Ibid*, pp 1000, 1001.
85   *Ibid*, p 1002, per Ward LJ.
86   *Ibid*, p 1001, per Ward LJ.
87   *Ibid*, p 1057.
88   *Ibid*, p 1010.
89   *Ibid*.

favour, but far harder to appreciate the apparent distinction between these two balancing exercises. While the court paid lip service to Mary's right to life, there is little doubt that her right to life was given less protection by the law than was Jodie's, perhaps understandably so. If the Court of Appeal felt it had no choice but to compare the value of the two lives, it would have been preferable for it to say so clearly.[90] Its failure to do so was at any rate entirely unsuccessful in disguising the fact.

Michalowski, for example, has strongly criticised the Court of Appeal for undertaking a balancing exercise between the conflicting interests of Jodie and Mary, and she notes that the 'determinative difference between Mary's and Jodie's lives was the degree of their disabilities and their ability to survive independently after a separation. The criterion on the basis of which the court distinguished the value of the two lives was therefore that of infirmity.'[91] As Michalowski notes, this distinguishing factor was expressly rejected as a legitimate consideration by Lord Mustill in *Bland*: 'the proposition that because of incapacity or infirmity one life is intrinsically worth less than another is the first step on a very dangerous road indeed, and one which I am not willing to take'.[92] In *Re A*, Michalowski argues, the Court of Appeal was willing to take a step on that dangerous road and in doing so undermined the sanctity of life.[93] Michalowski proposes a seemingly viable alternative to the balancing exercise undertaken by the Court of Appeal, namely that once it was decided that the operation was not in Mary's best interests, an alternative criminal law justification for the bodily intervention could have been sought.[94] This would have avoided the need to justify the prioritisation of Jodie's interests, and by implication, her right to life, over Mary's.

The focus upon the human rights of the twins in the *Re A* case is perhaps indicative of the time it was heard. The HRA was due to come into force in a few days time. Although all three judges denied that the HRA would make any difference to their decision, they did so on the basis that the 'fundamental importance of the right to protection of life is so ingrained in the English common law'.[95] This seems an unduly optimistic view of the common law. The right to life of Anthony Bland found little protection, or even recognition, in English common law, neither did the right to life of the young boy in need of a

---

[90] McEwan notes that 'the Court of Appeal attempt to disguise the fact that at every point of their argument they are engaged in a comparison of the respective rights to life of two human beings' (J McEwan, 'Murder by Design: The 'Feel Good Factor' and the Criminal Law' (2001) 9 *Med L Rev* 246, at p 248).

[91] S Michalowski, 'Sanctity of Life: Are Some Lives More Sacred than Others?' (2002) 22 LS 377, at p 397.

[92] *Bland*, n 1 above, p 891.

[93] Michalowski, n 91 above, p 397.

[94] Such as the doctrine of necessity relied upon by Brooke LJ. See E Wicks, 'The Greater Good? Issues of Proportionality and Democracy in the Doctrine of Necessity as Applied in *Re A*' (2003) 32 *CLWR* 15.

[95] *Re A*, n 82 above, p 1050, per Brooke LJ.

liver transplant in *Re T (a minor)*.[96] The reliance upon a best interests test determined by medical opinion is insufficient protection for a patient's fundamental right to life. The Court of Appeal's insistence in *Re A* that there is an inherent and equal value in all life does not assist in decisions about when, if ever, life should no longer be prolonged by medical intervention, and indeed it clouds the issue by implying that such questions need never arise.

V. Conclusion

The right to life is the most fundamental of all human rights but its enforcement at the end of life is inconsistent. The sound principle that every living person shares an equal right to life, regardless of lifespan and physical condition, faced an insurmountable hurdle in the conjoined twins case when a choice had to be made between two conflicting rights to life. The prohibition on the intentional deprivation of life (in Article 2 ECHR) has been stretched to breaking point with the judicial acceptance of the withdrawal of ANH from patients in PVS when the clear intention is to cause death. Even if the act/omission distinction is forced into service to excuse this apparent rights violation, a state's positive obligations under Article 2 to preserve life where there is a real and immediate risk to life seems to present an even stronger opponent. The incorporation of a best interests test into Article 2 is unconvincing because, even if life-sustaining medical treatment is no longer in the patient's best interests, as long as the patient (and crucially his brain stem) remains alive, he is owed the full gamut of rights, including a right to life. Even though the boundaries of life are not always clear, the law protects life from birth to brain stem death and in the intervening period individuals are entitled to respect for their autonomy, dignity and interests. It is this overall respect for the human being which has led many to argue that a right to life is of little value without a comparable right to die. The question of the sanctity of human life and its limitations now continues in the final chapter.

Recommended Further Reading:

J Finnis, '*Bland* – Crossing the Rubicon?' (1993) 109 *LQR* 329.
J Keown, 'Restoring Moral and Intellectual Shape to the Law after *Bland*' (1997) 113 *LQR* 481.
A Maclean, 'Crossing the Rubicon on the Human Rights Ferry' (2001) 64 *MLR* 775.

---

[96] [1997] 1 All ER 906 and see Chapter 5.

S Michalowski, 'Sanctity of Life: Are Some Lives More Sacred than Others?' (2002) 22 *LS* 377.

12

The Law and Ethics of Assisted Dying: Is There a Right to Die?

In the previous chapter, the issue of the right to life's application to end of life decisions was considered. The possibility was raised in that chapter that the right to life may encompass a broader right to self-determination in issues of life and death. This point will now be developed in this final chapter by consideration of the arguments for and against the existence of a 'right to die'. This is an ambiguous phrase but it is interpreted in this chapter to refer to a right to obtain assistance in dying. We will first set the issue in context by identifying the criminal law prohibitions on assisted dying. The remainder of the chapter will then evaluate the advantages and disadvantages (both for the law and society) of the legal recognition of a right to die. The chapter will end with a few words on the general utility of a human rights framework for emotive medico-legal issues such as this.

I. The Criminal Law Prohibition on Assisted Dying

Assisted dying, in all its diverse forms, has increasingly become the focus of medical, ethical and legal debate. The emergence of this debate is easily explained for, as Battin describes, it 'reflects a basic shift in the epidemiology of human mortality, a shift away from death due to parasitic and infectious disease . . . to death in later life of degenerative disease'.[1] In other words, we (at least in the developed world) are dying older and more slowly than before, from diseases that are 'marked by a terminal phase of dying'.[2] It is no wonder, then, that assisted dying has become an issue. The phrase 'assisted dying' is used here in an attempt to encompass a variety of situations. 'Euthanasia' is both too narrow and too

---

[1] MP Battin, *Ending Life: Ethics and the Way We Die* (Oxford, Oxford University Press, 2005) at p 18. Battin claims that heart disease and cancer alone now account for nearly two thirds of deaths in developed countries.

[2] *Ibid.*

broad a phrase (encompassing withdrawal of treatment in some definitions and excluding assisted suicide in others). We have already discovered during the course of this book that decisions about life-sustaining medical treatment can be taken either by the patient or the doctors and need not necessarily entail indefinite continuance of the treatment. For example, the previous chapter demonstrated that an incompetent patient may have life-sustaining treatment withdrawn if the treatment is no longer regarded as being in his best interests.[3] This, on some views, amounts to euthanasia of a passive variety. Similarly a competent adult patient is, as we discovered in Chapter 4, entitled to withdraw or withhold consent to life-sustaining treatment even if she knows that death will immediately ensue.[4] Both of these examples of end of life decisions involve the withdrawal of treatment but not all patients at the end of life are sustained by medical treatment. The notorious example is a comparison between the case of Ms B, a tetraplegic patient sustained by an artificial ventilator, and Dianne Pretty, a motor neurone sufferer facing a slow, lingering death. As was discussed in Chapter 4, Ms B was (eventually) able to validly refuse consent to the ventilation and thus die; Mrs Pretty, as we will see in this chapter, was denied any assistance in avoiding a lingering natural death by both English common law and the ECHR. As this chapter will attempt to explain, however, these two women were in starkly different, although equally unfortunate, situations both legally and ethically. Ms B was seeking to enforce her right to autonomy and consent; Mrs Pretty was arguing in favour of a right to be assisted to her death. She, and not Ms B, faced the considerable burden of the legal prohibition of intentional acts causing death or assisting a suicide. Furthermore, only Ms B was complaining to the courts of an unlawful assault upon her body. That the assault was well intentioned and came in the form of life-sustaining medical treatment should not distract us entirely from revulsion of a competent adult being subjected to an invasive treatment against her clearly expressed wishes.

English law is very clear in its prohibition of homicide. Any intentional act causing the death of another person falls foul of this prohibition. The motive of the perpetuator is, to that extent, irrelevant. So, if a doctor (or a relative) causes the death of a terminally ill patient in order to end that patient's suffering, he will face a charge of murder. The apparent harshness of this law, equating a mercy killer with a serial killer, is somewhat mitigated by both prosecuting and sentencing discretion, as well as by generally sympathetic juries. In *R v Cox*,[5] for example, a doctor was charged with attempted murder even though his patient had died, because the body had been cremated before suspicion arose and cause of death was impossible to determine. This introduced sentencing discretion because murder has a mandatory life sentence whereas attempted murder only has this as a maximum and the judge has a variety of other sentencing options

---

[3] *Airedale NHS Trust v Bland* [1993] 1 All ER 821.
[4] *Ms B v NHS Hospital Trust* [2002] 2 All ER 449.
[5] (1992) 12 BMLR 38.

available to him. Dr Cox was treating an elderly patient suffering from rheumatoid arthritis. This condition was not fatal but was extremely painful and she expressed the wish to die. Dr Cox injected her with potassium chloride which was potentially fatal and had no pain-relieving functions. On trial for attempted murder, the doctor was found guilty. However, he was not imprisoned and the judge instead exercised leniency to give him only a 12 month suspended sentence. Dr Cox's profession was even more lenient and the GMC did not strike him off the medical register. Dr Cox was, therefore, able to continue to practise medicine despite being convicted of attempting to murder one of his patients. Clearly both the judge and the GMC were swayed by Cox's good motive in seeking to relieve his patient's suffering. The case and its consequences are entirely unsatisfactory, however. If Dr Cox acted correctly – if society approves of what he did for his patient – then the law should not render his actions unlawful. If, however, the law is content to regard him as an attempted murderer, then the lack of consequences from his conviction is completely inappropriate. If he did nothing wrong, he should not be a convicted criminal; if he did do something wrong, he should not still be able to practise medicine. The mixed messages sent by the *Cox* case reflects the general uncertainty of society, divided on whether assisting a patient to die in order to relieve his or her suffering is heroic or criminal. At present the message seems to be that it is both.

The conviction of Dr Cox was extremely unusual as juries tend not to convict doctors of such serious crimes. The case against Cox was unusual, however, as he had used an entirely non-therapeutic drug. There was no room for doubt about his intentions. The (over)use of a therapeutic drug to cause death, on the other hand, raises the possibility of a double effect justification. The doctrine of double effect holds that an action with a good objective can be justified even if it will also have a bad effect. So, for example, giving enough drugs to effectively relieve pain may incidentally shorten life. This was the argument raised in *R v Adams*, an earlier case of a doctor prosecuted for treating a suffering patient with potentially fatal drugs.[6] Dr Adams had given an incurably, but not terminally, ill patient increasing doses of opiates leading to her death. He was charged with murder but acquitted, even though he benefited substantially from the patient's will and had lied on the death certificate. The judge, Devlin J, confirmed the doctrine of double effect and said that a doctor 'is entitled to relieve pain and suffering even if the measures he takes may incidentally shorten life'.[7] This has subsequently been approved by the House of Lords in *Airedale NHS Trust v Bland*[8] and so there is no doubt that the doctrine of double effect applies in English law. Traditionally there are four requirements of this doctrine: (1) the nature of the action must be morally good; (2) the bad effect must not be a means of achieving the good effect (for example, death as a way of relieving pain); (3) the good effect must be

---

[6] H Palmer, 'Dr Adams' Trial for Murder' [1957] *Crim LR* 365.
[7] *Ibid.*
[8] [1993] AC 789.

directly intended and the bad effect merely foreseen or tolerated; (4) the reasons for performing the good action must outweigh the unintended bad consequences (ie it must be a proportionate action).[9] The doctrine of double effect has been the subject of much academic criticism. For example, Price describes it as 'the primary catalyst for jurisprudential distortion'.[10] He argues, quite correctly, that 'sophistry and an absence of transparency pervade the judicial approach toward life-shortening pain relief procedures'.[11] The acquittal of Dr Adams and the conviction of Dr Cox, in respect of very similar acts, is not conducive to transparent and consistent law in this area. The fact that the law's sophistry (to use Price's word) reflects society's division on the ethical issues makes the law's approach understandable but no easier to justify.

The use of the double effect doctrine to prevent doctors facing criminal liability for causing what would otherwise be an unlawful death has become even more problematic in recent years due to the evolution of the meaning of intention in the criminal law. *R v Woollin* establishes that a jury may find the necessary intention if they feel sure that the doctor appreciated that death or serious bodily harm was a virtual certainty as a result of his actions.[12] This means that a doctor who foresees with virtual certainty that death will result from the provision of pain-relieving drugs has satisfied the *mens rea* for murder. It is not clear whether, and if so how, the doctrine of double effect operates within this transformed criminal liability context. Previously, one of the requirements for double effect was that a doctor intended the good effect of his actions (to relieve pain and suffering) but only foresaw the bad effect (death). Post-*Woollin* the latter suffices for the intention requirement and therefore it is hard to see how criminal liability can be avoided. As Ost argues, 'the current application of the doctrine of double effect as a means of legitimating the physician's actions creates something of an inconsistency and irregularity within the criminal law'.[13] She regards the doctrine as 'a curtain behind which judges can allow moral judgements to influence the conclusion as to the physician's legal culpability'[14] and this again raises the question of why the law prohibits an action if it is morally good. Clearly it is inappropriate for the law and morals to be out of sync in such a way, especially if it leads members of the judiciary to hide behind the 'curtain' of double effect. However, we should not be so quick to accept that assisted dying is a moral good. The English criminal law reflects what many regard as an ethical line between killing and letting die. The idea of a doctor as a killer, for however good a motive, is one that many patients regard as distressing. The Hippocratic

---

[9] See G Williams, 'The Principle of Double Effect and Terminal Sedation' (2001) 9 *Med L Rev* 41, at p45.

[10] D Price, 'Euthanasia, Pain Relief and Double Effect' (1997) 17 *LS* 323, at p 324.

[11] *Ibid*, p 339.

[12] [1998] 4 All ER 103, at 113.

[13] S Ost, 'Euthanasia and the Defence of Necessity: Advocating a More Appropriate Legal Response' [2005] *Crim LR* 355, at pp 357-58.

[14] *Ibid*, p 358.

Oath's infamous requirement of 'do no harm' may be of little weight in the contemporary argument but, as McCall Smith has recognised 'the criminal law makes the distinction between act and omission because it recognises that there are natural limits to moral obligations, and, further, because it appreciates that to equiparate act and omission liability would be to impose an unreasonable burden on people'.[15] Thus a doctor may withdraw life-sustaining treatment (whether by request or on medical evidence) and allow a patient to die, but cannot contribute to death by undertaking a positive act (unless the 'curtain' of double effect is available). Dworkin describes this distinction as seeming to be 'cruelly abstract'[16] and this is a very effective descriptor. The prohibition protects a vital abstract principle – that a doctor should not be a killer – but can often seem irrational when applied in practice to provide one person with an easier death and another person with a longer or harder one.[17] This prohibition on physician involvement in causing death is not only regulated by means of the homicide laws but also by the statutory offence of assisted suicide.

Suicide itself and, of greater practical significance, attempted suicide were decriminalised in the Suicide Act 1961 but section 2(1) of that Act contains an offence of counselling, procuring, aiding and abetting suicide. This offence covers those situations where the deceased took the final step to end his or her life, for example by taking an excessive amount of pills, but the perpetuator of the offence assisted in some manner, for example by supplying the pills. The offence will also be satisfied if there is encouragement to commit suicide provided that the intent is to assist suicide.[18] The dividing line between assisted suicide and murder is not always clear. For example, if the pills are placed in the mouth of the person wishing to commit suicide, does the person who places them there face liability for assisted suicide or for murder? While such uncertainty is undesirable, it is not crucial for our purposes because the key point is that assisting another person to die, regardless of who takes the final step, is unlawful.

This section started with an explanation of why the question of assisted dying is increasingly relevant to terminal patients but since then we have discovered that all forms of positive assistance in causing death are prohibited by the English criminal law, except where death results from the provision of pain-relieving pills prescribed primarily to relieve pain. If people are facing slower deaths with the increased physical and emotional suffering that it entails, it is understandable that there are increasing calls for a right to die. Rarely does this call mean what it

---

[15]   A McCall Smith, 'Euthanasia: The Strengths of the Middle Ground' (1999) 7 *Med L Rev* 194, at p 204. McCall Smith introduces this article as making 'about as provocative a statement as one might make in the columns of a legal journal', namely one in favour of the existing law (p 194).

[16]   R Dworkin, *Life's Dominion: An Argument about Abortion, Euthanasia and Individual Freedom* (London, HarperCollins, 1993), p 184.

[17]   The comparison between Dianne Pretty and Ms B again seems apt here.

[18]   See *AG v Able* [1984] QB 795.

says.[19] We will all die eventually and some of us will contribute to the inevitable, by smoking or driving recklessly or working too hard or by committing suicide. If there is no right to die, there is certainly no effective legal prohibition on it. What a 'right to die' really means is a right to receive some assistance in hastening death, perhaps by means of a doctor and a lethal injection; perhaps by means of the provision of sufficient pills to do the job oneself. The right to die is not really about death but the circumstances of it: when, where and how. It is a claim for a right to choose the nature of one's exit from this world, perhaps in order to ensure that it is consistent with our style of living, perhaps to cut short pain or suffering, perhaps to avoid being a burden or to preserve our sense of dignity. Of course, a large proportion of us will never be in a situation where we wish to exercise a right to die because we will die before we would wish to do so, for example by a sudden death in a road traffic accident, or we may choose to fight for life to endure as long as possible. But for patients like Dianne Pretty, facing an inevitably slow and painful death, the desire to claim for a right to die, before the suffering becomes too much, is overwhelming. Mrs Pretty was suffering from motor neurone disease and faced a lingering death. She was unable to commit suicide unaided and wanted her husband to assist her. He was willing to do so but they both sought a guarantee in advance that he would not be prosecuted for the offence of assisted suicide. The Director of Public Prosecutions refused to issue a guarantee that a prosecution would not be brought against Mr Pretty. The DPP argued that there was no such power to grant immunities from prosecution in advance of the prohibited activities being initiated. Mrs Pretty sought to challenge the DPP's refusal as contrary to the Human Rights Act 1998. A supplementary argument that the offence of assisted suicide found in section 2(1) of the Suicide Act 1961 was itself contrary to the HRA was also relied upon. While, as we have seen, English law has not traditionally protected a right to assisted death, the introduction of the Human Rights Act 1998 into English law opened a number of doors that, Pretty's lawyers argued, could lead to such a right. The remainder of this chapter will consider the most important lines of reasoning in favour of a right to assisted death:

(1) that the right to life implies self-determination about the end of life;
(2) that human dignity requires the relief of pain and suffering, by death if necessary;
(3) that autonomy requires freedom to decide how to die provided the rights of others in society can be adequately protected;
(4) that the denial of assisted suicide discriminates against those disabled persons unable to commit suicide unaided.

---

[19]   When I asked a friend's opinion on whether he thought he had a right to die, he replied 'just try to stop me'. The use of the phrase 'right to' is notoriously ambiguous.

These four lines of reasoning broadly correspond with the main arguments in the *Pretty* case,[20] and with Articles 2, 3, 8 and 14 of the European Convention on Human Rights respectively, but the following discussion will also incorporate some broader ethical and legal issues in determining whether there is any sound basis for a 'right to die' under English law.

II. Life and Death: A Right to Die as a Corollary of a Right to Life?

This first argument in favour of a right to assisted death is based upon the idea that the right to life protected in Article 2 ECHR (the application of which at the end of life was considered in the previous chapter) protects not merely life itself, but rather the choice of whether to live or not: a right to self-determination in relation to issues of life and death. In *Pretty*, the House of Lords easily dismissed this argument by emphasising that the right to life has the sanctity of life principle at its core. Lord Bingham said that Article 2's thrust is 'to reflect the sanctity which, particularly in western eyes, attaches to life. The article protects the right to life and prevents the deliberate taking of life save in very narrowly defined circumstances. An article with that effect cannot be interpreted as conferring a right to die ...'.[21] Lord Hope was more succinct, saying that Article 2 'is all about protecting life, not bringing it to an end'.[22]

One of the arguments raised by Pretty's lawyers to substantiate the claim that a right to life could be interpreted to include a right to die was a comparison with the interpretation of Article 11. This Article includes an explicit right to join a trade union which was interpreted by the European Court of Human Rights in the case of *Young, James and Webster v United Kingdom* to incorporate the right *not* to join a trade union.[23] By extrapolation it was argued in the *Pretty* case that the right to life could also include its apparent opposite: a right to die. When the case reached the European Court of Human Rights, the Court dismissed this argument. It held that Article 2 is distinguishable from Article 11 in respect of its interpretation to include a negative aspect because the right to life is not expressed as a freedom whereas the right to join a trade union is an aspect of Article 11's right to freedom of association.[24] The word 'freedom' implies a choice: to take advantage of the protected activity or not; whereas the right to life has no such choice at its heart. The European Court of Human Rights could not

---

[20]   *R (on the application of Pretty) v Director of Public Prosecutions* [2002] 1 All ER 1 (HL); *Pretty v United Kingdom* (2002) 35 EHRR 1 (ECtHR).
[21]   *Pretty* (HL), para 5.
[22]   *Ibid*, para 88.
[23]   (1981) Series A, No 44; 4 EHRR 38.
[24]   *Pretty v United Kingdom*, n 20 above, para 39.

escape the fact that Article 2 'cannot, without a distortion of language, be interpreted as conferring the diametrically opposite right, namely a right to die'.[25] The Court was swayed, therefore, by the commonsense meaning of a right to life and its apparent incompatibility with a right to die, which is regarded as the antithesis of the right to life. As Morris notes, the argument under Article 2 failed 'for very simple reasons: as a matter of ordinary, everyday understanding, the right to life just does not connote a right to end life'.[26] This point has been disputed by Coggon, however, who denies that a right to die is the opposite of a right to life: 'The opposite of life is death, so a diametrically opposite to the right to life would be a right to death'.[27] He notes that dying usually takes place simultaneously with living and so a right to die (in a particular manner) is not inconsistent with the protection of the right to life. In Coggon's view, therefore, a right to die 'is not logically or necessarily precluded by the right to life'.[28]

The difficulty which remains, however, is that both the House of Lords and the Strasbourg Court were insistent that Article 2 protects the sanctity of life.[29] It is more likely, therefore, that Article 2 could be pressed into service *against* assisted dying on the basis that permitting such assistance is incompatible with the state's obligation to protect life. By contrast, there is an argument that sanctity of life is not necessarily inconsistent with assisted dying. Dworkin raises this argument by emphasising how important it is 'that life ends appropriately, that death keeps faith with the way we want to have lived'.[30] For Dworkin, the sanctity of human life does not inevitably require its continuation but rather prioritises respect for the investment in life thus far:

> Anyone who believes in the sanctity of human life believes that once a human life has begun it matters, intrinsically, that that life go well, that the investment it represents be realised rather than frustrated. Someone's convictions about his own critical interests are opinions about what it means for his own human life to go well, and these convictions can therefore best be understood as a special application of his general commitment to the sanctity of life.[31]

On this basis the sanctity of life can support rather than preclude assisted dying because how we die is a crucial part of how we live and, as Dworkin famously states, '[m]aking someone die in a way that others approve, but he believes a horrifying contradiction of his life, is a devastating, odious form of tyranny'.[32] He further explains that because decisions about life and death are so important to

---

[25]   *Ibid.*
[26]   D Morris, 'Assisted Suicide under the ECHR: A Critique' (2003) 1 EHRLR 65, at pp 69-70.
[27]   J Coggon, 'Could the Right to Die with Dignity Represent a New Right to Die in English Law?' (2006) 14 *Med L Rev* 219, at p 225.
[28]   *Ibid*, p 226.
[29]   See the discussion in the previous chapter.
[30]   Dworkin, n 16 above, p 199.
[31]   *Ibid*, p 215.
[32]   *Ibid*, p 217.

us 'we think it crucial to make them in character, and for ourselves'.[33] These points suggest that, in order to treat life as sacred, we must respect an individual's own life (and death) choices. In principle this is a sound argument but it only takes us so far because in many respects English law already protects freedom over life and death choices. The crux of the issue for our purposes is whether protection for self-determination in life and death choices outweighs societal interests in preserving life because, even if sanctity of life can be interpreted along Dworkin's lines to include protection for a death consistent with the life already lived, it is also arguable that it incorporates some protection for the concept of 'life' itself having some inherent value. As such, a balancing exercise seems inevitable. This issue will be discussed further when we consider the role of autonomy in end of life decisions below but, first, we will consider the role of human dignity in the context of calls for a right to die with dignity.

III. A Right to Die with Dignity?

The concept of human dignity is one which we have encountered before in this book, for example in relation to the risks of commodifying human body parts.[34] It is recognised in the Preamble of the European Convention on Human Rights and Biomedicine (ECHRB) as being particularly significant in the medical context. The Preamble notes that 'the misuse of biology and medicine may lead to acts endangering human dignity' and this will be a particular concern in respect of end of life decisions where modern medicine may keep alive those patients who would previously have died much earlier from natural causes. Dignity is an ambiguous concept,[35] and it is entirely possible that it could be relied upon by both the hospice movement and those in favour of assisted dying: two movements which 'share the common goal of avoiding pointless pain and suffering at the end of life'[36] but disagree fundamentally about how to achieve this goal. This means that, while the concept of human dignity is vital within end of life decision-making, its role remains ambiguous.

Dignity of the human person is protected by means of Article 3 ECHR (as well as implicitly through other Convention rights such a right to respect of private life and a right to enjoy the rights and freedoms free from discrimination). Article 3 prohibits inhuman and degrading treatment or punishment. It is an absolute prohibition, which is non-derogable even in times of war or public emergency, and so sits in stark contrast to the more flexible protection of the right to life in

---

[33] *Ibid*, p 239.

[34] See Chapter 7.

[35] See D Feldman, 'Human Dignity as a Legal Value – Part I' [1999] *PL* 682; D Feldman, 'Human Dignity as a Legal Value – Part II' [2000] *PL* 61.

[36] H Biggs, *Euthanasia, Death with Dignity and the Law* (Oxford, Hart Publishing, 2001) p 171.

Article 2.[37] In *D v United Kingdom*,[38] the European Court of Human Rights made clear that Article 3 not only prohibits inhuman and degrading treatment from being imposed by the state, but also applies to situations where the suffering from a natural illness is exacerbated by the treatment of an individual by national authorities. In this case, the applicant was a man dying of AIDS and his complaint related to the authorities' attempts to deport him to the island of St Kitts where he would be denied the medical care and attention he was able to enjoy in the UK. The Court held that the deportation would expose the applicant to 'a real risk of dying under most distressing circumstances' and that this would amount to inhuman treatment, contrary to Article 3.[39] In the *Pretty* case, it was argued that *D v United Kingdom* provided a precedent for a right to die with dignity derived from Article 3 (and subsequently Munby J recognised such a right in *Burke*[40]). However, *D v United Kingdom* is distinguishable from the *Pretty* situation because in the former case the United Kingdom sought to take a positive step to intervene in the applicant's life (deportation) which would cause suffering; in *Pretty*, the state's only action was to prohibit assisted suicide. D's dignity could be assured by the state refraining from deporting him; whereas Pretty's dignity, she argued, could only be assured by her death. There appears to be a distinction here between D's desire to obtain *dignity in dying* and Pretty's desire to obtain *dignity by dying*.

It is not difficult to see why both the House of Lords and the European Court of Human Rights declined to recognise an Article 3 based 'right to die' in the *Pretty* case. Both courts emphasised that the authorities had not imposed any 'treatment' upon Dianne Pretty, inhuman or otherwise. As the Strasbourg Court explained, the extension of the meaning of 'treatment' to cover the UK's actions in this case would place a new construction on the concept of treatment which 'goes beyond the ordinary meaning of the word'.[41] And, while the Court recognised that it must take a 'dynamic and flexible approach to the interpretation of the Convention' due to its nature as a 'living instrument', it concluded that its interpretation 'must also accord with the fundamental objections of the Convention and its coherence as a system of human rights protection'.[42] Given the Court's rejection of any right to die under Article 2 and its interpretation of that provision as protecting the sanctity of life, the recognition of a right to die under

---

[37]   Article 2 is subject to a number of specified limitations for the benefit of the prevention of crime and public disorder.

[38]   [1997] 24 EHRR 423.

[39]   *Ibid*, para 53. Article 3 has also been interpreted as requiring states not only to refrain from subjecting people in its jurisdiction to inhuman or degrading treatment but also to take measures to ensure that individuals are not subjected to such treatment by private individuals. See *A v United Kingdom* (1998) Reports 1998-VI.

[40]   [2005] QB 424.

[41]   *Pretty v United Kingdom*, n 20 above, para 54.

[42]   *Ibid*.

Article 3 might be thought inconsistent.[43] In the House of Lords, it was also suggested, by Lord Hope, that the minimum level of severity of treatment had not been reached in Mrs Pretty's case.[44] This seems an unconvincing argument given the distressing death she would suffer without assistance, and her fears of it. The better reason for finding no violation of Article 3 is undoubtedly the argument that the state is not responsible for the 'treatment' suffered by Mrs Pretty. Given that the European Court of Human Rights focused on this point, a right to die with dignity has not been completely ruled out from the ambit of Article 3. The Court did not consider this issue in the abstract, holding instead that the UK had not inflicted any prohibited treatment onto Mrs Pretty.

It is unlikely that such a right to die with dignity will be developed under Article 3, however, except in the *D v United Kingdom* situation where the state is taking steps which will cause increased suffering during the dying process. This negative view is partly informed by the following section which explains the crucial role played by Article 8 and the principle of autonomy in respect of assisted dying but it is also a recognition of the inherent ambiguity in the concept of dignity which, as noted above, does not necessarily counsel in favour of assisted dying and certainly not for all patients. For some patients the thought of suicide, or another person taking away one's life, would be inherently *undignified*, perhaps because of a religious view that life is to be taken only by God and at a time that He alone chooses, or perhaps because fighting for life with every last breath is perceived by that individual as the most dignified exit from this world. Furthermore, there is an argument that death can never be dignified, signifying as it does the gradual destruction of each of the cells in our body.[45] If the concept of dignity in death is ambiguous and elusive, it may be preferable to focus upon what each individual would regard as a dignified (or the most dignified possible) death. However, this is less an issue of dignity and more an issue of autonomy. As Coggon recognises:

> it is perhaps incorrect to assert that this problem is an issue concerning dignity. It is
> arguably more to do with autonomy: overriding a person's desire to die, because it is

---

[43] A similar concern about coherency between Arts 2 and 3 arose in *Soering v United Kingdom* (1989) Series A, No 161; 11 EHRR 439 when the Court declined to interpret the death penalty as an inhuman or degrading punishment due to its status as an explicit exception to the right to life in Art 2. In *Soering*, however, the Court was able to find a way around this dilemma by holding that the 'death row phenomenon' (the circumstances surrounding the imposition and execution of the penalty, including the excessive delay between sentence and execution) could amount to inhuman or degrading punishment, in violation of Art 3.

[44] *Pretty v United Kingdom*, n 20 above, para 92.

[45] Biggs queries at one point in her book whether 'the whole process of dying despite the best efforts of modern medicine [is] so inherently undignified that no action can possibly succeed in providing dignity?' (Biggs, n 36 above, p 143.)

believed that death is contrary to his interests, even though he thinks it is necessary for his dignity, may not demonstrate disbelief in his dignity, but rather disbelief in his capacity to assess his dignity.[46]

It is, then, to the issue of autonomy, or self-determination, in matters of life and death to which we shall now turn.

IV. Autonomy, Private Life and Death

(a)   The Right to Respect for Private Decisions about Dying

We have discovered the key role played by the principle of autonomy throughout this book. As an ethical principle, it underlies the contemporary concept of human rights and it finds force in English law not only through the Human Rights Act but also, for example, through the case law on consent to medical treatment, the Human Fertilisation and Embryology Act 1990 and the Mental Capacity Act 2005. It is the HRA which is of greatest significance, however, because the principle of autonomy is at the heart of the ECHR, and it is Article 8 which gives most weight to arguments based upon individual autonomy. As we have seen in other contexts, Article 8 protects a right to respect for private life which has been interpreted so broadly as to incorporate a right to be free from state interference. The question of relevance for this chapter is whether Article 8 protects autonomy in respect of the dying process. When the House of Lords considered the issue in *Pretty*, it concluded that Article 8 could not have application in this context. The Lordships hearing the case reached a variety of views on this issue. Lord Bingham, for example, was inclined to rule out any application of Article 8 by emphasising that it is 'expressed in terms directed to protection of personal autonomy while individuals are living their lives, and there is nothing to suggest that the Article has reference to the choice to live no longer'.[47] This seems to be the majority view although Lord Hope took a slightly different approach by recognising that the way a person 'chooses to pass the closing moments of her life is part of the act of living, and she has a right to ask that this too must be respected'[48] but held that Article 8(1)'s positive obligations upon a state could not include an obligation to permit assisted suicide. All of the Lordships were agreed, however, that even if Mrs Pretty's Article 8(1) rights were engaged, which they all doubted, any interference would be justified under Article 8(2). This is an issue to which we will return below. First, it is crucial to consider the European Court of Human Rights' approach to this issue because

---

[46]   Coggon, n 27 above, p 226.
[47]   *Pretty* (HL) n 20 above, para 23.
[48]   *Ibid*, para 100.

the Strasbourg Court disagreed with the House of Lords and had no doubt that Article 8(1) was engaged in the *Pretty* case.

The Strasbourg Court held that Mrs Pretty 'is prevented by law from exercising her choice to avoid what she considers will be an undignified and distressing end to her life. The Court is not prepared to exclude that this constitutes an interference with her right to respect for private life as guaranteed under Article 8(1) of the Convention.'[49] The Court also made the interesting point that, while the principle of sanctity of life underlies much of the Convention, Article 8 is the provision under which notions of the quality of life take on significance.[50] It is important that the Convention contains a counterweight to sanctity of life considerations. One of the advantages of a human right approach is that it enables a balancing of individual autonomy against a societal interest such as the sanctity of life. As Blake has noted, 'it is really only within the rubric of human rights that personal autonomy can be openly and accurately weighed in the balance'.[51] It is fitting, therefore, that the European Court of Human Rights should recognise the potential significance of Mrs Pretty's Article 8 autonomy interests to the question of whether she should be entitled to receive assistance in dying. Having recognised that Article 8(1) was engaged, the Court now had to proceed to consideration of whether the interference with Mrs Pretty's rights was justified under Article 8(2) and it is here that a balance needed to be struck.

(b) Proportionate State Interference: Protecting the Rights of the Vulnerable

Article 8(2) permits interference with an Article 8(1) right provided that it is prescribed by law and necessary in a democratic society for one of a number of specified legitimate aims. There is no doubt that the prohibition on assisted death is prescribed by the law and so the key issue in *Pretty* was whether this prohibition is necessary in a democratic society and this was decided with reference to the specified legitimate aim of protecting the rights of others. The UK government argued that the prohibition on assisted dying protected the vulnerable members of society. The Strasbourg Court accepted that 'states are entitled to regulate through its operation of the general criminal law activities which are detrimental to the life and safety of other individuals'.[52] But the key issue for the Court under Article 8(2) is always the question of the proportionality of the interference with an individual's Article 8 rights. When considering whether the prohibition on assisted suicide was a proportionate interference with Mrs Pretty's right to determine for herself questions of life and death, the Court

---

[49]   *Pretty v United Kingdom*, n 20 above, para 67.
[50]   *Ibid*, para 65.
[51]   M Blake, 'Physician Assisted Suicide: A Criminal Offence or a Patient's Right?' (1997) 5 *Med L Rev* 294, at p 302.
[52]   *Pretty v United Kingdom*, n 20 above, para 74.

was influenced by the UK's 'system of enforcement and adjudication which allows due regard to be given in each particular case to the public interest in bringing a prosecution, as well as to the fair and proper requirements of retribution and deterrence'.[53] In other words, the need for the DPP's consent to prosecute and discretion in sentencing provide essential safeguards to mitigate the arbitrariness of the absolute prohibition on assisted suicide. This argument is not convincing to some commentators who take the view that the proportionality requirement under Article 8(2) is not so easily satisfied. Morris, for example, gives great weight to the importance of the manner of our death which in his view must reflect the life we have led. He argues, therefore, that:

> the burden on the state to justify interference under paragraph 2 should be peculiarly heavy. What it should have to show is that the infringement is so necessary that it is worth not only interfering with an individual's right to choose how he passes the closing stages of his life, but also that it is worth interfering with everything else he has done throughout his life to assert or define his own meaningful and lucid sense of self.[54]

The issue underlying this debate is whether the rights of others, particularly the most vulnerable persons in society – the ill, the elderly and the mentally incapacitated – are genuinely threatened by an exception to the general prohibition on assisted dying. The Strasbourg Court assumes that such a threat exists and that the blanket prohibition on assisted dying in the UK is a proportionate response to this danger. However, the Court fails to adequately investigate the existence of such a threat. At the crux of the issue is the so-called slippery slope argument propounded by, among others, John Keown.

A slippery slope argument is an argument which purports that standard A may lead to standard B, where A is usually good or of uncertain merit and B is bad. The question is whether we should prevent A in order to avoid B. Keown argues that the acceptance of one type of euthanasia or assisted dying will inevitably lead to the acceptance of other forms of euthanasia. For example, the legalisation of physician assisted suicide (PAS) and voluntary active euthanasia (VAE) would lead to non-voluntary or involuntary euthanasia.[55] Smith explains that Keown's slippery slope objection to euthanasia is actually divisible into two distinct types of slippery slope arguments: a practical slippery slope based upon evidence from states which have already legalised some forms of assisted dying; and a logical slippery slope based upon an argument of logic (which Smith argues is an 'argument from consistency' rather than a true slippery slope argument).[56] If we look, first, at Keown's practical slippery slope argument, we can see that this

---

[53]   *Ibid*, para 76.

[54]   Morris, n 26 above, p 82.

[55]   See J Keown, *Euthanasia, Ethics and Public Policy* (2002, Cambridge, Cambridge University Press) pp 72–7.

[56]   On these two arguments see, respectively, SW Smith, 'Evidence for the Practical Slippery Slope in the Debate on Physician Assisted Suicide and Euthanasia' (2005) 13 *Med L Rev* 17; SW Smith,

argument is based upon evidence from the Netherlands which he interprets as proving that legalised PAS and VAE leads to a change in public attitudes towards assisted dying and a lessening of the theoretical distinction between one type of euthanasia and another. The legal position in the Netherlands is invaluable in investigating the potential threat to vulnerable members of society in legalising assisted dying so an overview of this is now necessary.

The Dutch Criminal Code prohibits euthanasia (and assisted suicide) as a distinct crime to murder or manslaughter.[57] In the 1984 case of *Schoonheim*,[58] the Dutch Supreme Court recognised, for the first time, a defence of necessity to the crime of euthanasia and applied it to a doctor who committed a mercy killing of a 95 year old patient. Following this judicial relaxation in the enforcement of the prohibition on euthanasia, the Dutch Parliament introduced a reporting procedure for doctors committing euthanasia, and the public prosecution service adopted a policy of not prosecuting doctors for this offence provided they had met due care requirements.[59] Thus began a period of tolerance of VAE and PAS within the Netherlands which made it unique amongst states. Finally in 2000 a new law, the Termination of Life on Request and Assisted Suicide (Review Procedures) Act, was passed which added a statutory defence to euthanasia and physician assisted suicide along similar lines to that already de facto existing. Section 293 of the Dutch Criminal Code now provides that, while it remains an offence to 'take the life of another person at that other person's express and earnest request', there is a justification if the act is committed by a physician who fulfils due care criteria and notifies the municipal pathologist. The due care criteria are found in section 2(1) of the new Act and require that the doctor be satisfied that the patient has made a voluntary and well considered request; be convinced that the patient was suffering unbearably and without hope of recovery; inform the patient about the situation and the prospect of improvement; come to the decision that there is no other reasonable solution; consult another independent doctor; and terminate the patient's life with due medical care and attention.[60] The question of whether the due care criteria are met is now a matter for Regional Review Committees and the prosecution service will only be passed information about an assisted death if the committee decides that the due care requirements have not been met. De Haan's illuminating study of the law on euthanasia in the Netherlands concludes that the new Act is merely another step in an ongoing process of legal change and public debate about the

---

'Fallacies of the Logical Slippery Slope in the Debate on Physician Assisted Suicide and Euthanasia' (2005) 13 *Med L Rev* 224 (hereinafter referred to as Smith (Practical) and Smith (Logical)).

[57]   Sections 293 and 294 of the Criminal Code respectively.

[58]   HR 27 Nov 84, NJ 1985, 106.

[59]   See J De Haan, 'The New Dutch Law on Euthanasia' (2002) 10 *Med L Rev* 57, at p 60.

[60]   Section 2(2) permits the patient's request to be in the form of an advance directive and yet states that the due care requirements still apply. De Haan queries how the requirement of unbearable suffering can ever be satisfied if the request was made in advance and the patient is no longer conscious (*ibid*, p 65).

issue: 'The Dutch government simply now formally and unambiguously recognises what has been going on for a decade, which is that euthanasia is practiced on a large scale in the Netherlands ...'[61]

As mentioned above, Keown uses evidence from the decriminalised practice of VAE and PAS in the Netherlands to support his argument that there is a slippery slope from this to killing without request.[62] Smith, however, takes issue with the evidence provided by Keown. For example, Smith gives great weight to comparative studies which indicate that doctors in the Netherlands are less likely to support euthanasia for reasons other than pain or suffering (such as the patient feeling a burden) than doctors in the US.[63] The evidence about whether the decriminalisation of PAS and VAE have led to higher rates of terminations of life without an explicit request is also disputed. Studies show that the rates of non voluntary/ involuntary euthanasia are higher in Australia, Belgium and Denmark than in the Netherlands.[64] One argument of Keown's which is accepted by Smith, however, is that the guidelines for euthanasia in the Netherlands, including the crucial reporting requirement, have been repeatedly breached. No one can deny that this is a serious cause for concern. While it may be possible to design better, stronger guidelines,[65] the overriding impression from the somewhat conflicting studies and arguments of the Netherlands legacy is that legalising some forms of assisted dying will not eradicate the danger of abuse and may indeed provide greater opportunities for it to occur. There may not necessarily be a slippery slope towards involuntary deaths but the task of protecting the vulnerable will not be easy. From a human rights perspective, this suggests that the need to protect the rights of others under Article 8(2) before permitting individual autonomy in respect of death presents a serious challenge for lawmakers. The Dutch approach of due care criteria and reporting requirements seems no more infallible than the UK's approach of a blanket prohibition on assisted dying (which, after all, did not prevent Harold Shipman, or countless other more well-intentioned doctors, from ending life without request).

By contrast with the practical slippery slope argument, Keown's logical slippery slope argument relies upon logic rather than interpretation of disputed studies. Keown argues that 'the real, rather than the rhetorical, justification for VAE is not the patient's autonomous request but the doctor's judgment that the request is justified because death would benefit the patient'.[66] Therefore, as the patient's request 'serves merely to trigger the doctor's judgment about the merit

---

[61]   *Ibid*, p 67.

[62]   See Keown, n 55 above, Chapters 9-13.

[63]   See Smith (Practical), n 56 above, pp 26-7, discussing a study by Williams *et al*, 'Attitudes and Practices Concerning the End of Life' (2000) 160 *Archives of Internal Medicine* 63-8.

[64]   See Smith, n 56 above, pp 36-8.

[65]   Smith notes that the guidelines in Oregon, which has also legalised PAS, do not seem to suffer the same fate (*Ibid*, p 40).

[66]   Keown, n. 55 above, p 77.

of the request',[67] the justification can, in Keown's view, be just as easily applied to situations where the patient cannot make a request. If, on the other hand, autonomy rather than the doctor's judgement is the real justification, then Keown queries why it applies only to those individuals who are terminally ill or suffering unbearably.[68] Whether this is properly regarded as a slippery slope argument or an argument from consistency, as Smith argues, it can easily be countered by an insistence that BOTH autonomy and some sense of clinical need (in the doctor's judgement) are required to justify an assisted death.[69]

This point becomes even clearer if we return to the human rights perspective of Article 8. Individual autonomy, inherent in the right to respect for private life, is protected in Article 8(1) (and, as the Strasbourg Court recognised, it is engaged by the prohibition on assisted dying in English law) but an interference with it can be justified if it is necessary in a democratic society to protect the rights of others, prevent crime or protect public health (inter alia). A limitation on a general freedom to make life and death decisions can, therefore, be quite tightly defined, perhaps to include any assistance from another person in the absence of unbearable suffering, perhaps to include, as the current English law does, any assistance from another person in all circumstances. Neither of these scenarios would fall into the logical slippery slope or fail at the argument from consistency hurdle. Self-determination in all matters is a fundamental human right but in a democratic society it has to be balanced against other weighty societal needs. The UK government in the *Pretty* case succeeded in convincing the Strasbourg Court, as well as the House of Lords, that it was necessary and proportionate to limit Mrs Pretty's autonomous choices about her death by means of a blanket prohibition on all assisted dying.

Many commentators take issue with the judicial acceptance of this. Morris, for example, concludes that the criminalisation of assisted suicide is disproportionate under Article 8(2). He provides a number of reasons for this which are worth quoting in full:

> first, the sheer weight of the importance of the contended right; second, the lack of any conclusive evidence that lifting the ban on assisted suicide would do harm to the vulnerable; third, the fact that even if there is a risk of this, the state may still guard against it by less general, less intrusive means than blanket prohibition; and fourth although there may not yet be a consensus in favour of decriminalising assisted suicide, there certainly is no consensus in prohibiting it in toto either.[70]

We have already considered the first two of these points and must concede their veracity. The final two criticisms require further explanation. The third point –

---

[67] *Ibid.*

[68] *Ibid,* p 79.

[69] H Lillehammer, 'Voluntary Euthanasia and the Logical Slippery Slope Argument (2002) 61 *CLJ* 545; Smith (Logical), n 56 above, p 231.

[70] Morris, n 26 above, p 90.

that any risk to the vulnerable could be countered by less intrusive methods – is a point which flows naturally from the preceding discussion. To permit PAS in tightly defined circumstances, including only where there is unbearable suffering and the patient is unable to take his or her own life unaided, would seem a sensible solution to the dilemma of assisted dying. It would introduce greater respect for the exercise of individual autonomy at the end of life but would, provided it was strictly enforced, present little (although undoubtedly some) risk of harm to vulnerable patients. The Assisted Dying Bill introduced into Parliament in 2005, drafted along those lines, would have been a welcome compromise and it is regrettable that it was defeated (and particularly regrettable that it was defeated on religious and arguably undemocratic grounds[71]). Morris's final criticism of the *Pretty* judgments is the failure of either court to confront the lack of consensus on the issue of assisted dying. In addition to the Netherlands, other European countries now have a policy of partial legalisation, or at least tolerance, of forms of assisted dying.[72] This is only of limited relevance, however, because a lack of consensus will only encourage the Strasbourg Court to grant a wide margin of appreciation (or measure of discretion) to each state. With such a discretion, the UK would be perfectly entitled to prioritise the sanctity of life and the protection of the vulnerable over individual autonomy in respect of assisted dying. However, the increase in tolerance for (at least some forms of) assisted dying in Europe may herald a future relaxation of the prohibition in the UK. While it used to be the Netherlands which was regarded as the exception to the rule, it is not inconceivable that in years to come the UK may look increasingly out of step with its European neighbours if it continues to maintain such a strict prohibition on all forms of assisted dying. If that time comes then the Strasbourg Court may be less inclined to accept the UK government's arguments that its blanket prohibition is proportionate under Article 8(2).

---

[71]   The Bill was defeated in the House of Lords by 48 votes after a concerted lobbying campaign by church leaders amongst others. In addition to contributing to (or perhaps stalling) the ongoing debate on assisted dying, the circumstances of the Bill's fate raised a debate over the composition of the legislature and the role of religious representatives within it.

[72]   The Belgian Act on Euthanasia 2002 legalised voluntary euthanasia and in Switzerland the criminal offence of assisted suicide in Art 115 Swiss Penal Code is only committed if undertaken with self-serving ends (which has led to a perception that assisting a suicide with honourable motives is not prohibited). For further detail on the legal position of assisted dying throughout Europe, see H Nys, 'Physician Involvement in a Patient's Death: A Continental European Perspective' (1999) 7 *Med L Rev* 208.

V. Discrimination of the Disabled: Suicide versus Assisted Suicide

Even if it is accepted that the interference with Mrs Pretty's Article 8 right of self-determination is proportionate and thus justified under Article 8(2), there is a possibility that Article 8 could be violated in conjunction with Article 14. Article 14 is the prohibition of discrimination clause in the ECHR. It must always be pleaded in conjunction with one of the other articles because it only prohibits discrimination in the enjoyment of the rights and freedoms found in the Convention. In the *Pretty* case, it was argued that the prohibition of assisted suicide amounted to discrimination on the grounds of disability in respect of Article 8's right to respect for private life. The basis of this argument is that suicide is no longer illegal. Therefore, an able -bodied individual can choose to end his or her life and the state will not interfere with this private decision. However, if an individual is unable to end her own life because of illness or disability, which is the position in which Mrs Pretty found herself, then the law prohibits anyone from offering assistance.

Some commentators have sought to argue that suicide is a fundamental human right in itself, largely due to its perceived connection with human dignity.[73] However, Lord Bingham made very clear in *Pretty* that English law confers no right to commit suicide.[74] He emphasised that the decriminalisation of an act does not create a human right to undertake that activity, and this must be the correct view. Pedain takes issue with the significance of this conclusion and claims that the fact that there is no right to suicide is misleading:

> people have what can best be classified as a liberty to commit suicide protected under Article 8 as falling within the scope of activities by which we exercise our personal autonomy. Nevertheless, what matters is that most of us can in reality exercise our liberty to commit suicide while those who lack a sufficient degree of physical mobility to kill themselves unaided cannot. What needs to be shown is that there is sufficient justification to restrict the liberty of such persons more severely than the liberty of the able-bodied.[75]

Both the House of Lords and the Strasbourg Court looked at this matter slightly differently and asked themselves whether a special exception to the crime of assisted suicide should be made for disabled persons. Both courts concluded that it should not. The House of Lords made the comparison with provisions

---

[73] See MP Battin, *The Least Worse Death* (1994, Oxford, Oxford University Press) although she recognises the complexity of the issue and distinguishes between suicides which are dignity enhancing and those which are not.

[74] *Pretty* (HL), n 20 above, para 35.

[75] A Pedain, 'The Human Rights Dimension of the Dianne Pretty Case' (2003) 62 *CLJ* 181, at p 197.

criminalising drunkenness or misuse of drugs or theft which do not exempt those addicted to alcohol or drugs, or the poor and hungry.[76] The Strasbourg Court was influenced by the fact that there is 'objective and reasonable justification for not distinguishing in law between those who are and those who are not physically capable of committing suicide'.[77] This justification is that to exempt some persons from the assisted suicide offence 'would seriously undermine the protection of life which the 1961 [Suicide] Act was intended to safeguard and greatly increase the risk of abuse'.[78] This is arguable, however, given that the 1961 Act also decriminalised suicide, which suggests that the Act was not entirely about protecting life but also about protecting autonomy. Pedain also argues that respecting a choice to commit suicide with assistance by another person does not necessarily entail a reduction in the value of life: 'The *reason* why we respect her choice remains the same reason that makes us respect the choice of able-bodied persons to commit suicide: not that it is *the right* choice, but that it is *her* choice.'[79] The UK government's response to this would no doubt be that suicide is always the wrong choice and the fact that the law no longer seeks to (further) punish individuals who have tried, but failed, to end their lives, does not mean that it is a choice worthy of respect. As will be clear, at the heart of the discrimination argument is the conflict between individual autonomy and the sanctity of life and the question of to what extent a private choice to end life should involve the public authorities. For English law the answer to that question is when a second person becomes involved. In general this seems a reasonable answer but, as argued above, a narrowly defined exception for those physically unable to take their own life and subject to unbearable suffering would not necessarily undermine the general rule that involvement in another's death is wrong.

VI. Conclusion

English law is generally unforgiving of assisted dying. Unless one of the general principles of medical law, such as the need for consent to medical treatment or the doctor's duty of care to relieve pain, apply then English law makes no concession to the needs or wishes of a dying patient. It is for this reason that both Ms B and the patient of Dr Adams were legally entitled to be treated by their doctors in a way which hastened their deaths but Mrs Pretty could not be assisted by either her husband (as she wished) or a doctor and had to endure a longer dying process. There is some logic in this distinction and hasty comparisons are

---

[76]   *Pretty* (HL), n 20 above, para 36 (per Lord Bingham).
[77]   *Pretty v United Kingdom*, n 20 above, para 88.
[78]   *Ibid.*
[79]   Pedain, n 75 above, p 203.

unhelpful. However, we have seen throughout this book that individual autonomy plays, and must play, a central role in the law governing healthcare. It is for this reason that a limited and strictly policed exception to the general prohibition on assisted suicide is justifiable. As we have seen, the need to protect the vulnerable leads to seemingly irresolvable debates about slippery slopes but a general criminal prohibition on assisted suicide with an exception if performed by a doctor following strict guidelines to ensure a voluntary and well considered autonomous request by a patient enduring unbearable suffering and unable to commit suicide unaided is a justifiable relaxation of the societal interest in preserving life. It would be misleading and ultimately unhelpful, however, to regard such an exception as comprising a 'right to die'. The detailed discussion of the various potential bases for a right to die in the ECHR has revealed the theoretical and practical obstacles in protecting assisted dying as a fundamental human right. Both the value of 'life' and the nature of 'dignity' are debatable and counsel caution in using Articles 2 or 3 to build a 'right to die'. What is clear, however, is that autonomous choices must prima facie be protected, and this will include choices about life and death and the dying process.

The European Court of Human Rights in the *Pretty* case denied the existence of any right to die under the European Convention and it was right to do so but the Court accepted that choices about how to die are an aspect of an individual's private life and thus entitled to respect by the state under Article 8. The balance which has to be struck under Article 8 (between the first and second paragraphs) is difficult but vital and reflects the balancing exercise inherent throughout the entire Convention (and human rights law more generally). A human rights perspective on medical law encourages us to start from an assumption that protecting the rights and freedoms of the individual patient is the most important consideration. But it also requires that we accept interferences with those patient rights where necessary within a democratic society to protect the other conflicting interests of society. In this way, a human rights framework requires a continual reconciliation between concepts such as sanctity of life and autonomy; individual freedom of choice and the rights of others; health and self-determination. This chapter concludes with the argument that (despite the pressing need for legal recognition of a limited exception to the general prohibition on assisted dying) there exists no 'right to die' under the ECHR or English law. More broadly, this book concludes with the argument that consideration of end of life decisions within a human rights framework helps us to see what is important for both the individual and the democratic society in which he or she lives. There may be no right to die but the right to life, to dignity, and to self-determination apply throughout an individual's life, including (perhaps most crucially) at its very end. The fact that they are not, and cannot be, absolute rights does not detract from their value or from the importance of ensuring that the law, the judiciary and the medical profession recognise and accept the fundamental place of human rights in English medical law.

Recommended Further Reading

M Battin, *Ending Life: Ethics and the Way We Die* (Oxford, Oxford University Press, 2005), Chapter 1.

D Morris, 'Assisted Suicide under the European Convention on Human Rights: A Critique' (2003) 1 *EHRLR* 65.

A Pedain, 'The Human Rights Dimension of the Dianne Pretty Case' (2003) 62 *CLJ* 181.

J Coggon, 'Could the Right to Die with Dignity Represent a New Right to Die in English Law?' (2006) 14 *Med L Rev* 219.

Bibliography

APPLEBAUM, PS, LIDZ, CW and MEISEL, A, *Informed Consent: Legal Theory and Clinical Practice* (Oxford, Oxford University Press, 1987).

BARTLETT, P, *Blackstone's Guide to the Mental Capacity Act 2005* (Oxford, Oxford University Press, 2005).

BATTIN, M, *The Least Worst Death: Essays in Bioethics on the End of Life* (Oxford, Oxford University Press, 1994).

BATTIN, M, *Ending Life: Ethics and the Way We Die* (Oxford, Oxford University Press, 2005).

BEAUCHAMP, TL and CHILDRESS, JF, *Principles of Biomedical Ethics*, 5th edn (Oxford, Oxford University Press, 2001).

BELOFF, MJ and MOUNTFIELD, H, 'Unconventional Behaviour: Judicial Uses of the European Convention in England and Wales' [1996] *EHRLR* 467.

BEWLEY, S, 'Restricting the Freedom of Pregnant Women' in DL Dickenson (ed), *Ethical Issues in Maternal-Fetal Medicine* (Cambridge, Cambridge University Press, 2002).

BEYLEVELD, D and BROWNSWORD, R, *Human Dignity in Bioethics and Biolaw* (Oxford, Oxford University Press, 2001).

BEYLEVELD, D and HISTED, E, 'Betrayal of Confidence in the Court of Appeal' (2000) 4 *Med L Int* 277.

BIGGS, H, *Euthanasia: Death with Dignity and the Law* (Oxford, Hart Publishing, 2001).

BLAKE, M, 'Physician Assisted Suicide: A Criminal Offence or a Patient's Right?' (1997) 5 *Med L Rev* 294.

BOYD, KM, 'HIV Infection and AIDS: The Ethics of Medical Confidentiality' (1992) 18 *JME* 173..

BRAZIER, M, 'Patient Autonomy and Consent to Treatment: The Role of the Law?' (1987) 7 *LS* 169.

——'Rights OF HEALTHCARE' IN R BLACKBURN (ed), *Rights of Citizenship* (London, Mansell Publishing. 1994).

—— 'Retained Organs: Ethics and Humanity' (2002) 22 *LS* 550.

—— *Medicine, Patients and the Law*, 3rd edn (London, Penguin, 2003).

BRAZIER, M and BRIDGE, C, 'Coercion or Caring: Analysing Adolescent Autonomy' (1996) 16 *LS* 84.

BRAZIER, M and MIOLA, J, 'Bye-Bye *Bolam*: A Medical Litigation Revolution?' (2000) 8 *Med L Rev* 85..

BRIDGE, C, 'Religious Beliefs and Teenage Refusal of Medical Treatment' (1999) 62 *MLR* 585.

BRIDGEMAN, J, '"Learning from Bristol": Healthcare in the 21st Century' (2002) 65 *MLR* 241.

—— 'After Bristol: the Healthcare of Young Children and the Law' (2003) 23 *LS* 229.

BUCHANAN, AE and BROCK, DW, *Deciding for Others: The Ethics of Surrogate Decision-Making* (Cambridge, Cambridge University Press, 1990).

CAMPBELL, T, 'The Rights of the Mentally Ill' in T Campbell, D Goldberg, S McLean and T Mullen et al (ed), *Human Rights: From Rhetoric to Reality* (Oxford, Blackwell, 1996).

CASE, P, 'Confidence Matters: the Rise and Fall of Informational Autonomy in Medical Law' (2003) 11 *Med L Rev* 208.

CHALMERS, D and SCHWARTZ, R, '*Rogers v Whittaker* and Informed Consent in Australia: A Fair Dinkum Duty of Disclosure' (1993) 1 *Med L Rev* 139.

COGGON, J, 'Could the Right to Die with Dignity Represent a New Right to Die in English Law?' (2006) 14 *Med L Rev* 219.

CONWAY, H, 'Dead, But Not Buried: Bodies, Burial and Family Conflicts' (2003) 23 *LS* 423.

DE CRUZ, P, 'Adolescent Autonomy, Detention for Medical Treatment and *Re C*' (1999) 62 *MLR* 595.

—— 'The Terminally Ill Adult Seeking Assisted Suicide Abroad: The Extent of the Duty owed by a Local Authority' (2005)13 *Med L Rev* 257.

DAVIES, M, 'Selective Non-Treatment of the New-Born: In Whose Best Interests? In Whose Judgement? (1998) 49 *NILQ* 82.

DE HAAN, J, 'The New Dutch Law on Euthanasia' (2002) 10 *Med L Rev* 57.

DICEY, AV, *Introduction to the Study of the Law of the Constitution*, 10th edn (London, Macmillan, 1959).

DOUGLAS, G, *Law, Fertility and Reproduction* (London, Sweet and Maxwell, 1991).

DRAPER, H, 'Women, Forced Caesarians and Antenatal Responsibilities' (1996) 22 *J Med Eth* 327.

DWORKIN, G, *The Theory and Practice of Autonomy* (Cambridge, Cambridge University Press, 1988).

DWORKIN,R, *Life's Dominion: An Argument about Abortion and Euthanasia* (London, HarperCollins, 1993).

ERIN, CA and HARRIS,J 'An Ethical Market in Human Organs' (2003) 29 *J Med Eth* 137.

FEEK,CM, MCKEAN, W, Heneveld, L, Barrow, G, Edgar, W and Paterson, RJ, 'Experience with Rationing Health Care in New Zealand' (1999) 318 *BMJ* 1346.

FELDMAN, D, 'Privacy-Related Rights and their Social Value' in P Birks, *Privacy and Loyalty* (Oxford, Clarendon Press, 1997).

—— *Civil Liberties and Human Rights in England and Wales*, 2nd edn (Oxford, Oxford University Press, 2000).

FINNIS, J, '*Bland*: Crossing the Rubicon?' (1993) 109 *LQR* 329.

FORD, M, 'The Personhood Paradox and the Right to Die' (2005) 13 *Med L Rev* 80.

FOVARGUE, S and MIOLA, J, 'Policing Pregnancy: Implications of the *Attorney-General's Reference (No 3 of 1994)* (1998) 6 *Med L Rev* 265.

FOX, M, 'A Woman's Right to Choose? A Feminist Critique' in J Harris and S Holm (eds), *The Future of Human Reproduction: Ethics, Choice, and Regulation* (Oxford, Clarendon Press, 1998).

FRANKEL, S, Ebrahim, S and Smith, GD, 'The Limits to Demand for Health Care' (2000) 321 *BMJ* 40.

FREEMAN, MDA, 'Sterilising the Mentally Handicapped' in MDA Freeman (ed) *Medicine, Ethics and the Law* (London, Stevens, 1998).

FREEMAN, M, 'Does Surrogacy have a Future after Brazier?' (1999) 7 *Med L Rev* 1.

——, 'Denying Death its Dominion: Thoughts on the Dianne Pretty Case' (2002) 10 *Med L Rev* 245.

GARWOOD-GOWERS, A, 'Removal and Use of Body Materials for Transplantation and Research Purposes: The Impact of the Human Rights Act 1998' in A Garwood-Gowers, J Tingle and T Lewis, *Healthcare Law: The Impact of the Human Rights Act 1998* (London, Cavendish Publishing, 2001).

GLOVER, J, *Causing Death and Saving Lives* (London, Penguin, 1977).

GREEN, S, 'Coherence of Medical Negligence Cases: A Game of Doctors and Purses' (2006) 14 *Med L Rev* 1.

GRUBB, A, 'The New Law of Abortion: Clarification or Ambiguity?' [1991] *Crim LR* 659.

——, 'I, Me, Mine: Bodies, Parts and Property' (1998) 3 *Med L Int* 299.

——, 'Access to Fetal Material: Property Rights and PACE' (2003) 11 *Med L Rev* 142.

GUNN, M, 'The Meaning of Incapacity' (1994) 2 *Med L Rev* 8.

GURNHAM, D, 'Losing the Wood for the Trees: *Burke* and the Court of Appeal' (2006) 14 *Med L Rev* 253.

HAGGER, L, 'Some Implications of the Human Rights Act 1998 for the Medical Treatment of Children' (2003) 6 *Med L Int* 25.

HAGGER, L, Woods, S and Barrow, P, 'Autonomy and Audit: Striking the Balance' (2004) 6 *Med L Int* 105.

HALE, B, *From the Test Tube to the Coffin: Choice and Regulation in Private Life* (London, Sweet and Maxwell, 1996).

——, 'A Pretty Pass: When is there a Right to Die?' (2003) 32 *CLWR* 1.

HARRIS, DJ, O'BOYLE, M and WARBRICK, C, *Law of the European Convention on Human Rights* (London, Butterworths, 1995).

HARRIS, J, *The Value of Life: An Introduction to Medical Ethics* (London, Routledge, 1985).

——, 'QALYfying the Value of Life' (1987)13 *J Med Eth* 117.

——, 'Double Jeopardy and the Veil of Ignorance – A Reply' (1995) 21 *J Med Eth* 151.

——, 'Would Aristotle have Played Russian Roulette?' (1996) 22 *J Med Eth* 209.

——, 'Rights and Reproductive Choice' in J Harris and S Holm (eds), *The Future of Human Reproduction: Ethics, Choice, and Regulation* (Oxford, Clarendon Press, 1998).

——, 'Micro-Allocation: Deciding Between Patients' in H Kuhse and P Singer (eds), *A Companion to Bioethics* (Oxford, Blackwell, 1998).

——, 'Human Beings, Persons and Conjoined Twins: An Ethical Analysis of the Judgment in *Re A*' (2001) 9 *Med L Rev* 221.

——, 'Law and Regulation of Retained Organs: The Ethical Issues' (2002) 22 *LS* 527.

HARRIS, JW, 'Who Owns My Body?' (1996) 16 *OJLS* 55.

HERVEY, TK and MCHALE, JV, 'Law, Health and the European Union' (2005) 25 *LS* 228.

HOYANO, LCH, 'Misconceptions about Wrongful Conception' (2002) 65 *MLR* 883.

IRVINE OF LAIRG, LORD, 'The Development of Human Rights in Britain under an Incorporated Convention on Human Rights' [1998] *PL* 221.

——, 'The Patient, the Doctor, their Lawyers and the Judge: Rights and Duties' (1999) 7 *Med L Rev* 255.

JACKSON, E, *Regulating Reproduction: Law, Technology and Autonomy* (Oxford, Hart Publishing, 2001).

——, *Medical Law: Text, Cases and Materials* (Oxford, Oxford University Press, 2006).

JONES, M, 'Informed Consent and Other Fairy Stories' (1999) 7 *Med L Rev* 103.

JONES, M and KEYWOOD, K, 'Assessing the Patient's Competence to Consent to Medical Treatment' (1996) 2 *Med Law Int* 107.

KENNEDY, I, *Treat Me Right: Essays in Medical Law and Ethics* (Oxford, Clarendon Press, 1991).

——, 'The Fiduciary Relationship and its Application to Doctors and Patients' in P Birks (ed), *Wrongs and Remedies in the Twenty-First Century* (Oxford, Clarendon Press, 1996).

KENNEDY, I and GRUBB, A, *Medical Law*, 3rd edn (London, Butterworths, 2000).

KEOWN, J, 'Restoring Moral and Intellectual Shape to the Law after *Bland*' (1997) 113 *LQR* 481.

——, *Euthanasia Examined: Ethical, Clinical and Legal Perspectives* (Cambridge, Cambridge University Press, 1997).

——, *Euthanasia, Ethics and Public Policy: An Argument Against Legalisation* (Cambridge, Cambridge University Press, 2002).

——, '"Morning After" Pills, "Miscarriage" and Muddle' (2005) 25 *LS* 296.

LAWS, J, 'Is the High Court the Guardian of Fundamental Constitutional Rights?' [1993] *PL* 59.

——, 'Law and Democracy' [1995] *PL* 72.

LEE, RG and MORGAN, D, *Human Fertilisation and Embryology: Regulating the Reproductive Revolution* (London, Blackstone Press, 2001).

LESTER, A, 'Fundamental Rights: The United Kingdom Isolated?' [1984] *PL* 46.

LEWIS, P and CHARNEY, M, 'Which of Two Individuals Do You Treat When Only their Ages are Different and You Can't Treat them Both?' (1989) 15 *J Med Ethics* 28.

LIDDELL, K and HALL, A, 'Beyond Bristol and Alder Hey: The Future Regulation of Human Tissue' (2005) 13 *Med L Rev* 170.

LONGLEY, D, 'Diagnostic Dilemmas: Accountability in the National Health Service' [1990] *PL* 527.

LOUGHREY, J, 'Medical Information, Confidentiality and a Child's Right to Privacy' (2003) 23 *LS* 510.

———, 'The Confidentiality of Medical Records: Informational Autonomy, Patient Privacy and the Law' (2005) 56 *NILQ* 293.

MACKINNON, CA, 'Reflections on Sex Equality under Law' (1991) 100 *Yale LJ* 1281.

MACLEAN, A, 'The Individual's Right to Treatment under the Human Rights Act 1998' in A Garwood-Gowers, J Tingle and T Lewis, *Healthcare Law: The Impact of the Human Rights Act 1998* (London, Cavendish Publishing, 2001).

MACLEAN, A, 'Crossing the Rubicon on the Human Rights Ferry' (2001) 64 *MLR* 775.

MARSTON, G, 'The United Kingdom's Part in the Preparation of the European Convention on Human Rights, 1950' (1993) 42 *ICLQ* 796.

MASON, JK, *Medico-Legal Aspects of Reproduction and Parenthood*, 2nd edn (Aldershot, Dartmouth Publishing, 1998).

MASON, JK and BRODIE, D, '*Bolam, Bolam* – Wherefore Art Thou *Bolam*?' (2005) 9 *Edin LR* 298..

MASON, JK, MCCALL SMITH, A and LAURIE, G, *Law and Medical Ethics*, 7th edn (Oxford, Oxford University Press,2006).

MASON, K and LAURIE, G, 'Consent or Property? Dealing with the Body and its Parts in the Shadow of Bristol and Alder Hey' (2001) 64 *MLR* 711.

MATTHEWS, P, 'The Man of Property' (1995) 3 *Med L Rev* 251.

MCBRIDE, J, 'Protecting Life: A Positive Obligation to Help' (1999) 24 *Eur Law Rev HR Survey* 43.

MCCALL SMITH, A, 'Euthanasia: The Strengths of the Middle Ground' (1999) 7 *Med L Rev* 194.

MCCONNELL, ML, 'Abortion and Human Rights: An Important Canadian Decision' (1989) 38 *ICLQ* 905.

MCEWAN, J, 'Murder by Design: The "Feel-Good Factor" and the Criminal Law' (2001) 9 *Med L Rev* 246.

MCGEE, A, 'Finding a Way Through the Ethical and Legal Maze: Withdrawal of Medical Treatment and Euthanasia' (2005) 13 *Med L Rev* 357.

MCKIE, J, Kuhse, H, Richardson, J and Singer, P, 'Double Jeopardy and the Use of QALYs in Health Care Allocation' (1995) 21 *J Med Eth* 144.

——, ' Double Jeopardy, the Equal Value of Lives and the Veil of Ignorance: A Rejoinder to Harris' (1996) 22 *J Med Eth* 204..

——, 'Another Peep Behind the Veil' (1996) 22 *J Med Eth* 216..

MCLEAN, S, 'The Right to Reproduce' in T Campbell, D Goldberg, S McLean and T Mullen (eds), *Human Rights: From Rhetoric to Reality* (Oxford, Basil Blackwell, 1986).

MCMAHAN, J, 'Brain Death, Cortical Death and Persistent Vegetative State' in H Kuhse and P Singer (eds), *A Companion to Bioethics* (Oxford, Blackwell, 1998).

MERRY, A and MCCALL SMITH, A, *Errors, Medicine and the Law* (Cambridge, Cambridge University Press, 2001).

MICHALOWSKI, S, 'Court-Authorised Caesarean Sections: The End of a Trend?' (1999) 62 *MLR* 115.

——, 'Sanctity of Life: Are Some Lives More Sacred Than Others?' (2002) 22 *LS* 377.

MILLER, L, 'Two Patients or One? Problems of Consent in Obstetrics' (1993) 1 *Med L Int* 97.

MONTGOMERY, J, 'Time for a Paradigm Shift? Medical Law in Transition' (2000) 53 *CLP* 363

—— *Health Care Law*, 2nd edn (Oxford, Oxford University Press, 2003).

——, 'Law and the Demoralisation of Medicine' (2006) 26 *LS* 185.

MORGAN, D, 'Abortion: The Unexamined Ground' (1990) *Crim LR* 687.

——, *Issues in Medical Law and Ethics* (London, Cavendish, 2001).

MORRIS, A and SANTIER, S, 'To Be or Not To Be: Is that the Question? Wrongful Life and Misconceptions' (2003) 11 *Med L Rev* 167.

MORRIS, D, 'Assisted Suicide under the European Convention on Human Rights: A Critique' (2003) 1 *EHRLR* 65.

MUNZER, SR, 'An Uneasy Case Against Property Rights in Body Parts' in EF Paul, FD Miller Jr and J Paul (eds), *Property Rights* (Cambridge, Cambridge University Press, 1994).

NAFFINE, N, 'The Legal Structure of Self-Ownership: Or the Self-possessed Man and the Woman Possessed' (1998) 25 *JLS* 193.

NEWDICK, C, *Who Should We Treat? Rights, Rationing and Resources in the NHS*, 2nd edn (Oxford, Oxford University Press, 2005).

NYS, H, 'Physician Involvement in a Patient's Death: A Continental European Perspective' (1999) 7 *Med L Rev* 208.

O'DONOVAN, K and GILBAR, R, 'The Loved Ones: Families, Intimates and Patient Autonomy' (2003) 23 *LS* 332.

OLIPHANT, K, 'Defining "Medical Misadventure": Lessons from New Zealand' (1996) 4 *Med L Rev* 1.

OST, S, 'Euthanasia and the Defence of Necessity: Advocating a More Appropriate Legal Response' [2005] *Crim LR* 355.

OTLOWSKI, M, *Voluntary Euthanasia and the Common Law* (Oxford, Oxford University Press, 1997).

OVEY, C and WHITE, RCA, *The European Convention on Human Rights*, 4th edn (Oxford, Oxford University Press, 2006).

PATTINSON, SD, *Medical Law and Ethics* (London, Sweet and Maxwell, 2006).

PEDAIN, A, 'The Human Rights Dimension of the Dianne Pretty Case' (2003) 62 *CLJ* 181.

PHILIPSON, G, 'Transforming Breach of Confidence? Towards a Common Law Right of Privacy under the Human Rights Act 1998' (2003) 66 *MLR* 726.

PLOMER, A, 'A Foetal Right to Life? The Case of *Vo* v *France*' (2005) 5 *HRLR* 311.

PRICE, D, 'Assisted Suicide and Refusing Medical Treatment: Linguistics, Morals and Legal Contortions' (1996) 4 *Med L Rev* 270.

——, 'Euthanasia, Pain Relief and Double Effect' (1997) 17 *LS* 323.

——, 'From Cosmos and Damian to Van Velzen: The Human Tissue Saga Continues' (2003) 11 *Med L Rev* 1.

——, 'The Human Tissue Act 2004' (2005) 68 *MLR* 798.

QUICK, O, 'Outing Medical Errors: Questions of Trust and Responsibility' (2006) 14 *Med L Rev* 22..

RHODEN, N, 'The Judge in the Delivery Room: The Emergence of Court-Ordered Caesareans' (1986) 74 *Cal L Rev* 1951.

ROBERTSON, JA, *Children of Choice: Freedom and the New Reproductive Technologies* (Princeton, Princeton University Press, 1994).

SAVAGE, W, 'Caesarean Section: Who Chooses – the Woman or her Doctor?' in DL Dickenson (ed), *Ethical Issues in Maternal-Fetal Medicine* (Cambridge, Cambridge University Press, 2002).

SAVAS, D and TREECE, S, 'Fertility Clinics: One Code of Practice?' (1998) 3 *Med L Int* 243.

SAVULESCU, J, 'Is the Sale of Body Parts Wrong?' (2003) 29 *J Med Eth* 138.

SCOTT, R, *Rights, Duties and the Body: Law and Ethics of the Maternal-Fetal Conflict* (Oxford, Hart Publishing, 2003).

——, 'Prenatal Screening, Autonomy and Reasons: The Relationship between the Law on Abortion and Wrongful Birth' (2003) 11 *Med L Rev* 265.

SEABOURNE, G, 'The Role of the Tort of Battery in Medical Law' (1995) 24 *Anglo-AMLR* 265.

SEYMOUR, J, *Childbirth and the Law* (Oxford, Oxford University Press, 2000).

SHELDON, S, *Beyond Control: Medical Power and Abortion Law* (London, Pluto Press, 1997).

SHELDON, S and WILKINSON, S, 'Termination of Pregnancy for Reason of Foetal Disability: Are There Grounds for a Special Exception in Law?' (2001) 9 *Med L Rev* 85.

SIMPSON, AWB, *Human Rights and the End of Empire: Britain and the Genesis of the European Convention* (Oxford, Oxford University Press, 2001).

SINGER, P, *Rethinking Life and Death: The Collapse of our Traditional Ethics* (Oxford, Oxford University Press, 1995).

——, *Unsanctifying Human Life: Essays on Ethics* (ed H Kuhse) (Oxford, Blackwell, 2002).

SKENE, L, 'Proprietary Rights in Human Bodies, Body Parts and Tissue: Regulatory Context and Proposals for New Laws' (2002) 22 *LS* 102.

SMITH, SW, 'Evidence for the Practical Slippery Slope in the Debate on Physician Assisted Suicide and Euthanasia' (2005) 13 *Med L Rev* 17.

SMITH, SW, 'Fallacies of the Logical Slippery Slope in the Debate on Physician Assisted Suicide and Euthanasia' (2005) 13 *Med L Rev* 224.

STEINBOCK, B, *Life Before Birth: The Moral and Legal Status of Embryos and Fetuses* (Oxford, Oxford University Press, 1992).

SYRETT, K, 'Nice Work? Rationing, Review and the "Legitimacy Problem" in the New NHS' (2002) 10 *Med L Rev* 1.

TEFF, H, 'Consent in Medical Procedures: Paternalism, Self-determination or Therapeutic Alliance?' (1985) 101 *LQR* 432.

——, 'The Standard of Care in Medical Negligence: Moving on from *Bolam*?' (1998) 18 *OJLS* 473.

TULLOCH, G, *Euthanasia: Choice and Death* (Edinburgh, Edinburgh University Press, 2005).

WALLBANK, J, 'Too Many Mothers? Surrogacy, Kinship and the Welfare of the Child' (2002) 10 *Med L Rev* 271.

WELLS, C, 'On the Outside Looking In: Perspectives on Enforced Caesarians' in S Sheldon and M Thomson (eds) *Feminist Perspectives on Health Care Law* (London, Cavendish, 1998).

WHITTY, N, 'Rights of Personality, Property Rights and the Human Body in Scots Law' (2005) 9 *Edin LR* 194.

WICKS, E, 'The UK Government's Perceptions of the European Convention on Human Rights at the Time of Entry' [2000] *PL* 438.

——, 'The Right to Refuse Medical Treatment under the European Convention on Human Rights' (2001) 9 *Med L Rev* 17.

——, 'The Greater Good? Issues of Proportionality and Democracy in the Doctrine of Necessity as applied in *Re A*' (2003) 32 *CLWR* 15.

——, *The Evolution of a Constitution: Eight Key Moments in British Constitutional History* (Oxford, Hart Publishing, 2006).

WICKS, E, Wyldes, M and Kilby, M, 'Late Termination of Pregnancy for Reason of Fetal Abnormality: Medical and Legal Perspectives' (2004) 12 *Med L Rev* 285.

WILLIAMS, G, 'The Fetus and the Right to Life' (1994) 53 *CLJ* 71.

——, 'The Principle of Double Effect and Terminal Sedation' (2001) 9 *Med L Rev* 41.

WOOLF, LORD, 'Clinical Negligence: What is the Solution? How can we Provide Justice for Doctors and Patients?' (2000) 4 *Med L Int* 133.

WRIGHT, M and MOODIE, P, 'Confidentiality, Codes and Courts: An Examination of the Significance of Professional Guidelines on Medical Ethics in determining the Legal Limits of Confidentiality' (2000) 29 *Anglo-AMLR* 39.

Index